Bahudhā and the Post 9/11 World

India is a great nation with a very rich culture, heritage and philosophy. It is important to combine these values of tradition with the technological and scientific development. B.P. Singh is a person who has attempted to translate the values of this culture into his life.

—His Holiness the Dalai Lama
Nobel Peace Laureate

B.P. Singh deserves commendation for his eloquent and powerful words and presentation. This book will bring about a positive and harmonious approach in addressing terrorism. ... Warm felicitations to the author for his masterpiece.

—Surjit Singh Barnala
Governor of Tamil Nadu

The scholarly and reflective account of how to come out of the kind of problems that we face in the world today finds a clear diagnosis in the book. ... A defining work ... well substantiated ... logically explained ... and accessibly written. I hope this book will find serious readership everywhere.

—N. Ram
editor-in-chief, *The Hindu*

An interesting and a very readable book.

—Karan Singh
Ex member of Parliament

Balmiki Prasad Singh puts forward the view that consciously we must work for propagating the values of a global family. It is our duty to in calculate the *Bahudhā* approach in our society.

—Radha Burnier
President, Theosophical Society, Chennai

The fundamental issue facing the world today is unbeatably, 'How to live?' or more appropriately 'How we all ought to live?' This crucial question finds an answer in B.P. Singh's book.

—*The Tribune*

What is the panacea for a world so globalized, yet with nations so unequal, living in mutual distrust, fear and, worse, terror? Is there a way to curb, if not eliminate totally, the clashes in the name of religion, region, language, community and caste? The answer is Bahudha. ... Balmiki Prasad Singh blends knowledge of philosophy with four decades experience as a civil servant.

—*The New Straits Times Online*

One's belief in a religion as the only truth or the superiority of one's religion over all others leads the world to an impasse. Balmiki Prasad Singh's labours are not in vain, because however distant the prospect, the world needs to be reminded that there is another way to reorder things.

—S. Nihal Singh
The Week

Very valuable work done ... I would definitely recommend the book because it explains the spirit of *Bahudhā* as it has evolved and as it is practiced in this country.

—K. Subrahmanyam,
Strategic affairs analyst and thinker

B.P. Singh makes the ancient multilayered concept of *Bahudhā* breathe current air. For those fighting persistent poverty to containing newly emerging terrorist threats, the book helps us to reflect on the way we think of our world.

— Ela R. Bhatt, Founder,
Self Employed Women's Association (SEWA)

B.P. Singh's book has the unique quality of drawing upon the philosophical foundations of *Bahudhā*, living with plurality, and weaving it into a coherent blueprint for rebuilding the post-9/11 world ... An enlightening read.

—Imtiaz Ahmad, Former Professor of Sociology,
Jawaharlal Nehru University, New Delhi

Drawing upon sources ranging from the ancient roots of Indian culture to his own experience as an international civil servant, B.P. Singh ... provides an essential framework for addressing the core 21st century global conflict. ... An important book that should be widely read.

—Phillips Talbot, Diplomat and President Emeritus,
The Asia Society, USA

Bahudhā and the Post 9/11 World

BALMIKI PRASAD SINGH

OXFORD
UNIVERSITY PRESS

OXFORD
UNIVERSITY PRESS

Oxford University Press is a department of the University of Oxford.
It furthers the University's objective of excellence in research, scholarship,
and education by publishing worldwide. Oxford is a registered trade mark of
Oxford University Press in the UK and in certain other countries.

Published in India by
Oxford University Press
2/11 Ground Floor, Ansari Road, Daryaganj, New Delhi 110 002, India

First Edition published in 2008
Oxford India Paperbacks 2020

ISBN-13: 978-0-19-013004-6
ISBN-10: 0-19-013004-0

Typeset in Nalandagaramond 10/12
by Sai Graphic Design, New Delhi 110 055
Printed in India by Rakmo Press, New Delhi 110 020

Dedicated to

Ralph Buultjens
Akhlaqur Rahman Kidwai
Bindeshwar Pathak
Samdhong Rinpoche

in friendship and with admiration

Contents

Foreword

Our world today requires us to accept the oneness of humanity. In the past, isolated communities could afford to think of one another as fundamentally separate. Some could even exist in total isolation. But nowadays, what happens in one part of the world rapidly affects people in many other places too. Within the context of our new interdependence, self-interest clearly lies in considering the interest of others.

Many of the world's problems and conflicts arise because we have lost sight of the basic humanity that binds us all together as a human family. We tend to forget that despite the diversity of race, religion, ideology and so forth, people are equal in their basic wish for peace and happiness. However, this will not be achieved by merely talking or thinking about it, nor by waiting for someone else to do something about it. We each have to take responsibility as best we can within our own sphere of activity. As free human beings we can use our unique intelligence to try to understand our world and ourselves. But if we are prevented from using our creative potential, we are deprived of one of the basic characteristics of a human being.

Human beings naturally possess diverse temperaments and interests. Therefore, it is inevitable that different religious traditions emphasize different philosophies and modes of practice. Since the essence of our diverse religious traditions is to achieve our individual and collective benefit, it is crucial that we are active in maintaining harmony and mutual respect between them. Concerted efforts to this end will benefit not only the followers of our own faith, but will create an atmosphere of peace in society as a whole. Cultivating harmony, respect, and tolerance is something that we can each start doing in our own lives and in our own actions.

India is perhaps the one country whose civilization and culture have survived intact from their first beginnings. It is a civilization that has given rise to a long series of great teachers endowed with both human intelligence and a sense of responsibility towards the community. As a consequence, different schools of thought and practice have evolved, some born here and others arriving from abroad. Because India and her people have, from ancient times, cherished a rich and sophisticated philosophy of non-violence at the core of their hearts, tolerance and pluralism have also flourished.

Today, India is self-sufficient, economically vibrant, and the world's largest democratic country. It is a force to be reckoned with not only in Asia, but also in the world. It is a country in which we can see *Bahudhā*, which my friend and the author of this book Balmiki Prasad Singh has defined as something close to pluralism, as a living reality. Therefore, India has a very important role to play. It can be a model for other nations and peoples who are still striving to build civil societies, to institutionalize democratic values of free expression and religion, and seeking to find strength in diversity. India can also take the lead amongst other nations by formulating principled, courageous, and imaginative policies on regional and international issues.

The tragic events of 11 September 2001 and subsequently, have provided us with a very good opportunity. There is a worldwide will to oppose terrorism. We can use this consensus to implement long-term preventative measures. This will ultimately be much more effective than taking dramatic and violent steps based on anger and other destructive emotions. The temptation to respond with violence is understandable, but a more cautious approach will be more fruitful.

In today's reality the only way of resolving differences is through dialogue and compromise, through human understanding and humility. We need to appreciate that genuine peace comes about through mutual understanding, respect and trust. Problems within human society should be solved in a humanitarian way, for which non-violence provides the proper approach.

26 May 2007   HIS HOLINESS THE DALAI LAMA

Preface

It was during my tenure as Executive Director, World Bank, at Washington DC, that the catastrophe of 9/11 took place. In the aftermath of the tragedy, it became fashionable for every thinktank to discuss two questions: 'What went wrong?' and 'Why people hate us [Americans]'? I happened to attend one such meeting barely ten days after the catastrophe. The gathering was impressive, I was seated almost opposite the Chairperson. The guest speaker had concluded on the sombre note of the need for building a coalition of nations against terrorism. He also spoke of the radicalization of Islam, values of religious pluralism, and the need for tolerance. The presentation over, the Chairperson asked for comments and looked at me. She said that India may have the answer in view of its heritage of pluralism and originality of mind, and gave me the floor. I was not prepared. I recall having said then that 'while India may have the answer, I do not' and went on to narrate my experiences in handling terrorism in India.

I have been contemplating this theme since then with a view to exploring an enduring framework for a global public policy—a policy for harmony among different people and societies in the post 9/11 world as seen through the lens of the Indian experience.

It is said that when the student is ready the teacher will appear. I was drawn to an attitude that has greatly contributed to the enrichment of Indian life: 'respect for another person's view of truth with hope and belief that he or she may be right'.[1] This is best expressed in the Rigvedic hymn that enjoins

Ekam Sad Vipra Bahudhā Vadanti[2]
The Real is one, the learned speak of it variously

Etymologically speaking, the word *Bahudhā* is derived from the word *bahu*, and *dhā* is suffixed to it to make it an adverb. 'Bahu' denotes many ways or parts or forms or directions. It is used to express manifoldness, much, and repeatedly. When the word is used with the root *kri*, it means to make manifold or multiply. Bahudhā is also used as an expression of intermittent continuity in various time frames. It is used to express frequency, as in 'time and again'. In the present work, the word Bahudhā has been used to suggest an eternal reality or continuum, a dialogue of harmony, and peaceful living in society.

Pluralism could be the closest equivalent to Bahudhā in the English language. Pluralism has been described in various ways in history, sociology, and politics—cultural pluralism, political pluralism, and pluralistic societies. Pluralism has also been seen in the context of the coexistence of nation-state and ethnicity, equality, and identity issues.

The Bahudhā approach recognizes that there is a distinction between plural societies and pluralism. Pluralism is an inevitable ingredient of democratic societies. The role of religion, language, and ethnicity is very significant in plural societies. Pluralism in this context is an imperative for both developed and developing societies.

Pluralist societies are necessarily multi-ethnic, multi-religious, and multilingual societies. In such societies, there are various boundaries: racial, linguistic, religious, and at times even ideological. The Bahudhā approach does not believe in annexation of boundaries or assimilation of identities and propagation of a simplistic world view. It merely facilitates dialogue and thereby promotes understanding of the collective good. The realization of one's own identity may sustain boundaries and yet, at the same time, understanding of other identities may help formulate a public policy of harmony. The Bahudhā approach is conscious of the fact that societies without boundaries are not possible.

The great struggles of the twentieth century were against colonialism, fascism, and communism. The twenty-first century has a different conflict—a conflict between forces of fundamentalism and those of tolerance and peace.

With the fall of the Berlin Wall in 1989, there was a feeling of euphoria that peace had descended upon the world; that the time had come for diversion of funds from military budgets to develop-mental purposes. It also appeared that the forces of globalization and the liberalization of the market economy would secure the removal of poverty. But suddenly the importance of military conflict as a factor in our lives re-emerged, with the invasion of Kuwait by Iraq in 1991.

In today's world, the power of the militarily weak to create unrest and destruction has emerged as a global phenomenon. Economic power and the use of military force have proved inadequate agents for the preservation of peace. The moot question is how to cope with an enemy that is physically weak, but endowed with a 'do or die' mentality.

Today, we face not only the problems of terrorism and suicide squads but also of poverty, disease, illiteracy, and environmental degradation. Of the six billion people that inhabit the earth, five billion are in the developing countries. Near a billion people struggle to survive on less than a dollar a day. More than a 100 million children are illiterate. Almost three million people die annually from HIV/AIDS, with over two million of those deaths occurring in sub-Saharan Africa. Today, half of the world's population is under the age of twenty- five years. Many are unemployed. Millions are disillusioned by what they see as an inequitable global system. Clearly, the need for change is paramount.

We are witnessing phenomenal changes in global politics— unprecedented demands are being made upon traditional diplomacy and democratic approaches rooted in electoral politics. In fact, the instruments of traditional diplomacy are unable to cope with many of the fast emerging challenges. Democratic political processes are also under stress. All this calls for new, bold, and imaginative statecraft from world leaders. Notwithstanding unresolved territorial disputes and autonomy issues in different parts of the world, major nation-states are forging new partnerships and increasingly competing in trade. Regional alliances are also emerging. In these times of unprecedented change, we need to transcend old doctrines, and our language of dialogue too has to be reconstructed.

With the demise of colonialism and the collapse of the Soviet Union, democratic governance has emerged as the most important form of social and political ordering in the world. A major objective of democracy in a multi-religious and multi-ethnic society is to ensure that different faiths and cultures co-exist and flourish. Good governance in a democracy does not do away with alternative and opposing visions but deals with them in a manner that prevents physical conflict and violence. Argument and dialogue are important components of such a manner.

Today, in the age of terrorism and an unsafe world, there is a fresh need to understand the core meaning of our religions, to reshape our educational system, and to strengthen the United Nations (UN) in a manner that can help us to build a better future.

The re-emergence of religion as a vital force in the twenty-first century, both at the individual and community levels, needs to be taken into account in the formulation of a public policy of harmony. Blinkered visions about religion in general or about a particular religion is likely to create disaffection in society and make difficult the task of building a harmonious world order. Religion is a potent force. As an agent for the generation of peace and happiness, it generates goodwill among people, and helps them to lead a life of spirituality and fulfilment. In recent years, we have seen how people like Mahatma Gandhi and Martin Luther King have used it for achieving justice and freedom. Swami Vivekananda and Mother Teresa have been inspired by their religious faiths to serve the poor, the derelict, and the discarded. It is religious faith which has driven the Dalai Lama to propagate the message of love and peace not only among his Tibetan people (including those living in exile in India) but also in distant lands.

As an agent of destruction, religion is being used by radical leaders to spread hatred and inflict violence. Primarily, all faiths have emerged or been created to underpin a moral universe in which love, compassion, peace, and caring guide human conduct. Religion is to be an ennobling influence that leads men, women, and children to have respect for human beings, animals, and natural objects. In this background the recent phenomenon of suicide killings has indeed become a matter of concern. It is difficult to imagine that the young *jihadi*s are totally impelled by a yearning for paradise. In reality, they are mostly misguided by political aspirations.

In this context, scholars have rightly seen links between funda-mentalist movements and social conflict. For example, the eminent religious scholar Karen Armstrong[3] views the fundamentalism of the twentieth and twenty-first centuries as a reaction against scientific and secular culture. Modernization and rapid economic changes have been painful processes for several individuals and societies who have long been marginalized due to centuries of imperialist exploitative mechanisms. Fundamentalists openly proclaim that they are battling against forces that threaten their sacred values.

All major religions—Hinduism, Buddhism, Judaism, Christianity, and Islam—have fundamentalist elements, but it is militant Islam that is currently drawing maximum attention. Those who see links between terrorism and Islam need to take note of the fact that the Quran considers the killing of an innocent person a crime against humanity; it preaches tolerance and respect for all faiths. Far from promoting a clash of civilizations, the Quran celebrates social and cultural diversity. Jews, Christians, and Muslims lived peacefully for several centuries under Islamic rule in Spain. Similarly, Hindus and Muslims lived harmoniously under the rule of the Mughal Emperor Akbar and others in India.

While fundamentalist religious forces are likely to continue to dominate political discourse for some time to come, it is not likely to be a permanent feature of the world social and political order. As fundamentalism cannot satisfy growing human aspirations or meet the challenges of modernization, the present hold of extremist organizations over its followers in the Islamic world would gradually loosen and eventually recede substantially. We have strong mystical traditions in Islam that have found eloquent expressions in Sufi ideas and religious disciplines (to which Wahhabis and other fundamentalist groups are strongly opposed) that could be supported. The alienation of Muslims living in Europe and USA needs special attention as they feel alienated from their traditions. The problem gets accentuated as they are not fully accepted in the society where they live. In the prevailing situation both the civil society and the government needs to be sensitive. Intellectuals, women, and youth must be encouraged to play a greater role in the social and political affairs of their land. The more democratic the world becomes, the less would be the threat of terrorism and suicide killings.

Mahatma Gandhi, more than any other public figure in con-temporary history, supported an attitude towards religion that goes beyond toleration. He did this in several ways by encouraging greater knowledge and deeper commitment about one's own faith and tradi-tions and also that of others. He wanted believers to realize that loyalty towards one's own religion did not justify it being superior than other religions. He stated that every religion is imperfect but a beautiful expression of human aspirations of love rather than hatred. Mahatma Gandhi believed that a religiously plural society contains enormous resources as long as religion is not regarded as the primary maker of identity. His technique of non-violent conflict resolution—*satyagraha*—was a dialogic process, inviting negotiation and compromise.

More than two millennia before Mahatma Gandhi, Gautama Buddha wanted a rational approach to conflict resolution. In matters of religion, he advocated the Bahudhā approach of dialogue and understanding. To quote:

if others speak against me, or against my religion, or against the order, there is no reason why you should be angry, discontented or displeased with them. If you are so, you will not only be using yourselves into danger of spiritual loss, but you will not be able to judge whether what they see is correct or not correct![4]

Education has a central role to play in building a harmonious society. Education must begin at home as it is here that intolerance towards other faiths has its origins. We know that it is not only love and compassion but also hatred and intolerance that are widespread. Just as people can be taught to hate, they can also learn to treat others with love, dignity, and respect. In fact, the issue of a public policy of harmony is critically linked with education. There is an urgent need to focus on the educational curriculum in order to purge it of content that spreads hatred and/or distorts history. Effective education also demands the development of a creative mind and scientific temper.

Resolving conflict, however, goes much beyond education. Towards this end, the UN has to be strengthened in terms of its Charter so that it becomes an effective conflict resolution organization. The global political order must reflect the best interests, rules, and practices that states hold in common.

The UN is the best forum for generation of understanding among nation-states in the realm of politics and economy. It can also be a forum where dialogue among nations can be initiated and sustained. Such dialogues can support efforts towards peace and attempts to resolve conflicts between groups and nations.

As we look towards the future, it appears that the prevailing state system would continue to be a primary body. An international order based on the rule of law and consent of nation-states can alone be an effective conflict resolution mechanism.

*   *   *

During my research on manifestations of the Bahudhā philosophy in the works of Rabindranath Tagore, I found a powerful observation in the 'Introduction' to *Gitanjali* by W. B. Yeats. He writes:

We write long books where no page perhaps has any quality to make writing a pleasure, being confident in some general design while Mr. Tagore, like the Indian civilisation itself, has been content to discover the soul and surrender himself to its spontaneity.[5]

This made me wonder whether to pursue writing this book. Was I judicious in accepting the challenge of trying to seek the soul of civilizational harmony? I knew then and I am conscious now that the Bahudhā approach is not a discovery but at best a reassertion of an old truth about the pluralist approach in society, religion, and politics. In writing this book, I realize that I have not been able to raise myself to that sublime level where one has 'discovered the soul' or has 'surrendered oneself to [the] spontaneity' of civilizational harmony. Those are the tasks of the great universal philosophies. Mine is just an individual's effort to seek a way of reconciling the disturbing disorder of our times. This work is not a technical study of either history or philosophy. My effort is to record what I have found relevant in the Indian and world experiences that could provide ways and means for the formulation of public policies that could bring more harmony into societies. Nevertheless, I have been selective in choosing events and personalities and I am conscious of the fact that one's own cultural baggage affects one's outlook. My aim was not to glorify either the past or an individual but only to draw lessons from their successes and failures. William Faulkner does not exaggerate when he says: 'The past is never dead; it is not even past'.[6]

India has been living through this pluralistic challenge longer than several other nations. In terms of faith, well before the advent of Christianity and Islam, India was a significant playing field of civilizational encounters between Hinduism, Buddhism, and Jainism. Both Judaism and Christianity came to India in the first century AD. Islam commenced its entry through the coastal towns of peninsular India from the eighth century onwards. In the ninth century, when the Zoroastrians of Persia felt that their religion was being threatened by the invading Muslims, they moved to the north-west coast of India. Their descendants, known as Parsis, still live there. The birth of Sikhism in fifteenth century India had the avowed objective of bringing peace to conflicting encounters between Hinduism and Islam. In the last century, when the Tibetans felt a threat to their religion and culture, they chose India to be their new home. Multiculturalism, then, is a basic feature of India's civilizational experience.

The Indian civilizational experience in respect of pluralism or multiculturalism does not advocate a melting pot approach that facilitates domination of values and norms of the numerically strong and assertive community over others. The most important feature of pluralism is that people believe in their multiple identities. India's strength has always been to absorb external influences. It is not surprising, therefore, to see Indians speaking of Shakespeare and Tulsidas in the same vein, and without any strain, in seminar rooms as well as private homes.

Multiculturalism as practised in India is not atheistic in character but is a blending of religions. Mahatma Gandhi, a devout Hindu, highlighted this aspect of communitarian life in India when he had passages read from the holy books of all the major religions at his prayer meetings. Secularism in India establishes that the state shall be neutral in matters of religion. But multiculturalism goes beyond that—it demands the flowering of different faiths and belief patterns. Secularism and multiculturalism are not in conflict. It is this openness of the Indian experience that provides the basis for constructing a public policy of harmony. It establishes that disputes shall be settled through dialogue and there shall be a free flow of ideas and thought processes from different parts of the world.

One of the lessons of 9/11 is that we are living in an interdependent world. The futility of promoting violence and conflict in the name of religion is obvious to all except a few. It is here that public opinion needs to be groomed. We have to recognize that many factors drive public opinion, including education and media, and that a global view is required. There is a need for dialogue among the people of the world. Dialogue may or may not lead to consensus but it certainly creates understanding and relationships among people. The answer to terrorism lies not in repression, which only generates hatred and causes hindrances in the path of dialogue and peaceful change. Respect for the rights, beliefs, and cultures of all human beings can go a long way in facilitating and enhancing processes of negotiation and eventually in securing peace and harmony.

It is difficult to visualize a world where there will be no use of force. But, surely, military force should be only a last resort when all other methods to resolve conflict have been exhausted. While terrorism may gradually recede, the long-term threats to world peace are from poverty, inequality, environmental degradation (including global warming), disease, and illiteracy.

The message of this book relates to dialogue and compassion more than the mechanics of politics, statecraft, and diplomacy. And yet I am aware that without the rule of law, understanding and love cannot permeate social life. The process of dialogue would either be closed or cease to be a creative process and its value as a conflict resolution mechanism would get severely restricted. A progressive and peaceful world can only be one where both small and big nations receive a place under the sun and achieve a sense of recognition and worth.

Each book has its own destiny. I cannot predict the impact it will create or the attention it will receive. But my deep conviction of the relevance of the Bahudhā approach makes me hope that it will make some contribution to human affairs. In many ways, the writing of this book has been a *swantah sukhai* (pursuit of self-happiness). My thoughts and words have opened new doors of exploration for me. I hope it leads others to new possibilities too! In that spirit, I offer it to my readers.

NOTES

1. B.P. Singh, 'Bahudhā and the Post-9/11 World', speech delivered at Gandhi Smriti and Darshan Samiti, New Delhi, 2004, p. 7.
2. *Rig Veda* (I. 164–46).
3. Karen Armstrong, *The Great Transformation: The Beginning of Our Religious Traditions*, Alfred A. Knof, New York/Toronto, 2006, pp. xi–xviii.
4. S. Radhakrishnan, *Gautama the Buddha*, annual lecture on Master Mind, Oxford University Press, Oxford, 1938, p. 12.
5. W.B. Yeats, 'Introduction to Gitanjali (Song Offerings)' by Rabindranath Tagore, Rabindra Bhavan, Visva-Bharati, Shantiniketan, 23 December 1999, p. 13.
6. R.G. Collingwood, *The Idea of History*, Clarendon Press, Oxford, 1993, specially 'History as Re-enactment of Past Experience' in this book for detailed analysis of this idea, pp. 282–301.

Acknowledgements

During the three years that it took to write this book, I have incurred many debts to the Government of India and public institutions, to friends and scholars, and to many people and public leaders.

My gratitude goes to the Indira Gandhi National Centre for Arts (IGNCA), New Delhi and the Department of Culture, Government of India, whose support made the researching and writing of this publication possible. Shri Jagmohan, Dr L.M. Singhvi, Professor I.N. Choudhury, Dr K.K. Chakravarty, Dr B.K. Bhattacharya and Professor G.C. Tripathi of IGNCA and the IGNCA library family made valuable contributions.

The dynamic Director of Gandhi Smriti and Darshan Samiti (New Delhi), Dr Savita Singh invited me to deliver a lecture on 'BahudhŒ and the Post-9/11 World' on 7 November 2003 and published a monograph, which also formed part of the background literature for the global convention on peace and non-violence held on 31 January and 1 February 2004 at New Delhi.

I am immensely grateful to several editors who published my work on the BahudhŒ approach in *Mainstream, Man and Development, Social Change, Dialogue, Gaganachal, Bhavan's Journal,* and several Hindi and English newspapers.

I was fortunate to have Dr Kailash Chandra Mishra as Research Officer and Shri Raman Pathak as Programme Officer of this project. My research team led by Kailash did an excellent job in obtaining the views of ordinary rural people in terms of conflict resolution mechanisms and issues pertaining to harmony, peace, and happiness. Without Raman Pathak's tireless and committed efforts, it would have been impossible to finalize the manuscript.

Several events and individuals have contributed to my compre-hension and knowledge of the BahudhŒ approach. As a child, I had heard my grandfather, Hridaya Narain Singh, repeatedly stressing the need for free movement of two 'birds' in our social domain: *sabhyata* (civilization) and *sahanubhuti* (empathy). Over the years, a large number of people have enriched my understanding of the subject, including four esteemed individuals to whom this book is dedicated. They are Professor Ralph Buultjens, teacher, scholar, and thinker;

Dr Akhlaqur Rahman Kidwai, scientist and long time governor of Bihar, West Bengal, and Haryana; Dr Bindeshwar Pathak, social reformer and founder of the Sulabh Sanitation Movement; and Professor Samdhong Rinpoche, a monk and gifted leader and administrator (elected Prime Minister of the Government of Tibet in exile for the second term in India). The lives and works of each one of them in respective fields of human activity have been guided by the BahudhŒ approach.

I am deeply grateful to three outstanding editors who read through the manuscript with care and compassion, namely Jehanara Wasi, Rama Goyal, and Ambassador Placido d' Souza, the last formerly of the Indian Foreign Service.

I encountered several difficulties in writing this book: shortage of funds, illness in the family, and dislocation of staff and place of work. Fortunately, when I moved my place of work from IGNCA to the India International Centre (IIC), my friend H.K. Kaul, Chief Librarian at IIC, rose to the occasion in support. I am deeply indebted to him and his entire team.

A personal note of thanks for my family. As always, my family has supported me in my work in myriad ways. My wife Karuna graciously endured my preoccupation with this book and provided a carefree environment at home. My children—Sumita and her husband Paras, Rajeev and his wife Kirti, and Pritty and her husband Rajeevranjan—were most supportive of my work. My six grandchildren showed enormous curiosity in what BahudhŒ is all about. My granddaughter, Gauri Singh, in particular, constantly enquired about the progress in writing and was jubiliant when it was finished. The blessings of my father and the love and affection of my family have always sustained me and my work in public administration and academia. The BahudhŒ study too has been nourished by this love and affection.

Prologue to the Paperback Edition

Unexpected happenings do take place in relation to a new publication. *Bahudhā and the Post 9/11 World* was published by Oxford University Press (OUP) in April 2008. The book release event was organized by OUP New York in the magnificent hall of the Indian Consulate there. I had warmly accepted the invitation to join in. Meanwhile, I received an email from Niko Pfund, the head of OUP, New York, stating that a friend of his was deeply impressed with Bahudhā. He was a manufacturer of chocolates and wanted his new chocolate to be named Bahudha chocolate. Niko wanted my approval and also the amount of royalty that should be paid to me. I told him no royalty is required except that the company may provide two pieces of Bahudha chocolate to everyone joining the book launch event and this was done.[1] After conclusion of the function, I got worried as to whether the Bahudha chocolate would eclipse the Bahudhā approach that I have propounded after four years of research and contemplation! Some of my friends in New York also gave me the news that one liquor shop in the downtown area in New York has renamed itself as Bahudha Bar and another one as Bahudha Restaurant. Thankfully, soon thereafter there were several encouraging developments from different countries, including the USA. In fact, the Bahudhā approach has been receiving global appreciation since then.

On my return from the USA, I got in touch with OUP Delhi for organising a launch event in India and the auditorium of Nehru Memorial Museum and Library, New Delhi, was chosen. His Holiness the Dalai Lama, who has penned a magnificent foreword to this book, was invited to be the chief guest of the event. At this event, His Holiness the Dalai Lama spoke highly about the Bahudhā approach and its relevance in the present day world. He went on to declare that he does not know as to how long his books will survive but this book, *Bahudhā and the Post 9/11 World*, will be in circulation for at least the next 200 years![2]

SIKKIM, STATUE OF UNITY, AND BAHUDHĀ

On 8 May 2008, I was appointed as governor of Sikkim. My wife, Karuna, and I moved to Gangtok, the capital of Sikkim before the swearing-in ceremony. I was sworn in at a glittering function at the Raj Bhavan campus on 9 July

2008. Raj Bhavan at Gangtok has a rich and inspiring history. Its majestic location, with a view embracing the Kanchenjunga mountain range and Gangtok valley, is a constant reminder of how human aspirations can blend with the magnificence of nature.

Sikkim, which has borders with Tibet, Bhutan, Nepal, and the Indian states of West Bengal and Arunachal Pradesh, became a state of the Indian Union on 16 May 1975. Special provisions with respect to the state of Sikkim were incorporated under Article 371F of the Constitution of India[3] which inter alia includes special powers of the governor of Sikkim.[4] My five-year-long stay at Raj Bhavan gave me the time and favourable ambience to think and reflect beyond the challenges of governance, social cohesion, and also strategic issues facing Sikkim and other north-eastern states. I also had occasions to reflect upon the Bahudhā approach in the context of Sikkim and its neighbouring lands and also on issues of vital concern to the people of India and the world in the twenty-first century. Another advantage was getting ample opportunities to deliver lectures in India and abroad on topical subjects, a responsibility that I still enjoy.

Sikkim, a part of the Himalayas has enchanting landscapes that include India's highest mountain range in India Kanchenjunga and millions of varieties of flowers and breath-taking mountain slopes and waterways. No wonder it has attracted several extremely gifted people, including sages, mendicants, painters, and poets, from time to time. I wish to highlight only four of them. The most famous among them is Guru Padmasambhava, an eighth-century Buddhist master who was a student of and teacher at Nalanda University. He preached Buddhism in Tibet and also in Sikkim, Bhutan, Nepal, and other places in India. He attained the status of a godhead and his idol is placed next to Lord Buddha in various monasteries. Another pathfinder and teacher of global eminence was the founder of the Sikh religion, Guru Nanak (1469–1539). He visited Sikkim and travelled up to Gurudongmar Lake located at an altitude of 5,138 m in north Sikkim.[5] Nicholas Roerich (1874–1947), the famous Russian painter and philosopher, well-known all over the world for his enchanting painting of Mount Kanchenjunga,[6] spent many years in Darjeeling, an area which Sikkim had ceded to Bengal (now West Bengal) at the behest of the East India Company. Joseph Dalton Hooker (1817 – 1911) also needs to be mentioned here. He was a British botanist who traversed the entire Himalayan mountain range from Sikkim to Arunachal Pradesh and Nepal, and extensively reflected upon the rich Himalayan forests and its biodiversity wealth.[7]

A very unique invitation that I received at the beginning of my stay in Sikkim was to deliver the inaugural address at the annual Pang Lhabsol festival in the first half of August 2008. The meeting was organized in the Municipal Hall of Gangtok and its deliberations were to be broadcast all over Gangtok. On the way I saw that a large number of students had already gathered not only outside the hall but also at different places in the city. Chief Minister Pawan Chamling and his council of ministers were also present.

The Pang Lhabsol festival is unique among festivals and is a living part of Sikkim's history, society, and culture. It was on a day in the month of August in the thirteenth century that a solemn social pact of unity and brotherhood was made at Kabi Lungchok between the Lepcha tribes led by their chieftain Thekong Thek and the Bhutia tribes under the leadership of Khye Bumsa. The majestic and venerated Mt Khangchendzonga was accepted by both sides as its principal witness. Today the Statue of Unity is a tourist spot located 17 km from Gangtok on the North Sikkim Highway.[8] Over the years, Pang Lhabsol has emerged as a Day of Unity in Sikkim among people who live in the state. In fact, this festival is now being celebrated jointly by Lepchas, Bhutias, Nepalis, Vyaparis, and people of different ethnic groups and believers of different faiths including Buddhism, Hinduism, Sikhism, Christianity, and Islam. This unique festival also symbolizes respect for nature.

The institution of Pang Lhabsol, so imaginatively crafted in the thirteenth century, reminded me of the Bahudhā approach that I propounded after 9/11 in a different global environment. At the function I also had a deep sense of regret that I did not know of this unity celebration of Sikkim although my team of researchers and I had traversed different parts of India, which are discussed in Chapter 7 of this book, titled 'Among People'.[9]

Over the centuries human efforts have raised monasteries, temples, gurdwaras, churches, mosques, institutions of learning, and health care and communication networks. The world has also witnessed World Wars and continuing conflicts between religions and even among sects of a particular religion, race, and ethnicity. In fact, the world is moving at such a rapid pace that it would be unrecognizable to a person of, says, the thirteenth century, or even of the seventeenth or eighteenth centuries. There has been rapid progress in every field of human activity, including in ways of living.

CHANGING WAYS OF LIFE: NATION STATES, CONFLICTS, AND BAHUDHĀ

As a student of political science in Patna University, I was encouraged to think about the origins of society and civilization, religious beliefs, politics, and state formation processes. One of the conclusions that I drew then, and which have remained with me, is that the person who would have first conceived of an organized authority must have been moved by an immense feeling of insecurity and a deep sense of fear of nature as well as of the treachery of his fellow creatures. The propitiation of spirits and even prayers to God may not have been able to mitigate the prevailing mood of insecurity. During conversations several persons might have shared this vision and the idea of an organized authority might have been found attractive. No wonder, over the millennia, the concept of the state has engaged some of the finest minds of the world.

In contemporary history, three thinkers among numerous others have elucidated this idea comprehensively to describe the nature and role of the state: Thomas Hobbes (1588–1679), John Locke (1632–1704), and Jean-Jacques Rousseau (1712–1778). These thinkers conceptualized a thesis of a *social contract* and went on to elaborate the obligation of the state to provide security to its citizens and more.

Thomas Hobbes in his book *Leviathan* (published in 1651) envisaged a 'state of nature' and famously said that in a 'state of nature', human life would be 'solitary, poor, nasty, brutish and short'. In the absence of political order and law, everyone would have unlimited natural freedoms, including the 'right to all things' and thus the freedom to plunder, rape, and murder. There would be an endless 'war of all against all'. To avoid these, free individuals sought security in return for subjecting themselves to an absolute sovereign, though the orders of the sovereign may well be arbitrary; at times, even tyrannical. In short, Hobbes saw absolute government as the only alternative to the anarchy of a state of nature. Locke and Rousseau argued that one gained civil rights in return for accepting the obligation to respect and defend the rights of others. It needed to be appreciated that law and political order are not natural but human creations. The social contract and the political order it creates are simply the means towards an end—the benefit of the individuals involved and legitimate only to the extent that they fulfil their part of the agreement. Hobbes went on to argue that as the government is not a party to the original contract, citizens are thus not obligated to submit to the government when it is too weak or does not act effectively to suppress factionalism and civil unrest. According to Locke, when the government fails to secure natural rights of citizens, they could, in turn, withdraw their obligation to obey, or effect change in the leadership through elections or other means including, when necessary, even violence. Locke believed that natural rights were inalienable, and therefore the rule of God superseded government authority. Rousseau supplemented this proposition and developed the theory of 'general will' and advocated that democracy (self-rule) was the best way to ensure welfare of citizens while maintaining individual freedom under the rule of law.

Philosophers such as Immanuel Kant (1724–1804), Georg Wilhelm Friedrich Hegel (1770–1831), and Karl Marx (1818–1883) gave new meaning and context to the relationship between individuals and the state. Karl Marx, in particular, formulated the theory of economic interpretation of history and envisaged class struggle between the haves and have-nots, the establishment of dictatorship of the proletariat, and finally the withering away of the state, yielding the place for a classless society. The intellectual journey from Hobbes's descriptions of state of nature to Karl Marx's classless society makes for fascinating reading that has influenced not only happenings on the ground but have also shaped the role of the nation states and other human formations.

CONTEMPORARY TIMES: CONFLICTS AND THE NEED FOR BAHUDHĀ

The modern concept of the nation state, however, originated in the seventeenth century. It is a product of a series of peace treaties signed between May and October 1648 that ended the Thirty Years' War (1618–1648) in the Holy Roman Empire and the Eighty Years' War (1568–1648) between Spain and the Dutch Republic at Westphalia, a region in Germany. The salient features of the Westphalia treaties were: (*i*) the concept of sovereign states; and (*ii*) the need to have a balance of power to check the aggression of nation states. It provided impetus to the growth of nationalism and geopolitics.

The balance of power gets disturbed when a nation state acquires disproportionate military and economic clout, for powerful nation states are rarely satisfied with the prevailing distribution of power among them. They strive to change the balance in their favour. Meanwhile, old suspicions that can lead to conflict and religious concerns that may have fuelled conflict into war in the past are still operating. Besides, one nation state cannot be certain of the intentions of its neighbours and others. In fact, geopolitics and distrust never go away. In reality, conflicts do take place and states rise, fall, rise again, and compete with one another.

At the beginning of the nineteenth century and after the downfall of Napoleon Bonaparte (1769–1821), the European leaders perceived the need to have a dialogue amongst them to create a balance in a way that could prevent future wars and maintain peace and stability in the continent. A meeting of ambassadors of European states under the chairmanship of Austrian leader Klemens von Metternich was held in Vienna from November 1814 to June 1815, popularly referred to as the Vienna Congress of 1815. It succeeded in establishing peace in Europe for some time. However, geopolitics and suspicion surfaced again and that led to the First World War (1914–19).

The First World War ensured that peacemaking no longer lay in the hands of a few great powers and their landed elites. It was also no longer a solely European business. The Americans, excluded from Vienna as irrelevant, however, were in Paris in force. In fact, President Woodrow Wilson of the United States was the dominant presence. There were European leaders and others there too. The Paris Peace Conference convened at the end of the First World War succeeded in establishing for the first time an international organization called the League of Nations.

The industrial revolution had already made a deep impact on both society and global economic trends. It also led to the growth of democracy. However, geopolitics and ambition of domination over others led to the collapse of the League of Nations. Democracy too was subverted. The world witnessed the rise of dictators in Germany, Italy, and Japan. All these resulted in the outbreak of the Second World War in 1939. This was a war between the Allied powers (the UK, France, Russia, China, and the USA) and the Axis powers (Germany, Italy, and Japan). The War engulfed different regions of the world between September 1939 and September 1945: a period of six years and one day. A large number of combatants and civilians died as never before in any conflict or war. The Second World War resulted in victory of the Allies and collapse of Nazi Germany and fall of Japanese and Italian empires. Nuclear weapons were used for the first time in this war.

Wars and conflicts shook human consciousness in the twentieth century. In fact, the twentieth century became the most violent century in human history. Naturally, it generated a feeling of bewilderment, introspection, and questioning as to whether wars and human suffering were really inevitable. People genuinely wondered what had happened to the strength and wisdom of the human spirit. Not surprisingly since the end of the Second World War people all over the world made sincere efforts towards building a lasting future of peace.

The global scene changed dramatically. Leaders and statesmen, namely, Franklin Delano Roosevelt (1882–1945) of the USA, Winston Leonard Spencer Churchill (1874–1965) of the UK, Joseph Vissarionovich Stalin (1878–1953) of Russia, and Chiang Kai-shek (1887–1975) of China joined hands to refashion the world order. The United Nations Organization (UNO) was set up on 24 October 1945 to

save succeeding generations from the scourge of war', and 'to reaffirm faith in fundamental human rights, in the dignity and worth of the human person, in the equal rights of men and women and of nations large and small, and to establish conditions under which justice and respect for the obligations arising from treaties and other sources of international law can be maintained, and to promote social progress and better standards of life in larger freedom.[10]

The framers of the UN Charter were deeply conscious of the need to strike a balance between state sovereignty and the power of intervention by the United Nations (UN), a multilateral organization. As a result, it was categorically stipulated in the UN Charter that the use of military force against a sovereign state is to be resorted to by the Security Council only in extreme situations for the purpose of enforcing and keeping the peace.

Recognizing the importance of management of the world economy and economic development of member states, the Bretton Woods Convention recommendations led to the establishment of the International Monetary Fund (IMF) and the World Bank and General Agreement on Tariffs and Trade (GATT), from which emerged the World Trade Organization (WTO).

The establishment of the UN on 24 October 1945 in New York and subsequently of the IMF and the World Bank in Washington DC, and of GATT and later WTO in Geneva constituted landmark events in history.

Things have changed dramatically since 1945, particularly for the two countries that were widely regarded as responsible for World War II, Germany and Japan. Two cities of Japan, Hiroshima and Nagasaki, were subjected to atomic bombings during the war and Germany was divided after the war. Both countries adopted peace-oriented constitutions with self-denying ordinances regarding their military capabilities and intentions. Today they present a different picture of peace, progress, and unity.

Ways of living and conduct with each other also underwent major changes. The arc of geopolitics was moving simultaneously. The erstwhile allies started parting company. It led to the emergence of the USA and the Soviet Union as rival superpowers and the commencement of the Cold War. Strangely but successfully it held balance among powers. However, as time moved on two significant events took place. On 9 November 1989 the Berlin wall was pulled down and East Germany was united with West Germany restoring the 1945 position. Another big development was the dissolution of the Soviet Union on 26 December 1991 resulting in Russia and 15 new republics that were earlier parts of the Soviet Union. During the Cold War era (1946–91), the world had become bipolar: there was more or less a clear division in ideology as well, that is, democracy versus communist system, and a large number of recently independent countries from colonial rule which had declared themselves as non-aligned. All these led to one world euphoria. This was best described as the 'end of the history' by Francis Fukuyama's. He wrote: 'We may be witnessing the end of history as such: that is, the end point of mankind's ideological evolution and the universalization of Western liberal democracy as the final form of human government.'[11]

In contrast, an opposite point of view was soon articulated by Samuel P. Huntington. He beautifully described the new phenomenon in his book *The Clash of Civilizations and the Remaking of World Order* as follows:

The world became different in the early 1990s, but not necessarily more peaceful Change was inevitable, progress was not. A similar illusion of harmony flourished, briefly, at the end of each of the twentieth century's other major conflicts. World War was the 'war to end wars' and to make the world safe for democracy. World War II, as Franklin Roosevelt put it, would "end system of unilateral action, the exclusive alliances, the balances of power, and all the other expedients that have been tried for centuries – and have always failed.[12]

Huntington further argued:

In the post–Cold War world, the most important distinctions among peoples are not ideological, political, or economic. They are cultural. Peoples and nations are attempting to answer the most basic question humans can face: Who are we? And they are answering that question in the traditional way as human beings have answered it, by reference to the things that mean most to them. People define themselves in terms of ancestry, religion, language, history, values, customs, and institutions. They identify with cultural groups; tribes, ethnic groups, religious communities, nations and at the broadest level, civilizations. People use politics not just to advance their interests but also to define their identity. We know who we are only when we know who we are not and often only when we know whom we are against.[13]

He concluded: 'In the emerging era, clashes of civilization are the greatest threat to world peace, and an international order based on civilizations is the surest safeguard against world war.'[14]

My own thinking was that there was reason to be optimistic. In 1998, I shared my views in my book *India's Culture: The State, the Arts, and Beyond.* I wrote: 'In the last decade of the 20th century culture emerged as a third factor in determining the status of a nation in the world after market and military strength, the market having replaced military strength from its position of supremacy in the post–Cold War World.'[15]

I met Samuel P. Huntington twice during 1997–8 in New Delhi to discuss the viability of the theory of harmony among civilizations in the modern world. Francis Fukuyama also called on me to discuss this theme of harmony among civilizations in June 2001 at Washington DC.

Interestingly, my forecast that culture would come to dominate world affairs did materialize, but not in the manner that I had visualized. And this is how it happened.

Mahatma Gandhi had instructed his followers that India's Independence movement was against the servitude and exploitation of the colonial order and not against the British themselves. Senior leaders of the new republic such as Jawaharlal Nehru, Vallabhbhai Patel, Abul Kalam Azad, Rajendra Prasad, and B.R. Ambedkar concentrated their energy and time in drafting and debating the constitution for independent India and on establishing institutions in the fields of the sciences and arts, literature, philosophy, and technology, and most significantly on the participation of ordinary citizens in democratic governance.

This constructive phenomenon was not experienced in several newly independent countries of Asia and Africa, nor among the nation states which emerged after the dissolution of the Soviet Union in 1991. In these countries, there was deep resentment against the cruelty inflicted by colonialists and dictators on their people and against economic exploitation by imperialist powers. In these circumstances, fundamentalists in several countries fomented hatred and hostility and used religion and traditional values to support their ideas.

To my mind the future of peace and harmony in the twenty-first century is directly linked to issues concerning (*i*) poverty and increasing inequality; (*ii*) ecology, global warming, and climate change; (*iii*) nuclear weapons, emerging technology of warfare, and continuing arms race among nation states; (*iv*) geopolitics and nationalism; and (*v*) religious extremism.

One has to appreciate that geopolitical plates are moving rapidly since 1945. The UN, the international body set up in 1945 for keeping peace, has not been able to either limit and prevent war in several places. States continue to threaten each other with force (now including nuclear weapons), notwithstanding prohibitions prescribed in the UN Charter and international law, and also despite the availability of institutions and mechanisms for peaceful conflict resolution. The 'state of perpetual peace' is nowhere in sight.

The flashpoint came on the morning of 11 September 2001 when aircraft flown by Al-Qaeda crashed into the USA's World Trade Center at New York and the Pentagon, its defence headquarters in Washington DC, and one crash-landed in field in southern Pennsylvania; a new era thus began. The attack, which lasted just 1 hour and 42 minutes, forced the world to look at the threat to world peace posed by religiously motivated violence. It became a landmark not only in the lives of those who were physically affected and had barely survived, but also of millions of others around the world. Soon commenced the military attack on Afghanistan. The regime change in Afghanistan was followed by the invasion of Iraq, and finally, almost ten years later, the entry of the US navy seals in Abbottabad in Pakistan on 1 May 2011, leading to the capture and killing of Osama bin Laden, the leader of the Al-Qaeda.

UN AT 75: DOES IT PROVIDE GUARANTEE FOR WORLD PEACE?

At 75, the UN, which had vowed to resolve conflicts at the time of its birth seems to be weak. It is true that since the establishment of the UN in 1945, the world has managed to avoid a Third World War. But we also saw that both during the North Korea crisis and in the aftermath of the killing of a top Iranian General in Baghdad, the UN Security Council simply looked on. There is a very real fear that if the UN, particularly the Security Council is not reorganized to reflect the current political and economic power of member states of the UN, its effectiveness to guarantee world peace will further get weakened.

ARE WARS GOING TO END?

We have already entered into the third decade of the twenty-first century. Many people in the world are deeply concerned about the onset of World War III. During the last two decades the world has witnessed unfolding contours of World War III between the USA and North Korea and between the USA and Iran. There have been several other flashpoints of conflagration such as those between Israel and Palestine, India and Pakistan, and perpetual violent events in Afghanistan and several countries in the Middle East. How could this situation be altered?

An answer to this question has baffled many creative minds including Albert Einstein and Sigmund Freud. The 'Einstein–Freud Correspondence (1931–1932)' is instructive in this behalf. Historically, conflicts of interests between one person and the other are resolved in principle by recourse to violence. The superior force prevailed everywhere. In course of time, rule of law came into operation giving powers to the state to settle disputes. Similarly conflicts among the states are to be resolved by international organizations. But today the rule of law is not obtained in many parts of the world or even within a country. Fortunately, the cultural development of mankind has been in progress for centuries. Nation states, however, are at different levels of development.

Sigmund Freud articulated this phenomenon beautifully when he concluded his letter to Einstein in 1932 with the following observation:

How long have we to wait before the rest of men turn pacifist? Impossible to say, and yet perhaps our hope that these two factors—man's cultural disposition and a well-founded dread of the form that future wars will take—may serve to put an end to war in the near future, is not chimerical. But by what ways or byways this will come about, we cannot guess. Meanwhile we may rest on the assurance that whatever makes for cultural development is working also against war.[16]

The fundamental issue of the twenty-first century became how to promote an environment that is conducive to maintenance of peace and harmony. Peace is not simply the absence of war or cessation of conflicts among nation states. Peace is an essential quality that should characterize human activities as the world faces several issues: political, religious, economic, and cultural. Peace can be secured firmly only in a wider environment where injustice, inequality, and exploitation are tackled effectively and there is freedom of expression and dignity of human life.

Similarly, as the Second World War was finally coming to a close and the world leaders were busy giving shape to the new global political order to save the succeeding generations of mankind from scourges of war, there was realization at various levels, including among military leaders, about the futility of war. A typical example from among the military leaders was the statement of General Douglas MacArthur before the US Congress on 19 April 1951. He thoughtfully stated:

Men since the beginning of time have sought peace, Various methods through the ages have been attempted to devise an international process to prevent or settle disputes between nations. From the very start, workable methods were found insofar as individual citizens were concerned; but the mechanics of an instrumentality of larger international scope have never been successful. Military alliances, balances of power, leagues of nations, all in turn failed leaving the only path to be by way of the crucible of war. The utter destructiveness of war now blots out this alternative. We have had our last chance. If we will not devise some greater and more equitable system, Armageddon will be at the door. The problem basically is theological and involves a spiritual recrudescence and improvement of human character that will synchronize with our almost matchless advances in science, art, literature, and all material and cultural developments of the past 2,000 years. It must be of the spirit if we are to save the flesh.[17]

Keeping all these challenges in view, I have propounded the *Bahudhā approach* in the aftermath of the 9/11 tragedy of the USA.

ORIGINS OF THE BAHUDHĀ APPROACH

The Bahudhā approach has interesting origins. At the time of the 9/11 catastrophe in the USA, I was executive director of the World Bank in Washington DC. In the aftermath of the tragedy, it became fashionable for every think tank to discuss two questions: 'What went wrong?' and 'Why people hate us (Americans)?' I happened to attend one such meeting during September 2001 itself in Washington DC. The gathering was impressive; I was seated almost opposite the chairperson. The guest speaker had concluded on the sombre note outlining the need for building a coalition of nations against terrorism. He also spoke of the radicalization of Islam, values of religious pluralism, and the need for tolerance. After the presentation was over, the chairperson asked for comments and looked at me. She said that India may have the answer in view of its heritage of pluralism and originality of mind, and gave me the floor. I was not prepared. I recall having said that 'while India may have the answer, I do not' and went on to narrate my experiences in handling terrorism in India. I was aware of the inadequacy of my response. For the real question was: What could we do to achieve harmony in a world so globalized, yet with nations so unequal, living in mutual distrust, fear, and worse terror?

Since then I started contemplating this theme with a view to exploring an enduring framework for a global public policy—a policy for harmony among different peoples and societies in the post 9/11 world as seen through the lens of the Indian civilization experience.

THE BAHUDHĀ APPROACH

An attitude that has greatly contributed to the enrichment of harmonious life in India is 'respect for another person's view of truth with hope and belief that he or she may be right'. This is best expressed in the Rigvedic hymn that was enjoyed more than three millennia ago: *Ekam Sad Vipra Bahudhā Vadanti* (The Real is one; the learned speak of it variously).

Pluralism is the closest equivalent of Bahudhā in English. But Bahudhā denotes much more than pluralism as dharma conveys more than religion.

The Bahudhā approach recognizes that there is a distinction between plural societies and pluralism. Pluralism is an inevitable ingredient of democratic societies. The role of religion, language, and ethnicity is very significant in plural societies. Pluralism in this context is an imperative for both developed and developing societies.

Pluralist societies are necessarily multi-ethnic, multi-religious, and multilingual societies. In such societies, there are various boundaries: racial, linguistic, religious, and, at times, even ideological. The Bahudhā approach does not believe in annexation or transgression of boundaries or assimilation of identities and propagation of a simplistic world view. It merely facilitates dialogue and thereby promotes understanding of the collective good. The realization of one's own identity may sustain boundaries and yet, at the same time, understanding of other identities may help formulate a public policy of harmony. The Bahudhā approach is conscious of the fact that societies without boundaries are not possible.

The culture of Bahudhā is deeply rooted in the inculcation of a special attitude from an early age. Dialogue requires a state of mind where one can strongly believe in one's own way of looking at issues while simultaneously accommodating another's point of view. It is this mental discipline that makes one willing to consider the validity of another person's view point.

In short, the Bahudhā approach is both a celebration of diversity and an attitude of mind that respects another person's point of view. Democracy and dialogue are central to this approach.

Diversity demands celebration of different religions, gods and goddesses, and belief systems. It also promotes a feeling that the world would be a dull and over-uniform place if there was only one religion, one god, one language, one folklore, and one folktale. The human species cannot be all of one belief or faith or system: humanity is diversity—something we too often forget.

It is up to us to move towards a clash of civilizations or harmony among them; to indulge in wanton destruction of forests or to conserve them; to permit oligarchs to control the destiny of future generations or to give people a say in the formulation of policies which affect their lives; to allow killing of innocents at the hands of terrorists or to control it firmly; to teach hatred or love; and so on.

In this matrix, our perception as well as our approach needs to change radically to avoid collapse of the existing international order. This is both for self-preservation and collective survival. The emotional frontier is becoming as important as our geographical frontiers. A tolerant world calls for appreciation of differences and similarities of others with one's values and belief systems.

The great human achievements of technology need to be fused with enhanced powers of humane, compassionate, and moral judgement. The challenge is clearly before all of us and we have to harness spiritual energy to make the world a better place to live.

A brief analysis of the global scene (particularly in the twenty-first century) would help appreciate the enormousness of the challenge and the relevance of the Bahudhā approach.

THE GLOBAL SCENE AND THE BAHUDHĀ APPROACH

Looking at the emerging world in terms of major civilizations it seems that four of these—the Western, the Chinese, the Indian, and the Islamic—will continue to influence global geopolitics and culture. Notwithstanding some signs of decline, Western civilization, the originator of major innovations for the past three centuries, will continue to play an important role in global affairs. The Indian and Chinese civilizations have had a very rich past and they are major demographic centres in the world. As regards Islam, there is *negative perception* particularly in the West today. Believers in Islam, who are some 1.5 billion Muslims, a fourth of the world's population, are widely seen as austere, intolerant, and prone to violence. Their achievements in art, architecture, astronomy, mathematics, medicine, poetry, and music are rarely highlighted. The Middle East as a whole, once testament to the Arab genius for civilization, is viewed as authoritarian and narrow-minded. The Arab Spring did not improve the situation; instead it turned out to be an Arab winter, as much of the region has turned in on itself, becoming more introverted. Fortunately, cities such as Dubai and Doha today and old classics of the golden era of Islamic civilization give us some hope.

Many believe that the twenty-first century will belong to Asia and that economic and political power will shift from the West to the East. This shift power would largely be towards China and India. The three Asian giants—China, India, and Japan—will make manifold contributions to the global society as time passes. In the emerging world of the twenty-first century there will be multiple centres of power. All nation states are not going to be equal, and great powers are still going to exist. The geopolitics in the era of globalization has clearly established that the only global order that has any chance of ensuring peace is a pluralist one which accepts that there are open and closed societies, and free and authoritarian ones.

Notwithstanding the declaration of peaceful behaviour by the Chinese leadership, there are apprehensions with regard to its territorial goals. In recent years, Vietnam, India, Japan, and the Philippines have all complained about Chinese incursions into disputed areas. Beijing is engaged in 'land reclamation' projects across the South China Sea, creating full-fledged islands that are likely equipped with military facilities to reinforce its claims of territorial waters far from the Chinese mainland.

Many observers fear that China will alter the international order. Is this fear misplaced? As I see it, China desires to have a leading role, but it would also like to operate within existing norms and will not lay down its own rules. It may be mentioned that China has been a permanent member of the Security Council for several years. Like the USA and other major powers, it has exercised the veto power to protect its strategic interests and to help its allies. It is natural to expect that like any other great power, China will use these institutions in future as well to promote its geopolitical objectives. Some other observers also entertain the hope that in the long run China will adopt some liberal policies and that would create comfort in China's neighbourhood, including in India, Japan, Vietnam, and in Southeast Asia.

It may be mentioned that China and India were civilization-states in the past. Confucius advocated that the rulers must be benevolent. India has a long tradition of Hindu and Buddhist philosophy which advocates peace and primacy of dharma over military force. India has never gone to another country bearing arms throughout its ageless history. Michael Wood appropriately writes in this regard: 'History is full of Empires of the Sword, but India alone created an Empire of the Spirit.'[18]

In the coming years, Asia's three biggest economies—China, India, and Japan—are likely to present new growth models. The fact that these countries are led by strong and experienced leaders is significant: China's Xi Jinping; India's Narendra Modi; and Japan's Shinzo Abe. The reformation in the economy and technological progress that the trio seeks to accomplish in their respective countries could be a growth driver of the world's economy, a hope that is supported by the poor and the unemployed in these countries and other parts of the world.

The pace of democratization of information and technology (despite some areas of 'no-entry') has come to mean that anyone can get his or her hands on anything that would help him innovate and become a centre of power and influence. Notwithstanding this phenomenon, one can still reasonably hold the view that the USA would continue to play a major role in the twenty-first century in several fields including the world economy, science and technology, culture, and the democratic way of life. However, the twenty-first century would be different from the twentieth century as the USA would be increasingly required to share global influence with many other countries.

China, India, Japan, Russia, Germany, Brazil, South Africa, Indonesia, and Iran are going to play dominant roles in world affairs in the twenty-first century. The increase in the share of world trade of these countries and augmentation of their military strength would enable them to have a greater say in political as well as economic organs of global governance.

RISE OF CHINA AND THE THUCYDIDES TRAP IN THE TWENTY-FIRST CENTURY

The Greek general, strategic thinker, and historian Thucydides (441 BC) reflecting upon the causes of the Peloponnesian war wrote: 'What made war inevitable was the growth of Athenian power and the fear which this caused in Sparta.' This analysis has been called the 'Thucydides Trap' which refers to a situation when a rising power causes fear in an established power and that escalates toward war. In today's context the question is: Would the rise of China as an economic and military power challenge the supremacy of the sole superpower the USA and lead to war?

For the seven decades following World War II, a rules-based framework has defined the world order. It has ensured a world without war among great powers. Today, several scholars think that China, the new superpower, is increasingly questioning this order. In a recent book titled *Destined for War: Can America and China Escape Thucydides's Trap*, Graham Allison asserts that 'China and the United States are currently on a collision course for war—unless both parties take difficult and painful actions to avert it.' It is worth recalling that in the last century a rising Germany had rattled Britain's established position on the top and that resulted in World War II.[19]

In the present-day world, Xi Jinping of China and Donald Trump of the USA personify their country's aspirations for greatness. Allison asks:

Will Presidents Trump and Xi, or their successors, follow in the tragic footsteps of the leaders of Athens and Sparta or Britain and Germany? Or will they find a way to avoid war as effectively as Britain and the US did a century ago or the US and the Soviet Union did through four decades of Cold War? Obviously, no one knows. We can be certain, however, that the dynamic Thucydides identified will intensify in the years ahead.[20]

Amidst these assertions, the growth of China's economic and military strength under an authoritarian–capitalist system, theoretically wedded to communist ideology, makes an interesting picture. Since 1980, China has made phenomenal progress both as an economic and military power. China took full advantage of the growing potential of unrestricted global commerce to emerge as the number one trading nation and the second-largest economy in the world. In fact, China has attained this new position of an economic powerhouse while complying with the rules of the WTO, which it joined in 2001. China has built a powerful military. Its military budget has risen from USD 17 billion in 1990 to USD 152 billion in 2017—a 900 per cent increase in twenty-five years.

In 1946, China christened itself as the People's Republic of China and adopted the authoritarian model of polity management under the Communist Party of China (CPC). The Chinese state since then has continued to control its economy and has succeeded in expanding the market share of Chinese enterprises both in China and abroad. The USA and the Western countries had, however, visualized that trade and technology support to China on liberal commercial terms would eventually turn China into a Western-style market economy. This did not happen. Instead, China has continued as an authoritarian, one-party state. The two institutions which control and back the Chinese nation state are the Communist Party of China (CPC) and the People's Liberation Army (PLA).

China is a permanent member of the UN Security Council with veto power. It has used this position to promote its strategic interests. Already China is exercising considerable political influence in Asia thanks to its enormous powerful economic clout. Malaysia, South Korea, and Vietnam have upgraded diplomatic and military relations with China. The phenomenal rise of China as a global power has forced Japan to come out of the dilemma of continuing the post–Second World War policy of dependence on the USA for its security. It is considering rearming itself more heavily, perhaps even with nuclear weapons. China's rise is weighing heavily on the Association of Southeast Asian Nations (ASEAN) too. Beijing's pressure has tilted states such as Cambodia towards China and weakened the USA's ties with the Philippines and Thailand. China is confronted with a string of American allies and partners: South Korea, Japan, Taiwan, the Philippines, Singapore, and Vietnam.

The Communist Party's raison d'être and source of legitimacy since the beginning of market reforms in the late 1970s have been successful economic modernization and the maintenance of social stability during that process. In 2013 China announced the 'One Belt One Road' (OBOR) initiative that would lead to ports, railways, roads, and airfields linking China to Southeast Asia, Central Asia, the Middle East, and Europe. It is meant to be either fully or in parts a kind of new Silk Road that would greatly expand China's economic and diplomatic influence. Sixty-four countries have joined this initiative. Besides setting up manufacturing units and modernizing its defence infrastructure, China has also invested very significantly in upgrading its public institutions, including in the areas of health care and education.

China is likely to remain an authoritarian country, and its success will probably encourage other authoritarian regimes to resist the pressure to change. At the same time, however, it is aware that the political and economic architecture created after World War II and the present-day global trading system have facilitated its growth and economic success enormously. The Chinese youth educated in Chinese universities, as well as abroad, understand the significance of peace, stability, and development in Asia and in other parts of the world. Above all, China's age-old traditions, the fact that it is a 'civilization state', and the prevalence of Buddhist philosophy in several parts of the country give one hope that it will not cause any major conflict in the coming decades of the twenty-first century.

Looking at the history of China since 1946, one cannot rule out border skirmishes and trade conflicts between it and its neighbours. Given this background, I do not see a full-fledged war between China and the USA or with its neighbours in the coming decades that the 'Thucydides Trap' envisages, though the chances are that it will continue to be a lively metaphor in academic discourse.

SOUTH ASIA: WILL THERE BE A NEW ERA OF AMITY?

It must be acknowledged that in twentieth-century South Asia, primordial loyalties of religion, ethnicity, caste, and sect were aroused and dominated the social and political discourse, alongside the movement for freedom from British rule. This period also witnessed the spread of modern education and the development of fresh insights into India's civilizational attainments recorded in several languages, especially Sanskrit, Tamil, and Pali.

The 1940s witnessed a hardening of attitudes among the leaders of the Congress and the Muslim League. It may be recalled that as time went on, two contrasting visions about the future of India emerged: one, advocating the integrity of India based on Hindu–Muslim unity and the other the creation of Pakistan based on the two-nation theory. These sentiments found powerful exposition in the Congress Presidential address made by Maulana Azad in 1940 and the Muslim League Presidential address delivered by Md. Ali Jinnah in the same year.

In his address, Maulana Azad asserted that

it was India's historic destiny that many human races and cultures should flow to her, finding a home in her hospitable soil, and that many a caravan should find rest here. ... Eleven hundred years of common history (of Islam and Hinduism) have enriched India with our common achievements. Our languages, our poetry, our literature, our culture, our art, our dress, our manners and customs, the innumerable happenings of our daily life, everything bears the stamp of our joint endeavour. ... These thousand years of our joint life have moulded us into a common nationality. ... Whether we like it or not, we have now become an Indian nation, united and indivisible. No fantasy or artificial scheming to separate and divide can break this unity.

The vision of Md. Ali Jinnah was sharply different. In his presidential address, he declared that

it is a dream that Hindus and Muslims can evolve a common nationality, and this misconception of one Indian nation has gone far beyond the limits, and is the cause of most of our troubles, and will lead India to destruction, if we fail to revise our actions in time. The Hindus and Muslims belong to two different religious philosophies, social customs and literature. They neither intermarry, nor interdine together, and indeed they belong to two different civilizations which are based mainly on conflicting ideas and conceptions. Their aspects on and of life are different.

These two statements were, in fact, the manifestos of the Congress and the Muslim League. The conflict over these visions became central to the outcome of the freedom struggle. Simply put this led to communal divide between the Hindus and the Muslims, which in turn stiffened attitudes of communities towards each other, leading to political division of the country. On 15 August 1947, India attained freedom, but was divided into two countries, India and Pakistan. The Partition was accompanied by unprecedented violence, with more than one million Hindus and Muslims dead. The shame of violence was widespread. In many ways, we are still grappling with the legacies of these notions.

The British withdrew hastily. Winston Churchill, no friend of Indian Independence, termed it a 'shameful flight'. This Partition created more than 11 million refugees. This cataclysmic event was followed by the Pakistani attempt to capture the state of Jammu & Kashmir forcibly. Pakistan continues to be in control of a large tract of the state. In 1971, after a bloody civil war brought on by the inept and callous military and political leadership, Pakistan lost control over its eastern half, which became a new country, Bangladesh. That war which resulted in the creation of Bangladesh witnessed the killing of over half a million of its fellow Muslim citizens by the Pakistani army. There continue to be a number of territorial disputes and repeated incidents of cross border terrorism originating from Pakistan. The consequences and ramifications continue to impact other neighbouring countries, particularly Afghanistan and China.

The Partition of India, a decision taken in haste by a handful of men, has proved to be a monumental failure. The people of the region, where millions are still living below the poverty line, are in dire need of improvement in their economic condition. The painful question that continues to haunt us is whether the Partition of India was merely a division of one nation into two, or the breaking-up of a civilizational ethos that had held good for centuries.

I have always viewed Partition both as a political failure as well as a civilizational one. Should the youth of South Asia not ponder over their contemporary history and focus on how they might cooperate in building a better future?

It may be mentioned that the primordial loyalties of religion, ethnicity, caste, and sects were aroused and dominated social and political discourse in South Asia alongside the movement for freedom from the British rule in the twentieth century. It also saw the spread of modern education and fresh insights into India's civilizational attainments recorded in several languages: Sanskrit, Tamil, and Pali, among others.

The Partition created an unprecedented crisis and continues to do so. In particular the Partition raised mind-walls and spread hatred. Today, the situation in India's neighbourhood is not conductive to peace as Pakistan not only provides safe havens to terrorist outfits but uses terrorism as an instrument of state policy. All these are directly related to Partition. The Pakistan Army, the Mullahs, among others have developed vested interests to persist with these divides. It has caused armed conflicts between India and Pakistan (in 1947, 1965, 1971, and 1999). In 1971 Pakistan was divided into Pakistan and Bangladesh on the grounds of language. The inept and callous military and political leadership accelerated the process.

Thankfully a new wind has started blowing, although it is weak. People are looking at their past afresh and entertaining new ambitions fuelled by forces generated by information technology and from movement of capital and technology. Would globalization and its twin sisters technology and capital, supported by new innovations in education, create a new set of social relations, and a fresh approach towards unity and harmony in society, polity, and economy in South Asia? Would the new elite of India, Bangladesh, and Pakistan overcome the partition crisis in this century?

Since the inauguration of the democratic Republic, faith in India's rise at the global level has gained strength and today it looks like a clear possibility. There is little doubt that India, with strong and sensible political leadership both at the centre and in the states, can accelerate the pace of its economic and industrial progress.

Of course, India's immense diversity—multiplicity of religions, languages, castes, and belief patterns—presents enormous challenges as it makes decision-making processes slow, thus increasing the difficulty of arriving at a unity of approach necessary for implementation. This results, at times, in delaying concerted action on important national issues. However, this plurality is not such a disadvantage. The various cultural traits and practices as well as religious beliefs that have poured into India throughout the ages have created a kind of synthesis which needs to be accommodated when political and administrative decisions are taken. If handled well by well-meaning leaders, the presence of diversity in our society can be utilized to bring about a rich and harmonious way of life.

India's march towards progress and celebration of diversity has been guaranteed by democracy and the rule of law. In fact, India's political stability can be strengthened by a strong and decisive political leadership through its democratic institutions and pluralist ethos. Creative leadership igniting the minds of youth can accelerate both the pace of progress and the construction of an inclusive society in India.

India has been a civilization state since the beginning of the state formation processes. To many it seems unlikely that the republic would recapture the territory that made Mughal or British India a confederation of nation states along India's historic boundaries during the twenty-first century. Towards the end of the twentieth century we saw how the energy of the country's youth and the dynamism of its entrepreneurs were released. The aspirational class of young men and women in Bangladesh and Pakistan may support the idea of a confederation as a way of conciliation. At a deeper level, there may be a positive response to the call that civilizational oneness could unites us against religion and ethnicity, recently created political boundaries (1947 and 1971), and the will of the armed forces.

If we look at the global scene we find that in this part of the world interplay of ideas, religion and culture, and scientific advancement gives India and its neighbouring states a unique position. India has been home to Hinduism, Buddhism, Jainism, Islam, Sikhism, and others for several centuries. In its neighbourhood, the people of Nepal profess Hinduism. Bhutan is a Buddhist state, as are Sri Lanka and Myanmar to a large extent. An overwhelming majority of people in Pakistan, Bangladesh, and Afghanistan are believers of Islam. All these nation states have a history of civilizational unity within their geography and with each other. During the last seven decades, the working of democracy in India and other countries of the region has imparted new meaning and content to harmonious living among people of different faiths and ethnicities in tune with the Bahudhā spirit.

Even after seven decades, the wounds of Partition are alive. Thus it is no wonder that any aggressive assertion of faith-based identity provokes fears in the society. It is therefore essential to fashion our political discourse and think in larger terms of citizenship and fundamental rights, which duly take into account and protect religious and cultural rights of every person and community. All over the world minorities have benefited substantially by articulating their concerns in the framework of citizenship and basic rights rather than demanding special and exclusive treatment.

Towards this end, we have to realize that it is the duty of the present generation to strengthen forces of amity and harmony among communities. Mohammad Ali Jinnah founded Pakistan in 1947 and reiterated his promise that the Muslims of the subcontinents would now finally be able to fulfil their cultural and civilizational destiny notwithstanding the bloodbath of ethnic cleansing and sectarian violence that took place. His fundamental premise was that Hindus and Muslims could never live together. The creation of the new state of Bangladesh in 1971, carved out of Pakistan, was recognition of the fact that Islam cannot be a state. There are other forces such as language, shared history, and living experiences which are equally relevant. It became evident that Pakistan was created out of a false premise and that Islam constituted a nation. It was a misnomer then as well as today. In case of the subcontinent, one has put it eloquently that 'Islam as nation' was thrown out in the Bay of Bengal in 1971. People are not happy that Pakistan has developed a habit of renting itself to powerful nation states such as the USA, Saudi Arabia, China, and others. It may be mentioned that earlier the comment that 'all countries have armies, but in Pakistan, an army has a country' was resented by Pakistanis. This comment is now even heard in Pakistan freely.

The crying needs of the people for good education, health care, employment, and dignity cannot be secured by military rulers. The people of the region are also fully aware that the South Asian Association for Regional Cooperation (SAARC) has not fulfilled the objectives for which it was created. For the partition attitudes come in the way of positive directions. We have to create a Confederation of South Asian Nations and even think of linking it up with ASEAN countries. The other alternative is to consider the lines of the European Union. I have faith in modern minds among the youth, teachers, scholars, and political leaders that they can think out of the box and become agents of change. It is up to the new generation of youth who are well educated and trained not only in their own countries but also abroad to take a lead in this regard.

BAHUDHĀ IN MODERN TIMES

Bahudhā and the Post 9/11 World, since it was published in 2008, has not only received aplomb but has also been subjected to critical analysis both within India and outside. A large number of post-publication commentaries (published in newspapers and seminar notes) have come to me; I have enjoyed reading these while drawing benefit towards expansion of my own understanding of the subject in the wider human context of peace and progress. Questions have been raised as to whether violence in our world and the acquisition/pursuit of weapons of mass destruction are not beyond Bahudhā philosophy? Is Bahudhā not an ideal which no country is willing to practice? Can any country risk its application unilaterally? The ever increasing threats of destabilization, including by highly motivated non-state actors, make it impossible for any country to follow the Bahudhā approach. To several of them, hope is idealism and clashes and conflicts are real.

An overwhelming majority of commentaries on and reviews of *Bahudhā and the Post 9/11 World* have praised the book as the need of our time and a magnificent contribution to knowledge. An explicit endorsement came from Professor Sabyasachi Bhattacharya, an eminent historian of India. He said:

B.P. Singh's argument is just the opposite of the work of Samuel Huntington entitled 'The Clash of Civilizations and the remarking of the World Order'. ... While B.P. Singh sees in pluralism the resolution, the prospect of resolution of national and international discord, Huntington emphasized that conflict, which is inherent in politics, is inevitable. The inevitability of conflict is written very large in Huntington's book. B.P. Singh's book is about the long history of Bahudhā from the Vedic times through Buddhism to the Panchsheel principles of Jawaharlal Nehru. Thus, these two represent contending alternative approaches to the world around us today, as well as alternative approaches to understand the past history. But here are many things which are wrong in Huntington's thesis and many things which are right in what B.P. Singh tell us. If we accept the conflictual account as the only true interpretation of history, the practical consequence is to sow the seeds of further conflict. The emphasis on pluralism as a value has the potential of creating a moral climate more suitable for resolving the conflict. That is the choice before us and in B.P. Singh's book we see a reasonable argument which tells us why our choice should be in favour of an approach which is built upon the concepts of Bahudhā. In fact, in social sciences we cannot get away from making moral choices. B.P. Singh's notion of Bahudhā has the potential of opening a line of thinking that involves both the moral choice and intellectual endeavour.[21]

Things in the second decade of the twenty-first century (in fact after the publication of *Bahudhā and the Post 9/11 World*), particularly in the realms of geopolitics, economics, and technology, have been moving fast and at considerable expense. In fact, since the tragic events of 9/11 in the USA and further violence in Afghanistan, Iraq and Syria have accorded a commanding position to religion- and ethnicity-based terrorism in the game of geopolitics.. When geopolitics dominate a region or the global scene, state systems, whether democratic or authoritarian, come under severe stress and peace is threatened. Further complications come about as a result of the interplay of historical legacies, radical views, and religions as witnessed since 2010.

Three events of the second decade of the present century in particular establish the changing realities of geography and nationalism and the complexities of religious phenomena. First, the merger of Crimea into Russia in March 2014 generated fears about peace and tranquillity in Europe and beyond. Second, China's claims over the South China Sea as well as islands that Japan, the Philippines, and Vietnam consider their own are also developments reminiscent of the games of geopolitics of the preceding century. Third, the Islamic State of Iraq and Ash-sham (ISIS), a jihadi militia of Sunni Muslim groups in Syria set up in June 2014, conquered large parts of territory in Syria and across northern and western Iraq. It was clear that Iraq and Syria by themselves could not contain the ISIS, as military conflicts between Sunni and Shia sects as well as Christians and Muslims have spread to several countries in the Arab world and North Africa. Fortunately, the ISIS menace is now under control thanks to proactive steps taken by the USA and other powers, including killing of ISIS leader Abu Bakr Al-Baghdadi on 26 October 2019. But the Islamic State (IS) is alive, for geopolitical tensions, civil conflicts, and foreign interventions have been a source of power for jihadist groups such as the Al-Qaeda and the IS. The group still has affiliates and arms in several parts of the world such as Afghanistan, Egypt, and Nigeria. The Shia–Sunni sectarianism that the IS tried to exploit is still burning across West Asia. They have enough reasons to indulge in violence. For the IS, violence is linked to their survival. The group is likely to retain its need to kill in order to survive.

There is also a threat to a rules-based world order. Authoritarian countries such as China and Russia continue to follow global codes, but from time to time they would also like to have such changes in the rules that would suit promotion of their interests. Iran and North Korea have shown proclivities to defy the rules. The USA too under the leadership of Donald Trump is in a defiant mood to pursue objectives of 'America first'. How to save the rules-based liberal world order? The leaders and strategic thinkers and officials in France, Germany, Italy, the United Kingdom, and the EU in Europe; India, Japan, Indonesia, and South Korea in Asia; and also Brazil, South Africa, Australia, and Canada are the obvious candidates to give ideas as well as to provide leadership.

HERITAGE OF EVIL?

Another matter of great worry is the cult of violence that is taking deep root. A group of radical Islamists has advocated terrorism and violence as instruments of achieving world government based on Islam. This is comparatively a new phenomenon. Terror is founded on the idea that only killing guarantees meaning. All else seems feeble, uncertain, and inadequate. On that foundation are built the various motivations used to justify the acts of terror. There are no distinctions of class or age. For the dictum is: 'In this garden no one entered except those who wanted to be an assassin.'[22] It casts a special responsibility on all of us, including upon leaders of Islam. We must not allow this evil to become heritage.

SOME OPTIMISTIC DEVELOPMENTS

There is something eternal about geopolitics. It never disappears. It only changes its character and takes new stances. These developments will be for fresh dialogues and conciliatory approaches.

The future of harmonious living demands sharing of a perspective that accommodates different points of view and respect for the ideals of Bahudhā. Several hopeful developments have taken place in recent times as well.

World leaders are well aware of and concerned about peace, ecology, and dignity of life and are making efforts towards finding solutions. Concerted efforts are being made to achieve the targets defined by the Millennium Development Goals (MDGs) adopted in 2000. In the year 2015 world leaders assembled again at the UN and resolved to further the development agenda and adopted 17 Sustainable Development Goals (SDGs) and 169 targets. This was emotively titled 'Transforming Our World—2030 Agenda for Sustainable Development'.

NORTH KOREA AND USA RELATIONS

Fresh conflicts that emerged in the Korean peninsula since 2008 had brought with them the threat of the use of nuclear weapons of mass destruction. The spat between North Korea and the USA had reached a new low and witnessed use of foul and seriously undiplomatic language from both sides. In fact, in the closing months of 2017, North Korea, South Korea, and the USA faced the catastrophic prospect of a war situation that none of them wanted. The rest of the world was in fear of a potential nuclear conflict. Things moved dramatically in a positive direction and on 12 June 2018 US President Donald Trump and North Korea Supreme Leader Kim Jong-un met at Singapore and signed a joint statement agreeing to security guarantees for North Korea and peaceful relations among others. Earlier in March 2018, Moon Jae-in, the South Korean president, paid a visit to North Korea and at a public forum spoke of peace and made a plea for Korean unity. These were totally unexpected developments and showed the strength of the Bahudhā approach. The talks are continuing and their outcome would have a bearing upon both regional and global peace.

US–CHINA TRADE WAR

The bonhomie between the USA and China is over. In 2018, President Trump of the USA in a policy statement declared China as a strategic rival. Today China and the USA are engaged in a trade war by altering the terms of earlier tariffs placed on goods traded between them. And yet there is some optimism, although talks at official levels between the two countries are on—an essential prerequisite of the Bahudhā approach.

SUPPORT OF CHINA TO CIVILIZATIONAL DIALOGUE

China's President Xi Jinping in his address on 14 May 2019 at the conference of Asian Civilizations Dialogue debunked the 'clash of civilisations' theory and appealed for harmonious dialogue and coexistence between civilizations. He said:

It someone thinks their own race and civilization is superior and insists on remoulding or replacing other civilizations, it would be a stupid idea and disastrous act. ... We should hold up equality and respect, abandon pride and prejudice, deepen our knowledge about the differences between our own and other civilizations, and promote harmonious dialogue and coexistence between civilisations.[23]

SOUTH ASIA

History is a great teacher. It may be mentioned that the events of 9 November 1989, when the Berlin Wall came down, hold a special significance for Germans. For this was the first non-violent turn to liberty and democracy in German history. Similarly, the dissolution of the Soviet Union on 26 December 1991 restored national sovereignty of fifteen countries which constituted the Soviet Union; and pro-democracy revolutions that commenced earlier toppled communist order in Eastern and Central Europe previously and tore down the infamous Iron Curtain. This is a significant achievement of modern European history and needs to be conserved.

In the context of South Asia, real-life happenings at times are full of human brotherhood. It is difficult not to be moved by common civilizational expressions when you see a painting or hear a song covering economic and/or emotional bonds of commonality outside your country, for these constitute statements of the road not travelled in the last seven decades and more. The recent two happenings are worth recalling.

On 9 November 2019 two momentous events took place: one related to the Sikh religion and the other concerned with Hinduism and Islam. On this day, the Kartarpur Corridor was inaugurated, which was the realization of the long-cherished dream of Sikhs, almost in Bahudhā spirit. On the same day, the Supreme Court of India passed a judgment allowing the construction of the Ram temple at Ayodhya on the hitherto disputed site between Hindus and Muslims. These two events have made a deep impact on the followers of three major religions—Hinduism, Islam, and Sikhism—in India, Pakistan, Canada, and beyond.

RAM JANMABHOOMI–BABRI MASJID DISPUTE

Lord Ram, also referred to as Raja Ramachandra, is the seventh avatar of Lord Vishnu, the supreme Hindu god. Lord Ram was born at Ayodhya in Uttar Pradesh, a state of the Indian Union. His mother was Kaushalya and father Dasharatha of the Ayodhya Kingdom of ancient India. Lord Ram is the central figure of the ancient Hindu epic *Ramayana*, which is extremely popular in South Asian and Southeast Asian cultures. It is widely believed that the Ram temple that existed on the birthplace site on a plot of land measuring 67 acres of land was vandalized and a mosque was built on it in 1528–29 by general Mir Baqi, on orders of the Mughal emperor Babur. The mosque was popularly referred to as Babri Masjid. An irate Hindu mob pulled down the mosque on 6 December 1992. This led to fierce legal disputes between the contending parties since then. The Supreme Court of India, through the 'constitution bench' consisting of five judges, unanimously decided to allocate the entire 67 acres of land for construction of the Ram temple and directed the government to give five acres of land for construction of a mosque. On that day, with its verdict on the Ram Janmabhoomi–Babri Masjid case, the Supreme Court brought closure to one of the most contentious chapters in India's contemporary history.

It may be mentioned that over the years, the site has become as sacred to many Hindus as Mecca is to the Muslims. Several efforts for mediation were undertaken by both the communities to work out an amicable solution. This, however, did not succeed, but did ease the situation considerably.

Few disputes had divided the country as starkly on religious lines as this one. In fact, communal conflict that ensued between Hindus and Muslims after the Babri Masjid demolition in 1992–3 led to loss of 2000 innocent lives and huge amount of public and private property.

The Supreme Court in this judgment has shown virtues of clarity and decisiveness marked by unanimity and balance to uphold national unity in terms of the constitutions of India. It famously observed:

For a case replete with references to archaeological foundations, we must remember that it is the law which provides the edifice upon which our multicultural society rests. At the heart of the Constitution is a commitment to equality upheld and enforced by the rule of law. Under our Constitution, citizens of all faiths, beliefs and creeds seeking divine provenance are both subject to the law and equality before the law. The Constitution does not make a distinction between the faith and belief of one religion and another. All forms of belief, worship and prayer are equal.[24]

The Supreme Court verdict has provided an opportunity for building harmony and trust among the Hindus and Muslims. The way forward, therefore, is for both communities to move on to build a secular and progressive India.

Kartarpur Corridor
Guru Nanak (1469–1539), the founder of Sikhism and the first of the ten Sikh Gurus, was born at Talvandi and died at Kartarpur. After the Partition of

India, both these places came under Pakistan, a Muslim majority country. Gurudwara Kartarpur Sahab was raised at Kartarpur in 1925, well before the Partition. For the past seven decades, India and believers of Sikhism have been demanding a corridor between India and Pakistan for believers to visit and pay their respect at Gurudwara Kartarpur Sahab without any hindrance. The inauguration of the Kartarpur Corridor on 9 November 2019 was the realization of this long-cherished dream.

It may be mentioned that Guru Nanak was a votary of Hindu–Muslim unity, and before him two outstanding poets namely Ramananda (1400–1470) and his disciple Kabir (1940–1518) also strove for fusion of Hinduism and Islam. In the opinion of all three of them, God may be spoken of in many ways—as Allah or Brahman, Ram or Rahim. But the great name of God is Truth. In this background it is maturely hoped that the Kartarpur Corridor will be a confidence-building measure between India and Pakistan. It cannot be compared with the fall of the Berlin Wall but it will be a travesty of hope if Kartarpur became a military project for Pakistan. Besides political leadership the youth of India and Pakistan must keep Kartarpur as a positive force to improve relations between India and Pakistan and that would ensure all-round progress of the people.

I am aware of the 'hate speech' delivered by Pakistan Prime Minister Imran Khan at the UN General Assembly on 28 September 2019 in the aftermath of the abrogation of Article 370 of the Constitution of India providing for special status to Jammu and Kashmir. He also warned of a spectre of a war between the two nuclear-armed neighbours. In this background, the inauguration of the Kartarpur Corridor is indeed a big event in terms the Bahudhā spirit.

PEACE IN AFGHANISTAN AND ITS IMPACT ON SOUTH ASIA

After 9/11, new institutions of democratic governance were set up replacing the traditional system of administration by tribal chieftains. The US administration and troops sent after 9/11 have played an important role in this regard. The USA, under internal political pressures for withdrawal of their troops from Afghanistan, was negotiating a peace agreement with Taliban and the democratically elected Afghanistan government.

After years of violence, an initial peace agreement in Afghanistan appears to be in the realm of possibility. Nine rounds of talks between the Taliban and US officials have focused on the terms for a ceasefire, the withdrawal of foreign troops, and counterterrorism assurances by the Taliban. Fortunately, the talks which were postponed by the USA are likely to be resumed. In a surprise move, US President Donald Trump visited Afghanistan on 28

November 2019 and declared that US–Taliban talks are back on track.[25]

Finally, on 29 February 2020 the Afghan peace deal was signed between the officials of the USA and the chief of the Taliban at Doha, the capital of Qatar, ending the Afghan War that began with the US-led attack on Afghanistan on 7 October 2001. The US Secretary of State was present at the signing ceremony. The agreement provides for full withdrawal of the US and North Atlantic Treaty Organization (NATO) forces in the next fourteen months. The agreement envisages that the details of the settlement on the ground would be worked out by the Taliban with the Afghan government led by President Ashraf Ghani. This comprehensive ceasefire is expected to determine the role of the Taliban in future governance of Afghanistan. Obviously, too much faith has been laid on the Taliban by the USA.

Many fear, with good reason, that the return of the Taliban could threaten the progress made by women over two decades to secure equal rights to education, employment, and political participation. Also at risk are the democratic institutions and practices the Afghans have put into place since the Taliban were overthrown after the 9/11 terror attacks.

Under Taliban rule, girls above the age of eight were barred from schools, and women were banned from working and forcibly confined to their homes. In public, women had to be completely shrouded and were not permitted to speak above a whisper. Women were also punished severely for any semblance of independent conduct.

To enable political stability in Afghanistan, democratic institutions need to be affirmed and strengthened.

FORCES OF NATURE: THREAT TO THE END OF THE WORLD

The ecological crisis facing us is very serious. Today there is a credible threat to human survival from global warming and climate change with the potential to damage the lives and habitats of billions of people in different parts of the world.

Four events of the twenty-first century need to be particularly referred to: (*i*) bushfires in Brazil and Australia in 2019; (*ii*) extinction of certain species; (*iii*) outbreak of pandemic SARS (Severe Acute Respiratory Syndrome) in Hong Kong in 2002–3; and (*iv*) the coronavirus pandemic, popularly referred to as COVID-19.

The magnitude of destruction caused by the Australian bushfires was hard to comprehend. More than 6.3 million hectares of land were affected by the fires. In 2019, the Amazon rainforest saw a tremendous surge in fires.

It may be mentioned that a large number of species have already become extinct. We can recount here are some of the species that became extinct in

2019: three bird species, two frogs, a shark, a famous snail, and one of the world's largest freshwater fish.

The outbreak of SARS in Hong Kong in 2002–3 that had killed nearly 800 persons globally was declared a pandemic.

We are currently facing a coronavirus pandemic, popularly known as COVID-19, which first commenced from Wuhan in China in November–December 2019. COVID-19 was declared a pandemic by the World Health Organization (WHO) on 12 March, 2020. It has engulfed the entire world. It has infected over 2 million and has killed nearly 150,000 people, and the numbers are rising. (WHO figures as on 17 April 2020 are 2,206,348 infected and 148,649 dead.) COVID-19 has made a deep impact on the global economy, the global balance of power, and the very process of globalization. It has adversely affected travel and trade, resulted in a global slowdown, and, in fact, possible recession in the economy. All these have led to the deprivation of the lower and middle classes as well as daily wage earners of their means of livelihood.

The post-COVID world would be a different world. It has emphasized in clear terms that we are all interdependent and have to work for sharing economic benefits as well as fruits of science together on this planet, irrespective of religious, ethnic, economic, and cultural divides. It needs to be refashioned with hope and courage and respect for nature. We should employ science and human ingenuity with determination to overcome the present state of despondency. It is imperative to highlight that the post-COVID world will need far-sighted leadership and efficient institutions of governance.

Human beings have the capability to destroy their own environment but also the ability to rise above petty interests and to use technology for reversing the process of destruction of plant species and minimize carbon emissions. Nation states have to find ways of development that do not destroy nature, because nature is the ultimate source of all development. If nature is gone, development will become meaningless. Therefore, development must be in harmony with the conservation of nature. Science and technology have given us the capacity to accomplish this goal.

These four recent events have given us signals that if ecological problems are not attended to urgently the world may not need world wars to destroy itself!

There is thus an imperative requirement to contemplate and work towards building an ecological civilization that would outline the ways of living in harmony with nature. Dialogue and a belief in collective good mark the culture of Bahudhā, an approach that celebrates diversity and harmonious living.[26] It is necessary to build trust and social cohesion as these are crucial in multicultural societies and they in turn strengthen the forces of peace and stability.

TRUST AND SOCIAL COHESION

Talking about development, the Nobel laureate Kenneth Arrow reflected that 'much of the economic backwardness in the world can be explained by the lack of mutual confidence'.[27] The low level of trust implies low economic performance. This premise is also upheld by the World Values Survey (WVS) located in Stockholm, Sweden. In their report of 2019, it has highlighted the impact of values of trust on social, economic, and political life.[28] Decline in trust and social collection makes adverse impact on economy and other pursuits of life. I have witnessed as a young district officer in Assam how Marwari traders transacted their business on trust to their mutual benefit and provided hospitality to one another. Similarly, as governor of Sikkim (2008–13) it was my privilege to strengthen the processes of harmony between forces of democracy, culture, ecology, and administration. Thus, it is no wonder that Sikkim has become not only one of the best run states of India but also a model state. The concept of Gross National Happiness (GNH) of Bhutan also emphasizes trust and social cohesion as relevant to achieving happiness. These are axiomatic truths. The Bahudhā approach of respect for each other's religion, belief systems, and ways of living facilitate augmentation of trust; the social cohesion doctrine could be used to facilitate it.

The study of society and the behaviour of people have always fascinated me. I am aware that both peace and conflict characterize humanity and also the fact that ideas do influence the course of history. My approach to history and politics is based on my deep optimism that the world must and could be improved.

It is no longer possible to lead an isolated life in our current global society. People of different faiths and beliefs live together. It is, therefore, necessary to understand each other's needs, aspirations, faiths, and belief practices. We have to learn to live together in concord in spite of traditional differences of religion, civilization, nationality, class, and race. To accomplish this, we have to know each other, which includes knowing each other's past. We must learn to recognize and, as far as possible, understand the different cultural configurations in which human nature has expressed itself through indifferent religions, civilizations, and nationalities.

We have to acknowledge that compassion, love, and respect are intrinsic, just as hatred and brutality also are. Those biological attributes cannot be extinguished but we have the potential to augment our capacity to promote compassion and good neighbourliness. What is required is that good and intelligent individuals both among believers and non-believers should come forward to teach people how to control negative emotions. This is only possible when we shed the divisive '*us*' and '*them*' attitude.

TOWARDS BETTER DISCOURSE

In my view the problem lies in over-emphasizing the commonly shared belief among believers of various religions that there is only 'one truth'. There may not be any problem in supporting this view so long as it relates to the quest for truth. Problems arise in practice. Most religions have a single 'god' and a single 'scripture'. The believer of such a religion thinks that their 'god' is supreme and that their 'scripture' contains all the truth.

Simultaneously, we have to discard ideas such as 'my god is superior to yours', 'teaching hatred can secure national integrity', and 'using terrorist groups in pursuit of national goals', and dismantle infrastructure that 'breeds hatred and imparts training for terrorist acts'.

Overemphasis on *ekam sad* (one truth) has led to fundamentalist positions. It has caused religious wars in the past and rise of fundamentalism in today's world. I have thus shifted the emphasis from '*ekam sad*' to '*Bahudhā*'. I believe that the Bahudhā approach is the need of our time. Let us celebrate diversity and inculcate an attitude into ourselves to respect another person's point of view with hope and belief that he or she may perhaps be right.

I see the relevance of the Bahudhā approach both for religious and secular issues. In fact, I have consciously taken it out from the religious closet of conflicts among religions and conflicts within a religion to the secular realm. Dialogue is essential to resolve differences of views pertaining to geopolitical issues such as territorial disputes or even to arrive at a conclusion about the role of the state in the affairs of citizens.

Secular society must allow religious pursuits, as is being done in a number of countries. Accordingly, I hold the view that the Bahudhā approach could facilitate the quest of truth in a religious order and secular behaviour in society simultaneously. The need is to understand and respect all religions and at the same time to uphold the rule of law.

The Bahudhā approach, I believe, can flourish when decent and ethical people that include a large segment of the global population of non-believers support it. It is relevant to all those persons who believe that one can be a very good person and citizen without being religious.

Should we not make Bahudhā a global creative venture, a cornerstone of liberal democracy and a plural world? Such questions need to be asked and answered. It is no surprise to me that I found the best answers in age-old knowledge systems, because people of goodwill have invested intellectual and spiritual energies in constructing them throughout history, not just in India but in other parts of the world as well.

PROMOTING BAHUDHĀ SPIRIT

This approach which I call the Bahudhā approach could be secured particularly through (*i*) religious harmony, including inter-faith meetings and dialogue for peace and prosperity of the world; (*ii*) educational programming, including taking a fresh look at text books for promotion of harmony; (*iii*) strengthening of international political architecture of the UN and its agencies; (*iv*) the use of military power in terms of the UN Charter; and (*v*) fortification of regional and global economic organizations for securing sustainable and inclusive development through dialogue with stakeholders and nation states.

IMPORTANCE OF RELIGION AND GOODWILL AMONG PEOPLE

Religion is a potent force. As an agent for the generation of peace and happiness, it facilitates goodwill among people, and helps them to lead a life of spirituality and fulfilment. In recent years, people such as Mahatma Gandhi and Martin Luther King have used it for achieving justice and freedom. Swami Vivekananda and Mother Teresa were inspired by their religious faiths to serve the poor, the derelict, and the discarded. It is religious faith which has driven the Dalai Lama to propagate the message of love and peace not only among his Tibetan people (including those living in exile in India) but also in distant lands.

Inter-faith dialogue is essential and could be accomplished by adopting the following three methods:

(i) *Meeting of practitioners of different faiths*: This would lead to mutual sharing of spiritual experiences such as warm-heartedness, forgiveness, compassion, contentment, and self-discipline. Such meetings will bring to light the fact that essentially all faiths are the same in their message.

(ii) *Coming together of spiritual leaders on the same platform*: Let them advocate in one voice the need to work for harmony and peace in the world. This would inspire their followers to feel the oneness and not the divide among faiths.

(iii) *Group pilgrimages of people from different faiths to the sacred sites of all spiritual traditions*: This would be very helpful in establishing commonality of approach.

The task of holding religious freedom and maintaining social harmony do not belong exclusively to politicians, administrators, policemen, and diplomats. In case of terrorism, religious leaders must go beyond condemnation. For that, initiatives have to be taken by the mainstream religious leaders and concerned citizens by setting an example of dialogue and communication with each other. This requires honest and robust relationships between religious leaders and social groups. Such relationships can be built only by protecting minorities in each society (fully recognizing that minority in a particular place may be majority in another place and vice-versa).

EDUCATION FOR HARMONY THROUGH WORLD CLASSROOM?

Education has a central role to play in building a harmonious society. The Vedic worldview entertained the idea that *the world is one family* (*Vasudhaiva Kutumbakam*). My enquiries revealed that this was a floating verse of the people which later formed part of Upanishadic literature.[29] In many ways this idea could be associated with the idea of a world classroom.

Education about harmony and tolerance must begin at home, as it is here that intolerance towards other faiths has its origins. We know that it is not only love and compassion but also hatred and intolerance that are widespread. Just as people can be taught to hate, they can also learn to treat others with love, dignity, and respect. In fact, the issue of public policy of harmony is critically linked with education.

There is an urgent need to focus on the educational curriculum in order to purge it of content that spreads hatred and/or distorts history. Effective education also demands the development of a creative mind and scientific temper.

Utilizing education as an instrument of harmony is not an easy task. The educational curriculum, in particular, has become in several countries an ideological battleground. The interpretation of historical events often excites religious and ethnic groups who start taking positions that are not always rational. Yet, education is the most dependable resource for preparing the youth for initiating dialogue.

INTERNATIONAL POLITICAL ARCHITECTURE: THE UNITED NATIONS

Resolving conflict, however, goes much beyond education. Towards this end, the UN has to be strengthened in terms of its Charter so that it becomes an effective conflict resolution organization. The global political order must reflect the best interests, rules, and practices that nation states hold in common.

As we look towards the future, it appears that the prevailing nation state system would continue to be a primary structure. An international order based on the rule of law and consent of nation states can alone be an effective conflict resolution mechanism.

The UN is the best forum for generation of understanding among nation states in the realm of politics and economy. It can also be a forum where dialogue among nations can be initiated and sustained. Such dialogues can support efforts groups and nations.

The UN needs to be reorganized in several ways: by expanding the Security Council to reflect present-day political and economic realities and by funding a permanent peacekeeping force.

USE OF FORCE

A question is often posed about the role and relevance of the military in the construction of an environment for creative dialogue among civilizations. In the post 9/11 world, it is quite obvious that the ugly face of terrorism has given full justification for a strong military posture by governments. In fact, the rise of terrorist activities in different parts of the world demands it. It, however, does not mean that military intervention can be taken in an arbitrary fashion.

In this context, the theory of preventive war enunciated by the USA in its National Security Document of September 2002 explicitly defining its unilateralist approach to terrorism needs to be examined. The UN Charter calls upon member states to attempt to settle disputes peacefully; and failing that, to make reference to the Security Council for appropriate action including use of military force in terms of Article 51. The categorical position emerging out of Article 51 is that states refrain from the use of military till an armed attack takes place. This has been repeatedly violated but it needs to be respected for building a harmonious world.

BAHUDHĀ AND NON-BELIEVERS

Out of over 7 billion people living on the earth, more than 1 billion people are non-believers, such as agnostics, atheists, and anti-religionists. In the perception of non-believers, religion is only a social or cultural formality. However, ethical and moral beliefs and respect for rule of law are very strong among these non-believers.

The information technology revolution and phenomenal increase in rationality has changed the religious temper not only of Western society but other areas of the world as well. The concerned citizens who care for harmony in society but who are also religious are realizing that religion in a secular state and a secularized culture is almost always a private matter. They also realize that spiritualism of an earlier era based on rituals cannot be replicated in totality today.

Diversity celebrates different religions, gods and goddesses, and belief systems. It also promotes a feeling that the world would be a dull and over-uniform place if there was only one religion, one god, one language, one folklore, and one folktale. We are all at different levels of human consciousness and in terms of history, the human species is characterised by immense diversity

The challenges before us are colossal, by any reckoning. Politics is the most formidable driver of change as well as harmony. It is my hope that the twenty-first century shall have better drivers than what we had in the previous one. Would that happen?

Leaders endowed with spiritual resources can strengthen the cause of peace and people's welfare. They can think outside the traditional boxes of faiths and scriptures, paradigms of democracy and dictatorship, and so on by invoking the paramount need of the people to live in peace. Such leaders can make a positive influence in society and polity management. In such a situation love and compassion, non-violence, and respect for other person's point of view shall prevail and guide human affairs. Let us combine statesmanship and good governance with the wisdom of the world's faiths and the principles of spiritual practice. Virtues such as honesty, generosity, courage, fortitude, and empathy are core strengths or capacities that are needed in order for a social system to function well and result in political, social, and economic development.

Would the twenty-first century have enough leaders in different walks of life to take our people to follow the right path? Or would the world be guided by demagogues and fascists, a phenomenon that we witnessed in the twentieth century? The challenge is clearly before all of us and we have to harness spiritual energy to make the world a better place to live. The achievements of technology must be fused with enhanced powers of humane, transcendent, and moral judgment.

How do we move towards a better world? One is aware that the twenty-first century will not succeed in replacing the love of power by the power of love, notwithstanding the fact that the power of love is enormous and that the world needs it. We must not get disenchanted or be filled with despair in the face of the enormity of the challenge. Optimism is crucial.

I am aware that there are people who think hope is irrational. They would like to submit to the movement of time and accept whatever turn it takes.

I have been in administration all my life and have known public leaders of both kinds: those who work to promote their conviction and a larger number of others who see the opportunity of holding public office as a means of self-aggrandizement and worse. This could be changed only when far-sighted people with full conviction move to public office.

I believe that both institutions and individuals are important. Institutions mould character and individuals provide resilience and flexibility to institutions. To preserve and strengthen, hope calls upon our wisdom and our energy. The need is to nurture the moral strength of men and women and their leaders to live with compassion and to spend their energies working for peace and genuine development.

One positive trend is that the present generation of people think about the future. And the more we think about the future, the more we expand our outlook of what we should do to save it. I am not visualizing a 'borderless world'. All I am advocating is that we bring down mind walls that divide people and create hatred. This seems to be an achievable target provided we work in that direction. I am aware of citizens in different parts of the globe who at the psychological level believe and practice for the welfare of everyone.

It is my belief that the dogs of war and conflict will bark and may occasionally bite as well but will not prevail as they did in the preceding century.

I strongly feel that strengthening open societies where dialogue has primacy and where the spirit of understanding another's point of view is cultivated leads to a better world. Fundamentalism or that a particular view of the world must prevail is the worst of all ideologies and must be discarded. The need is to develop a resolve that as a people we will not allow our respective faiths to be used as instruments of violence. We must have the moral strength to live in accordance with the teachings of compassion and spend all our energies working for peace and development.

The Bahudhā doctrine is the single most comprehensive one formulated after 9/11 tragedy to tackle the rise of terrorism and fundamentalism. It gives me pleasure and satisfaction as an innovator that when I apply this doctrine to meet global challenges in realms of religion, ecology, and geopolitics it is useful. It is thus no wonder that the famous Buddhist monk and scholar His Holiness the Dalai Lama visualized its relevance for next 200 years![30]

I am proud of the Bahudhā approach, its idea, and its relevance. I know the Bahudhā approach is moving slowly. I know a new approach takes time to grow. I am, however, not exasperated at its speed as I clearly see that its time has come.

NOTES

1. The maker of 'Bahudha Chocolate' was the Hershey Company, an important manufacturer of chocolates in the world.

2. The ambience in the hall was conducive too, particularly after Dr Bhupen Hazarika's invocation song calling on the two famous rivers of India namely Ganga and the Lohit (a tributary of the Brahmaputra river) to help in the process of change towards peace, progress, and development. Dr Bhupen Hazarika was conferred with India's highest award, the Bharat Ratna, in 2019 (posthumously).

3. Special provisions with respect to the state of Sikkim were incorporated in the Constitution of India by the Thirty-sixth Amendment Act, 1975 (w.e.f. 24 April 1975).

4. 'The Governor of Sikkim shall have special responsibility for peace and for an equitable arrangement for ensuring the social and economic advancement of different sections of the population of Sikkim and in the discharge of the special responsibility under this clause, the Governor of Sikkim shall, subject to such directions as the President may, from time to time, deem fit to issue, act in his direction' (See Article 271 F (g) of the Constitution).

5. This place is associated with both Guru Padmasambhava and Guru Nanak.

6. Nicholas Roerich's paintings of Mount Kanchenjunga are kept in the Moscow Museum.

7. During my tenure as additional secretary (1993–5), Government of India, I came across Hooker's pioneering works and later also read several reports of his as maintained in the archives of the Forest Research Institute (FRI), Dehradun. A circular was issued from my side to the Governments of West Bengal, Sikkim, and Arunachal Pradesh to erect the Hooker's Trail to encourage students, mountaineers, and tourists to undertake walks on the path traversed by him. I was happy to walk on his trail in 2009 in North Sikkim, at the time I was serving as governor.

8. Statues similar to the Statue of Unity have been raised at other places in Sikkim.

9. See pp. 192–221 of this book.

10. See Preamble of the UN Charter, available at https://www.un.org › sections › un-charter › un-charter-full-text).

11. Francis Fukuyama, *The End of History and The Last Man*, The Free Press, New York, 1992. See the introduction of the book entitled 'By Way of an Introduction' (pp. xi–xxii) which explains this argument admirably.

12. See Samuel P. Huntington, *The Clash of Civilizations and the Remarking of World Order*, Simon & Schuster, New York, 1996, p. 31.

13. Ibid, p. 31.

14. Ibid, p. 321.

15. See Balmiki Prasad Singh, *The 21st Century Geo-politics, Democracy and Peace*, Routledge, 2017, p. 5.

16. See 'Einstein and Freud Correspondence' on World Peace, available at https://www.frominsultstorespect.com.

17. See autobiography of Douglas MacArthur, *Reminiscences*, Mc Graw-Hill, New York, 1964, p. 404.

18. See 'India: The Empire of the Spirit' by Peter Spry-Leverton and Michael Wood. Available at https://www.youtube.com/watch?v=8Lex_eMC6wE, last accessed on 13 March 2020.
19. See Graham Allison, *Destined for War: Can America and China Escape Thucydides's Trap?* Houghton Miffin Harcourt, 2017, Preface.
20. Ibid.
21. See Balmiki Prasad Singh, *The Bahudha Approach: A Path Towards a Harmonious World*, Department of Information & Public Relations, Government of Sikkim, p. 35. Available at www.sikkimipr.org.
22. See Roberto Calasso, *The Unnamable Present*, translated from Italian by Richard Dixon, Farrar, Straus and Giroux, UK, p. 8.
23. See *The Hindu*, dated 15 May 2019.
24. See the 'Supreme Court of India verdict on 9 November 2019'. Available at https://en.wikipedia.org/wiki/Ayodhya_dispute, last accessed on 13 March 2020.
25. See *Economic Times*, dated 29 November 2019.
26. My thoughts on the subject have been encapsulated in my article 'Towards Building an Ecological Civilisation', *Economic & Political Weekly*, 30 March 2019, Vol. 54, No. 13. Available at https://www.epw.in/journal/2019/13/notes/towards-building-ecological-civilisation.html, last accessed on 13 March 2020.
27. See Todd A. Knoop, *Global Finance in Emerging Market Economies*, Routledge, 2015, Preface.
28. See www.worldvaluessurvey.org, last accessed on 13 March 2020.
29. The 'world is a family' verse is engraved in the entrance hall of the Parliament of India.
30. See paragraph 2 of this prologue and note no. 2 above.

I

A World in Need of Bahudhā

1

The World Today

You may say I am a dreamer,
But I am not the only one,
I hope some day you join,
And the world will be one.

—John Lennon[1]

Historical factors—religious, political, and economic—shape events, which in turn, determine the future course of history. Even as we must fully comprehend the past, there is no way in which the past can be separated from the present. The past and present (are entities which) always coexist and each informs the other, each implies the other, and each coexists with the other. And yet certain events carve out a niche for themselves. Amongst the many events witnessed by the world during 1989–2001, three stand out as being of immense significance. These are: the fall of the Berlin Wall in 1989; the transfer of Hong Kong to China in 1997; and the terrorist attack on the United States of America (USA or US) on 11 September 2001.

These events are both symbolic and substantive in nature. The transfer of Hong Kong to China marked the formal end of colonialism and the racial superiority theory in international affairs. It generated debates on the changing nature of imperialism and communism. In the minds of many it also aroused hopes for the resolution of the Tibet issue. The fall of the Berlin Wall meant the triumph of democracy and self-rule over communism and dictatorship. It also coincided with the era of globalization and integration of world markets. The attack on the US on 11 September 2001 was followed by military intervention in Afghanistan and Iraq by the US and its allies. The situation in Iraq, in particular, is still unfolding. The menace of cross-border terrorism in India is also receiving global attention. 9/11 reiterated that terrorism and religious fundamentalism are contemporary threats to world peace and harmony. These events have profoundly affected the lives of millions of people in the world and marked the course of contemporary history.

FALL OF THE BERLIN WALL

The proverbial 'curse of geography' applies to no other country more aptly than to Germany. Ever since Germany started on the road to power under the leadership of Frederick the Great in 1740, it has assumed various geographical shapes. But, it has always been an integral part of the heart of Europe, with vulnerable frontiers in an inhospitable neighbourhood: France in the west, Russia in the east, Austria-Habsburg in the south-east, and Britain looming across the North Sea. Germany's political architecture has been marked by rapid transformation: from the Wilhelmine Empire (1871–1918) to the Weimar Republic (that lasted until 1933), from Hitler's 'Third Reich' (1933–45) to its two successor states, the Federal Republic of Germany (FRG or West Germany) and the German Democratic Republic (GDR or East Germany), and back again to a reunified Germany in 1990. In between, the two World Wars not only curbed Germany's political ambitions but also ruined it economically.

The division of Germany (into FRG and GDR)[2] allowed the Soviet Union to maintain a massive military force in the East European countries, including the GDR. This enabled them not only to deter and defeat a military aggression but also to quash any ideological rebellion in the region.

Conditions in West Germany, including West Berlin, improved rapidly due to financial help under the Marshall Plan from the USA. In East Germany, many people suffered under the repressive Communist Party and due to lack of investments. Many East Germans moved stealthily to West Germany for better economic opportunities. More than 2.6 million East Germans escaped to West Germany between 1949 and 1961 (the total population of East Germany was about 17 million). The Berlin Wall, built to prevent the exodus of population from East Germany to West Germany, became operational on 13 August 1961.

Mikhail Gorbachev,[3] introduced an innovative policy based on restructuring (*perestroika*) and openness (*glasnost*). On his first official visit to West Germany as President of the Soviet Union in May 1989, Mikhail Gorbachev informed Chancellor Helmut Kohl that Moscow was no longer willing to use force to prevent the democratic transformation of its satellite states. This was the kiss of death for East Germany.

In September 1989, more than 13,000 East Germans escaped via Hungary within three days. Mass demonstrations against the government followed and Erich Honecker, East Germany's Head of State, had to resign on 18 October 1989. Egou Krenz's new government prepared a new law to lift travel restrictions for East German citizens.

At 6:53 p.m. on 9 November 1989, a member of the new East German government announced, at a press conference in East Berlin, that new travel plans would be put into force 'straightaway, immediately'.[4] Thousands of East Berliners proceeded to the border crossings. At Bornholmer Strasse, the people demanded that the border be opened, and at 10:30 p.m. the border was opened. That moment meant the end of the Berlin Wall. Soon other border-crossing points opened the gates to West Berlin.

Historic opportunities are often wasted or turned into disasters, primarily due to the ineptness of new leaders and their failure to cooperate. In the case of Germany's unification, the antithesis happened. The division of Germany disappeared along with the Cold War that had created it. Unification occurred with surprising ease and swiftness and, most importantly, without bloodshed.[5]

The significance of the Wall extended far beyond the city of Berlin and far beyond Germany. The Berlin Wall made an indelible impact on global politics, economics, and culture since its construction in 1945. The tearing down of the Wall was not only dramatic, but also a definitive historic triumph that closed an era in history. It redefined, for the better, the way millions of people would live their lives. It heralded the potential for a profound change in the way people and communities would resolve their conflicts and indeed, the way they would communicate among themselves and decide where to invest and where to travel to pursue their goals.

The fall of the Berlin Wall leading to the collapse of the Soviet Union in 1991, redefined the territory of the Soviet Union into present-day Russia and fifteen separate nations. If the success of the Bolshevik Revolution of 1917 meant the transformation of imperial tsarist Russia to that of the communist Union of Soviet Socialist Republics (USSR), or the Soviet Union in short, the fall of the Berlin Wall meant a new Russia shorn of an empire and the awe that had characterized the Russia of Nicholas II and Stalin. Eric Hobsbawm, the renowned historian, has viewed the collapse of the Soviet block and the Soviet Union as the end of an epoch in world history.[6]

The new Russia under the leadership of Boris Yeltsin, and now Vladimir Putin, has generated hope for envisaging a moderate and well-integrated Russia. Although Russia has not eradicated every fragment and habit of its authoritarian past, it has largely dismantled the infrastructure needed to underpin an authoritarian system and has legitimized democratic aspirations as never before. Russia is already a part of a globalized international economy. The growth of Russia's global trade as a percentage of its Gross Domestic Product (GDP), the flow of capital in and out of the country, and its involvement with international financial institutions have made economic considerations a far larger dimension of foreign policy.[7]

There is no doubt that a moderate and well-integrated Germany and Russia would be a positive factor in determining the kind of international order we shall have in the present century in more or less the same degree as policies pursued in foreign affairs by the US.[8]

A change of such tectonic magnitude as the breakdown of the entire post-war international order can only result from an unusual confluence of forces. But new arrangements can endure only when longer-term political and economic developments create an enabling environment. In 1989–90 both elements came together to bring about a new spirit of time that altered the political map of the northern hemisphere.

As students, we would often debate amongst ourselves[9] the respective merits and shortcomings, the superiority and inferiority of democracy and communism, capitalism and socialism, and the role of the State and the market. The fall of the Berlin Wall was decisive in promoting democracy, capitalism, and the free market. These three concepts have emerged as the most reliable instruments of political policy and economics. At this moment in history nations with responsible political leadership opted in favour of these three concepts. Several countries have balanced their budgets, cut subsidies, welcomed foreign investment, and lowered their tariff barriers. While the net outcome has not always been peace and happiness, a large number of thinkers in the Third World feel that the disappointment, anxiety, and resentment are temporary phases in the process of development. Hernando de Soto rightly sees it from a historical perspective when he writes:

But it is not only former communist and Third World countries that have suffered all of these problems. The same was true of the United States in

1783, when President George Washington complained about 'banditti ... skimming and disposing of the cream of the country at the expense of the many.'[10]

The most significant event in the capitalist growth process was formulation of property laws that included, among other things, sale and registration of land. Gordon Wood calls it 'something momentous' 'that released the aspirations and energies of common people as never before in [American] history'.[11] The new property law in the West led to successful capitalism when George Washington's dreaded 'banditt' were transformed into the beloved pioneers that American culture now venerates.[12]

Fundamentally, globalization is the closer integration of the countries and peoples of the world that has been brought about by the enormous reduction of costs of transportation and communication, and the breaking down of artificial barriers to the flow of goods, services, capital, knowledge, and (to a lesser extent) of people across borders. Globalization has been accompanied by the creation of new institutions that have joined with existing ones to work across borders.[13]

The East European countries moved rapidly away from Communism and regulated markets to democracy, private partnership of property, and free markets. Most of these countries have benefited immensely from self-rule and free markets. Life expectancy has increased and new employment opportunities have arisen. The globalization of ideas, of democracy, and of civil society has altered the way people think. However, the countries that recognized the role a government can play in development rather than relying solely on the notion of a self-regulated market have gained more. Others have not benefited as much. A large number of people have been left out from the march of progress and some have lost their jobs and have seen their lives become more insecure. Such people feel increasingly powerless.

There is no denying that national governments in developing countries need to improve the lives of the poor and to provide everyone access to healthcare, education, and a chance to succeed. This is a new challenge that several of the East European countries face. There is, however, an overall improvement in the availability of goods and services. On the whole, the situation is increasingly looking better for the future.

TRANSFER OF HONG KONG TO CHINA

On 30 June–1 July 1997, a very significant event took place that straddled Hong Kong's transition from a British colony to a Special Administrative Region of China.[14] At 11:59 p.m. on 30 June 1997, the British flag came down and at 12:01 a.m. the Chinese flag went up in Hong Kong.[15] This was followed by the entry of the People's Liberation Army into the Hong Kong and the reunification ceremonies, in which President Jiang Zemin of China and Tung Chee Hwa, the new Chief Executive of Hong Kong, participated. On this occasion, President Jiang Zemin observed that China would implement the 'one country, two systems' policy, and that Hong Kong would 'gradually develop a democratic system that stands Hong Kong's reality.'[16]

In a limited sense the transfer of Hong Kong to China raised questions about the future of democracy in Hong Kong; on the tenability of the 'one country, two systems' theory; and on the influence of Hong Kong's western culture on mainland China.

The rich history of Hong Kong—Pearl of the Orient—is inextricably linked with China. The territory was settled by Han Chinese during the rule of the Han dynasty in China. British contact began only when the East India Company made its first successful sea incursion into China in 1699. Hong Kong was formally ceded to Britain in 1842, under the Treaty of Nanking, when the territory became a colony of the British Crown or British colony. The Opium Wars[17] were ostensibly fought to liberalize trade to China. With a base in Hong Kong, British traders, opium dealers and merchants, launched the city which was to become the 'free trade' centre of the East. American opium traders and merchant bankers too joined in the trade.

Hong Kong came under Japanese rule briefly during the Second World War. At the end of the War, after the communist takeover of mainland China in 1949, millions of people emigrated from China to Hong Kong. Some of the new immigrants brought with them skills and capital, while others formed a vast pool of cheap labour. At the same time, many foreign firms moved their offices from Shanghai to Hong Kong. This helped Hong Kong in becoming a major manufacturing centre and a land of economic opportunities.

Hong Kong, since 1997, has gradually emerged as a premier investment funnel into China—the world's biggest developing market. There were, and continue to be, fears in mainland China about the encroachment of Hong Kong's freewheeling capitalism, pop culture, and strong western flavours, on the mainland. However, there are moderate elements as well in China who hold the view that Hong Kong can be a bridge between China and the West. It could facilitate the transfer of western technologies and old-fashioned culture, rather than the modern ways of life that include drugs and decadence.

China's literature is firmly rooted in its millennia-old traditions of storytelling. China's literati perceive Hong Kong as a cultural wasteland. Few writers from Hong Kong have managed to find a large audience across the border. Nonetheless, Hong Kong's liberating openness and enterprising spirit is bound to make a profound impact on the Chinese mindset. *The People's Daily* has begun trumpeting Hong Kong's 'benevolent market mechanisms'. Though the Communist Party's top newspaper does not promote the word 'capitalism', it does not shy away from quoting Adam Smith, the father of the free market. To a significant extent, this remarkable conversion of hardcore communists has been fuelled by countless exchanges between the mainland and Hong Kong.

The people of Hong Kong continue to show great appreciation for democracy. Hong Kong's citizens line up to vote in record numbers. Hong Kong's protest against the violent crackdown of the 1989 Tiananmen Square demonstrations in Beijing is well known. More than 1 million Hong Kong residents—nearly a fifth of the total population—marched in protest just hours after the People's Liberation Army moved on the demonstrators in and near the Square. Today more than 6.3 million of its inhabitants no longer entertain fears about the loss of their democratic rights as they did before the merger. Hong Kong remains a great city which is prosperous and free.

THE TIBETAN CRISIS

The transfer of Hong Kong to China showed that China's rightful claims over Hong Kong could be recognized without bloodshed. Does it have a message for the peaceful resolution of the Tibet–China imbroglio?

The march of the Chinese forces into Tibet on 7 October 1950, through its eastern border regions of Kham and Amdo, caused a crisis of great magnitude. The Tibetan people's resistance to this process of subjugation, which culminated in the 'Tibetan people's national uprising' on 10 March 1959, was suppressed. As a result of repressive measures taken by the Chinese authorities, the 14th Dalai Lama, Tenzing Gyatso, and a sizeable number of his followers took refuge in India in April 1959, and continue to reside here since then.

Notwithstanding the demand of the Tibetans for independence and self-determination, the Dalai Lama has launched a peaceful movement for freedom. He has conceded that Tibet is a part of China but wants the removal of threats to Tibet's culture, heritage, religious freedom, and environment. The Dalai Lama's representatives have visited Beijing and dialogues between them and the Chinese authorities are on. One cannot, however, predict a time frame within which the Tibet problem can be resolved but there are welcome signs. One only hopes that political autonomy comes early enough to the people of Tibet, so that they can live freely in terms of their culture and values, and not after everything is lost.

Colonialism and Imperialism

The transfer of Hong Kong to China can be viewed only as a 'symbolic' event heralding the end of colonialism. Yet, it has added to the debate as to whether colonialism and imperialism have actually ended and been relegated to the museum of history. Many believe, that to understand various political and economic events in the world today, a proper appreciation of the history of colonialism and imperialism is required.

The age of modern colonialism began in about 1500 AD, following the European discoveries of a sea route around Africa's southern coast (1488) and of America (1492). Colonialism soon emerged both as a political and an economic phenomenon whereby various European nations (England, France, Portugal, the Dutch Republic, and Spain in particular) discovered, conquered, settled, and exploited large areas of the world, including the present USA. Colonialism and imperialism were viewed by the people of the colonies—as the Indonesian nationalist leader Sukarno saw it—as 'a concept, an idea, a lust, a programme, a system, a policy of subjugating or controlling the country of another people or the economy of another nation'.[18] The form of control, however, varied from complete subjugation, as in India, to collaborative arrangements, as in China.

The process of rapid decolonization began from 1945 (USA got independence from the British colonial rule on 4 July 1776). This was facilitated after the Second World War by a number of factors. The US and the Soviet Union took up positions opposed to colonialism. Secondly, the mass revolutionary movements in countries like India, Indonesia, and several African countries, proved that the colonial system was untenable. Thirdly, the war-weary nations of

Western Europe eventually refused to make any further sacrifices to maintain overseas colonies.

Overnight the old colonial empires became independent nation-states, which led to fresh moral imperatives. A modern community, sweeping aside class and religion, and providing a sense of meaning and belonging to all, became the hallmark of the new order. In a narrow sense, the moral authority of the state has always rested on a claim to deliver public good, but under the freedom fighters-turned-leaders this became a national creed.

The establishment of the United Nations (UN) in 1945, based on the philosophy of sovereign equality of nation-states, was a major step forward. This political equality, however, did not take away gross inequality in wealth and natural resources among countries. The economic, educational, and health divide remains. There are several other challenges too. Happily today, human rights violations, as also the need for conservation of the ecology, are global concerns.

Fortunately, the vocabulary of the colonial era—including terms such as 'inferior', 'subject races', 'subordinate peoples'—and notions that 'certain territories and people require domination' are no longer in vogue. The colonial philosophy that 'there is a hierarchy of races and civilization', and that 'the best legitimation of conquest over native peoples is the conviction of superiority, not merely mechanical, economic, and military superiority but moral superiority', are fortunately dead and buried.

Imperialism did not become part of the 'past' once decolonization had set in motion the dismantling of the empires. Michael Barratt-Brown, in the preface to the 1970 second edition of his *After Imperialism* (1963), argues 'that imperialism is still without question a most powerful force in the economic, political and military relations by which the less economically developed lands are subjected to the more economically developed. We may still look forward to its ending'.[19]

Today the world is described in the context of developed, developing, and underdeveloped nations, notwithstanding 'the equality of nations' philosophy enshrined in the UN Charter. Edward Said has captured the nuances of this phenomenon aptly:

No one can deny the persisting continuities of long traditions, sustained habitations, national languages, and cultural geographies, but there seems no reason except fear and prejudice to keep insisting on their separation and distinctiveness, as if that was all human life was about. Survival in fact is about the connections between things; in Eliot's phrase, reality cannot be deprived of the 'other echoes [that] inhabit the garden'. It is more rewarding—and more difficult—to think concretely and sympathetically, contrapuntally, about others than only about 'us'. But this also means not trying to rule others, not trying to classify them or put them in hierarchies, above all, not constantly reiterating how 'our' culture or country is number one (or not number one, for that matter). For the intellectual there is quite enough of value to do without that.[20]

How we can do 'without that' is an important question before all of us.

9/11: ASSAULT ON THE UNITED STATES OF AMERICA

At 8:46 a.m. on 11 September 2001 an airliner, travelling at great speed and carrying some 10,000 gallons of jet fuel, plunged into the north tower of the World Trade Center (WTC) in lower Manhattan in New York. A few minutes later, at 9:03 a.m., a second airliner hit the south tower. The twin towers, where up to 50,000 people worked, collapsed less than 90 minutes later. At 9:37 a.m. that same morning, a third airliner slammed into the western face of the Pentagon. At 10:03 a.m., a fourth airliner crashed in a field in southern Pennsylvania. In this unprecedented terrorist attack, which became popularly known as 9/11, more than 2,600 people died at the World Trade Centre, 125 died at the Pentagon, and 256 died in the four planes. The death toll surpassed the Pearl Harbour attack of December 1941.

This terrorist attack was the handiwork of nineteen young Arabs, acting at the behest of Al-Qaeda, an Islamist extremist outfit headquartered in Afghanistan, under the leadership of Osama bin Laden. Islamist extremists had given ample warning of their intention to kill Americans indiscriminately and in large numbers. Plans to attack the US were developed with unwavering single-mindedness throughout the 1990s. Osama bin Laden saw himself as called upon 'to follow in the footsteps of the Messenger and to communicate his message to all nations, and to serve as the rallying point and organizer of a new kind of war to destroy America and bring the world to Islam'.[21] Immediately after 9/11 and ever since, terrorism has become a topic of debate all over the world.

Leftist interpretation of terrorist activity having its roots in poverty and exploitation does not fully explain the terrorist phenomena today. All the nineteen individuals responsible for the 9/11 attack hailed from middle-class backgrounds and several of them were educated in the West (US).

Poverty, combined with unemployment, among the youth has always been the cause of dissatisfaction against authority in developing countries. But there, causes have erupted in terrorist violence only when backed by ethnic or religious emotions. 9/11 occurred not because of a territorial dispute or property conflict between the US and the nineteen Arab extremists, but because they were charged with emotions.

It is rightly argued that terrorism cannot be tackled by weapons alone; what is required is a struggle for the hearts and minds of the people. It is important to realize that both terrorists' ideas and their weapons do damage. The terrorists want to defeat their perceived enemies without entering into any dialogue or rational debate. Against this background, a strong state which can launch an effective anti-terrorist campaign is a prerequisite. An effective government that provides education, healthcare, employment, and the rule of law is not liked by unlawful elements. In the context of terrorism, however, it is essential that the state is respected in every eventuality.

In the post-9/11 world, threats are not always visible. An organization like Al-Qaeda, headquartered in a country far removed from the US and with poor economic and military strength, could nevertheless build weapons of unprecedented destructive power and successfully use them against a powerful country like the US. Recent happenings in India, Indonesia, and several other countries have also proved that terrorism 'over there' could be converted into terrorism 'over here' through the resolute will of terrorists and their mentors.

THE IRAQ WAR AND THE WORLD

After 9/11, the immediate goal of the US was to dismantle Al-Qaeda's widespread and well-entrenched network (in Afghanistan and its neighbourhood) built by Osama bin Laden and his son-in-law Muhammad Omar, head of the Taliban. The US armed forces, together with the armies of its allies, acting on the mandate of the UN Security Council, succeeded in dismantling the Taliban regime within a short period (October–November 2001). They installed a civilian administration led by Hamid Karzai in December 2001. The focus then shifted to what President Bush declared as the 'axis of evil',[22] comprising of Iraq, North Korea, and Iran.

Iraq was singled out for military intervention. The US and the UK attacked Iraq in March 2003, after a war-sanctioning resolution failed to gain support in the UN Security Council. The US and the UK, with military ground forces of about 300,000 and ably supported by its air power, silenced the comparatively insignificant Iraqi resistance, and installed Ghazi Mashal Ajil al-Yawer as President of Iraq in May 2004. Saddam Hussein, the then President of Iraq, was subsequently captured by the US military on 13 December 2003. The war has, however, created a deep humanitarian crisis in Iraq and a deep political crisis in the international system.

Three reasons were advanced for the invasion of Iraq: Iraq's possession of Weapons of Mass Destruction (WMD); its partnership with Al-Qaeda; and the need to liberate the long-suffering people of Iraq from the atrocities of Saddam Hussein.

The unilateral decision by the US and the UK, to militarily intervene in Iraq, has raised several questions about the role of the UN. The establishment of the UN in 1945 was predicated on the belief that in future no one nation, or even a partnership of two or three nations, would assume the role of world arbitrator and policeman. This concept is now in jeopardy with the invasion of Iraq. The US action has introduced the dangerous theory of 'preventive' war in international relations, based solely on perceptions of national interests by the political leadership of a country.[23]

The distinction between 'preemptive' and 'preventive' is well worth preserving. 'Preemptive' war refers to a direct, immediate, specific threat that must be crushed at once. This means military action against another country initiated on the basis of incontrovertible evidence that attack from that country is imminent. 'Preventive' war refers to potential, future, and therefore speculative threats. The entire case for 'preventive' war rests on the assumption that there is accurate and reliable intelligence about the enemy's intentions and military capability. The Cold War, after all, was a manifestation of old-fashioned rivalry among sovereign states, visible entities with governments accountable for their decisions. But international terrorists are invisible and not accountable. They strike from the shadows and recede into them.

In 1932, when Einstein attempted to induce Freud to support pacifism,[24] Freud replied that there was no likelihood of suppressing humanity's aggressive tendencies. If there was any reason for hope, it was that people would turn away on rational grounds—that war had become too destructive and that there was no scope any more in war for acts of heroism.

Freud was partially correct. War (at least between great powers) has become far less likely, largely due to the supremacy of rationality over emotions. But this argument does not apply to the terrorism of today which is motivated by small groups and not nation-states always.

The threat to world peace can be overcome only through dialogue and by creating a climate where harmony can flourish.

TERRORISM IN INDIA

TERRORIST ATTACK ON INDIA'S PARLIAMENT

At 11:40 a.m. on 13 December 2001, five Pakistani terrorists entered the Parliament House Complex in New Delhi in a white Ambassador car.[25] When challenged by the security personnel present on the spot, they jumped out of the car and began firing indiscriminately. During the exchange of fire, nine persons from the security, watch and ward staff, and a gardener at Parliament House, lost their lives and 16 other persons were injured. All five terrorists were killed.

In the 13 December event, the members of the security forces made supreme sacrifices to prevent harm to the Parliament building and members of Parliament working inside it. The Indian people, instead of bursting into uncontrolled rage, showed admirable restraint and discipline and asked the police, the judiciary, and leaders of government to take appropriate measures to deal with the terrorist menace.[26]

The investigation of the case clearly established that this act of terrorism was the handiwork of Pakistan-based terrorist outfits who derived their support and sustenance from the Pakistani Inter Services Intelligence (ISI).

STATE-SPONSORED TERRORISM

The roots of terrorism as an instrument of state policy are seen, by many scholars and defence experts, in Pakistan's desire to 'take away' Kashmir from India. The Kashmir conflict is rooted in the colonial history of the subcontinent. Pakistan could not fulfil its ambition through military interventions in 1965 and 1971. The Simla Agreement concluded on 2 July 1972, in the aftermath of the 1971 Indo-Pak War and the partition of Pakistan into two sovereign nation-states of Pakistan and Bangladesh, provided a comprehensive framework for the normalization of relations between the two countries. The second paragraph of the Agreement states that the two countries 'resolved to settle their differences by peaceful means through bilateral negotiations or by any other peaceful means mutually agreed upon between them'.[27]

The Simla Agreement binds both governments to take all steps within their power to prevent hostile propaganda directed against each other and to respect each other's national unity and territorial integrity. But Pakistan, particularly since 1989, has followed a policy of proxy war against India. Towards this end, Pakistan has been extending support to fundamentalist elements in Jammu and Kashmir and by sending well-trained jihadi and armed irregulars into the Kashmir Valley. Pakistan has also committed overt aggression against India in the Kargil area in May 1999.

INDIA AND KASHMIR

After 9/11, Pakistan dramatically renounced its support for the Taliban and offered to get enlisted as a frontline state in the global war on terrorism led by the US. President Pervez Musharraf has since been forced to adopt a radical change in the country's pro-jihadi Kashmir policy which had been in place since 1989. In his 12 January 2002 speech, President Musharraf went so far as to say:

Pakistan rejects and condemns terrorism in all its forms and manifestations. Pakistan will not allow its territory to be used for terrorist activity anywhere in the world. No organization will be allowed to indulge in terrorism in the name of Kashmir.[28]

On 17 January 2004, while addressing a joint session of Parliament in Islamabad, President Musharraf declared jihad against Islamic extremism. He reminded the nation that 'a handful of elements with ulterior motives have been indulging in promoting the evil and are also attempting to defame the military as well as the public representatives'.[29]

Discussions with Pakistan on all outstanding issues, including Jammu and Kashmir, need to be pursued. Quiet diplomacy and back-channel liaison have their place. A resolution of the Kashmir issue has, however, baffled pundits as well as political leaders for over half a century. Accordingly, many believe and advocate that a political initiative, internal and international, is necessary as there is no military 'solution' to the Kashmir question.[30] An extended insurgency in Kashmir is likely to lead to continuing small-scale border skirmishes between India and Pakistan, with the ever-present possibility of inadvertent escalation and instability in the region stretching from

Afghanistan to the Punjab in India. It would also prevent India from moving ahead with settlement of its long-standing border dispute with China, as this involves portions of Kashmir as well.[31]

Pakistan's role in the US war on terrorism is bound to be crucial as it is located in the very region which is one of the main sources of Islamic terrorism. The founding ideals of Pakistan speak of modernity and moderation; it is imperative that the present generation be constantly reminded of this resolution.

WORLD VIEWS

After the end of the Cold War and much before 9/11 two divergent views about the future were well articulated. First, the end of the Cold War was sought to be viewed as the end of major conflicts in global politics and the emergence of a harmonious world. Francis Fukuyama, the most articulate exponent of this school of thought, called it 'the end of history'. He asserted that 'we may be witnessing the end of history as such: that is, the end point of mankind's ideological evolution and the universalization of Western liberal democracy as the final form of human government'.[32] He acknowledged that there might be some conflicts in future but the era of global conflict was over.

Antithetical to Fukuyama's view is the thesis of several other scholars who saw the end of the Cold War as heralding a new era of conflict. This view has come to be associated with Samuel P. Huntington. In his widely read article entitled 'The Clash of Civilizations?' published by *Foreign Affairs* in the summer of 1993, and later developed as a book under the title, *The Clash of the Civilizations and the Remaking of World Order*, Huntington saw emerging conflicts in civilizational terms. Although Huntington did not specifically talk about Islamic terrorists, he did visualize the fault lines clearly. In his words:

A global war involving the core states of the world's major civilizations is highly improbable but not impossible. Such a war, we have suggested could come about from the escalation of a fault line war between groups from different civilizations, most likely involving Muslims on one side and non-Muslims on the other.[33]

In the aftermath of this debate, there is a growing realization that the international order based on civilizations could be promoted only by accepting the philosophy of pluralism and not by supporting the thesis of the superiority of one civilization over the rest.

LOOKING BEYOND

Looking beyond these events and the conflict between different world views of a 'clash of civilizations' and 'the end of history', we find that the western countries in particular are apprehensive of jihadi terrorist attacks. This culture of fear is matched by a widespread feeling of humiliation among people living in the Arab world. Amidst all these the important fact about today's world is that the global economy is growing at great speed. Living standards of people are rising rapidly in developing countries. One sees tremendous hope and resolution about a better future among people in China, India, South Africa, Brazil, Mexico, and several other countries. At the same time, a fierce debate is raging in the world about terrorism and its links with religion and about the forces of democracy and globalization. These are analysed in the next chapter.

NOTES

1. John Lennon (1940–80), the songwriter, musician, and singer and member of the influential Beatles pop group. See *www.johnlennon. com*, the official John Lennon website.
2. Under the terms of the Agreements of 1944–5 signed by the United States, the Soviet Union, Great Britain, and France, a defeated Germany was divided into four occupation zones overseen by four Commanders-in-Chief, who together formed the Control Council. The premier city, Berlin, itself was divided into East Berlin with GDR and West Berlin with FRG. See *www.dailysoft.com/berlinwall*
3. President Ronald Reagan at the Brandenburg Gate, Berlin, declared on 12 June 1987, 'Mr. Gorbachev, tear down this wall'.
4. See *www.dailysoft.com/berlinwall/history/fall-of-berlinwall.htm*
5. 'The right-wing version of this experiment ended in 1945 with the defeat of Nazi Germany, while the left-wing version crumbled under the weight of its own contradictions when the Berlin Wall fell in 1989' (quoted from Francis Fukuyama, *State Building: Governance and World Order in the Twenty-first Century*, South Asian Edition, Profile Books, London, 2004, p. 4).
6. Eric Hobsbawm writes: 'A page in history has been turned. What has happened has been, far more often than not, quite unexpected. All of us have been mistaken more than once in our judgments and expectations. Some have found themselves agreeably surprised by the course of events, but probably more have been disappointed, their disappointment often sharpened by earlier hope, or even, as in 1989, by euphoria. Whatever our reaction, the discovery that we were

mistaken, that we cannot have understood it adequately, must be the starting-point of our reflection on the history of our times. These are cases—perhaps mine is among them—where this discovery can be particularly helpful. Much of my life, probably most of my conscious life, was devoted to a hope which has been plainly disappointed, and to a cause which has plainly failed: the communism initiated by the October Revolution'. See Eric Hobsbawm, *On History*, Abacus, London, 1997, p. 317.

7. Robert A. Pastor (ed.), *A Century's Journey*, Basic Books, New York, 1999, p. 188.

8. Ibid., pp. 189–90.

9. This refers to debates primarily in Indian universities in the 1950s and 1960s when the author received his education at Patna University.

10. Hernando de Soto, *The Mystery of Capital: Why Capitalism Triumphs in the West and Fails Everywhere Else*, Basic Books, New York, 2000, p. 9.

11. Gordon S. Wood, 'Inventing American Capitalism', *New York Review of Books,* 9 June 1994, p. 49.

12. de Soto, *The Mystery of Capital*, p. 10.

13. For a detailed analysis of globalization issues, please see Joseph E. Stiglitz, *Globalization and its Discontents*, W.W. Norton & Company, New York, 2002; and Jagdish Bhagwati, *In Defense of Globalization*, Oxford University Press, New York, 2004.

14. The abdication of British control over Hong Kong indicated the formal end of colonialism—a process which began with India's independence on 15 August 1947, under the leadership of Mahatma Gandhi. The handing over programme in Hong Kong closely followed the schedule adopted for India's Independence Day.

15. The handing over ceremony was also marked by the new Chief Executive of Hong Kong, Tung Chee Hwa, joining some 50,000 Buddhists in prayers at Hong Kong's stadium. The handing over ceremony continued smoothly despite fears of clashes between supporters of Hong Kong's independent status and pro-China elements.

16. See *http://en.wikipedia.org/wiki/Hong.Kong*

17. Ibid.

18. Quoted by Nicholas Tarling, *The Fall of Imperial Britain in South-East Asia*, Oxford University Press, Kuala Lumpur, 1993, p. 10. Also see Elie Kedourie, 'A New International Disorder', in H. Bull and Adam Watson (eds), *The Expansion of International Society*, Oxford University Press, Oxford, 1984, p. 352.

19. Quoted in Edward W. Said, *Culture and Imperialism*, Chatto & Windus, London, 1993, p. 341; Michael Barret-Brown, *After Imperialism* (rev. edn, Humanities, New York, 1970), p. viii.

20. Said, *Culture and Imperialism*, p. 408.

21. *The 9/11 Commission Report: Final Report of the National Commission on Terrorist Attacks upon the United States*, W.W. Norton & Company, New York, 2004, p. 48.

22. President Bush's State of the Union Address, The United States Capitol, Washington DC, 29 January 2002 (see *www.whitehouse.gov*)

23. Quoted in Arthur M. Schlesinger, Jr., *War and the American Presidency*, W.W. Norton & Company, New York, 2004, pp. 24–5. *The National Security Strategy of the United States of America*, issued by the White House in September 2002, introduces the policy of preventive wars as a part of its national security. The document *inter-alia* declares, 'Given the goals of rogue states and terrorists, the United States can no longer solely rely on a reactive posture as we have in the past. The inability to deter a potential attacker, the immediacy of today's threats, and the magnitude of potential harm that could be caused by our adversaries' choice of weapons, do not permit that option. We cannot let our enemies strike first'.

24. See Einstein-Freud correspondence at *www.cis.vt.edu/modernworld/d/Einstein.html*

25. For long, the white Ambassador car (an India-made automobile) has been the official vehicle of ministers and senior civil servants, and has been subjected to more lenient (soft) checking by security guards than any other vehicle. This has, however, changed somewhat since the attack on India's Parliament.

26. See N. Mukherji, 'December 13 Tenor over Democracy' (Foreword 'Manipulation of Fear' by Noam Chomsky), Promilla and Co. in association with Bibliophile South Asia, New Delhi and Chicago, 2005, pp. 2–5.

27. See Simla Agreement 2 July 1972 at *www.jammu-kashmir.com/documents/simla.html*

28. For the full text of Pervez Musharraf's speech, see *Dawn*, 12 January 2002, and online at *http//www.dawn.com/2002/01/12/speech020112.htm*

29. Ibid. K. Subrahmanyam Committee.

30. See Government of India report entitled: *From Surprise to Reckoning: Kargil Review Committee Report*, New Delhi, 1999, pp. 187–8.

31. Excerpts of an article entitled 'Avoiding War in Kashmir' by Sumit Ganguly in *Foreign Affairs*, vol. 69, no. 5, Winter 1990/91.

32. Francis Fukuyama, *The End of History and the Last Man*, Free Press, New York, 1993, pp. 4–18.

33. Samuel P. Huntington, *The Clash of Civilizations and the Remaking of World Order*, Simon & Schuster, New York, 1996, pp. 312–13.

2
Political 'Tsunamis' and After

ekam sad vipra bahudha vadanti[1]
The Real is one, the learned speak of it variously

—*Rig Veda*

The end of colonialism and the Cold War in the second half of the twentieth century and the rise of the demon of terrorism at the beginning of the twenty-first century, has created a tsunami-like impact on politics and international relations, economics, and cultural practices.

One of the legacies of dictatorship and fascist political culture relates to the cultivation of the belief that an opponent is not someone with whom you can enter into dialogue and negotiate, but an enemy whom you must destroy. Religious fundamentalists and terrorists are also actuated by similar strong feelings and indulge in meaningless violence and senseless killing of innocent people. We wonder therefore whether the end of the Cold War has really opened the door for peace-building.

The elimination of terrorism has become a matter of deep concern for all of us. Its links with primordial values of religion are sought to be understood. Although every religion has a fundamentalist group, after 9/11 particularly, the fundamentalist forces of Islam are receiving special attention from scholars and statesmen, media commentators, and even persons in uniform. At the same time, forces of modernization are integrating both markets and minds. There has been phenomenal economic progress in the world in recent years. Good governance and inclusive political order are resulting in democracy being viewed as the destiny of people.

With this background of crisis generated by terrorist attacks in different parts of the world, on the one hand, and rapid economic progress, on the other, people are turning their attention increasingly to the more fundamental question of 'how to live'. Questions are asked as to whether the past could be any guide in formulating a new public policy that would ensure harmony and good conduct and thus propel society not only to economic progress but also enable everyone to lead a life in terms of their genius and beliefs.

TERRORISM TODAY AND TOMORROW

Terrorism occupies centre-stage in global discourse today. The new breed of terrorists have no respect for human lives, including their own, and the rules of war that protect civilians in armed conflicts among nation-states are alien to their thought-processes. There are several terrorist groups operating in different parts of the world but Al-Qaeda has emerged as a major terrorist outfit with global reach and sophisticated capacity.

In the aftermath of the 9/11 tragedy, several initiatives have been taken at national as well as global levels to counter terrorist threats, dry up their resources, dismantle their networks, and destroy their hideouts. These efforts have met with varying degrees of success. Several terrorist leaders have been apprehended and their bank accounts frozen. Some of them will be facing trial for crimes against humanity. Efforts are also being made to counter extremism and intolerance by civil societies in various ways, including education and public debate. Even then terrorist attacks by individuals and fundamentalist groups are on the rise and, State-sponsored terrorism has not disappeared, even after military action in Afghanistan and Iraq.

Several US watchers view the elections in Iraq as a clear indication that the US is determined to stay in Iraq and carry forward the democratization process there. It is also a warning to all autocratic Arab rulers to evolve appropriate survival policies. Though the Bush administration considers the election as a victory for its West Asia policy, elsewhere in the world it is seen as a high-pressure policy of forcible democratization in the Islamic world. This is so, particularly in respect of Iran, which although does not have a liberal democratic constitution, does have a genuinely free and fair voting system.

In the past, terrorism was almost always the province of politically-backed groups of militants, like the Irish and Russian social revolutionary movements of 1900, but not any more. In fact, future terrorists are likely to be individuals or like-minded people working in very small groups. Such people may possess the technical competence to steal, buy, or manufacture the weapons they need for terrorist purposes. Such individuals may work alone or in small groups, making detection difficult and possible only by default. Thus, at one end of the scale, the lone terrorist has appeared, and at the other, state-sponsored terrorism is quietly flourishing. When the interests of the two coalesce, it becomes 'proxy' war—a war that is affordable at a time when open aggression has become an expensive and risky business/affair.

Advanced societies today are becoming increasingly dependent on the electronic storage, retrieval, analysis, and transmission of information. A large percentage of the transactions of the government, defence, the police, banking, trade, transportation, scientific technological, economic, and private sectors are on-line. This exposes vital areas of national life to mischief or sabotage by computer hackers and possible collapse of these functions. Hence, the growing speculation about infoterrorism and cyberwarfare which can become tools in the hands of terrorists.

This gives rise to the following question: Has terrorism become a substitute for the great wars of the nineteenth and twentieth centuries? Former UN Secretary General, Kofi Annan, constituted a high level panel under the leadership of Anand Panyarachun, former Prime Minister of Thailand, to assess threats to international peace and security; to evaluate how existing policies and institutions have performed in addressing those threats; and to make recommendations for strengthening the UN so that it can provide collective security for all in the twenty-first century.

Terrorists have drawn their strength from the lack of consensus among nation-states on a common definition of terrorism. The Panyarachun Report defines terrorism as:

any action ... that is intended to cause death or serious bodily harm to civilians or non-combatants, when the purpose of such an act, by its nature or context, is to intimidate a population, or to compel a government or an international organization to do or to abstain from doing any act.[2]

Adoption of this definition by member countries of the UN would indeed go a long way in tackling terrorism together in times to come.

The debate over why the attack of 11 September 2001 occurred has been characterized by different interpretations involving religion, politics, and foreign policy. Several leading intellectuals have observed that religion underlies both politics and human motivation in the Arab world. For this school of thought, Islam is the issue that explains terrorist attacks on the US installations as well as on the Indian Parliament, the killing of innocent children in Chechnya and massacre of tourists in Bali, as also suicide bombings and jihad. The other school of thought ascribes this state of affairs largely to the western control over oil resources of the Middle East and also its support to authoritarian rulers in different countries in the Arab world. US foreign policy is blamed for being partisan towards Israel and for its failure to ensure a separate state for Palestine. The truth perhaps lies somewhere in between.

The extremist point of view highlights the need to end states militarily as it sees a close link between terrorists and states where they can flourish. Leonard Peikoff, in his essay titled 'End States Who Sponsor Terrorism', affirms that:

the struggle against terrorism is not a struggle over Palestine. It is a clash of cultures, and thus a struggle of ideas, which can be dealt with, ultimately, only by intellectual means. But this fact does not depreciate the crucial role of our armed forces. On the contrary, it increases their effectiveness, by pointing them to the right target.[3]

This school of thought advocates military action in Iran and North Korea. However, there are many who do not believe that war can be a solution.

There is an apprehension that despite elections in Iraq, the US is not going to leave Iraq or allow it to be run by the Iraqi people. Experts are of the opinion that there are massive unexplored petroleum resources in Iraq. Once properly exploited, these may be the largest oil reserves in the world. The profits from these would naturally go to the US and UK energy corporations. Hence, controlling these resources would put the US in a very powerful position, in fact even more powerful than today, to exert influence over the world.

State Building After 9/11

In the post-9/11 period, the chief issue for global politics will not be how to cut back on 'stateness' but how to build it up. For individual societies and for the global community, the withering away or decline of the state is not a prelude to utopia but to disaster. Bill Clinton describes the new dilemma aptly when he writes:

I believe that the biggest problems to our security in the twenty-first century and to this whole modern form of governance will probably come not from rogue states or from people with competing views of the world in governments, but from the enemies of the nation-state, from terrorists and drug runners and organized criminals who, I predict, will increasingly work together and increasingly use the same things that are fuelling our prosperity: open borders, the Internet, the miniaturization of all sophisticated technology, which will manifest itself in smaller and more powerful and more dangerous weapons. And we have to find ways to cooperate to deal with the enemies of the nation-state if we expect progressive governments to succeed.[4]

One of the dominant trends in world politics after the fall of the Berlin Wall has been the attempt to move activities from the state sector to private markets or to civil society. But in several countries, particularly in the developing world, weak, incompetent, or corrupt governments are the source of severe problems. They are unable to handle a whole range of problems from poverty to AIDS and drugs to terrorism. As Francis Fukuyama argues:

The end of the Cold War left a band of failed and weak states stretching from the Balkans through the Caucasus, the Middle East, Central Asia, and South Asia. State collapse or weakness had already created major humanitarian and human rights disasters during the 1990s in Somalia, Haiti, Cambodia, Bosnia, Kosovo, and East Timor. For a while, the United States and other countries could pretend these problems were just local, but 11 September proved that state weakness constituted a huge strategic challenge as well. Radical Islamist terrorism combined with the availability of weapons of mass destruction added a major security dimension to the burden of problems created by weak governance.[5]

States throughout the less-developed world are weak, and the end of the Cold War led to the emergence of a band of failed and troubled states from Europe to South Asia. These weak states have become threats to international order because they are the source of conflict and grave abuses of human rights. They are also potential breeding grounds for a new kind of terrorism that has its reach in the developed world. Strengthening these states through various forms of nation-building is a task that has become vital to international security but one that few developed countries have mastered. The art of state-building is thus central to the future of world order.

In any event, this is likely to be a key component of national power, as important as the ability to deploy traditional military force for the maintenance of world order.[6] At the same time, cooperation among nation-states is bound to be crucial to contain terrorist attacks and also to build a world free from the menace of terrorism.

RELIGION

In the second half of the twentieth century, it was widely believed that once problems of poverty, hunger, and disease are overcome, thanks to the application of science and technology in human endeavour, religion would be a matter of the past or confined merely to private domain. This has proved to be wrong. Religion has returned to occupy an important place in human life in the twenty-first century.

In fact, whenever a change is required to be made in the general intellectual and moral climate of the day, scholars and statesmen, ordinary people and warmongers, pontiffs and villains have all accepted that religion has a powerful role to play. A belief in spiritual values has always been at the core of every religion. The commitment of individuals to their religion and its system of beliefs has been a matter of great political and social significance.

A large number of religions have grown over the years. Major religions that still survive are Hinduism, Judaism, Zoroastrianism, Buddhism, Christianity, and Islam—in the historical order of their appearance in the world. Discussing their origins, Arnold Toynbee significantly observes:

Hinduism and Buddhism originated within the Indic Civilization, Judaism within the Syriac Civilization, Zoroastrianism within the Iranian Civilization, and Christianity and Islam in a 'culture-compost' in which elements of the disintegrated Syriac and Hellenic Civilizations were mingled.[7]

Buddhism, Christianity, and Islam have all been whole-heartedly universalistic. Each of these faiths has succeeded in converting whole continents and embracing the regional domains of a number of different civilizations; Each of them has achieved this by means of the rudimentary vehicles of communication that were available before the 'annihilation of distance' through the modern advance of techno-logy.[8] The transformation of Christianity and Islam into religions for a large section of humanity was achieved through persuasion as well as conversion (at times adopting coercive means including monetary inducements). It was, however, not the intention of the founders themselves.

Religion is native to the human mind. Though it has taken many forms and is still evolving, its continuation is undoubted as long as human beings continue to be a blend of power and weakness. It should be noted that support to the fundamentalist approach is not an integral part of any religion or even its system of beliefs.

A lot may have and continues to happen in the name of religion that may not stand rational scrutiny, but the spiritual aspects of every religion have always unified mankind and had an ennobling effect. Secular values are often regarded as encompassed by religious values. Viewed thus, religion becomes the foundation of society and the traditional vision of life remains holistic.

The growth of religious fundamentalism and sectarian belief has largely undermined the value of religion and led many modern intellectuals to believe that religion or religiosity is the bane of a good enlightened life. For Mahatma Gandhi and the millions of Indians he represented, religion was indeed constitutive of society. To him every activity was governed by what he considered to be his religion. This is as true of many Indian Muslims, for whom the ultimate reality is spiritual and for whom, consequently, there is no such thing as a profane world. It is also true of many Sikhs, who deny the separation of spiritual goals from the pursuit of political power, and of many devout Hindus who see the cosmos as a single whole, a unity, comprising all creation animated by one spirit.[9] Let me state here that I am inclined to believe that the religious and traditional view of life has not really been the source of conflict between peoples, but that it is its perversion which has been so.

It is significant that the present Iranian President Muhammad Khatami, in his address to the United Nations in 1998, called for dialogue among civilizations and culture. He said:

Today the Iranian nation draws on its past to contemplate a better tomorrow while defying reactionary tendencies and, backed by principles and ideas rooted in its religious, national, historical and revolutionary heritage, and benefiting from positive achievements of contemporary civilization, marches, through trial and error, towards a promising future.

The Islamic Revolution of the Iranian people was a revolt of reason against coercion and suppression. Certainly a revolution which resorted to logic in the phase of destruction is much better disposed to resort to dialogue and reason in the phase of construction. Hence, it calls for a dialogue among civilizations and cultures instead of a clash between them.[10]

Coming as it does from the land of the Islamic Revolution, this approach is optimistic and needs to be further worked upon. One has to realize that it will never be possible for the world to have only one religion, and neither is it desirable. On 30 May 1913, Mahatma Gandhi wrote: 'Personally, I think the world as a whole will never have, and need not have, a single religion.'[11]

FUNDAMENTALISM AND ISLAM

'Islamic fundamentalism' is the current buzzword used by the media and politicians to label various Islamic groups. Earlier, in 1995 itself, the Secretary-General of North Atlantic Treaty Organization (NATO) made the following statement:

Muslim fundamentalism is at least as dangerous as communism once was. Please do not underestimate this risk . . . at the conclusion of this age it is a serious threat, because it represents terrorism, religious fanaticism and exploitation of social and economic justice.[12]

The debate as to why the attacks of 11 September 2001 occurred has been dominated by talks of civilizational conflict between the West and Islam. The argument of the 'clash of civilizations' by Samuel Huntington has been furthered to mean that religion drives both Islamic culture and politics and that the motivation for Islamist violence is religious fundamentalism. This, however, is far from correct.

This approach does not take into account the philosophy of love and compassion which is integral to Islamic mysticism popularly known as Sufism. The word Sufism simultaneously means 'occlusion' and 'enlightenment'. It is commonly referred to as 'Islamic spirituality' or 'Islamic mysticism'. Sufis believe that their teachings are the essence of every religion, and indeed of the evolution of humanity as a whole. The central concept in Sufism is 'love'. Sufism believes and propagates that only by following the path of spirituality can the good life be attained.[13]

There is much misconception about the concept of 'Muslim brotherhood'. Muhammad, on his pilgrimage to Mecca shortly before his death had proclaimed:

O men! listen to my words and take them to heart! Know ye that every Muslim is a brother to every other Muslim, and that you are now one brotherhood.[14]

This exhortation to Muslims by the Prophet provides even the humblest peasant or cobbler a dignity and courtesy from even those who are rich and powerful in the Islamic world. This is the essence of the democratic ethos of equality among human beings.

It is wrong to view fundamentalism as an exclusive Islamic phenomenon. Almost every major faith has a fundamentalist code, which opposes the problems of modernization and material progress. There is fundamentalist Judaism, fundamentalist Christianity, fundamentalist Hinduism, fundamentalist Buddhism, fundamentalist Sikhism, and even a fundamentalist Confucianism.

In every faith, fundamentalists assume prominence because they cater to disappointment and disenchantment and blame others for the ills in their society. The fundamentalists blame the processes of secularization and liberalization in society, which are particularly perceived by them as an imitation of western values. The root of all their frustration seems to be in their dislike of the western way of life.[15]

The fundamentalist strain took root in the Muslim world after the rapid modernization in the 1960s and 1970s propelled by unprecedented oil wealth, leading to integration of their economies with the global market. Fundamentalists have drawn strength and sustenance from the traditional education system. The madrasas have provided sustenance to the religious, narrow-minded sections. Hence it is necessary to reform and modernize the education system. Students in madrasas must be taught modern science so that these boys and girls are able to compete with the rest of the world.

Every attempt should be made to encourage Islamic principles which support dialogue among people. This should not only be restricted to believers but also encouraged among people in the neighbourhood. The focus must be on the principles of democratic norms and *shurah* (consultation). The fact that Islamic law promotes the principles of shurah and *Ijmah*—where the law has to be endorsed by consensus or *ummah*—could give legitimacy to the modern democratic systems.

The origins of Islam conveyed a strong message for the Arab world to create a just community in which all members, even the weakest and most vulnerable, high and low, were to be treated with respect. This social concern has always been an essential part of the visions of the world's great religions, which developed during what historians have called the Axial Age (700 BC–200 BC)—Taoism and Confucianism in China; Hinduism and Buddhism in the Indian subcontinent; monotheism in the Middle East; and rationalism in Europe.

The Prophet Muhammad lived in a society where one tribe fought another, in a murderous cycle of vendetta and counter-vendetta. To Prophet Muhammad this clearly established that in future the Arabs would have a single god. The Quran insisted that it was wrong to build a private fortune, but good to build wealth and create a society where the weak and vulnerable were treated with respect. Under this new religious Islamic order, 'a Muslim was a man or a woman who had made submission of their entire being to Allah and prayed that human beings behaved with one another with justice, equity and compassion'. The old tribal ethic had been egalitarian; Arabs did not approve of the idea of monarchy, and it was abhorrent to them to grovel on the ground like slaves. Social justice was, therefore, a crucial virtue of Islam. Muslims were commanded, as their first duty, to build a community (ummah) characterized by practical compassion, in which there was a fair distribution of wealth. This was far more important than any doctrinal teaching about God.[16]

There are an estimated 1.3 billion Muslims in the world today. My Muslim scholar friends tell me that the Quran can be understood properly only in Arabic, the language in which it was delivered. I am fully aware of the limitations of translation and that my understanding of the Quran through its English or Hindi versions may not be adequate. Huston Smith provides an insight into the Quran when he writes:

Unlike the Upanishads, it is not explicitly metaphysical. It does not ground its theology in dramatic narratives as the Indian epics do, nor in historical ones as do the Hebrew scriptures; nor is God revealed in human form as in the Gospels and the Bhagavad-Gita. Confining ourselves to the Semitic scriptures, we can say that whereas the Old and New Testaments are directly historical and indirectly doctrinal, the Quran is directly doctrinal and indirectly historical. Because the overwhelming thrust of the Quran is to proclaim the unity, omnipotence, omniscience, and mercy of God—and correlatively the total dependence of human life upon him—historical facts are in its case merely reference points that have scarcely any interest in themselves.[17]

Many Muslims look back at the century after the revelations to the Prophet Muhammad as a golden age. Its memory is strongest among the Arabs. As Philip Hitti notes:

Around the name of the Arabs, gleams that halo which belongs to the world-conquerors. Within a century after their rise this people became the masters of an empire extending from the shores of the Atlantic Ocean to the confines of China, an empire greater than that of Rome at its zenith. In this period of unprecedented expansion, they assimilated to their creed, speech, and even physical type, more aliens than any stock before or since, not excepting the Hellenic, the Roman, the Anglo-Saxon, or the Russian.[18]

Islam is both a faith and a code of conduct that governs all aspects of life. For many Muslims, a good government would be one guided by the moral principles of their faith. This does not necessarily translate into a desire for clerical rule and the abolition of a secular state. It does mean that some Muslims tend to be uncomfortable with distinctions between religion and state, though Muslim rulers throughout history have readily separated the two.

EXTREMISTS IN ISLAMIC COUNTRIES

The extreme Islamist version of history blames the decline of Islam's golden age on the rulers and people who turned away from the true path of their religion, thereby leaving Islam vulnerable to encroaching foreign powers eager to steal their land, wealth, and even their souls.

A decade of conflict in Afghanistan[19] (from 1979–89) gave Islamist extremists a rallying point and training field. Young Muslims from around the world flocked to Afghanistan to join as volunteers in what was seen as a 'holy war'—jihad—against an invader, the Soviet Union. The largest numbers came from the Middle East. Some were Saudis, and among them was Osama bin Laden.

After gaining independence from western powers after the Second World War, several countries in the Middle East assiduously worked for the revival of political institutions in terms of their glorious past and in accordance with their aspirations for self-rule. In several countries, a dynastic order prevailed over new aspirations such as in Saudi Arabia, Morocco, and Jordan where monarchies still survive. However, in many other countries such as Egypt, Libya, Iraq, and Yemen, monarchical orders were overthrown by secular nationalist revolutionaries.

The secular revolutionary regimes promised a glowing future for Arab socialism, such as that promoted by the Egyptian President Gamal Abdel Nasser (1918–70). Similar visions were propagated by the Ba'ath Party of Syria and Iraq. But very soon these regimes, and even the one in Egypt, became autocratic and unwilling to tolerate any opposition. Thousands of members of the Muslim Brotherhood were put into concentration camps. Reza Shah Pahlavi who reigned during 1921–41 in Iran deprived the ulama of their endowments and even forbade the Iranians to go on the *hajj*.

The bankruptcy of secular, autocratic nationalism was evident across the Muslim world by the late 1970s. Two major events took place after that: one in Iran in 1979 and the other in Saudi Arabia in the 1980s. Iran's 1979 revolution swept a Shia theocracy into power. In the 1980s, awash with sudden oil wealth, Saudi Arabia competed with Shia Iran to promote its Sunni fundamentalist interpretation of Islam, Wahhabism.[20]

The situation was equally volatile elsewhere. Confronted with a violent Islamist movement that killed President Anwar Sadat in 1981, the Egyptian government combined harsh repression of Islamic militants with harassment of moderate Islamic scholars and authors, driving many into exile.

Islamist revival movements gained followers across the Muslim world, but failed to secure political power except in Iran and Sudan. In Algeria, where in 1991, Islamists seemed almost certain to win power through the ballot box, the military pre-empted their victory, triggering a brutal civil war that continues till today.

The Kingdom of Saudi Arabia, always conscious of its duties as the custodian of Islam's holiest places, joined with wealthy Arabs from the Kingdom and other states bordering the Persian Gulf in donating money to build mosques and religious schools that could preach and teach their interpretation of Islamic doctrine. The Saudi rulers proclaimed that a constitution was unnecessary, since the government was based on a literal reading of the Quran. According to them, the ulama granted the state legitimacy and the kings enforced conservative religious values.

The unprecedented flood of oil wealth among Arab nations created problems of plenty. The leadership funded huge infrastructure projects and created subsidized social welfare programmes. These programmes established a widespread feeling of entitlement without a corresponding sense of social obligations. By the late 1980s, diminishing oil revenues, the economic drain from many unprofitable development projects, and population growth made these entitlement programmes unsustainable. The resulting cutbacks created enormous resentment among recipients who had come to view government largesse as their right. This resentment was further stoked by public understanding of how much oil income had gone into the pockets of the rulers, their friends, and their helpers.

By the 1990s, high birth rates and declining rates of infant mortality contributed to a large, steadily increasing population of educated young boys and girls without any reasonable expectation of suitable or steady employment. Many of them had been trained only in religious schools and lacked the skills needed by modern industrialized establishments. On a cultural plane, owing to their educational curricula they had little understanding of the rest of the world's thought, history, and culture. The modern education reflected a strong cultural preference for technical fields over the humanities and social sciences. Many of these young boys and girls, even if able to study abroad, lacked the perspective and skills needed to understand a different culture. Frustrated in their search for a decent living, and unable to benefit from their education in self-employment, some of these young men became easy targets for radicalization.

PAKISTAN AND RELIGIOUS FUNDAMENTALISM

Muhammad Ali Jinnah (1876–1948), the founder of Pakistan, was keen to build a democratic secular order in Pakistan but died soon after the country's independence. Another towering secular leader Liaquat Ali Khan (1896–1951), the first Prime Minister of Pakistan, was assassinated. These developments afforded the fundamentalists ample opportunities to assert themselves—and they did.

Unfortunately, democracy did not take deep root in Pakistan and military dictators assumed power and indulged in the game of pleasing fundamentalist elements. The subsequent emergence of elected political leadership did not improve the state of affairs in any enduring fashion. Secular democratic leaders such as Zulfiqar Ali Bhutto and his daughter Benazir Bhutto were forced during their tenure as Prime Ministers (1972–7 for the former and 1988–90 and 1993–6 for the latter) to make concessions to these fundamentalist elements to remain in office although their tenure too was short-lived.

The fundamentalist hold over the government was solidified during the rule of Muhammad Zia ul-Haq (1977–88). Madrasas and various religious institutions and outfits provided sustenance to the fundamentalist philosophy. General Zia's military regime sought to justify its seizure of power by a pious public stance and by encouraging unprecedented Islamist influence on education and society, and these tendencies continue to dominate society and polity in that country. This was a reaction to the policies pursued by the government of General Muhammad Ayub Khan (1958–69) who had nationalized religious endowments, placed restrictions on madrasa education, and promoted a secular legal system.

According to the 9/11 report:

from the 1970s onwards, religion had become an increasingly powerful force in Pakistani politics. After a coup in 1977, military leaders turned to Islamist groups for support, and fundamentalists became more prominent.

South Asia had an indigenous form of Islamic fundamentalism, which had developed in the nineteenth century at a school in the Indian village of Deoband.[21] The influence of the Wahhabi school of Islam had also grown, nurtured by Saudi-funded institutions. Moreover, the fighting in Afghanistan made Pakistan home to an enormous—and generally unwelcome— population of Afghan refugees; and since the badly strained Pakistani education system could not accommodate the refugees, the government increasingly let privately funded religious schools serve as a cost-free alternative. Over time, these schools produced large numbers of semi-educated young men with no marketable skills but with deeply held Islamic views.[22]

The greatest threat to Pakistan's future lies in its abysmal education system. Pakistani schools—and more particularly madrasas—are churning out fiery zealots, fuelled with a passion for jihad and martyrdom. It is reckoned that one million Pakistani children now attend madrasas where the syllabus consists solely of the Quran, jihad, and martyrdom.

The obstacles to educational reforms are great. For example, recent street rampages by Islamists forced Musharraf's former Minister of Education, Zubaida Jala, to declare herself a fundamentalist and denounce as unacceptable school textbooks that do not include Quranic verses on jihad.

Thirty years ago, university students noisily argued over ideological positions and competed for votes in student elections. Today, academic dialogue has been substituted by one group, defined by sectarian or ethnic beliefs, pitted against another. With Islamism as the only outlet for political involvement, these students are prime candidates for membership in extremist organizations. Unless political organizations are once again allowed to organize locally and nationally, and intelligence agencies stop harassing critics of state policies, this 'depoliticization' has the potential to push Pakistan further down the abyss towards instability.

The game of musical chairs between elected leaders and military coups has continued till recently in Pakistan. The present ruler of Pakistan, General Pervez Musharraf, too, led a successful coup and replaced the regime of Prime Minister Nawaz Sharif on 12 October 1999. After 9/11 Pakistan, under his leadership, has made a complete turnaround by becoming an ally of the United States in its war against terrorism, notwithstanding Pakistan's role of sponsoring terrorism as an instrument of state policy in Kashmir and as a close ally of Al-Qaeda and the Taliban regime in Afghanistan. A deep struggle between secular forces and the fundamentalists continues in Pakistan and it is very difficult to forecast its outcome.

RECENT CHANGES IN ISLAMIC COUNTRIES

Far-reaching changes have taken place since 9/11, both within Islamic countries and Muslim populations in the wider world. Events in Afghanistan, Iraq, Pakistan, and Palestine and the rise of intellectual and ideological groups in several Arab countries have transformed the terms of the discourse about Islam. Today new questions with regard to both the nature of Islam, and how it needs to be understood in an increasingly interactive world, are being asked. Islam is evolving in response to this change in the global environment.

Islamic studies were originally the province of theologians and of those who relied on textual sources in their work as members of the clergy or as social activists. In this kind of analysis, a great deal of emphasis was placed on the unity and commonality of beliefs, attitudes, and sentiments. But in the post-9/11 world, understanding Islam through the written text as interpreted by the clergy is being contested. Today, Islam is proposed to be understood in terms of the ground realities. The existence of 'folk' Islam as opposed to 'formal' Islam is quite significant here. The daily experience of a believer of Islam in the market place or in an office with believers of other faiths has its own bearing on the understanding of formal Islam. It is, therefore, not possible to accept the theological interpretation as an absolutist phenomenon. It certainly needs to be seen in terms of its wider social and cultural ramifications.

POLITICAL REFORMS IN THE ARAB WORLD

The 11 September 2001 terrorist attacks have created pressure for political reform in the Arab world. This pressure is coming from both the United States as well as from liberal intellectuals in the world. There is a growing conviction that Middle East democracy is the best antidote to Islamist terrorism. Fortunately, talk about political reform and democracy is noticed even in the Gulf monarchies where such issues have been taboo till only recently. The concerted measures initiated so far in most countries, however, are limited.

There are a few countervailing factors. The major constricting factor lies in the failure to resolve the Arab–Israeli conflict. Liberal Arabs perceive claims by the US of wanting democracy in the Middle East as hypocritical, pointing to what they see as American indifference to the rights of the Palestinians and unconditional support for Israel.

For their part, many Arab governments do not take US pressure to democratize their region seriously, believing that the need for oil and fear of upsetting regimes that recognize Israel will trump Washington's desire for democratic change.

The history of political experience has not been of much help either. Democracy in the Arab world is a relatively recent historical phenomenon. Arab rulers have been highly authoritarian. Arabs developed a political system based on Islam through the Caliph, an individual who served as supreme leader of all Muslims. Fortunately, newly independent countries in the Arab world in the 1960s and 1970s adopted the democratic philosophy of the time. Most Arab countries outside the Gulf displayed the combination of nationalism and socialism that constituted typical Third World ideology at the time. The triumvirate of Gamal Abdel Nasser in Egypt, Jawaharlal Nehru in India, and Marshal Tito in Yugoslavia was a major champion of this ideology. All this waned in the 1980s.

During the last decade, Islamist parties and candidates have participated in elections in several Arab countries (Algeria, Bahrain, Egypt, Kuwait, Lebanon, Morocco, and Yemen). These elections suffered from varying degrees of government interference, but there is no indication that the Islamists would have won in a more open environment. But Turkey, a country where an Islamist party assumed power with a large majority, is an encouraging example of democratic success.

In western societies, a small democratic cadre sufficed in the distant past as political participation was the preserve of public-minded intellectual elites and wealthy property owners. However, the Arab world of today is not the United States or Europe of the eighteenth century. The political elite face a growing challenge from Islamist movements that are developing a popular support base. As a result, democratic transformation also requires broad-based political parties and movements capable of transforming abstract democratic ideals into concrete programmes that resonate with a public whose main concern is employment and security.

DEMOCRACY AS DESTINY

One of the principal features of political consciousness of people of the twenty-first century consists of a belief that legitimate power of governance derives not from divine right, nor from naked threats, but from the will as well as consent of the people.[23]

The end of the Cold War also signalled the end of the belief that democracy can gain a foothold in a country only once it is developed economically, and that India was the solitary exception among developing countries. The dismal economic record of the communist states in Eastern Europe and the former Soviet Union, as well as that of Latin American military countries, and those of the strongmen rulers in Africa, clearly vindicated the theory that economic development cannot be guaranteed under autocratic rule.

Data compiled from the World Bank's *World Development Indicators* from 1960 to the present reveal a simple truth: low-income democracies have, on average, grown more rapidly than low-income autocracies over the past forty years. Outside eastern Asia, the median per capita growth rates of poor democracies have been fifty per cent higher than those of autocracies. Countries that have chosen the democratic path—such as the Dominican Republic, India, Latvia, Mozambique, Nicaragua, and Senegal—have typically outpaced their autocratic counterparts, such as Angola, the Republic of Congo, Syria, Uzbekistan, and Zimbabwe.

The advantage poor democracies have over poor autocracies becomes even more apparent when the debate moves from growth rates to broader measures of well-being. Development can also be measured by social indicators such as life expectancy, access to clean drinking water, literacy rates, agricultural yields, and the quality of public-health services. On nearly all these quality-of-life criteria, low-income democracies dramatically outdo their autocratic counterparts. A careful review of the data suggests that low-income democracies have another powerful advantage: they are better at avoiding calamities.

South Korea, Taiwan, Singapore, and Indonesia encouraged the private sector, pursued export-oriented growth strategies, and were heavily influenced by western democracies when they adopted their particular economic and political institutions. Moreover, China, by its appalling economic record through the late 1970s (when it began to adopt market-oriented economic policies) clearly demonstrated that authoritarianism is not the distinguishing characteristic of its growth.

Democratic leaders have incentives to respond to the needs of common citizens. The bread-and-butter issues of ordinary people figure prominently in the candidates' agendas. By contrast, the narrow clan and patronage-based support, on which autocratic leaders often rely for power, gives them little incentive to focus on the general well-being of society.

Information is best communicated through multiple and independent channels. For example, it was the active public education campaign undertaken by the Ugandan government and non-governmental organizations in the 1990s that dramatically reduced the transmission of HIV/AIDS in that country. Uganda was once the world leader in the percentage of adult population infected, at roughly thirty per cent, but by 2003, that rate had declined to seven per cent. By contrast, attempts to suppress information during the SARS epidemic in China allowed the disease to spread before the public became aware and concerted action could be taken. Once the epidemic was acknowledged, distrust of the government led many Chinese in infected areas to violate the government's quarantine. This example also confirms a larger proposition: democracies do a better job of correcting errors. Once private or public authorities make decisions in open societies, the results become known and corrective action, if needed, can be taken. Openness also reduces the scope for corruption.

Alleviating poverty and advancing democracy are long, difficult processes susceptible to periodic setbacks. But democracy brings political checks and balances, responsiveness to citizens' priorities, openness, and self-correcting mechanisms—all of which contribute to steady growth and superior living conditions.[24]

The spread of democracy to 117 countries in the world in the last few decades is significant from another angle as it inhibits governments from fighting each other. The democratic peace—the idea that democracies do not fight each other—also suggests that the critical division in the world is between democratic and non-democratic regimes. A burgeoning literature has tested and refined the thesis, developing variations, including the proposition that new fragile democracies might be more bellicose than dictatorships[25] and that narrowly based democracies might fight with more broadly based ones.

There is, however, a growing concern about the non-functioning of democratic governments. There are a number of scholars who feel that in several places a democratic government does not necessarily lead to more freedom for citizens. The weakening of the institutions of Parliament and legislatures and the increasing role of bureaucracies has led to restrictions on individual freedom. Bureaucracies, moreover, have failed to deliver quality services to

people, particularly in health and education. The right of citizens
to seek information from the government, and effective public
expenditure review, both by civil society groups and committees of
legislatures, have been advocated. The strongest fears have arisen
from the working of US democracy itself. Fareed Zakaria has
expressed the opinions of concerned citizens about the challenges
of modern democracies and its vulnerabilities in the following words:

Modern democracies will face difficult new challenges—fighting terrorism,
adjusting to globalisation, adapting to an aging society—and they will have
to make their system work much better than it currently does. That means
making democratic decision-making effective, reintegrating constitutional
liberalism into the practice of democracy, rebuilding broken political
institutions and civic associations. Perhaps most difficult of all, it requires
that those with immense power in our societies embrace their responsibilities, lead and set standards that are not only legal, but moral. Without
this inner stuffing, democracy will become an empty shell, not simply
inadequate but potentially dangerous, bringing with it the erosion of liberty,
the manipulation of freedom, and the decay of a common life.

This would be a tragedy because democracy, with all its flaws, represents
the 'last best hope' for people around the world. But it needs to be secured
and strengthened for our times.[26]

DEMOCRACY AND DEVELOPMENT

The new millennium began with the resolve of the international
community to set targets for meeting the most compelling of human
desires—a world free of poverty and of the misery it breeds—in the
form of the Millennium Development Goals (MDGs) adopted by the
UN member countries. Today, there is a strong desire among the
youth for development. The eradication of poverty is being rightly
viewed as central to stability and peace. Despite rapid economic
development in recent years, out of six billion people today, nearly
one billion people live on less than $1 a day and an additional 1.6
billion on less than $2 a day. There is mind-boggling inequality in
the world, both at the individual and nation-state levels.[27]

With this background, democracy has become much more
acceptable in recent years, both as an object of development in itself
and as a means towards economic growth. It is clear, for example,
that it is not authoritarianism per se that determines economic
growth but rather the quality of the authoritarian leader and the
technocrats advising him or her. Authoritarian countries as a group

might do well if they could all be run by leaders like Lee Kwan Yew. But authoritarian rulers are often like Mobutu Sese Seko, or Ferdinand Marcos, and it is, therefore, not surprising that authoritarian regimes pay scant regard to people's welfare as compared to democratic ones. Democratic regimes at least have some institutional checks against the worst forms of incompetence or rapacity: bad leaders can be voted out of office.[28]

During the last two decades many countries have overthrown authoritarian and dictatorial regimes and have embarked on the road to democracy. The answer to the question as to 'why we aspire for democratic government' is simple and can be stated unequivocally. Government is still central to our society. An efficient, effective, and democratic government is the best guarantor of social justice and an orderly society where a multiplicity of views can flourish. We know from experience that democratic governments are participatory, transparent, and accountable; they respect plural and diverse perspectives and allow freedom of choice, expression, and beliefs.

GLOBALIZATION

The end of colonialism and the Cold War accelerated the pace of globalization[29] not only in economic, financial, and trade domains, but also in social, cultural, and political arenas. The significant transformations in financial markets and production and business organizations in different parts of the world today mean that they are more global in character than ever. Globalization is not an event but a gradual and continuous expansion and integration of relations, largely through economic routes, having a bearing on society, culture, and politics.

From the women's movement to environmentalists, from mobile telephones to Internet connections, from advertisements to printed material, there is strong evidence that globalization is affecting society and culture. A further great change has been the huge outflow of information, which contributes to sharing; the world is now accessible, understandable and 'transparent' as never before.

Human destinies are now linked round the world not only by the politics of formal organizations such as the UN or the Bretton Woods institutions such as the International Monetary Fund (IMF) and the World Bank, but by science and technology through their complex networks, by commercial and industrial organizations, and by material practices.

The globalization thesis highlights the increasing integration of the world economy and the homogenization of products, tastes, and even ideas. The rapid flow of goods, services, technology, and capital among states tie countries together and compel people, firms, and governments to either adapt, compete, or fall behind.[30]

Multinational Corporations (MNCs), in particular, have played a significant role in international politics. The need for protection of information and technology assets has also facilitated the integration of relations between different countries. The sovereignty of states in many ways has been curtailed. The multilateral agencies in the global economy such as IMF, World Bank, and World Trade Organization (WTO), have greatly influenced the decisions of the nation-states. Governments no longer have a monopoly on the issues on which the future of their countries rests. Indeed, the number of cases in which businesses, more than governments, seem to be driving policy changes is steadily rising. Nevertheless, nationalism remains an important force. The world is still, in territorial terms, made up of separate states, each of which enjoys certain basic sovereign rights.

There is an increasing realization that markets cannot function without government regulation. For effective functioning a market must rely on the government to: protect private property rights; enforce contract; provide arbitration in case of disputes; manage and regulate patents and trade marks; facilitate the exchange of goods and services by setting standards for measurement; create the conditions for international trade; protect against theft and fraud; and above all, control money supply through manipulation of interest rates. There is absolutely no such thing as an unfettered free market and no society can leave the market uncontrolled.

The first responsibility of each nation-state is to ensure the security of its nationals and to promote national interests. Today USA, European nations, India, and several other developing countries are dependent on gas and oil imports from abroad. This also applies to food imports in respect of several countries. Economic globalization cannot succeed without political globalization. Without peace, there can be no trade or integration of markets. The principal challenge of globalization lies in the state providing job opportunities for everyone. The best way to ensure livelihood security and thus help the poor is not in simply letting the economy grow, but also in intervening imaginatively, so that there is work for everyone, and ensuring that the political economy also becomes inclusive. We need to work in a manner that does not allow globalization to create economic and social inequalities or even environmental hazards, but creates political, economic and cultural uniformity. The demanding task is to bring in a state of affairs that promotes the well-being of ordinary citizens without interfering with rapid economic growth. At a tactical level, it needs to be noted that terrorists, money launderers, and arms dealers are proving their ability to successfully network their operations. This has thrown up challenges to security agencies to deal with 'networked threats'.

HOW TO LIVE?

The fundamental issue facing the world is 'how to live'. Arnold Toynbee has rightly stated:

The same unprecedented scientific and technological advances that have unified the world by 'annihilating distance' have put it into Mankind's power to annihilate itself by making war with atomic weapons. We are now waking up to the truth that we have unintentionally put ourselves in a new position in which mankind may have to choose between the two extreme alternatives of committing genocide and learning to live henceforward as a single family.[31]

How do we control human nature that involves violent conflicts and threatens peace? How do we subordinate sectarian and ethnic loyalties to work for harmony among peoples? How can love and compassion be made to prevail over oppression and exploitation? How can people in different countries be made masters of their own destinies? How do we get engaged in dialogue on a constant basis? How do we step up the level and depth of dialogue? The need to work for harmony among people and to spread democratic govern-ance is widespread.

By the end of the twentieth century, many believed that democracy, secularism, and market forces had finally arrived. What many forgot was that several totalitarian regimes professing Communism and Fascism had once been secular. We also forgot, that until two centuries ago, the world had gotten along without democracy.

There are enormous challenges in removing poverty and building an equitable social order. There are fears of violence, of terrorism, of the revival of the balance of power philosophy that caused conflicts and wars in the past. We have to learn to live together in concord in spite of traditional differences of religion, civilization, nationality, class, and race. In order to live together successfully, we have to know each other, which includes knowing each other's past. We must learn to recognize and, as far as possible, understand the different cultural configurations in which our common human nature has expressed itself in different religions, civilizations, and nationalities.

Arthur M. Schlesinger, Jr., in his book *War and the American Presidency,* writes:

Hegel observed in the introduction to his *Philosophy of History,* 'People and governments never have learned anything from history, or acted on principles deduced from it.' Hegel exaggerated. For history is surely to the nation rather as memory is to the individual. As individuals deprived of memory become disoriented and lost, not knowing where they have been or where they are going, as a nation denied a conception of its past is disabled in dealing with its present and its future. . . .Yet history is subject to the same liabilities as memory—to the same whims, distortions, and corruptions that make memory self-serving, misleading, and unreliable. And the oracle of history, like the oracle of Delphi, is very often clouded and ambiguous.[32]

We cannot claim accuracy for our knowledge either about the past or about our understanding of conflict resolutions in the past. And yet, imperfect though we may be, we must try to delve into the past and learn both about human failures and wisdom.

THE BAHUDHĀ PHILOSOPHY

India, Egypt, Iraq, Greece, and China have been recognized as the five cradles of human civilization.[33] Among them, India and China have maintained their civilizational continuum. Historical enquiries and archaeological findings have clearly established that the Vedas, which are the collective designation for the ancient sacred literature of India, reflect the ideals of Hinduism and have shaped the nature and content of early Indian civilization. Their composition is now placed at about 1500 BC and may even go back to an earlier time.

The Vedas are four in number: *Rig Veda, Yajur Veda, Sama Veda,* and *Atharva Veda.* The *Rig Veda* is, on the whole, the most important as well as the oldest of the four Vedas. Vedic literature was followed by the composition of two great epics: the Ramayana and the Mahabharata. The Vedas, the Upanishads, the Ramayana, and the Mahabharata have been the principal instruments in shaping the Indian way of life ever since. This literature, in both prose and poetry, was transmitted orally from one generation to the other. Notwithstanding the fact that Sanskrit was the language of the elite, several of the *shloka*s and key expressions became the preserve of the common people and were handed down from generation to generation through dialogues in local dialects.

The pluralist approach towards all life is at the heart of India's civilizational endeavours. The Vedas and Upanishads as well as the oral traditions are full of ideals propagating harmonious ways of thinking. All these have invariably emphasized inclusiveness among all people, all societies, and all natural objects, including water, the earth, and the sky. It also talks about the unity of mind. This approach has been both an idea and a reality. The existence of plurality as an idea helps us understand our cultural diversity and incredible ethnic, religious, and linguistic varieties. As a reality, it enables us to participate in this diversity. It is not just simple tolerance for others' points of view but a seeking of understanding.

Purely from the people's point of view, I find that one attitude that has greatly contributed to the enrichment of Indian life and that is respect for another person's view of truth with the hope and belief that he or she may be right. This has been best expressed in the Rigvedic hymn which enjoins '*Ekam Sad Vipra Bahudhā Vadanti*'.[34]

I imagine this approach of 'one truth, many interpretations' was formulated by our *rishi*s, both in order to understand the complexities of natural objects and their inter-relationships, and for harmonious living in society among peoples of many-sided beliefs and practices, each claiming superiority over the other.

The most important feature of the Vedic world view is that it is essential to question everything and to test every teaching. What matters is not what you believe in but how you behave. There is emphasis on leading a compassionate life. All the sages preach about compassion and brotherhood. They stress that people must abandon or control their ego and greed, their violence and unkindness both in thoughts and deeds. They talk of a cosmic order where each one, including the Gods, is expected to behave in an orderly fashion.

The Bahudhā approach is central to the generation of an attitude which creates an environment for harmony among communities and religions, harmony between nature and humans, and enables a person to understand another's point of view about life and religion, science and spirituality. Whether one reads India's great epics or travels through the length and breadth of its sacred geography, one is struck by the fact that neither our literature nor our places of worship emphasize a singularity of approach to truth. The idea of 'the one in the many' is central to this thought process. In historical terms, this thought has found expression in Emperor Ashoka's (273–32 BC) Rock Edict 12 in a region of Gujarat in western India. It reads:

The faiths of all deserve to be honoured for one reason or another. By honouring them, one exalts one's own faith and at the same time performs a service to the faith of others. By acting otherwise, one injures one's language, faith and does disservice to that of others.

One cannot merely conclude from this that there has never been conflict between different world views in India. On the contrary, major civilizational encounters have occurred in South Asia, both supporting and, on some other occasions, jeopardizing the Bahudhā philosophy or pluralist approach.

It would be fruitful to examine the Indian experience at various levels and from several perspectives to enable us to formulate a public policy of harmony and peace. The following five chapters of the book are aimed at this endeavour.

NOTES

1. *Rig Veda* (I. 164–46)—the earliest among the four Vedas—composed in 1500 BC or even earlier. Its English translation is 'The Real is one, the learned speak of it variously'.
2. Anand Panyarachun Committee report entitled: *Report of the High-level Panel on Threats, Challenges and Change*, United Nations, New York, 2004, p. 49.
3. Leonard Peikoff, 'End States Who Sponsor Terrorism', dated 2 October 2001 on the Ayn Rand Institute website. (*www.aynrand.org*)
4. Sidney Blumenthal, *The Clinton Wars*, Viking, New York, 2003, p. 671.
5. Francis Fukuyama, *State Building: Governance and World Order in the Twenty-First Century*, South Asian Edition, Profile Books, London, 2004, pp. ix–xi.
6. Ibid., pp. 162–4.
7. Arnold Toynbee, *A Study of History: Illustrated* (The first abridged one-volume edition), Strand Book Stall, Bombay and Bangalore, 1995, pp. 334–5. Toynbee writes: 'The principal higher religions that still survive are Hinduism, Judaism, Zoroastrianism, Buddhism, Christianity, and Islam. They are named here in the historical order of their appearance in the world, but the beginning of the two oldest of them, namely Hinduism and Judaism, cannot be dated precisely, since these two, unlike the later four, were not originated by historically well-attested single founders who claimed, or have been claimed by their followers, to have made a revolutionary break with the past on the religious plane.'
8. Ibid., pp. 294–5.

9. T.N. Madan (ed.), *India's Religions: Perspectives from Sociology and History*, Oxford University Press, New Delhi, 2004, pp. 384–5.
10. Lloyd Ridgeon (ed.), *Major World Religions: From their Origins to the Present*, Routledge Curzon, London, 2003, pp. 284–5.
11. Madan, *India's Religions*, p. 384.
12. Ridgeon, *Major World Religions*, p. 278.
13. This thought has been best explained by the parable narrated by Jalal ud-din Rumi (1207–73). One is reminded of Rumi's well-known story of a group of men in India who had never seen an elephant. One day they came to a place where there was an elephant. In complete darkness they approached the animal, each man feeling it. Afterwards, they described what they thought they had perceived. Of course their descriptions were different. He who had felt a leg, imagined the elephant to be a pillar. The man who felt the animal's ear, described the elephant as a fan, and so on. Each one of their descriptions with respect to the various parts they had experienced was true. However, as far as accurately describing the whole, their conceptions had all fallen short. If they had a candle, the difference of opinions would not have come about. The candle's light would have revealed the elephant as a whole. Sufism provides that candle light. (For the full text of this narration see Franklin D. Lewis, *Rumi: Past and Present, East and West: The Life, Teaching and Poetry of Jâlal al-Din Rumi*, Oneworld Publications, Oxford, 2001, p. 5. The book makes a detailed analysis of Sufi thought).
14. Huston Smith, *Islam: A Concise Introduction*, HarperCollins, San Francisco, 2001, p. 57.
15. Fundamentalists nearly always feel assaulted by the liberal or modernizing establishment, and their views and behaviour become more extreme as a result.
16. Karen Armstrong, *Islam: A Short History*, Modern Library, New York, 2002, pp. 5–6.
17. Smith, *Islam: A Concise Introduction*, pp. 28–9.
18. Philip Hitti, *History of the Arabs*, 1937, rev. edn, St. Martin's Press, New York, 1970, pp. 3–4. Quoted from Smith, *Islam: A Concise Introduction*, p. 3.
19. The international environment for Osama bin Laden's efforts was ideal. Saudi Arabia and the United States supplied billions of dollars worth of secret assistance to rebel groups in Afghanistan fighting the Soviet occupation. This assistance was funnelled through Pakistan. The Pakistani military intelligence service (Inter-Services Intelligence Directorate, or ISID), helped to train the rebels and distribute the arms. But Osama bin Laden and his comrades had their own sources of support and training, and they received practically no assistance from the United States.
20. Wahhabism (sometimes spelled Wahabbism or Wahabism) is a

movement of Islam named after Muhammad ibn Abd al Wahhab (1703–92). It is a fundamentalist Sunni form of Islam and has become an object of increased interest because it is the major sect of the government and society of oil-rich Saudi Arabia. See *http://en.wikipedia.org/wiki/wahhabi*.

21. Deoband is a small city located in Uttar Pradesh, at a distance of about 150 km from Delhi. Darul Uloom, one of the biggest and most important schools of Islamic Studies, is situated here.

22. *The 9/11 Commission Report: Final Report of the National Commission on Terrorist Attacks upon the United States*, W.W. Norton & Company, New York, 2004, p. 48.

23. The term 'state' is often used interchangeably with 'nation' and 'country'. They are related but distinct. A 'state' is a sovereign political entity with a set of governing institutions. A 'nation' is a group of people with a shared culture and history. A 'country' is the territorial component of the state.

24. Joseph T. Siegle, Michael M. Weinstein, and Morton H. Halperin, 'Why Democracies Excel', *Foreign Affairs*, vol. 83, no. 5, September/October 2004, pp. 57–71.

25. Edward D. Mansfield and Jack Snyder, 'Democratization and the Danger of War', *International Security*, Vol. 20, No. 1, Summer 1995, pp. 5–38.

26. Fareed Zakaria, *The Future of Freedom: Illiberal Democracy at Home and Abroad*, Viking, New Delhi, 2003, p. 256.

27. The ten richest people on earth have a combined net worth of US $255 billion—roughly 60 per cent of the total income of sub-Saharan Africa. (*http://www.forbes.com/billionaires/* as on February 2005).

28. Fukuyama, *State Building*, p. 37.

29. For an insightful exploration of the many-sided effects of globalization, see Thomas J. Friedman, *The Lexus and the Olive Branch: Understanding Globalization*, Farrar, Straus, Giroux, New York, 1999, pp. 434–75.

30. World exports as a percentage of world product increased from about seven per cent in 1950 to twenty-one per cent in 1995. World Bank, *World Development Report, 1998/1999*, Oxford University Press, Washington DC, 1999, p. 23.

31. Toynbee, *A Study of History: Illustrated*, the first abridged one-volume edition, Strand Book Stall, Bombay and Bangalore, 1995. This thought has been well articulated in author's foreword to this work, pp. 10–14.

32. Arthur M. Schlesinger, Jr., *War and the American Presidency*, W.W. Norton & Company, New York, 2004, p. 121.

33. The terms 'civilization' and 'culture' have been used in this book referring to the people's overall way of life. Civilization has been viewed as culture writ large. They both involve values, norms, institutions,

and modes of thinking to which successive generations of people have attached primary importance.

34. The full text (and its English version) reads as follows:

इंद्रं मित्रं वरुणमग्निमाहुरथौ दिव्य: स सुपर्णो गुरुत्मान् ।
एकं सद्विप्रा बहुधा वदंत्यग्नि यमं मातरिश्वानमाहु: ॥

They have styled him (the Sun), Indra, Mitra, Varuna, Agni, and he is the celestial, well-winged Garuimat, for learned priests call one by many names as they speak of Agni, Yama, Matarsvanmahu, the Sun— The Sun is Sayana's interpretation: Yāska says Agni: but they are the same, and are the same as all the other forms, according to the texts, Ekaivā va mahān ātmā devatā sūryah, the divine sun is the one great spirit; and Agni sarvā devatāh, Agni is all the divinities. See Vishva Bandhu (ed.), Vishveshvaranand Indological Series-20, Vishveshvaranand Vedic Research Institute, Hoshiarpur, 1963, p. 1072.

II
Manifestations of Bahudhā Approach in India

3
The Vedic World View

Vasudhaiva kutumbakam [1]
The world is one family

— Floating Verse (authorship not known)

The longing for conflict-free and harmonious living is both an ancient and a continuing human aspiration.

Multiplicity of tribes and beliefs has been a special feature of the Indian society since early times. The earliest known Indian civilization, the Indus Valley Civilization, was already quite advanced by about 2500 BC. It decayed in the middle of the second millennium BC, perhaps because of invasion by people who described themselves as *Arya* (Aryan). Several scholars, however, deny the theory of an invasion by the Aryans but accept that the earliest known population flow into India was of the Aryans, pastoral people who migrated from Iran through Afghanistan to north-west India, beginning around 1500 BC or even earlier.

INDUS VALLEY CIVILIZATION

The first archaeological report on a settlement of the Indus Civilization was written in 1875 by Alexander Cunningham, Director General of the Archaeological Survey of India. It was, however, only in 1931 that the full significance of the excavations at Mohenjodaro and Harappa came to light with the report by John Marshall, one of Cunningham's successors. He wrote:

Never for a moment was it imagined that five thousand years ago, before even the Aryans were heard of, the Punjab and Sind were enjoying an advanced and singularly uniform civilization of their own, closely akin but in some respects even superior to that of contemporary Mesopotamia and Egypt. Yet this is what the discoveries at Harappa and Mohenjodaro have now placed beyond question.[2]

It is fairly obvious that a civilization as advanced as the Indus Valley does not just come into being: it is preceded by many years, decades, and even centuries of development. For a long time, Mohenjodaro and Harappa were the only two large townships belonging to this civilization that were excavated. Then, in the 1960s, archaeologists unearthed the ruins of Kalibangan in Rajasthan. The fourth major Harappan site to be discovered and excavated is at Lothal in Gujarat. The discoveries at Dholavira are in that same chain and have conclusively proved that the geographical extent of this civilization stretched well beyond the Indus Valley.

The excavations at several Indus Valley sites have clearly established that the geographical spread of this civilization comprised present-day India, Pakistan, Bangladesh, Afghanistan, Sri Lanka, and Nepal. There is ample evidence of planned communal living in cities dating back to at least 2500 BC. The culture was largely urban as well-planned streets and an impressive system of drains marked the urban establishments. Apart from the well-laid-out towns and cities, the elaborate social structure and the standard of living of the people of this civilization indicate that the system must have been maintained by highly developed trade and agricultural productivity in different parts of the region.

Our knowledge of the religion and culture of the Indus Valley Civilization is still incomplete and is, in fact, severely limited, as the Indus script has not yet been deciphered. However, one of the important indications of the gradual unification of India is the way the Aryan and non-Aryan mythologies merge and a common mythology develops.[3] The Indus Valley people seem to have worshipped deities, both male and female, that had some connection with later Hindu mythology. Similarly, the principal Aryan deities Shiva and Vishnu subsequently became the basis of popular Hindu worship. Sanskrit, the language of the Aryans, became the language of the Indian subcontinent and the mother of the Indo-Aryan languages of northern India.

The intellectual development in India after the entry of the Aryans and the subsequent development of Vedic culture were not a complete break from the Harappan culture. Archaeologists are of the opinion that the Vedic and the Dravidian-speaking peoples were in a 'contact situation' for a long period, perhaps of centuries, before the compilation of the *Rig Veda*.[4] In fact, relics of the Indus Civilization show the merging of many cultures and concepts—including the ancient civilizations of Egypt, Mesopotamia, and China.

The Vedic period (1500 BC–AD 1000) also witnessed the inter-mingling of the Aryans with autochthons. This had a decisive influence not only on religion and spirituality but also on patterns of agriculture, industry, trade, and overall productivity. It was during this period that the core values of Indian civilization were strongly defined, including the approach which called for respect for another's point of view that is enjoined in the Bahudhā philosophy. The Vedas and the Upanishads and the great epics—the Ramayana and the Mahabharata (including the Bhagavad Gita)—guided and determined the way of living and thinking of the elite as well as of the common people. Besides, during this era, there were notable advances in music, medicine, mathematics, and astronomy.

VEDAS

The most ancient works of the Vedic period are the four Vedas— *Rig Veda*, *Sama Veda*, *Yajur Veda*, and *Atharva Veda*. Each Veda contains four sections consisting of (i) Samhita or collection of hymns, prayers, benedictions, sacrificial formulae and litanies; (ii) Brahmanas or prose treatises discussing the significance of sacrificial rites and ceremonies; (iii) *Aranyaka*s or forest texts, which are partly included in the Brahmanas and partly considered as independent; and (iv) Upanishads.

The Vedas comprise of a whole body of literature that arose in the course of centuries and was transmitted from generation to generation through oral communication.[5] The people who composed these evocative hymns to nature and celebrated life are exuberantly referred to as Aryas, usually anglicized as Aryan, meaning 'noble'. Talking about the origins of the Vedas, Sri Aurobindo convincingly observes:

Veda, then, is the creation of an age anterior to our intellectual philosophies. In that original epoch, thought proceeded by other methods than those of our logical reasoning and speech accepted modes of expression, which in our modern habits would be inadmissible. The wisest then depended on inner experience and the suggestions of the intuitive mind for all knowledge that ranged beyond mankind's ordinary perceptions and daily activities. Their aim was illumination, not logical conviction, their ideal the inspired seer, not the accurate reasoner. Indian tradition has faithfully preserved this account of the origin of the Vedas. The Rishi was not the individual composer of the hymn, but the seer (drasta) of an eternal truth and an impersonal knowledge. The language of Veda itself is Sruti, a rhythm not composed by the intellect but heard, a divine word that came vibrating out of the Infinite to the inner audience of the man who had previously made himself fit for the impersonal knowledge. The words themselves, drsti and sruti, sight and hearing, are Vedic expressions; these and cognate words signify, in the esoteric terminology of the hymns, revelatory knowledge and the contents of inspiration.[6]

One of the tenets of Vedic philosophy is that every person takes birth with three *rina*s (debts), and that it is his/her sacred duty to redeem these debts. These debts are to the (i) *deva*s (celestials); (ii) *pitarah* (parents); and (iii) *samaja* (society). The debt to celestials is repaid by performance of *yajna*s (fire sacrifices), which includes conservation of nature and peaceful conduct towards other living creatures. The debt to parents is redeemed by becoming a diligent student and raising a family. The debt to society is discharged by helping the poor, and by providing money to the underprivileged in society. It would, therefore, appear that Vedic literature deems family, society, and ecology as integral to human life and conduct. This has found further expression in the Upanishads, Puranas, and the great epics such as the Ramayana and the Mahabharata.

UPANISHADS

Composed in 800 BC, Upanishads,[7] are the most classic texts and form the inner core of the Vedic world view. There are a large number of Upanishads, and of these, 108 are in print. Ten of these Upanishads (*Isvsya, Kena, Katha, Prasna, Mundaka, Mandukya, Taittiriya, Aitareya, Chandogya*, and *Brhadaranyaka*) have specifically influenced the development of Indian philosophy. The Upanishads throw light on different aspects of knowledge and experience. One highly significant assertion of the Upanishads lies in its assertion that the Brahman and the *atman* are the same: The Supreme manifests Himself in every soul, and the student of religion is dramatically told 'Thou art That' (*Tat tvam asi*).[8] The Upanishads in their totality impart to us a spirited vision as well as philosophical argument.

PURANAS

The Puranas were written to popularize the teachings or precepts of the Vedas. They contain the essence of the Vedas. The aim of the Puranas is to impress on the minds of the masses the teachings of the Vedas and to generate in them devotion to God, through concrete examples, myths, stories, legends, lives of saints, kings and great men, allegories and chronicles of great historical events. Puranas were meant not for scholars, but for the ordinary people who could not understand complex philosophy and who could not study the Vedas.[9]

The Puranas form the smrti tradition, which constitute those that are remembered. The Puranas are a combination of mythology and history, freely intermixed. Almost all the Puranas are in the form of a dialogue between an exponent and enquiries from listeners. There are several Puranas, of which eighteen are the most prominent.[10]

The Puranas can be described as a popular encyclopaedia of Hinduism, religion, philosophy, history, politics, ethics, etc. The purpose of the Puranas was, probably, to regulate society in a harmonious way.

THE RAMAYANA AND THE MAHABHARATA

It is widely believed that the Ramayana and the Mahabharata were already part of the collective Indian consciousness before 800 BC. However, their actual composition took place subsequently, some time between 300 BC and 300 AD.

The Ramayana, first composed in Sanskrit by Valmiki some time during the second millennium BC, consists of 24,000 couplets and is divided into seven *kanda*s or books. It contains ethical and philosophical conclusions epitomized in the life and deeds of Lord Ram and his wife Sita. The Ramayana is called *Adi Kavya* (the first epic) and has been translated into various languages, and Tulsidas's *Ramcharitamanas* in Hindi and particularly Kamba's Ramayana in Tamil have guided generations of Indians in differentiating right from wrong, moulding the attitude of children towards their parents and siblings, defining the duties of kings, and explaining the role of religion in this life and thereafter. The Ramayana spread beyond the confines of South Asia, and is a living part of the human consciousness in South-East Asian countries, and among people of Indian origin in Africa and Europe.[11]

The Mahabharata[12] consists of over a hundred thousand verses and is divided into eighteen *parva*s (books). It is widely believed that it was composed by Vyasa.[13] Historians are of the view that the composition of the Mahabharata in poetic verse was spread over a period of 800 years, from 1000 BC–200 BC.

The story of the Mahabharata[14] centres on a heroic battle between two Bharata families, the Kauravas and the Pandavas, with the hero-god Krishna, King Dhritarashtra, and the two insuperable archers—Karna and Arjuna—playing leading roles. The Mahabharata contains the teachings and beliefs of various tribes and societies of that era and is a rare work of history and mythology, politics and law, as well as philosophy and theology. Many great works of enduring value in poetry, painting, sculpture, music, drama, history, philosophy, cinema, and jurisprudence have been inspired by it and are cast in its image.

A part of the Mahabharata—the Bhagavad Gita (the Lord's holy song), comprising eighteen chapters—elucidates the spiritual law of action beyond the rigid confines of a single religion. It was revealed by Krishna to Arjuna on the battlefield of Kurukshetra (in Haryana). The philosophical significance of these great epics is central to the Indian psyche. The epic makes it amply clear that spiritual man need not be a recluse and that union with divine life may be achieved and maintained in the midst of worldly affairs. The principal obstacles of the union lie within and not outside. Once we internalize the thought, that we have only the right to perform but none claim to the fruits of our actions, that are in the hands of God, one enters into a new state of consciousness. This is important for conflict resolution within one's own mind. As Vamadeo Shastri has observed, the Bhagavad Gita is

a poem that is still universally read, praised, and quoted in educated Hindu society, in the form of truisms. And I ask, where else in poetry, or in religious legend, will you find a divinity, on the eve of a desperate battle, persuading the hero that it is his duty to fight, not for the promise of victory or the justness of his cause, but by demonstrating that life and death, the slayer and the slain, are philosophically indistinguishable. That the incongruity of such a discourse, at a time when the two warring sides were poised for imminent collision, has not affected the great power of the poem shows, I would like to point out, what solace the Hindu mind has drawn, at all time and in all places, from the story.[15]

In popular imagination as well as discourse, both the Ramayana and the Mahabharata are viewed as classics where, in the conflict between good and evil forces, good triumphs. In the Ramayana, the evil forces led by Ravana are defeated at the hands of Ram representing the virtues of *dharma* and righteousness. Similarly, in the Mahabharata, the Pandavas who are on the side of righteous demands, manage to vanquish, in the battle of Kurukshetra, the Kauravas, their cousins, who represent the evil forces.

Several scholars and thinkers, however, have different interpretations to offer, particularly with respect to the Mahabharata. In their perception, and perhaps rightly so, the Ramayana stands on a different footing. In the Ramayana the war is between humans and demons, unlike the Mahabharata where the war is fought between cousins. In the Ramayana the incarnation of Vishnu, Lord Ram, vanquishes Ravana and destroys his entire clan except Vibhishan who had earlier defected and taken refuge with Ram. In the Mahabharata, the efforts of Lord Krishna—a subsequent incarnation of Vishnu— for reconciliation fail, leading to war at Kurukshetra.

The message of the Mahabharata has been interpreted in many ways. Rajmohan Gandhi, in his book *Revenge and Reconciliation*, argues that in the Mahabharata:

revenge is a fact, reconciliation a fancy; forgiveness is preached, vengeance practised; healing is conceived, injury executed.[16]

Some other scholars have seen the destruction and loss of human lives in the Mahabharata in terms of '*purusartha dharma*'. According to M.A. Mehendale:

To my mind even the nucleus of the Mahabharata, divested of its didactic and philosophical tracts, has a message for posterity. This message is related to the Purusartha dharma. The epic tells us what it considers to be the dharma, as well as the apadharma, of a Kshatriya.[17]

Many others have seen it on a metaphysical plane. The reputed scholar V.S. Sukthankar argues 'that the epic war is a projection of the conflict within man. The epic war was fought on the Kurukshetra and the word used for the human body in the Bhagavad Gita is *kshetra* which is the place of the conflict'.[18] In other words, a battle goes on within man in his own lower nature, and it must be won.

The failure of god to resolve conflict in a peaceful manner is significant in the Mahabharata. It may be recalled that before the war, the Pandavas made a final attempt to peacefully settle the issue between them and the Kauravas. Krishna was sent as their spokesman to persuade Duryodhana to part with at least five villages, if not their entire share of the ancestral kingdom, and avert war. Krishna did not succeed in his mission.

The Mahabharata itself raises questions about Lord Krishna's sincerity. Gandhari, Duryodhana's mother, holds Krishna responsible for not preventing the war and curses him. She puts it across powerfully:

The Pandavas and Kauravas are all dead
Why did you allow this?
O Krishna, you could have stopped the war.
You had the tongue, you had the power.[19]

The creator of the Mahabharata has other characters to support this point of view. For example, Utanga, an old friend of Krishna, his eyes red with indignation at the destruction of life, argues:

Vasudeva (Krishna), were you there standing by and did you let all this happen? You have indeed failed in your duty.[20]

In many ways, the message of the First and Second World Wars is similar—that all wars are futile. Mahatma Gandhi and the famous translator of the Ramayana and the Mahabharata, C. Rajagopalachari, have something similar to say about the futility of war. To Mahatma Gandhi the message of the epic is the folly of war. As resentments in the Mahabharata war finally destroyed almost everybody, including Krishna and his clansmen, and left the world a virtual void, Gandhi draws from the Mahabharata the lesson that violence and revenge lead inexorably to a desert—a moral, emotional, and physical desert. The victors of war shed tears of sorrow and repentance and are left with nothing but a legacy of misery.[21] In the Preface C. Rajagopalachari writes:

The Mahabharata drives home—as nothing else does—the vanity of ambition and the evil and futility of ambition and hatred.[22]

It is inconceivable to have a society without conflicts. Conflicts have often been concerned with social issues or economic denials, and have several dimensions. Conflicts which were limited in the Rigvedic period or earlier to fights among tribes or with some outsiders have now progressed in scale, varying from a family tiff to a world war. The intensity of conflict is another important area. In the predominantly tribal and pastoral society of the Rigvedic era, conflicts among tribes involving agriculture or animal hunting were common. In the *Dharmashastras*, war was recognized as one of the legitimate modes of livelihood and went on to provide a rationale for the warrior class of Kshatriyas.[23]

The periods of the flourishing of the Indus Valley Civilization and its subsequent decay, the entry of the Aryans, and composition of the Vedas also experienced violence and conflicts. Ways and means were devised to resolve conflicts and to establish harmony. The plurality of approach adopted then contributed to the enrichment of India and her culture. This approach has also ensured an Indian continuum as a major living civilization in the world. Another notable feature of India's civilizational experience has been its capacity to learn and

absorb. The famous historian R.C. Majumdar captures this phenomenon admirably when he writes:

The icons discovered at Mohenjo-daro are those of gods and goddesses
who are still worshipped in India, and Hindus from the Himalaya to Cape
Comorin repeat even today the Vedic hymns which were uttered on the
banks of the Indus nearly four thousands years ago. This continuity in
language and literature, and in religious and social usages, is more prominent
in India than even in Greece and Italy, where we can trace the same
continuity in history. The social and religious ideas of ancient Greece and
Rome and their philosophy and outlook on life, in short, some of the most
essential factors which give individuality to a nation and preserve its
continuity, arc almost foreign to the peoples now inhabiting those lands.
An artificial continuity is no doubt maintained in those two countries, and
the link with the past is not altogether snapped, as in the cases of Egypt and
Mesopotamia. Nevertheless, the difference can only be regarded as one of
degree and not of kind; and neither Greece nor Italy offers a parallel to
India, in respect of either antiquity or continuity of civilization.[24]

Love, hatred, and conflict are intrinsic to the existence of human
beings. The vision of creating or grooming a society, well ordered
and peaceful in all respects, is Utopian. What is needed is a conflict
management or conflict resolution mechanism. The people of the
Vedic civilization had always tried to devise a series of mechanisms
to resolve conflicts and, as a result, could manage to create harmony
in several periods of Indian history. The Vedic sages strived to organize
the social structure and to provide a moral code that could ensure
social harmony.

There is enough evidence to show that conscious efforts were
made by the Aryans to build cordial relations with the Dravidians
and others. Towards this end, the gods and rituals of Dravidians and
other tribals were incorporated in the Aryan pantheon.

ORIGINS OF THE BAHUDHĀ APPROACH

The Bahudhā approach originated during the Vedic period as a public
policy of harmony in the midst of conflicts among tribes (in a society
devoid of state authority) and found lofty expression in several
Rigvedic hymns. Later the Puranas and the epics—the Ramayana and
the Mahabharata—carried this message forward. Folklore and tales,
forms of worship and rituals, works of art and architecture, edicts
and inscriptions emphasized the importance of dialogue among

people and respect for different faiths. Here we are not talking of an ideal society, but one with shortcomings where several social institutions, created for solving conflicts and for ensuring orderly progress, led to injustices and inequities, negating the Bahudhā approach. But several of them tried to focus on ways of harmonious living and a life of austerity and high thinking unparalleled in human history. At no stage did they abandon the pluralist approach which meant tolerance for other faiths and beliefs, and respect for the diversity of spiritual experiences. All these could be viewed in a fivefold perspective: (i) the vision of cosmic order; (ii) the idealism of harmony and peace; (iii) the institution of moral order; (iv) the social architecture; and (v) the political system.

COSMIC ORDER

A new vision of cosmic order was developed in the Vedas as a result of a series of encounters in the social, political, economic, and religious domains. This was *rta*—harmony. The famous philosopher R. Panikkar calls it order. He writes

It is order, in a way similar to the order of the Christian scholastics which combines the Greek taxis and the intelligent, creative, and provident power of the patristic-medieval God. . . . It is sovereignly free. It is not constricted by any law.[25]

The Rigvedic vision of rta is of a cosmic order in which all parts throb with dynamic life and play an effective role subservient to the whole. In a pioneering work on the subject, Jeanine Miller reflects:

Vedic man conceived life as a web of divine forces, each object focusing, in varying degrees, the same divine force as he himself, all governed by the law of equilibrium; hence, that every deed of his had repercussions extending far beyond his present awareness. At the cosmic level rta is the law of harmony; at the human level, the law of truth, righteousness, justice; at the personal level, integrity, the manifestation of the human conscience, the silent voice that guides conduct and points to the right.[26]

IDEALISM OF HARMONY AND PEACE

The inspiring ideals of peace and harmony were sought to be made integral to the individual way of life as well as to social and political organizations. It was repeatedly emphasized that these ideals could be best attained by concord, not only with one's own people but also with strangers. To achieve this, objectives that were common to all human beings were formulated and dialogue processes devised, to enable people of different sections of society to participate, in order that they could work and live together. Since early society was pastoral and agricultural in nature, earth, ecology, and cattle were of primary importance and dominated public concerns.

The following prayers/hymns would give us a broad conception of the ideals of peace and harmony that dominated the thought processes of the Brahmins in the Vedic period. These ideals became the kernel of social and political order, as well as prayers of the elite of those times.

Peace be the earth, peaceful the ether, peaceful heaven, peaceful the waters, peaceful the herbs, peaceful the trees. May all Gods bring me peace. May there be peace through these invocations of peace. With these invocations of peace, which appease everything, I render peaceful whatever here is terrible, whatever here is cruel, whatever here is sinful. Let it become auspicious, let everything be beneficial to us.[27]

Let us have concord with our own people, and concord with people who are strangers to us; Asvins, create between us and strangers a unity of hearts. May we unite in our midst, unite in our purposes, and not fight against the divine spirit within us. Let not the battle-cry rise amidst many slain, nor the arrows of the War-God fall with the break of day.[28]

What, O earth I dig out of thee,
quickly Shall grow again.
May I not, O pure one,
Pierce thy vital Spot (and) not thy heart![29]

Enjoy things of this world with the spirit of renunciation in you. Don't be avaricious. Whose wealth is all this? It is all God's. We take nothing with us. Regard yourselves only as trustees and not owners of the wealth.[30]

Do not injure the beings living on the earth, in the air and in the water.[31]

The Prithvi Sukta in the *Atharva Veda* contains highly powerful ecological invocations in literature. In it the Vedic seers solemnly declare the enduring filial allegiance of humankind by proclaiming, 'Earth is my mother, I am her son'.[32] The Vedic seers regarded the Earth as 'sacred space' for the consecrated endeavours and aspirations of humankind and for the practice of restraint and responsibility. On it rests the Vedic vision of a world filled with the purity of the spiritual environment and the sanctity of environmental spirituality and morality. Such a world can only be sustained by the exacting discipline of truth, harmony, and rectitude, based on a conception of cosmic and comprehensive peace. This is well conceived in the famous Vedic hymn of peace:

We invoke and imbibe Om, the primordial sound of cosmic harmony and pray for Peace and Harmony in Heaven; Peace and Harmony in the Sky and on the Earth; Peace and Harmony in the Waters; Peace and Harmony in the Herbs, the Vegetation and the Forests; Peace and Harmony among the Peoples and the Rulers of the World; Peace and Harmony in Spiritual Quest and Realisation; Peace and Harmony for one and all; Peace and Harmony Everywhere and in Every Thing; Peace, True and Real Peace, Let that Peace repose in my inner space, Peace of Peace, Everlasting Peace, We pray for Peace.[33]

The vision of rta, or of cosmic wholeness, was linked to doctrines of dharma and *karma*, of the law of cycles, and of the essential oneness of all creatures with the ultimate source. In the doctrine of karma, we clearly see the interconnectedness of all actions and their counter-balancing of one another—as you have sown so are you reaping, as you are sowing so will you reap. Dharma prescribes one's duty–vocation function stand in life, the regulations of conduct, codes of ethics, each appropriate to, or in strict accordance with, one's inherent truth, the innermost law of one's being, *svadharma*. This was further amplified in the theory of the *varna*s and *ashram*s. Rta in its cosmic sense becomes specialized as dharma in a social or human sense, but a dharma which is not imposed by anyone from outside, but seen as the inner law which governs all, and which, if followed by man in his life, results in harmony, in establishing on earth the divine harmony.[34]

MORAL ORDER

OBJECTIVES OF LIFE

The Vedic view of the individual and his relation to society is determined by four objectives of life: (a) *dharma* (ethical living); (b) *artha* (economic pursuits); (c) *kama* (desire and enjoyment); and (d) *moksha* (spiritual freedom).

These four objectives of life relate to different aspects of human nature and aspirations. Through millennia the core of human nature has remained the same. Its aspirations continue to be in the realm of emotions, intellect, material gains, and spiritual progress and thus are well covered under the four objects of life as broadly comprehended by Indian savants.

Dharma

Etymologically speaking, dharma formed from the root *dhr* (to hold), means that which holds a thing and maintains it in being. Dharma or virtue is conformity with the truth of things; *adharma* or vice is opposition to it. Dharma is not a religious creed or cult. Each man and group, each activity of the soul and body has its dharma. While man is justified in satisfying his desire, which is essential for the expression of life, at the same time to conform to the dictates of his desires is not the law of his being. He will not get the best out of them if he does not conform to the dharma or the rule of right practice.

Dharma is the foundation for the edifice of society. It is the code of conduct that sustains society and secures the welfare and happiness of all individuals. This can be possible when all members of society are imbued with the spirit to strive for the welfare of all. There can be none superior or inferior. 'All the brothers have gathered together to increase the well-being of all'. In order to work harmoniously to attain this common goal of human welfare, the method of allotting work to individuals on the basis of one's aptitude and capacity was devised, and this is popularly referred to as *Varnashramadharma*.

Artha

Artha relates to wealth and material well-being. Though economic pursuits are not an end in themselves, they help to sustain and enrich life. Economic insecurity and individual freedom do not go together.

Artha is the source of human livelihood. Artha excludes wealth or property acquired illegally through theft, cheating, or through foul or unfair means such as tax evasion or exploitation. This is so, because *artha* through exploitation is contrary to dharma.

Kama

Kama refers to the emotional being of man, his feelings and desires. If man is denied his emotional life, he becomes a prey to repressive introspection and lives under the continual strain of moral torture. When the reaction sets in, he will succumb to a wildness of ecstasy which is ruinous to his sanity and health. Similarly, Kama grows by indulgence: the more one indulges in desires and sensual enjoyment, the more it whets the appetite of the senses. It is, therefore, absolutely essential that kama is regulated by dharma.

Moksha

Moksha is the principal objective of man. The Upanishads tell us that there is nothing higher than the person. The physical body is not his whole or real being. It is only an instrument for the use of the spirit which is the truth of his being. To find the real self, to exceed his apparent, outward self, is the greatness of which man alone of all beings is capable.[35] Krishna's advice was not to give up actions, but to rid oneself of one's desires for the fruits of any actions (*niskamakarma*). Detachment and moksha do not mean indifference. Niskamakarma does not mean cessation of activity: it means karma without selfish or personal interest.

VARNASHRAMADHARMA, FOUR STAGES OF LIFE AND KARMA

The Vedic teachers further prescribed the attainment of these eternal pursuits through the categorization of: (i) individuals into four varnas known as varnashramadharma, namely, Brahmin (the learned class), Kshatriya (the warrior class), Vaishya (the economic class), and Shudra (the service class); (ii) the four stages of life, that is *brahmachari* (the student), *grihastha* (the householder), *vanaprastha* (the recluse), and *sannyasin* (the free man); and (iii) the law of *karma*.

VARNA SYSTEM

The Brahmins, Kshatriyas, Vaishyas, and Shudras had different occupations. Brahmins were responsible for providing vision, wisdom, and faith in society as teachers, priests, and guides. The works of a Kshatriya included courage in battle, generosity, and noble leadership. Trade, agriculture, and the rearing of cattle were the occupations of a Vaishya. The work of a Shudra was to provide service to all the other three varnas.

The first three varnas were called the twice-born. Being twice-born meant that one came of age in a religious sense, allowing him to follow the Vedic religion, be eligible to learn Sanskrit, study the Vedas, and perform Vedic rituals. According to the *Laws of Manu*,[36] boys were 'born again' when a sacred thread was bestowed around the waist at specific ages: eight years for Brahmins, eleven years for Kshatriyas, and twelve years for Vaishyas. The numerals to be written in words equivalent of coming of age for girls was marriage. The Shudras were denied the 'sacred thread' and hence were outside the pale of the 'twice-born'.

The Vedas mention the change of varna in rare circumstances when an individual acquired higher knowledge. Maharsi Vyasa—the writer of the Mahabharata—was born to a fisherwoman and a Brahmin man without any recognized marriage. The famous wise man of the Mahabharata, Vidura, was the son of a Shudra woman. That same Vidura is described as the very incarnation of Dharma.[37] In fact, when King Dhritarashtra wanted religious instruction, he approached Vidura for it.[38] Other instances of men who became Brahmins by virtue of their higher knowledge were Vishwamitra,[39] Parasara,[40] Kvaish Aylush,[41] and Satyakam Jabala.[42]

According to *Manusmriti,* when the 'twice-born' came of age, they entered into the four ashrams or stages of life.

(i) The first was the brahmacharya, or the stage of the student (brahmacharin). The student was supposed to go and live with a teacher (*guru*), who was a Brahmin, to learn Sanskrit, science, mathematics, philosophy, and rituals. The dharma of a student included being obedient, respectful, celibate, and nonviolent.

(ii) The second stage was that of the grihastha, or the stage of the householder. This was a crucial stage for raising a family and also pursuing economic, social, and religious pursuits. The role to be played by a priest as a grihastha would certainly differ from that of a warrior or from a farmer. It is during this stage that a girl became a wife and mother.

(iii) The third stage was vanaprastha, or the stage of the forest dweller. This was to be entered into optionally if (ideally) one's hair became grey and one's skin wrinkled. The children and grandchildren were then meant to perpetuate the family. Husbands and wives could leave their affairs and possessions with their children and retire together to the forest as hermits.[43]

(iv) The fourth stage was the sannyasa, or the stage of the wandering ascetic (sannyasin or *sadhu*). If a man desired, he could continue on to this stage, but his wife would have to return home; traditionally she was not to stay alone as a forest dweller or as a wanderer on the highways.

An orderly workplace at home or outside is fully articulated in the theory of varnashramadharma, where the definition of one's duty has reference not only to one's caste, but also to the particular stage in one's life. A productive working environment was dependent on the fact that every individual must understand and recognize the duties he was expected to perform and act accordingly.[44]

The division of responsibility was essential because it promoted individual security and happiness as well as the stability of the social order. Each man's dharma had its own role in the larger and more complex network of the social structure. Therefore, by observing the rule of his own dharma, a man showed an awareness of others in society as well. If anybody acted against his dharma, he not only caused disturbance in society but also impaired social harmony and upset the equilibrium.

The fear of anarchy led to the elevation of dharma to a divine status, and this in turn gave it an even higher status than the king and the government.[45] To further safeguard the position of dharma, another concept was introduced—that dharma is protected by *danda* (literally a rod or staff, signifying punishment).[46] The concept of dharma rooted in varna was extended to every aspect of human activity.

OVERVIEW

The *varnadharma* was an attempt to establish a social law or a systematic functioning of society that would ensure its well-being. It was stated that society was made up of four orders. A fifth order added later was identified with the untouchables.

On the basis of varna the elite became a closed group with minimal or no upward mobility. Recruitment to each group was strictly through birth. The elite were drawn from the first three orders—Brahmin, Kshatriya, and Vaishya.

Some historians maintained that the Aryans had inherited, perhaps from the Indo-European times, the system of varna, and applied the same to the Indian socio-economic context.

This grouping on the basis of division of labour gradually gave a new identity to the people belonging to different tribes. Since the functions, rights, and duties of every varna were well defined, clashes were unlikely. Priests and intellectuals were placed at the top but were not given any political power or power to rule. They were simply the guides and mentors of the royal power. The Kshatriyas were satisfied with their lot at the second place because they virtually wielded power. Most of the people lived as farmers cultivating the land and paying taxes and revenue to the kings.

Down the ages all the *jatis* or professional groups of the artisans, in addition to the traders and cowherds got a new affiliation, a new sense of belonging to a particular class or varna besides remaining in their own jatis. The varna system did not disturb the identity of the jatis. Instead, it gave them a new overarching, overriding, wider group-identity with a feeling of belonging and brotherhood, especially in relation to people who were not members of their own tribes.

With the system assuming a classical form and a pan-Indian dimension, a number of ethnic groups attempted to become part of it. This was usually achieved through the process of first inviting Brahmins from the Madhyadesa and getting genealogies composed in Sanskrit. The ruling elite belonging to a particular tribe from one region were connected with the earlier tribes of India. In the next stage, the whole tribe was assimilated into the system as either Kshatriyas or a part of it as Kshatriyas and a part as Vaishyas, whereas their priests automatically received the status of Brahmins.

A number of gods and goddesses worshipped today do not find any mention in ancient texts. On the other hand, mighty Aryan gods such as Indra and Varuna have faded into oblivion. The mother goddess is worshipped all over India in many forms with separate names and even with iconic representations. Most of them now have non-Brahmin priests in their temples and even have their own exclusive rituals of worship.

The resilience of the Indian ethos to absorb new groups of people and institutions and fit them into various categories of dharmas is evident in Vedic literature. It is the rta aspect that lent dharma its mystical quality, and it stood for the ideal in the conduct of man. As society grew and expanded, dharma also had to accommodate itself to the changes in society.

It is generally said that, if there had been only the various classes and castes without the overriding concept of dharma, ancient Indian civilization would also have met the same fate as other ancient civilizations such as the Sumerian and Egyptian. Assimilating and re-identifying, not discarding or destroying, has been the basic *mantra* of Indian heritage. Multiculturalism and the coexistence of many races, languages, religious beliefs has been the strength of Indian society.

SOCIAL ORDER

Family, Village, and Caste

The social order during the Vedic period revolved round the institutions of joint family, village, and caste. In fact, these three social institutions grew during the Vedic period and have survived since then. Of the three, it is the family which has been viewed most positively over the centuries, in both public and academic discourse. Attitudes to the caste system have been critical and at times, even hostile. The village stands in between both as an object of admiration and criticism, the latter due to exploitation of the lower castes by the higher castes in the village.

In the Vedic period and even earlier, the family grew as a site of biological reproduction. This has continued to be the principal *raison d'etre* of the family. This institution not only expresses and represents the character of the members of the family but in the totality of its achievements has conserved the valued aspects of Indian culture and tradition.

The Indian family system, however, has varied from region to region. Even during the Vedic period it was possible to identify four main types of family or kinship organizations in India: (i) the Dravidian type in the south; (ii) the Indo-European or Sanskritic type in the north; (iii) a mixed central zone between the two; and (iv) a tribal type on the periphery of the Indian subcontinent.

Except in some tribal societies, the family has been patriarchal in nature. This may be attributed to the fact that it was initially constituted by a group of people related in the main line, and subject to the absolute power of the senior-most male member. A major function of the family is that of care and nurturance—of the young, the handicapped, the sick, the unemployed, and the aged.

FAMILY AND THE STATUS OF WOMEN

The Vedic family was patriarchal. The father was the head of the family and controlled the activities of his children, including their marriages. Attempts were, however, made to maintain harmony between males and females, and the idea of equality was categorically expressed in the *Rig Veda*.[47]

The Upanishads refer to several women philosophers, who entered into dialectics (*shasthrartha*) with their male colleagues. The dialogue between Vachaknavi,[48] who challenged Yajnavalkya,[49] is well documented. Gargi[50] and Maitreyi[51] were also reputed scholars of Vedic lore.

Seclusion of women was unknown in the Vedic times. Young girls mixed with young boys and had a decisive voice in the selection of their husbands.

INSTITUTION OF MARRIAGE

The Vedic pathfinders enunciated highly ethical principles regarding the institution of marriage. Most of the ancient scriptures prescribe various forms of marriages. Some of these forms are Brahma Vivah,[52] Prajapatya,[53] Arsa,[54] Daiva,[55] which do not require self effort and are mostly arranged by parents. In fact, marriages arranged by parents were contemplated and emphasized, such as, for example, in the institution of *svayamvara* where the bridegroom was required to fulfil certain conditions of expertise, strength, power, and knowledge as prescribed by the bride's parents. Parents encouraged young men and women who loved each other to enter wedlock. Emphasis was laid on the bride and groom being compatible and having a similar level of intelligence, ability, and proficiency. The dowry system was not mentioned anywhere. However, there is a reference to voluntary gifts given to the daughters by their parents in the *Rig Veda*.[56]

After the girl's marriage, the parents were not expected to interfere in the family affairs of their daughters in the interests of peace and harmony of the patriarchal family of their sons-in-law. Children were to be known after their father, and the girl was to live after marriage only with her husband in the joint family, which included his parents, grandparents, brothers, and sisters. As has been mentioned in the floating verses, the 'wife is verily a home'.[57]

The economic and political role of the household as an intermediate unit between the individual and the state is prominently acknowledged in public policy and administration, with public goods and services being routinely allocated to the household as if it were a single unit of consumption.

Sociologists maintain that the undivided family might have expanded over several generations to become a self-organized 'brotherhood of relatives' and thus the village community.

VILLAGE

The number of villages increased over time and dotted the landscape. The village provided a community life beyond the family for those of diverse age groups and professions. As a physical entity, the village represented a conglomeration of houses huddled together and surrounded by fields. The villagers knew each other and were bound together over generations through times of festivals as well as disasters. The nuclear village settlements varied in size, with populations ranging from 1000 to even 50,000.

The birth of an individual in a family simultaneously conferred on him or her not only membership of the family but also of the caste and sub-caste in his village. Some of these relationships were built by an individual and some were obtained through inheritance. The primary economic activity in the village being agriculture and handicrafts, these relations were primarily organized around agriculture where caste became the main social institution for mediating relations with other villagers. The village and caste, therefore, together provided an elaborate scheme for the social organization of life. The broad basis of the mode of production was thus formed by the unity of small-scale agriculture and the handicraft industry.

Even to this day, an important aspect of Indian village society is the strong interpersonal bond between any two persons based on the pattern of 'family relationship', which transcends varna (social group) and jati (caste) structure. Here the people who belong to different castes and different social groups are 'brothers', 'sisters', 'uncles', 'aunts', 'nephews', and 'nieces' to each other and not only address each other by these terms but also behave towards each other in a manner appropriate to these relationships.[58]

The village as a moral entity expresses itself internally as a coordinating unit along multiple dimensions of social life, and externally through an assertion of its collective identity, prestige, and claims in the competitive sphere of polity and development. A village is communitarian in the sense that numerous interactions occur among the same set of people beyond the interest group formations, which bind the villagers together in reciprocal ties repeated over generations. However, wider ties of kinship, neighbourhood, and ritual intersecting economic and political ties often represent the prestige of the village in a region. The life cycle rituals especially those relating to marriage and death, not only led to the generation of collective sentiments among villagers but also bound them closely.

Members of village communities made public use of common facilities, including common property resources, as a part of their collective life. Encroachment over common resources by locally powerful people often created fissures in the communitarian character of the village.

During the Vedic period, the exchange of goods was conducted mainly in villages. The village as a 'little republic' has been the focus of attention of various sages and seers even in the Vedic period and subsequently thereafter. Different units within the structure of the village community are activated when a common calamity such as drought or flooding occurs. Kinship, neighbourhood, and caste also provide the ready-made primordial ties to cope with displacements occurring in the wake of floods, famines, and other calamities.

THE CASTE SYSTEM

It is widely believed that the caste system is a degeneration of the varna system. On the other hand, there is enough evidence to suggest that there were different castes and communities even during the Rigvedic period.

In the vast corpus of Hindu religio-legal texts known as the Dharmashastra,[59] the unequal rights and duties of the four varnas are set out in detail. So too are those of the untouchable Chandalas, who are outside the four-class system and are the object of extreme stigmatization. From the famous *Manusmriti*, which attained its final form about 2000 years ago, it is reasonable to infer that in India two millennia ago there existed a large number of distinct castes, which the Brahmin lawgivers wished to fit into the varna scheme.[60]

The hierarchical caste system is one of the most distinctive institutions of Indian society. In this system, every individual is born into one and only one caste, of which he or she remains a member until death. In other words, castes are ascriptive status groups with no individual social mobility between them. Castes are normally endogamous, so that husband and wife belong to the same caste, which is also their children's caste. If marriage does take place across caste boundaries, then it is usually but not invariably hypergamous.

In theory, the caste system defines a division of labour, but in practice many occupations are caste-specific, especially in the services and artisan sectors. For example, throughout India there are castes of washermen and carpenters who have a virtual monopoly in their work, so that almost all laundry is done by persons belonging to the *dhobi* caste, and similarly carpentry is done by members of the *barhai* caste. It is fairly rare for members of one caste to take up the traditional occupation of another, but it has always been common for people of every caste not to pursue their own caste occupation. In particular, employment in the vast agricultural sector is not specifically assigned to particular castes, even though many landlords and peasant farmers belong to the traditional landholding castes, and many agricultural labourers belong to the lowest castes. Almost all occupations in the modern sectors of the economy are also caste-free in the sense that members of any caste can take them up, although recruitment is often done disproportionately from particular castes. Nevertheless, the extent to which castes actually are closed occupational groups, in the past or present, should not be exaggerated: the division of labour has never been fully determined by caste.

CIVIL SOCIETY

Civil society institutions were envisaged to facilitate dialogue among people. Two important social institutions were *sabha* and *vidatha*. These institutions have played major roles in addressing social issues and in the resolution of conflicts.

The sabha was a political and social assembly, which provided a forum where all citizens irrespective of caste, creed, sex, religion, and varnas could attend and deliberate on social and political problems. After deliberations, the conclusions arrived at in the sabha were conveyed to the ruler. It was within the jurisdiction of the sabha to advise the ruler to punish smugglers, bribe-takers, adulterators, rapists, and those who cornered food for material gain.[61] The *Yajur Veda* provided a social prayer in this behalf which reads:

May we acquire mundane and celestial joy and felicity, it should help in performing our noble deeds and duties, creating concord and peace everywhere.[62]

The vidatha was a religious institution. It was a place where issues concerning divinity, goodness, soul, spirit, nature, and other spiritual matters were deliberated.

OVERVIEW

The Vedic social order is predicated on social inequality. At the top are the Brahmins and at the bottom are the various Untouchable castes, now known as Harijans, Dalits, or Scheduled Castes (their official designation). Between the Brahmins and Dalits is a wide range of other castes. All these generalizations are subject to numerous qualifications because there is a great deal of regional and local variation in the structure of the caste system and its relationship with other social institutions.[63]

Two features of the Vedic social order, which have harmed Indian society and polity immensely over the centuries, are the creation of a class of 'untouchables' outside the varna system and the denial of education to various segments of society including women.

Declaring or describing someone as an untouchable has racial connotations and is a highly derogatory form of conflict resolution mechanism. It negates the concept of equality and also makes a direct attack on human rights. It has a degrading impact all round, including on the society itself which upholds this system.[64]

The denial of education to large various social groups, including women, in the name of the varna system has led to the spread of ignorance and illiteracy among the people. This has contributed in large measure to India's extreme backwardness and poverty. The lack of education and access to scriptures and books has adversely affected the untouchables, the Dalits, the backwards, and the women and also generated a tremendous sense of insecurity among them, and especially women.

All this is contrary to the lofty ideals of peace and brotherhood that characterize the hymns of the *Rig Veda*. Lack of effective condemnation of these extremely discriminatory practices could again be attributed to major activities in society being controlled by the hegemonic hierarchy of the upper castes and the lack of education among the masses.

All these features of the conflict resolution mechanism in Vedic society are against the concept of the Bahudhā philosophy, which pre-supposes an environment conducive to dialogue and discussion whereas untouchability and the denial of education are totally at variance with this approach.

POLITICAL SYSTEM

STATE

The origins of the state as the final authority in India as in other civilizations are shrouded in mystery. Early Hindu theories explain the origin of kingship as being essentially the need for a leader, particularly in a conflict or in a war-like situation. The contract theory of the origin of the state is also mentioned in the early Brahmanical literature. However, the first clear and developed exposition of this theory is found in the Buddhist canonical text *Digha Nikaya*.[65] It envisages a situation where people gradually entered into a series of agreements among themselves and set up the institutions of family and property. But this gave rise to a new set of problems, as theft and other forms of undesirable conduct appeared. Therefore, people assembled and agreed to choose as chief a person who was the best favoured, the most attractive and the most capable. On their request, that person consented to be indignant where one should be rightly indignant, to censure that which should be rightly censured, to banish him who deserves to be banished.

Considerations of preserving family, property, and the varna system played the most vital part in the origin of the state. The traditional account of the state of nature and the circumstances leading to the rise of coercive authority, the conditions obtaining in a kingless society, the concept of the main duties of the monarch all point to the same conclusion. As the author of the *Leviathan* aptly put it:

Before the names of just and unjust can have place, there must be some coercive power.[66]

The Vedic period, especially in its early years, was essentially an age of primordial collectivities that cannot be considered political in the modern sense. Institutions such as the *gana*, the vidatha, the sabha, the *samiti*, and the *parishad* were mainly tribal in character. Of these, the vidatha seems to have been of the greatest antiquity among the Indo-Aryans and contains memories of even pre-Rigvedic times. The presence of women on the parisad may have been a pre-Aryan trait.

In post-Vedic times, from *c.* 600 BC onwards, varna, or social class, superseded tribal elements and emerged as an important factor in law and politics. The origin and growth of the Dharmashastra law were conditioned by the varna system, and accordingly civil and criminal laws discriminated between one varna and another. The need for combination and cooperation between the Brahmins and the Kshatriyas was repeatedly emphasized, although in actual politics sometimes the Kshatriyas and, at other times, the Brahmins enjoyed the upper hand. The Vaishyas or the Shudras, however, never acquired any dominant role in politics.

Two sets of political order clearly emerged during the Vedic period. First, the republican form of governance grew up among the Licchavis of Vaishali area. The other was of a large state-system headed by a monarch, epitomized by the Magadha empire.

That a clan-based society should opt for a system that was more egalitarian and less autocratic than a large state-system headed by a king was a natural option. Several small republics, mostly in Bihar and Uttar Pradesh, such as those of the Licchavis, Sakyas, Koliyas, and Videhas, flourished. There were open samitis in which both males and females participated. There were also special sabhas and parisads where entry was more restricted. Buddha spoke very highly of the republic of the Licchavis and revealed an important feature, on which depended its strength and security in the following dialogue:

And the Blessed One said to him: 'Have you heard, Anand, that the Vajjians (Confederacy of Republics at Vaishali) hold full and frequent Public assemblies?' 'Lord, so I have heard', replied he.

So long Ananda, rejoined the Blessed One, 'as the Vajjians held these full and frequent public assemblies, so long may they be expected not to decline, but to prosper'.[67]

The ideological basis for kingship, however, was emphasized from two separate elements. The element of contract leading to the installation of a chief or king was a vital element in Buddhist sources and in the laws of Manu. Brahmanic sources, however, have focused on the element of divine sanction. In Brahmanic tradition, kingship was pioneered by the gods. A *raja*, was to be chosen by his peers, his role was principally a military one, but his authority had divine sanction. In north India, in the mid-first millennium BC, both republics and other small kingdoms functioned and monarchy was not essential to state formation. However, Brahmanical support to the monarchy ultimately led to its supremacy.

In the Ramayana, Lord Ram returned to Ayodhya after fourteen years and ushered in a resplendent system of order, justice, and prosperity under his rule. The resultant *Ramrajya* quickly became and is still the Indian political ideal invoked by countless politicians and thinkers.

Dharma plays a major role in Ramrajya. It prescribes for individual conduct in its relations with members of the family such as parents, brothers, and other relatives. It guides the relations of the individual with his neighbours, his village, and his entire community. There is a feeling of belongingness not only with the state administrative set-up that administers justice and supervises general duties, but with society and the king.[68]

The Ramayana greatly contributed to legitimization of monarchical rule in India as well as in South-East Asia. Ayodhya became the model of a royal capital and this concept also travelled to other countries. For example, Thailand's ancient capital was known as Ayuthia and adopted many other features of this Indian kingdom.

The rule of dharma is central to the Mahabharata as in the Ramayana.

The king and his dharma (rajadharma) have a sacred character in the Mahabharata. The Mahabharata has expressed the ideal with great clarity and precision. Shanti Parva says:

The proper function of the king is to rule according to Dharma (the law) and not to enjoy the luxuries of life.[69]

Bhishma says that the king is appointed by Vishnu himself, and he partakes of his divinity and is, therefore, to be obeyed.[70] Manu mentions that, in the absence of a king, stronger people consume weaker ones like the bigger fish devouring the smaller ones.[71] The king is even considered to be the maker of heaven on earth.[72] Thus, prosperity in the land and of his subjects depend on him.[73]

Vidura—the wise counselor—in his several interventions in the Mahabharata enunciates the duties of the king and the principles of statecraft. To him:

A wise king should be able to discriminate between right and wrong with the help of his intelligence. He should keep control over friend, stranger and enemy by gift, conciliation, disunion and punishment.[74]

The main stages in the history of ancient Indian polity can be identified. The earliest stage was that of the tribal system in which tribal assemblies, which had some place for women, dominated the social and political scene. The age of the *Rig Veda* was primarily a period of assemblies. The second stage saw the break-up of the tribal polity under the stress of constant conflicts. The third stage was marked by the formation of the full-fledged state. There arose the large territorial monarchies of Kosala and Magadha in the mainland and tribal oligarchies in north-western India and at the foot of the Himalayas. One of the principal features of this large state-system was the presence of a body of armed personnel to safeguard the territorial and political interests of the state and an organized machinery for collection of land revenue. The organized bureaucracy became an additional feature of the centralized state-system in view of the expanding economic activities of the state during the Maurya period. The influence of religion is perceptible throughout, though it becomes more prominent in the post-Maurya and Gupta times when deliberate attempts were made to attribute divine powers to the head of state.

THE VEDIC EXPERIENCE AND RELEVANCE OF A BAHUDHĀ APPROACH

The Vedic age is the most seminal one in the history of India for it decisively shaped human behaviour, created social structure and a mindset that continue to influence us to this day. The sages of the Vedic era created spiritual technology and unique conflict resolution mechanisms that brought in harmony between nature and human beings.

The Vedic experience in conflict resolution may seem unrelated to modern-day realities as these thoughts and institutions may not provide direct answers to present day questions, and yet at the same time their relevance as intellectual quests and their quality of approach are of considerable relevance and great value in our immediate efforts to create a harmonious world.

This quality of approach was possible because the sages and saints of that era never thought in terms of exclusiveness. They knew their actions would have repercussions in society and the world in general. These sages were not dreamers but practical people; several of them were teachers of statecraft and politics. They did not think only of their own welfare, but prayed for the welfare of the whole human race to which they belonged. Their prayers were 'Let all be happy, let all be healthy, let all have good fortune and let nobody suffer'.

The Vedic sages were convinced that compassion and concern for human beings as well as natural objects were integral to a good policy. They adopted a rational approach and advocated that what was told needed to be scrutinized first. The critical enquiry coupled with practical and effective action were the cornerstones of harmonious order.

The ancient sages had feared that a single written scripture could lead to orthodoxy. On the other hand, a compassionate and non-violent lifestyle based on the experiences of the learned men and women could provide a better solution.

The Vedic sages and saints accepted the multiplicity of aboriginal gods and the different rituals which originated outside the Aryan tradition, and yet justified them and incorporated several of them in their sacred texts. Accordingly, many sects professing diverse beliefs came to exist within the Hindu fold of that era. It brought together both the Aryans and the non-Aryans. The emotional attitudes of worshippers of the old forms were transferred to the new. The contact of cultures did not result in complete domination of one by the other. There was accommodation. All these facilitated the evolutionary growth of the Hindu order and enormously contributed to its continuity on the one hand and emotional satisfaction of its old and new followers on the other. For what counted then, and is relevant today, is human conduct and not necessarily beliefs.

The method of religious and social progress of the Vedic period had several democratic features. It allowed each group to get to the truth through its own tradition by means of discipline of mind and morals. Each group had its own tradition and this did not interfere with building a homogeneous village or society. The Vedic sages and seers clearly saw that each religious rite or social institution (both tribal and non-tribal) were conditioned by the social structure and pattern of beliefs in which their followers had lived. It recognized that history had made them what they were, and they could not suddenly be different. As a result of this realization, these people followed the plurality of gods and beliefs. A south Indian folk song aptly expresses the Indian experience of that era when it says:

Into the bosom of the one great sea
Flow streams that come from hills on every side,
Their names are various as their springs,
And thus in every land do men bow down
To one great God, though known by many names.[75]

There was no attempt to silence or stifle a person or to forbid him even to question the fundamental principles of the Hindu order. As a result, while there is only one philosophy being discussed and promoted, one sees also the *advaita* alongside the *dvaita* philosophy being argued and sponsored. The Vedic order never discarded someone since he or she wrote a wrong scripture or did not observe a particular ritual.

The lessons to be learnt from this experience are highly relevant today. For we are still seeking ways and means by which people following different faiths and belonging to different cultures can live together in peace and harmony. It was realized then, and it needs to be recognized now, that we cannot have harmony and peace as long as we assert that we are in possession of the light and that others are groping in the dark. For such an approach will not promote the brotherhood of free nations of peoples, differing profoundly in life, mind, habits and institutions, under a single global political architecture such as the United Nations.

When there are a series of experiences containing valuable lessons and explaining the nature of truth in different languages with different emphasis, the Bahudhā approach of 'one truth, many interpretations' alone could help resolve our differences. The need is to believe in a unity of spirit between multiple belief systems that have guided individuals of different faiths. The world would be much poorer if one God and one way of worship was prescribed for everyone; or if one language and one dialect were to become the mode of human expression; if one folklore or set of songs were prescribed to be sung by everyone.

Modern technology has created a global society which is interconnected by markets and politics and through the internet. It needs to be strengthened with a spiritual consciousness. There can be no simple answers but the Vedic experience teaches us that the Bahudhā approach in dialogue and the spirit of compassion would be of considerable help.

NOTES

1. The full text of the verse reads as follows:

   अयं निज: परोवेति
   गणना लघुचेतसाम् ।
   उदारचरितानं तु
   वसुधैव कुटुम्बकम् ॥

   Ayam nijah paroveti
   Gananaa laghuchetsām
   Udaracharitanam tu
   Vasudhaiva kutumbakam.

   In 'Vasudhaiva Kutumbakam'—'vasudhaiva' means 'the entire creation or entire earth' and 'kutumbakam' is the Sanskrit world for 'family'. 'Vasudhaiva Kutumbakam' means the world or entire creation is a Family.

   This is a floating verse, often quoted to express the harmony of human relations and associated with the Vedic world view. This verse is also found mentioned in the *Hitopadesah* along with other floating verses.

   The *Hitopadesah* or friendly counsel is a wonderful rendering of India's animal fables. These fables were originally written in order to instruct young Indian Princes in their duties as rulers. Hitopadesah is similar to the *Panchatantra.* Both *Hitopadesah* and *Panchatantra* were written in Sanskrit. The *Panchatantra* was probably put together around the year 3000 CE, although it is difficult to date precisely. The oral story telling tradition that finally produced the *Panchatantra* and the *Hitopadesah* is the same oral story telling tradition that led to the Buddhist jataka stories. See Narayana Pandita, *Hitopadesah*, Chaukhamba Sanskrit Pratishthan, Delhi, 1987 (reprint edition), p. 36.

2. Quoted in B.P. Singh, *India's Culture: The State, The Arts and Beyond*, Oxford University Press, New Delhi, 1998, p. 177.

3. K.M. Sen, *Hinduism*, Penguin Books, London, 1961, p. 18.

4. Bridget Allchin and Raymond Allchin, *The Rise of Civilization in India and Pakistan*, Select Book Service Syndicate, New Delhi, by arrangement with Cambridge University Press, London, 1983, p. 355.

5. The Indian scriptures and the subsequent knowledge related thereto have their origins in the *sruti* and *smriti* traditions. The Vedas are believed to be divine revelations (*smriti*). The great seers of ancient times who had perfected themselves had heard these internal truths in their hearts and they taught these truths to disciples by telepathy and later wrote in books. The term *smriti* signifies an oral tradition wherein the teachers passed to their students the texts which they had received from their masters. The Puranas and other great works belong to this category.

A. Smirti (revealed scriptures)

1. The Vedic hymns (*mantras*), grouped into four collections (*samhitas*) known as the Vedas, as listed above.

2. The seven Brahmanas (treatises on ritual and folklore), one or more for each Veda. Annexed to the Brahmanas are (a) the Aranyakas (forest meditation documents) and (b) the Upanishads.

3. The six *Angas* (further explanations, especially explanations of the Brahmanas). Included in the Angas are (a) the *Kalpa Sutras* (pronouncements on the ages of the world), which themselves include the *Dharma Sutras* (pronouncements on duty or justice), and (b) works on ceremonies, grammar, and astronomy.

B. Sruti (traditional scriptures)

1. The four *Upangas* (additional explanations), which include (a) about 20 Dharmashastras (poetic treatises on duty or justice, attributed to Manu, Yajnavalkya, and others; see Chapter IV of the present volume); (b) the *Nyaya* and *Mimamsa Sutras* and other epitomes (see Chapter IV of the present volume); and (c) the 18 Puranas (cosmogonies, legends, etc.).

2. The four Upavedas (supplements to the Vedas), one for each Veda, on archery, music, sculpture, medicine, etc.

(William Gerber (ed.), *The Mind of India*, Southern Illinois University Press, Carbondale and Edwardsville, 1967, pp. 2–3).

6. Sri Aurobindo, *The Secret of the Veda* (*The Complete Works of Sri Aurobindo*, Vol. 15), Sri Aurobindo Ashram Publication Department, Pondicherry, 1998, p. 10.

7. Upanishad means the inner or mystic teaching. The term Upanishad is derived from *upa* (near), *ni* (down), and *s(h)ad* (to sit), i.e., sitting down near. Groups of pupils sit near the teacher to learn from his secret doctrine. In the quietude of the forest hermitages the Upanishad thinkers pondered on the problems of deepest concerns and communicated their knowledge to fit pupils near them. Shankaracharya derives the word Upanishad as a substitute from the root *sad*, 'to loosen', 'to reach', or 'to destroy' with *upa* and *ni* as prefixes and kvip as termination. If this determination is accepted, Upanishad means *brahma*—knowledge by which ignorance is loosened or destroyed. The treatises that deal with brahma-knowledge are called the Upanishads and so pass for the Vedanta.

It needs to be mentioned that the Upanishads undoubtedly admit of different interpretations, although there is a certain uniformity of leading concepts running through the Upanishads. This is to be understood in the context that their authors belonged to different periods of time and came from different sections of society.

8. *Tat Tvam Asi*—One of the four *mahavakyas*, great teachings of the Upanishads.

9. The word Purana means 'ancient'. Panini grammatically dissolves this word as that which happened before. It may mean 'an old narrative' which speaks of ancient traditions. The use of *itihsa* and purana together suggests that the line of demarcation between these two branches of knowledge is very thin and both together mean the records of ancient events. Later on, legends, stories, and myths were added to these and a Puranasamhita was prepared by Badrayana. (See the *Vishnu Purna* III.6.15.)

10. *Matsya Purana, Padma Purana, Naradiya Purana, Vishnu Purana, Varaha Purana, Vamana Purana, Bhavishya Purana, Brahma Purana, Shiva Purana, Devi Purana, Skanda Purana, Markandeya Purana, Garuda Purana, Agni Purana, Kurma Purana, Brahmanda Purana, Bhagvata Purana, Linga Purana,* etc. fall under this particular category.

11. The story of Ram is narrated in all Indian languages and regions. The Ramayana has evolved in different languages, idioms and cultures. Though the basic storyline remains the same, several minor deviations are found in different versions due to poetic licence and literary form. In the process, the story of Ram acquired the hues of these different regions, taking on a regional flavour, for example, in those of Thailand, Indonesia, Myanmar, Malaysia, Cambodia, and Vietnam.

12. The Mahabharata is a unique creation of India and has no equal in world literature. It represents a corpus of some 200,000 lines, eight times the size of the *Illiad* and the *Odyssey* put together, that has influenced and captivated the minds of almost all Indians for about

two millennia. Thanks to Peter Brooks' laudable efforts the story, and the underlying unique human drama, has been staged in cities like Paris, New York, and Glasgow in recent years with great success. Its popularity is no longer restricted to the geographical boundaries of India.

13. Vyasa is said to be the writer of the Mahabharata and son of the sage Prasara and Satyavati. 'Vyasa does not signify one person. It is a title. Every Dwapara Yuga witnesses the birth of a Vyasa. He bears the title till the next Dwapara Yuga emerges. This Vyasa was actually Krishna Dwaipayana—'Krishna' because he was dark-skinned, 'Dwaipayana' because he was born on an island in the Yamuna. He was called 'Veda Vyasa' for it was he who classified the Vedas into four branches. His hermitage was in Badari and he was therefore 'Badrayana'. Thus, men called him by many names.

14. The television shows serializing the Ramayana and the Mahabharata in India proved so popular that at the time of their telecast, traffic in towns used to come to a standstill! In rural areas, working people and children invariably sat spellbound in front of a television set at a community centre or in a home. They wept and laughed as the situation demanded and even the electricity supply, which is irregular at the best of times in the rural areas, would function normally during the telecast. Perhaps the employees of the Electricity Board did not wish to incur the wrath of the public—and of the gods—by their failure to ensure the uninterrupted viewing of the epic tale!

15. Vamadeo Shastri, *Asiatic Studies* (2 volumes). Both the volumes of this book were first published in 1882 and reprinted in 1976 by Cosmo Publications, New Delhi, pp. 21–2. Vamadeo Shastri is the assumed name of Alfred C. Lyall.

16. Rajmohan Gandhi, *Revenge and Reconciliation: Understanding South Asian History*, Penguin Books, India, 1999, p. 16.

17. Quoted from the Bulletin of the Deccan College Postgraduate and Research Institute's Diamond Jubilee Volume [Vols 60–1 (2000–1)], Pune.

18. Ibid.

19. P. Lal, *The Mahabharata of Vyasa*, Vikas, New Delhi, 1980, p. 294.

20. C. Rajagopalachari, *Mahabharata*, Bharatiya Vidya Bhawan, Bombay, 1968, p. 310.

21. J. J. Bakker, *Gandhi and the Gita*, Canadian Scholar's Press, Toronto, 1993, p. 29.

22. Rajagopalachari, *Mahabharata*, p. iv.

23. While it is needless to cite examples of several inter-tribal and intra-tribal conflicts in Rigvedic society, the case of the battle of ten kings or Dasarajna fought on the Ravi is well known. In it, each of the allies and their adversaries appear as a mixed group consisting of Vedic and non-Vedic peoples.

24. R. C. Majumdar, 'Indian History: Its Nature, Scope and Method', *The History and Culture of the Indian People: The Vedic Age* (ed.), Bharatiya Vidya Bhawan, Bombay, 1951. (Quoted from the Fifth Edition 1988, p. 38).

25. Quoted from the Foreword by Raimundo Panikkar in Jeanine Miller, *The Vision of Cosmic Order in the Vedas*, Routledge & Kegan Paul, London, 1985, p. xviii.

26. Miller, *The Vision of Cosmic Order in the Vedas*, p. 285.

27. *Atharva Veda*, X.191.4.

पृथिवी शान्तिरन्तरिक्षं शान्तिद्यौः शान्तिराप: शान्तिरोषधय: शान्तिर्वनस्पतय:

शान्तिर्विश्वे में देवा: शान्ति: सर्वे में देवा: शान्ति: शान्ति: शान्ति: शान्तिभि: ।

ताभि: शान्तिभि: सर्व शान्तिभि: शमयामोऽहं यदिह घोरं यदिह क्रूरं

यदिह पापं तच्छान्तं तच्छिवं सर्वमेव शमस्तु न: ॥

28. *Atharva Veda* VII.52.1–2.

संज्ञानं न: स्वेभि संज्ञानमरणेभि: ।

संज्ञानमश्विना युवमिहास्मासु नि यच्छतम्

सं जानामहै मनसा सं चिकित्वा युष्मिहि मनसा दैव्येन

मा घोषा उत् स्थुर्बहुले विनिर्हते मेषु: पप्तदिन्द्रस्याहत्यागते ॥

Give us agreement with our own, with strangers give us unity:
Do ye, O Asvins, in this place join us in sympathy and love.
May we agree in mind, agree in purpose: let us not fight against the heavenly spirit.
Around us rise no din of frequent slaughter, nor Indra's arrow fly, for day is present!

29. *Atharva Veda*, XII.1.12.

यत् ते मध्यं पृथिवि यच्च नभ्यं यास्त ऊर्जस्तन्व: संबभूव: ।

तासु नो धेह्यभि न: पवस्व माता भूमि: पुत्रो अहं पृथिव्या: ॥

पर्जन्य: पिता स उ न: पिपर्तु ॥ १२ ॥

Also see *Atharva Veda*, XII.1.35.

यत् ते भूमे विखनामि क्षिप्रं तदपि रोहतु ।

मा ते मर्म विमृग्वरि मा ते हृदयमर्पिपम् ॥

Let what I dig from thee, O Earth, rapidly spring and grow again.
O Purifier, let me not pierce through thy vitals or thy heart.

30. *Yajur Veda* 40:1.

ईशा वास्यमिदं सर्वं यत्किंच जगत्यां जगत्।

तेन त्यक्तेन भुण्जीथा मा गृध: कस्यस्विद्धनम्॥

Enveloped by the Lord must be This All—each thing that moves on earth.
With that renounced enjoy thyself. Covet no wealth of any man.

31. *Yajur Veda*.

32. 'Mata Bhumih Putroham Prithivyah'.

33. *Atharva Veda* XIX.9.14.

पृथिवी शान्तिरन्तरिक्षं शान्तिद्यौं: शान्तिराप: शान्तिरोषधय: शान्ति:

वैनस्पतय: शान्तिर्विश्वे मे देवा: शान्ति: सर्वें मे देवा शान्ति: शान्ति:
शान्ति: शान्तिभि: । ताभि: शान्तिभि: सर्व शान्तिभि: शमयामोऽहं
यदिह घोरं यदिह क्रूरं यदिह पापं तच्छान्तं तच्छिवं सर्वमेव-शमस्तु न: ॥ १४ ॥

Earth alleviation, air alleviation, heaven alleviation, waters alleviation, plants alleviation, trees alleviation, all Gods my alleviation, collective God my alleviation, alleviation by alleviations. By these alleviations, these universal alleviations, I allay all that is terrific here, all that is cruel, all that is wicked. This hath been calmed, this is not auspicious. Let all be favourable to us.

34. Miller, *The Vision of Cosmic Order in the Vedas*, pp. 294–5 further reflects: The fundamental idea of the one law that constitutes the foundation of life, the very structure of the universe and pulsation of the One Absolute Principle from whom proceed the many, first as a duality, then as a plurality, in ordered sequence; and the possibility for man of realizing, through supra-normal insight or vision and through righteous living, through the integration of his whole being, and through the ritualistic ordering in symbolic gestures, certain truths that lie beyond the scope of ordinary, mundane experience and perception; all this forms the background of the hymns of the *Rig Veda* and was to be taken up, developed and expounded in a different language in the Brahmins, the Upanishads, the *Vedanta Sutras*, the epics and the Puranas.

35. *Bhagavata Purana* says,
कामस्य नेन्द्रिय-प्रीतिर्लाभो जीवेत यावता । जीवस्य तत्त्वजिशासा नार्थो यश्चेह कर्म्मभि: ॥ १० ॥
वदन्ति तत् तत्त्वविदस्तत्त्वं यज्ज्ञानमद्वयम् । ब्रह्मेति परमात्मेति भगवानिति शब्द्यते ॥ ११ ॥
तच्छद्द्धाना मुनयो ज्ञानवैराग्ययुक्तया । पश्यन्त्यात्मनि चात्मानं भक्त्या श्रुतगृहीतया ॥ १२ ॥
The chief end of life here is not the attainment of heaven popularly known to be the result of pious duties. It is the desire to enquire into truth (I.2.10).

36. Known as the *Manusmriti* it is one of the eighteen smritis of the Dharmashastra (or 'laws of righteous conduct'), written *c*.200. Smritis mean 'what is remembered' and applied to Hindu texts other than the Vedas, including epics, the Puranas, and science and grammar treatises.

37. Mahabharata, Adi Parva, 64.91.
(Ref. Sriman Mahabharatam, Adi Parva-I, edited by T.R. Krishnacharya and T.R. Vyasacharya, Sri Satguru Publications, Delhi, 1985, p. 108.

38. Mahabharata, Udyoga Parva, 33–41.
वीक्षमाणं मुनिं दृष्ट्वा प्रोवाचेदं वचस्तदा ।
जन्म शोकाभितप्तायाः कथं ज्ञास्यसि कथ्यताम् ॥
                                —The Mahabharata, Adi Parva 64.91
(Ref. Krishnacharya and Vyasacharya, p. 108.)

39. One of the seven venerated sages of Hindu mythology. He was a Kshatriya (warrior caste) by birth, but transcended into the Brahmin

priestly caste with his tough penance. He was the sage to the royal dynasty wherein Ram was born, and went to the forest with Ram to kill the demons that bothered him. He is known as a prominent sage and rival of the sage Vashistha.

40. A sage who begot Vyasa through Satyavati before she married Shantanu.
41. A maharishi and highly learned Aditya was born to a Shudra father and mother and became a Brahmin.
42. A sage was born of a prostitute—Jabala—and later became a renowned rishi, even though he retained the name of his mother with his name. He is therefore rightly remembered as Satyakam Jabala.
43. This did not involve the complete renunciation of the world, for husbands and wives could still have sex (once a month), and a sacred fire was to be kept and minimal rituals performed.
44. The king's duty was to protect his people and if a king failed to do so, then the people were justified in deserting him (Mahabharata, XII.57). However, the right to revolt in the Hindu tradition was whittled down to a moral right with the merest of legal sanctions, probably arising out of a fear of anarchy. The Brahmins were permitted to express their disapproval of an oppressive ruler, and on occasion this expression could be extended to the populace. The justification for such action did not emerge from an anxiety to protect civil rights, but rather to oppose the abuse of power on the part of the ruler (*Bhagavata Purana*, IV.14).
45. One of the functions of the state was to uphold dharma (*Arthashastra*, III.1.38).

चतुर्वर्णाश्रमस्यायं लोकस्याचाररक्षणात् ।

नश्यतां सर्वधर्माणां राजा धर्मप्रवर्तक: ॥ ३८ ॥

धर्मश्व व्यवहारश्व चरित्रं राजशासनम् ।

विवादार्थश्वतुष्पाद: पश्चिम: पूर्ववाधक: ॥ ३९ ॥

When all laws are perishing, the king here is the promulgator of laws, by virtue of his guarding the right conduct of the world consisting of the four varnas and four ashramas.

46. Mahabharata, Shanti Parva, 59.
47. *Rig Veda* (V.61.8). The commentator explains this passage thus: 'The wife and husband, being the equal halves of one substance, are equal in every respect; therefore, both should join and take equal parts in all work, religious and secular.' Every hymn of the *Rig Veda* is attributed to a rishi. Though most of these hymns were the work of male rishis, the *Rig Veda* contains hymns which were also revealed by women seers. The latter were called *rishikas* and *brahmavadinis*. The *Rig Veda* (V.7.9) refers to young maidens completing their education as *brahmacharinis* and then acquiring husbands.
48. A woman philosopher of Upanishadic times who challenged Yajnavalkya.

49. The seer of a Veda Samhita from Surya, the revealer of Brahma Jnana to Janaka, Maitreyi and others, Yajnavalkya hails supreme among sages of sacred memory. He was from Mithila and stands distinguished both in the *srutis* and in the *smritis*. He is especially known for his unsurpassed spiritual wisdom and power.
50. A great female scholar of Vedic lore; also known as one of the revealers of Vedic wisdom.
51. Wife of Sage Yajnavalkya, Maitreyi was fond of discussing the nature of Brahman—ultimate knowledge. She is, therefore, aptly known as Brahmavadini. Brahmavadinis were products of the educational discipline of brahmacharya, for which women were also eligible.
52. After a student bachelor completed his studies, his parents approached the parents of a girl who belonged to a good family and asked them to give away their daughter in marriage to their son—to make a gift of their daughter to him. The girl's family did not give any dowry or jewellery to the boy's family. Of the eight forms of marriage, the Dharmashastras regard this as the highest.
53. Prajapatya is one of the eight forms of marriage recognized by the Dharmasastras. In prajapatya there is no trading and *kanyadana* is a part of it as in the brahma ceremony. But from the name prajapatya it must be inferred that the bride's menarche is imminent and that a child must be begotten soon after the marriage. For this reason the bride's father goes in search of a groom, unlike in the brahma type.
54. This form of marriage, 'arsa', suggests that it is concerned with the sages.
55. Marrying a girl to a *rtvik* (priest) during a sacrifice is called 'daiva'. The parents, in this type, after waiting in vain for a young man to turn up and ask for their daughter's hand, go looking for a groom for her in a place where a sacrifice is being conducted. This type of marriage is considered inferior to brahma.
56. *Rig Veda*, X.85.
57. न गृहं गृहमित्याहुः
    गृहिणिगृहमुच्यते ।
58. It is regrettable that this aspect of our society is getting progressively weaker every day owing to political machinations.
59. Hindu law has been codified in the Dharmashastra literature, frequently referred to as the Law Books. Of these the most significant for our purposes are the Dharmashastras of Manu, Yajnavalkya, and Narada. Buddhist concepts of law were never codified in any single source. Legal ideals are, however, found in the Buddhist Canon, particularly in the *Vinaya-pitaka.*
60. Once upon a time, India had 3,000 castes and 25,000 sub-castes. There were 1,800 Brahmin castes in India. Even different Brahmin castes did not mingle socially or otherwise, in ancient times.

61. *Rig Veda*, X.86.4.
62. *Yajur Veda*, III, 43.

उपहूता इह गाव उपहूता अजावय: ।

अथो अन्नस्य कीलाल उपहूतो गृहेपु न: ।

क्षेमाय व: शान्त्यै प्रपद्ये शिवश्च शग्मश्च शंयो: शंयो: ॥ ४३ ॥

Here have the cows been called to us, the goats and sheep have been called near,

And in our home we have addressed the meath that sweeteneth our food.

I come to thee for safety and for quiet. May joy be ours, felicity, and blessing.

63. In contemporary India, the hierarchical structure of the caste system is under stress. While in politics the significance of caste has increased, in most other respects, except in arranged marriages, caste is no longer a critical determinant of people's life chances as it used to be.

In many rural and urban settlements throughout India, there are populations of Muslims or other non-Hindus that are internally divided into ranked, endogamous groups. These groups, often referred to as jati, are commonly integrated into their local caste hierarchies alongside the Hindu castes, and their rank frequently depends on their putative caste status prior to conversion. For example, the Muslim Meos in parts of north Rajasthan and south Haryana, despite their conversion to Islam long ago, regard themselves as Rajputs. There are several other instances as well.

The Constitution of India, adopted in 1950, guarantees for all citizens the fundamental right of equality before the law, freedom from discrimination on grounds of race, caste, sex or place of birth, and equality of opportunity in public appointments. The Constitution also specifically abolishes untouchability. Another section of the Constitution lays down 'special provisions' for the reservation of seats in parliament and state legislatures, and of posts in government services, for the Scheduled Castes (SCs) and Scheduled Tribes (STs). The same section also mentions other 'backward classes', but neither defines them nor specifies provisions on their behalf.

In 1990, the issue of reservations for Other Backward Classes (OBCs) took a dramatic turn with the decision of the National Front government to implement the recommendations of the Mandal Commission Report issued ten years earlier, beginning with the reservation of 27 per cent of jobs in central government services and public undertakings for the OBCs. This new quota was in addition to the 22.5 per cent already reserved for SCs and STs. The introduction of the new reservations for OBCs profoundly affected political developments during the 1990s, and the term 'mandalization' has been coined to describe the way in which caste has become a more potent factor in the political process throughout India.

64. The Constitution of India rightly denounces untouchability and laws framed therein make it a penal offence for those who practise untouchability.

65. The Digha Nikaya, or 'Collection of Long Discourses' (Pali digha = 'long') is the first division of the *Sutta Pitaka*, and consists of 34 *suttas*, grouped into three *vaggas*, or divisions:
    a) *Silakkhandha-vagga* : The Division Concerning Morality (13 suttas)
    b) *Maha-vagga* : The Large Division (10 suttas)
    c) *Patika-yagga* : The Patika Division (11 suttas)

66. Quoted in Robert D. Kaplan, *The Coming Anarchy*, First Vintage Book Edition, New York, 2001, p. x.

67. Quoted from B.P. Singh's Sardar Patel Memorial Lecture, 1999 entitled 'Democracy, Ecology and Culture: The Indian Experience'. From the Mahaparinibbana Sutlam (in Pali), Ch. 1 of the *Digha Nikaya* (part II), N.K. Bhagwat (ed.), Bombay, 1936, pp. 60–2. English translation from *Sacred Books of the East*, Vol. XI, trans. by T.W. Rhys Davids, Oxford, 1900, pp. 3–4. Also available in *Dialogues of the Buddha*, Part II, trans. by T.W. Rhys Davids and C.A.F. Rhys Davids, London, 1910, pp. 79–80.

68. The story of Lord Ram's life, including his relationship with his parents, brothers, teacher, subjects, advisers, etc. has gripped the minds of generations of Indians and still continues to be a talisman. Family feuds and personal conduct are sought to be evaluated in buses and bazaars, huts and palaces in the light of the story of Lord Ram's life. None can overemphasize the way Sant Tulsidas's epic *Ramcaritamanas* immortalized this story in Hindi-speaking regions of the country.

69. Quoted from M. Ram Jois, *Dharma: The Global Ethic*, Bharatiya Vidya Bhawan, Mumbai, 1996, p. 46.

70. Mahabharata, Shanti Parva.
    धर्माय राजा भवति न कामकरणाय तु।

71. *Manusmriti*, VIII.20.2.26–6.97
    G. Buhler gives following translation of this verse:

    A Brahmana who subsists only by the name of his caste (jati), or one who merely calls himself a Brahmana (though his origin be uncertain), may, at the King's pleasure, interpret the law to him, but never a Shudra.

    The Sacred Books of the East, translated by various Oriental scholars, and edited by F. Max-Muller, Vol. XXV. *The Laws of Manu*, translated by G. Buhler. Oxford Press 1886, p. 255.
    जातिमात्रोपजीवी वा कामं स्याद्ब्राह्मणाब्रुवः ।
    धर्मप्रवक्ता नृपतेर्न तु शूद्रः कथंचन ॥
    वैदिकैः कर्मभिः पुण्यैर्निषेकादिर्द्विजन्मनाम् ।
    कार्यः शरीरसंस्कारः पावनः प्रेत्य चेह च ॥ २६ ॥

Caturvarnyasya Dharmah [Dharma of the Four Varnas] 2.25–11.266

3.1) Dharmavidhih [Rules Relating to Dharma] 2.25–10.131.

3.1.1) Anapadi Karmavidhih [Rules of Action in Normal Times] 2.26–9.336

3.1.1.1) Brahmanasya Caturvidhah Dharmah [Fourfold Dharma of a Brahmin] 2.26–6.97

esa vo bhihito dharmo brahmanasya caturvidhah |
punyo ksayaphalah pretya rajnam dharmam nibodhata || 6.97

I have explained to you above the fourfold Law of Brahmins, a Law that is holy and brings imperishable rewards after death. Listen now to the Law of kings.

72. *Kamandaka*, I.9.

73. Mahabharata, Udyoga Parva, 63.10.

अथाब्रवीन्महाराजो घृतराष्ट्रः सुदुर्मनाः ।
विदुरं विदुषां श्रेष्ठं सर्वपार्थिवसंनिधौ ॥

(Sriman Mahabharatam, Krishanacharya and Vyasacharya, p. 119.

74. A great devotee who heard Srimad-Bhagavatam from Maitreya Muni. The great men of the world regarded Vidura as mahatma who was unparalleled in his knowledge of dharma, sastras, and statesmanship, and was totally devoid of attachment and anger. Bhishma appointed him while he was still in his teens as the chief counsellor of King Dhritarashtra. Vyasa has it that no one in the three worlds could equal Vidura in virtue and knowledge.

75. Charles E. Gover, *The Folksongs of Southern India*, Higgenbotham, Madras, 1871, p. 165.

4
The Pathfinders

Appa dipo bhav[1]
Be ye lamps unto yourselves

—Gautama Buddha

The Polish poet and Nobel Laureate Wislawa Szymborska, in her poem 'The Turn of the Century', has raised a very pertinent question:

How to live—someone asked me this in a letter,
someone I had wanted
to ask that very thing.
Again and as always,
and as seen above
there are no questions more urgent
than the naïve ones.[2]

At the risk of oversimplification as to 'how should we live?', three ways were clearly stipulated by savants of the Vedic era. The first relates to karma or action, which covered the entire gamut of human activity from agriculture to warfare, and the second to rituals that prescribed *yajna* to propitiate nature and the gods. The third relates to attitude—the Bahudhā attitude—and it is in this attitude of accommodation and tolerance, in this temper of the mind governing human beings that strong foundations of a harmonious society can be laid. One could imagine that this approach was formulated by the rishis both in order to point to the ultimate reality and also for harmonious living in society among people of diverse beliefs and practices, each claiming superiority over the other.

The Bahudhā philosophy is central to the generation of an attitude. Such an approach helps create an environment for harmony among communities and religions, harmony between nature and men, that enables a person to understand the other's point of view in the realms of life and religion, science and spirituality.

In its long history, Indian thought processes have undergone major changes spurred both by internal developments and by external contacts. Social conflict and external aggression have been a feature of history. Notwithstanding this, the Bahudhā philosophy has found eloquent expression in India. For our purposes this could be viewed from the following perspectives:

  (i) the pathfinders: Lord Mahavira, Lord Buddha, and Guru Nanak;
 (ii) the builders: Swami Vivekananda, Mahatma Gandhi, and Rabindranath Tagore;
(iii) the rulers: Ashoka, Akbar, and Jawaharlal Nehru;
(iv) among people: field visits.

IN THE LIGHT OF GODS AND GURUS

There is a growing realization, even among rationalists who do not attach much value to religion, that a moral regime is necessary to deter people from indulging in unrestrained self-aggrandisement. The evolutionary nature of human behaviour too has shown that a deity could help rein in mankind's worst impulses, bring out the best in us, and give us a sense that there is someone awake in the cosmic house watching us and judging us. The belief that good karma brings desirable results not only in this life but also in the after-life has been a major motivation for making one walk on the path of righteousness and virtue.

The Hindu and the Buddhist approaches to God that have dominated the Indian consciousness are different in nature. The Hindus have always advocated the idea of the oneness of God, and yet the *Rig Veda* identified such diverse gods as Agni, Indra, and Varun. In later times, the Rigvedic gods receded into the background and the trinity of Brahma, Vishnu, and Mahesh acquired prominence. Of this trinity, Hindu belief talks about only the incarnations of Vishnu in the world, of which there have been ten in number since time immemorial.[3] The Hindus believe that whenever there is a decline in dharma (righteousness) and a rise in adharma (immoral acts), Lord Vishnu manifests himself. Lord Krishna eloquently explains the concept of *avatara*[4] in the Bhagavad Gita in the following words:

Yada yada hi dharmasya
Glanir bhavati bharata
Abhyutthanam adharamasya
Tadatmanam srjamyaham[5]

Whenever there is a decline in religious practice and a predominant rise of irreligion—at that time I descend Myself. To deliver the pious and to annihilate the miscreants, as well as to establish the principles of religion, I Myself appear, millennium after millennium.

In Buddhism and Jainism, the majesty of God is neither expressly stated nor is it explicitly denied. The existence of the universe, as also its eternal nature, is emphasized. Mahatma Gandhi captures the Buddhist approach admirably when he reflects:

I have heard it contended times without number and I have read in books claiming to express the spirit of Buddhism, that the Buddha did not believe in God. In my humble opinion such a belief contradicts the very central fact of the Buddha's teaching. Confusion has arisen over his rejection, and just rejection, of the base things that passed in his generation under the name of God. He undoubtedly rejected the notion that a being called God could be actuated by malice, could repent of his actions, and like the kings of the earth could possibly be open to temptations and bribes and could have favourites.

God's laws are eternal and unalterable and not separable from God Himself. It is an indispensable condition of His very perfection. Hence the great confusion that the Buddha disbelieved in God and simply believed in the moral law.[6]

The belief in transmigration of the soul is one of the basic tenets of Indian religious thought and is shared by Hinduism, Buddhism, and Jainism. According to the Buddhist belief a person is bound to samsara, karma is his (means for) going beyond. As one's karma of the present life determines his birth in the following one is really the child not only of one's parents but also of what one did in his previous birth.

The theory of transmigration finds expression in the selection process of the Dalai Lama. On the death of the Dalai Lama the spiritual leaders go in search of a special child, and once he is recognized he is proclaimed to be the new Dalai Lama. For example, Buddhist spiritual leaders recognized Tenzin Gyatso, His Holiness the fourteenth Dalai Lama, at the age of two years as the reincarnation of the thirteenth Dalai Lama. He was, accordingly, brought to Lhasa, the capital of Tibet and enthroned in 1940.

Christianity also advocates the theory of God as the Creator of the universe but it does not go far in supporting the theory of the avatara of Hindu mythology. However, the resurrection of Jesus Christ after his crucifixion would support the theory of a kind of brief avatara of God on earth.

Both Lord Mahavira and Lord Buddha relied on religion, logic, and experience and asked people to seek the truth in their own minds. They did not accept or deny the existence of God but saw the eternal and unalterable character of physical phenomena. Buddha believed in the natural law of universal possession of each being, determined by the pre-existing condition of virtue, and happiness, vice and suffering being organically related.

Islam advocates that Allah (God) is the Creator of the universe and 'there is no God except Allah', and hence no multiple gods. Towards understanding the majesty and exalted position of God and His works, people should accept what Prophet Muhammad has taught. Islam does not entertain or subscribe to the incarnation theory nor does it support image worship.

For various reasons—economic, social, and political—the limitations of the Vedic world view started becoming evident. An increasing number of people were convinced that the sacrificial rituals of their ancestors no longer worked for them. The social injustices of the varna system, more particularly vis-a-vis the untouchables and women, began to come to the fore. A sharp decline in the intellect and character of several Brahmins was seen, and their inadequacies became more apparent as they did not measure up to their role in the religious and cultural domain in accordance with the standards set by the ancient system.

The principal concern then was to control the natural forces that had a bearing on economic activity as well as human health through rituals and magic. This approach was viewed as both timeless and changeless but it worked only occasionally. In the changing society the priests increasingly lost respect. The old order, based on traditional values, began to crumble. Many were disturbed by the violence and ruthlessness of the new society in which kings had become very powerful and the economy was dominated by merchants, who were moved by greed and engaged in aggressive competition among themselves.

A materialistic approach to life was also being advocated by some scholars. The Lokayata school, of which Carvaka is the best-known exponent, advocated the good life. A well-known expression attributed to Carvaka states:

Live well, as long as you live. Live well even by borrowing, for, once cremated, there is no return.[7]

In fact, an impressive array of prophetic and philosophical geniuses in India began to make supreme efforts to find a solution with a view to reorder society and polity. Of them, the two most significant ones are Mahavira and Gautama Buddha.

Incidentally, this is the period which historians call the 'Axial Age'—about 600–400 BC—a period of intense intellectual and religious development that continues to reverberate till today. The great sages of this age taught humanity new ways to cope with suffering in life and to live harmoniously. The new religious systems that emerged during this period, namely Jainism and Buddhism in India, were also marked by similar reformation movements in other civilizations of the world. Taoism and Confucianism in China, Monotheism in Iran and the Middle East, and Greek rationalism in Europe, all helped people to look at the problems facing society from a new perspective. This massive transformation in approach towards religion and society facilitated an accelerated pace in economic development, particularly in India, China, Iran, and Greece. In other words, the axis of the world's thoughts moved from a study of nature to a study of the life of man, particularly his economic, social, and political pursuits.

LORD MAHAVIRA (599–527 BC)

Lord Mahavira was born in Kaundinyapura, close to Vaishali, in a family of the ruling elite, and was named Vardhamana by his parents. His father, Siddhartha, was a ruler and his mother was Devananda. After his marriage, Vardhamana was blessed with a daughter. At the age of twenty-nine, following the death of his parents, Vardhamana renounced the world and became an ascetic for thirteen years and subjected his body to all kinds of mortification. He then entered, while meditating, into the emancipated state of *Kaivalya*, meaning 'absolute aloneness'. After enlightenment, he came to be known as Mahavira (Great Hero). By a steady process of austerity, discipline, self-purification, and understanding, he raised himself to the position of a man who had attained divine status. He was also referred to as *Jina* (conqueror), because he had overcome the limitations of human existence and conquered his own self.

Lord Mahavira became the founder of Jainism[8] in the line of *tirthankar*[9] (path-maker or finder) and was twenty-fourth in that order. Tirthankars in the Jain belief system are great spiritual teachers who appear periodically to enlighten and help mankind. His followers are called 'Jains', or those who follow the Jina. Lord Mahavira went on to emphasize the need for non-violence or ahimsa in private as well as public life. In his view, the three elements of right faith, right knowledge, and right action together are necessary for the attainment of salvation. The Jain teachers ask us to undertake five vows: not to kill anything, not to lie, not to take what is not given, to preserve chastity, and to renounce pleasure in external things. But the most important of them all is the vow of ahimsa, the vow of non-violence, of non-injury to living beings. The Jains regard ahimsa as the virtue of all virtues, '*ahimsa parmo dharmah*'. Ahimsa is strength and power that grows with patience, and self-control or restraint (*samyama*).

The finest expression of the Bahudhā philosophy in Jainism is to be found in Lord Mahavira's theory of *Anekantavada*, which recognized the multifaceted nature of reality. The Jains tell us that the absolute truth or *kevala-jnana* is our ideal.[10] So far as we are concerned, we know only part of the truth. *Vastu* is *anekadharm-atmakam*; it has several sides to it; it is complex; it has many qualities. The complete truth is not to be found in these views. It is only realizable by souls who have overcome their own passions. This fosters the spirit which makes us believe that what we think right may not after all be right. It makes us aware of the uncertainty of human hypotheses. It makes us believe that our deepest convictions may be changeable, ephemeral, or transitory.

The principle of anekanta symbolizes the fact that no element is either different from or the same as the total. It is both separate and integrated. A person is not entirely different from this universe; yet, he is not the same. We are undeniably connected—that is why we lead both dependent and independent lives.

The Anekantavada was explained through the theory of relativity called '*sapta-bhangi*' or '*sapta bhanginaya*'. It could be explained as: (i) relatively, it is; (ii) relatively, it is not; (iii) relatively, it both is and is not; (iv) relatively, it is indescribable; (v) relatively, it is and is indescribable; (vi) relatively, it is not and is indescribable; (vii) relatively, it both is and is not and is also indescribable. The theory also says that a thing may be one as well as many, eternal as well as momentary.

In addition to the above, Jainism also developed the philosophy of *syadvada*. This envisaged the necessity of an integrated view in order to arrive at a final judgement about an object possessing many characteristics. According to syadvada, each modal truth is valid as far as it goes, and, instead of being annulled, it is supplemented and transfigured by the other six modal truths, all the seven together giving us a full range of the complex truth concerning a particular problem of a fact in reality. Syadvada is a 'system of philosophy' that 'strives to incorporate the truth of all systems' as well as a 'method by which it (that is, incorporating the truth of all systems) is made. It is not a loose piece of mosaic work but an organized body of thought. The effort is to make the parts hang together in an organized or systematic closeness in order to understand several aspects of truth.

Several Hindu philosophers and logicians have criticized the doubts about truth that are entertained in the Jain philosophy of anekanta-vada.[11] A most powerful argument is that existence and non-existence, unity and plurality, eternity and momentariness cannot belong to the same thing, just as light and darkness cannot remain at the same place or just as the same thing cannot be hot and cold at the same time. In this backdrop, how can a person act on a doctrine whose matter is altogether indeterminate? S. Radhakrishnan rightly denounces the light and darkness analogy in relation to anekantavada. He writes:

they are not related to each other as light is related to darkness; they are related to each other as the different colours of the spectrum are related to one another. They are not to be regarded as contradictories, they are to be taken merely as contraries. They are alternative readings of reality.[12]

The supporters of anekanta believe that this idea is conveyed by the sevenfold statement as a whole; and it expresses the nature of reality in several steps, because no single mode of doing so is adequate for it.[13]

There is no doubt that in the anekantavada approach the present and interrelation of many interpretations is specially provided for. For our purposes, anekantavada—the doctrine of manifoldness—serves the purpose of the pluralist approach to life and its problems.

Anekantavada was directly related to Mahavira's philosophy of non-violence, which encompassed both physical and mental aspects.[14] Mahavira understood that the roots of violence lie in the human psyche.[15] He believed that a dogmatic or absolutist approach to human issues would generate conflict and disharmony. He recognized the fact that there are several aspects to truth and, accordingly, absolute truth cannot result from any one viewpoint. He, therefore, wanted respect for different belief systems.

Wars start in human minds and often with human speech.[16] Jainism teaches us that non-violence begins with the self, in one's thoughts and language, and in one's own actions. A peaceful world based on respect and care for all living beings is possible only when we extend this personal non-violence to the socio-political and ecological domains, and translate the non-violence for the self into non-violence for all. How do we cultivate this positive frame of mind?

We have to recognize that ordinarily violence is rooted in dogmatic but mistaken knowledge claims that fail to recognise other legitimate perspectives. Anekantavada provides us with an alternative episte-mology to support dialogue among people of diverse viewpoints. Such an epistemology allows us to respect the views of others. It does not mean conceding that all views are valid. It does suggest, however, that logic and evidence determine the validity of a given view. Anekantavada allowed the Jain thinkers to maintain the validity of the Jain view of reality, and to respectfully criticize the views of others, and their own views in terms of weaknesses. Such episte-mological respect for the views of others has a great potential to eliminate violent argument between ideological opponents by methodically both disarming and persuading them.

Anekantavada allows us to accept a pluralistic approach to reality. Being open-minded to others' beliefs does not mean a weakening of one's own world view. It only demands dialogue without pre-conceived notions or exclusive approaches.

The term anekanta consists of two words *aneka* (more than one) and *anta* (qualities, attributes or ends). When we say that an object has infinite attributes, we are actually saying that an object is capable of undergoing infinite modifications. Anekanta signifies the inter-dependence of substance and modes. It is not possible to have the existence of only substance or only mode. Reality is made up of both substance and mode, permanence and change. Therefore, every mode is as much a part of reality as substance is or vice-versa. Anekantavada allows us to overcome the apparent internal contradictions between eternal and non-eternal, substance and mode, and helps us recognize their dependence on one another for existence.

In practical life, such an approach to reality encourages us to keep our minds open, and discourages us from adopting a fundamentalist stand where one considers one's view as superior to those of others. An approach imbued with anekantavada spawns tolerance. Thus, in this sense, anekanta is also an essential precondition of ahimsa. The application of the philosophy of anekanta to the larger world helps in advancing towards a peaceful, harmonious, and non-violent world order. Such an attitude will certainly decrease enmity towards others and promote an increasing degree of amity among human beings.

The mental discipline with which one looks at a range of perspectives naturally results in a balanced and secular understanding of reality. This understanding encompasses the insight that other beings are not 'other' to themselves; that they are themselves just as much as we are ourselves. The history of conflicts and wars teaches us that one-sided and fanatical views in religion and politics have been at the root of terrible violence. Multiplicity of perspectives as enshrined in anekantavada allows dialogue and reconciliation in the quest for truth. It searches for the solution of a problem and asks contending parties to see both the strengths and weaknesses in their claims.

Jainism does not recognize that the universe was created by any god or gods. However, the Jains agree with the Vedic belief that after death a person is reborn in a human, animal, or other form according to his or her previous deeds. The emphasis on absolute non-violence also led to vegetarianism and a life free from the rule of priests and pandits. Mahavira believed in the equality of men and women and founded orders of celibate monks and nuns.

Mahavira's teachings greatly influenced intellectuals and princes and spread over several parts of India, including south India. Jainism is very popular among the commercial class of Gujarat in western India. Mahatma Gandhi, who belonged to this class, was influenced by the Jain teachings of non-violence.

The world is facing new dimensions in the post 9/11 world. Instead of regarding different faiths as alternatives or varying aspects of one fundamental reality, they are seen in the context of the clash of civilizations. The need of the hour is to cultivate the spirit as well as a capacity to discriminate between right and wrong and try to work for a greater synthesis between different stands in different religions and among different nation-states. Towards this self-control, the practice of ahimsa and also tolerance and appreciation of others' point of view as enshrined in the Bahudhā approach become necessary.

LORD BUDDHA (563–483 BC)

Lord Buddha, a contemporary of Mahavira, was born in the year 563 BC in Lumbini in Nepal Tarai near Kapilavastu in the Himalayan foothills and was named Siddhartha. His father was King Suddhohana of the Sakya tribe and the Gautam clan, and his mother Maya was a

Lichchhavi princess. At the age of nineteen years, he was married to Princess Yashodhara and was later blessed with a son, Rahul. At the age of twenty-nine years, Siddhartha left his home to seek enlightenment and peace. He received instructions from gurus at Vaishali and Rajagriha and later practised penances and austerities at Uruvela (near Gaya) for six years but without any results. It was, however, at Bodh Gaya after a period of seven weeks' continuous meditation, sitting under a *pipal* tree, that Siddhartha obtained supreme enlightenment at the age of thirty-five years. Thereafter, he became the Buddha or the Enlightened One. He went on to Sarnath where he preached his first sermon to five Brahmins who had been his companions for six years at Uruvela. His preaching is well known as *dharma-chakra pravartana* (setting in motion the wheel of law).[17]

Gautama Buddha[18] explained the four noble truths, the eightfold path of duty, the need to follow the middle path to avoid the extremes of the pursuit of pleasure, on the one hand, and worthless austerities on the other.

The four noble truths are: (i) misery (*dukkha*); (ii) cause of misery (*dukkha-samudaya*); (iii) negation of misery (*dukkha-nirodha*); and (iv) the path which leads towards the negation of misery (*dukkha-nirodha-gamini-pratipada*).

The eightfold path comprises (i) right speech, (ii) right action, (iii) right means of livelihood, (iv) right exertion, (v) right mindedness, (vi) right meditation, (vii) right resolution, and (viii) right point of view. The first of these three paths lead to *shila* (physical control), the next three to *samadhi* or *chitta* (mental control), and the last two to *prajna* (intellectual development).[19]

The five holy men of Sarnath who received these instructions became Buddha's first followers. In the remaining forty-five years of his life, Buddha travelled around north India teaching the masses and debating with many other religious teachers the four noble truths, the eightfold path, and dharma. Buddha always spoke in the people's language Prakrit and not in Sanskrit. Many people became his followers but stayed with their jobs, homes, and families. These lay followers provided food and shelter for others who decided, like Buddha, to give up ordinary life and become wandering monks wearing saffron robes. The community of monks and nuns became known as the *sangha*.

The gospel of Buddha spread rapidly. Buddha's impressive personality, use of the common people's language, and his communication skills made his gospel spread fast. It is another matter that Buddha's dialogue and discussions were recorded well after his *maha pari nirvana* in Pali and these formed the basis of Buddhism in Sri Lanka, Myanmar, Cambodia, and Vietnam where the Hinayana form of Buddhism prevails. Similarly, some hundred years after Buddha, several scholars recorded the Buddhist precepts and practices in Sanskrit. These Sanskrit writings of Buddhist scholars in India spread to China, Japan, Tibet, and Central Asia and provided the kernel for the growth of the Mahayana form of Buddhism.

Though Buddha never fancied himself as the founder of a new religion, he did claim that he had extinguished the fires of greed, hatred, and delusion. As Mahatma Gandhi wrote:

In Hindu culture, I venture to submit, Buddhistic culture is necessarily included, for the simple reason that the Buddha himself was an Indian, not only an Indian, but a Hindu amongst Hindus. I have never seen anything in the life of Gautama to warrant the belief that he renounced Hinduism and adopted a new faith.[20]

He further reflected:

Another thing that Gautama taught was that all that caste means today—as it meant in his time also—was wholly wrong. That is to say, he abolished every distinction of superiority and inferiority that was eating into the vitals of Hinduism. But he did not abolish Varnashramadharma—Varna dharma is not caste.[21] ...I hold that there is nothing in common between caste and Varna. Whilst Varna gives life, caste kills it, and untouchability is the hatefullest expression of caste. You will, therefore, banish untouchability from your midst. I wish you will take immediate steps to declare every man to be absolutely equal with the rest of you. You are denying Buddhism, you are denying humanity, so long as you regard a single man as an untouchable.[22]

BAHUDHĀ AND THE MIDDLE PATH APPROACH

One of the finest expressions of the Bahudhā philosophy is to be found in the doctrine of Gautama Buddha's 'middle path'. According to this doctrine of the golden mean, the correct or right course of action is always some middle point between the two extremes of excess (too much) and deficiency (too little). There is, however, no evidence to suggest that the Upanishads had any direct influence over the *madhyam nikai* (middle path) doctrine of Buddhism.

It is interesting to note that similar approaches were propounded in China and Greece in the pre-Christian era. Confucius (550–479 BC) believed in virtuous living by what he called the 'doctrine of the

mean' (Chung Yang or 'constant middle'): for every action, there are
two extremes which must be avoided, and what lies at a proper
distance between these two extremes is virtue, and the right way to
act. Lao Tze,[23] an older contemporary of Confucius believed, and
accordingly advocated, that the right way (Tao) consists in reversion
from extremes. This helped cultivate forbearance and resilience
among the Chinese people in adversity. In a similar way, in Greece,
Aristotle (384–322 BC) developed this doctrine of the mean to be
applied in determining the right course of action in a number of
different situations.

There is nothing to indicate that Buddha and his 'middle path'
doctrine were known to the Chinese savant Confucius or to the Greek
philosopher Aristotle. This astonishing coincidence in approach
among the leading men of three civilizations (Indian, Chinese, and
Greek) establishes that commonality in findings about truth is
independent of race, environment, or age.

The doctrine of the middle path, which emphasizes moderation
in all things, accommodation of antithetical points of view, and
primacy of a common-sense approach, is not without its possible
misuses. To arrive at the middle path is not to effect a compromise
but to attain a harmonious view among conflicting interpretations.
This is a difficult task. At a deeper level, it denotes unity of mind and
thought.

Buddha's middle way has also received treatment from the
perspective of high logic and philosophy. The most significant among
them is that of Nagarjuna who lived in south India in approximately
the second century and founded the Madhyamika, or middle path
schools of Mahayana Buddhism. Our view of the middle path,
however, relates to matters of practical relevance in day-to-day life
and not to high logic and philosophy.[24]

During the time of Lord Mahavira and Lord Buddha the conflict
resolution mechanism of Indian society received new ideas and institutions. This is reflected in three areas: (i) the increasing importance
of compassion and rationalism in dharma; (ii) establishment of a non-
violent order; and (iii) the rise of strong states.

DHARMA

The concept of dharma has to be seen in the context of the idea of
rta. In the Vedic period, the idea of rta gradually extended from the
physical order to the moral order of the world and covered law,
custom, and etiquette. Rta, the moral order, is not a creation by god

but is itself divine. In Buddhism, greater stress is laid on dharma, in the same manner as the Upanishads had earlier propounded that there is nothing higher than dharma. In Buddhism, dharma or it is higher than the king. Buddha emphasized the ethical aspect of dharma. For him, dharma or righteousness is the guiding principle of the universe. It is not a mere theory but is the reality underlying the sense determining it.[25]

Buddha provided an institutional mechanism for the sangha—the Buddhist order of *bhikkus*—to help establish the supremacy of dharma in public life. In the sangha, compassion and kindness would be the guiding factors along with discipline, meditation, holding frequent assemblies, showing respect to the senior bhikkus, and so on. A famous saying is as follows:

Buddham sharanam gacchami.
Dharmam sharanam gacchami.
Sangham sharanam gacchami.[26]

It's translation reads:

I go for refuge to the Buddha, to the Dharma, and to the Sangha.

In Buddha's conception of dharma, there was no place for priest-craft and ritualism. This was a clear departure from the Vedic era. Several of the rituals and ceremonies associated with the Vedic value system and practised by the common people at the time of birth, marriage, death, harvesting and particularly animal sacrifices and food offerings disappeared.

COMPASSION

Love and kindness are the very basis of society. Hatred, the Buddha said, was never appeased by more hatred—it could only be defused by friendship and sympathy.

Our ordinary sense of love and compassion is actually very much involved with attachment. The deep feeling of compassion and love for one's own wife or husband, parents, and children is related to attachment, and has a very limited circle. Again it is centred on a filial relationship—because they are my mother, my father, my children, I love them. In contrast to this is a clear recognition of the importance and rights of others. Developed from that viewpoint, compassion will reach even enemies.[27]

Compassion is the real essence of religion. All religions emphasize improvement of human beings, a sense of brotherhood and love. If one can practise compassion, then the essence of religion is automatically followed, whether it is the Hindu, Buddhist, Christian, or Islamic way. The important thing is that in daily life one must practise the essentials of religion—non-violence, love, and compassion—and on that level there is hardly any difference between Buddhism, Christianity, or any other religion.

RATIONALISM

Buddha attached greater importance to rational enquiry than perhaps any other religious leader in history. The Buddha says in a sutra:

Monks and scholars should
Well analyse my words,
Like gold (to be tested through) melting, cutting and polishing,
And then adopt them, but not for the sake of showing me respect.[28]

By this Buddha meant that even if a particular doctrine is set forth in scriptures, one must examine whether or not it meets the test of reasoning. If it conflicts with reasoning, or is at variance with new realities, it is no longer appropriate to assert its primacy and follow its dictates. This applies to Buddha's sayings as well.

A fundamental change in attitude is necessary. Basically, a Buddhist attitude on any subject must be one that accords with the facts. If, upon investigation, one finds that there is reason and proof for a point, then one should accept it. It does not mean that there are not certain points that are beyond the powers of human deductive reasoning. However, when we investigate certain descriptions as they exist in sacred texts and find that they do not correspond to reality, then we must accept the reality, and not the literal scriptural explanation.

Buddha, like Socrates, was never content to accept traditional certainties as final, however august they might be. Socrates questioned everything, infecting his interlocutors with his own perplexity, this being the beginning of new ideas and institutions. In a similar fashion, Buddha believed that every individual must find the truth in his own way, and must question everything, even Buddha's own words and sayings. This new rationality had no place for blind faith.

By nirvana, Buddha meant conquest of hatred and ignorance. Though subject to physical ailments and other vicissitudes, nothing could touch the inner peace of one who had attained nirvana. Nirvana did not mean personal extinction: what had been snuffed out or extinguished was not one's personality, but the fires of avarice, hatred, and delusion. Buddha wanted everyone to work towards the goal of nirvana, and the institution of sangha was a place where bhikkus worked towards this goal.

Buddha was, thus, creating an alternative way of living where compassion and kindness, rationality and self-enquiry, harmonious living and brotherhood played major roles. This was a new religion. The new moral order that he tried to promote is well expressed in this poem in the Pali canon:

Let all beings be happy! Weak or strong, of high, middle or low estate,
small or great, visible or invisible, near or far away,
alive or still to be born—may they all be entirely happy!
Let nobody lie to anybody or despise any single being anywhere.
May nobody wish harm to any single creature, out of anger or hatred!
Let us cherish all creatures, as a mother her only child!
May our loving thoughts fill the whole world, above, below,
Across—without limit; a boundless goodwill towards the whole world,
unrestricted, free of hatred and enmity.[29]

Towards the end of his life, Buddha told his colleagues: 'Let the *dhamma* and the discipline that I have taught you be your teacher when I am gone'. He had always told his followers to look not at him but at the dhamma[30]—he himself had never been important. Then he turned to the crowd of bhikkus who had accompanied him on this last journey, and reminded them yet again 'Decay is inherent in all component things! Work out your salvation with diligence!'[31] This was the last word of the Tathagata.

NON-VIOLENCE

According to Buddhism, non-violence is not just the absence of violence, rather it is a positive mode of attitude and action that gives life constructive shape and further entails goodness for others and oneself. All non-violent actions are motivated by compassion and altruism. Such an attitude not only restrains the person from indulging in violence but driven by the force of love and compassion, also makes him strive to benefit other beings to the utmost extent, both in terms of quantity and quality. The eightfold path enables one to lead a constructive non-violent way of life.

Non-violence is a fundamental teaching of Buddhism. Buddha's thinking was clear about the wider application of non-violence. He would spend hours in the forest alone, reflecting on the power of benevolence. He stated:

(Buddha) insists on an active and systematic cultivation of the spirit of goodwill for all kinds and conditions of men and even for animals and other sentient creatures.[32]

It is our moral responsibility to be concerned for the well-being of all sentient beings. By developing a sincere kind heart, we can make this world a better place to live in. A good heart is the true source of all happiness. To resort to a weapon is the easiest way one can think of protecting oneself as it is the direct consequence of fear and a sense of enmity. Compassion and a good heart transcend the realm of enmity where the weapon has no place. Living a life with non-violence is the most constructive approach towards harmonious living.

THE ANGULIMALA EPISODE

Among Buddha's several unique experiences, perhaps his close encounter with Angulimala[33] provides fresh insights into how a courageous, creative, and compassionate society could overcome terror, and is of great relevance in the present-day context.

Angulimala was born into a family of the untouchable community and suffered degradation and discrimination, which turned him into a terrorist.[34] He indulged in indiscriminate killings and wore a necklace (*mala*) made of human fingers (*anguli*), and thus came to be known as Angulimala. In his regular wanderings, Buddha and his followers set up their camp at Jeta Grove on the outskirts of Savatthi, close to a forest from where Angulimala operated. Buddha came to Savatthi seeking food for his mid-day meal and knocked at the door of a devoted disciple, Nandini. Buddha noticed fear in Nandini's face. On enquiry, Nandini told Buddha that Angulimala had been terrorizing the town and murdering people. On his return journey Buddha encountered Angulimala, but he smiled and kept on moving. Angulimala shouted, 'Who are you? Why aren't you running away from me? Don't you know I am going to kill you without blinking an eye, and thread your fingers into my necklace?' Buddha paused for a moment and said, 'Yes, I know who you are'. He added, 'I am always ready to die. Dying harms no one. But killing? How do you feel about killing others, Angulimala? Have you looked deeply into your feelings about killing?' Angulimala observed that 'the rich are cruel to the poor. The high castes are vicious and deceitful to the lower castes. Why should I love them? I will not stop until I have killed them all'. The conversation continued and Angulimala found himself perplexed. Buddha told Angulimala that though he rebelled against the oppression of others, yet he himself was oppressive. Buddha asked Angulimala, 'How can terror bring freedom?' Buddha reassured Angulimala that 'as you were the cause of your suffering, you are also the key to your happiness, your source of joy'. This conversation changed Angulimala.

Later, Buddha introduced Angulimala to Ananda saying: 'We have a new friend, Ahimsaka ('The Nonviolent One'). Please give him a robe and a bowl, and train him in the ways of a monk'.

DECLINE OF BUDDHISM

The disappearance of Buddhism by the tenth century or so despite Buddhism having been a state religion in India for a significant period, and the outstanding leadership provided by Ashoka in this sphere, is still a matter of profound interest to students and researchers. In the *Discovery of India*, Jawaharlal Nehru addressed this question and went on to elaborate it in the following manner:

How did Hinduism succeed in absorbing, as it were, a great and widespread popular religion, without the usual wars of religion which disfigure the history of so many countries? What inner vitality or strength did Hinduism possess then which enabled it to perform this remarkable feat? And does India possess this inner vitality and strength today?[35]

In his comments on the theme of the disappearance of Buddhism from India, Nehru emphasizes two aspects on the matter. Firstly, Hinduism was at no time wholly displaced by Buddhism and there was no widespread or violent extermination of Buddhism in India. In his perception, Buddhism died a natural death in India. Secondly, under Ashoka's state patronage, Buddhism spread rapidly and became the dominant religion in India and spread to other countries. But simultaneously there was a revival of Brahmanism and a great cultural renaissance under the imperial Guptas in the fourth and fifth centuries AD which led to the reassertion of Hinduism.

Although both Buddha and Mahavira ignored the gods, they were not atheists. They both admitted the existence of a supernatural force as well as the doctrine of transmigration though they interpreted its mechanics in their own way. Mahatma Gandhi and A.L. Basham offer different explanations for the disappearance of Buddhism from India. Mahatma Gandhi reflected as follows:

It is my deliberate opinion that the essential part of the teachings of the Buddha now forms an integral part of Hinduism. It is impossible for Hindu

India not to retrace her steps and go behind the great reformation that Gautama effected in Hinduism. By his immense sacrifice, by his great renunciation and by the immaculate purity of his life, he left an indelible impress upon Hinduism, and Hinduism owes an eternal debt of gratitude to that great teacher.[36]

According to A. L. Basham:

As early as the Gupta period Buddhist monks often took part in Hindu processions. The Buddhist family, which gave its chief support to the local monastery, would at all times rely on the services of brahmans at births, marriages and deaths. If for a time Buddhism became to all intents and purposes a separate religion, denying the Vedas, the ordinary layman might not see it in that light. For him Buddhism was one of many cults and faiths, by no means mutually exclusive, all of which led to salvation, and all of which were respectable and worthy of honour. Thus, in medieval North India, the Buddha came to be looked on as the ninth of the ten incarnations of the great god Vishnu, and Buddhism gradually lost its individuality, becoming a special and rather unorthodox Hindu sect, which, like many others, did not survive. Hinduism, relying for its strength mainly on independent brahmans and ascetics, and on domestic ceremonies, suffered from the Muslim invasion, but was not seriously weakened by it. Buddhism, by now mainly concentrated in large monasteries, and already rapidly declining in influence, could not stand up to the change. In the first rush of the Muslim advance down the Ganges Nalanda and other great monasteries of Bihar were sacked, libraries were burnt, and monks were put to the sword. The survivors fled to the mountains of Nepal and Tibet, and Buddhism in India was dead.[37]

Several other explanations have also been offered for these phenomena of history. First, Buddhism was not only entirely a product of India but its philosophy was in line with the Vedas and the Upanishads. Buddhism, in fact, emphasizes in its social domain those parts of the Upanishads that ridicule the priest-class and ritualism and minimizes the importance of caste. Secondly, the Mahayana school of Buddhism accommodated the Brahmanical system and forms. It also, like the Hindus,[38] made Buddha a God. Thirdly, under Ashoka's state patronage, Buddhism spread rapidly both within India and outside and when the process of its decline in India commenced it was accompanied by migration of Buddhist scholars and monks from India to China. Fourthly, there was a major revival in Hinduism and it attained great heights under the leadership of Shankaracharya in the eighth century. It was the genius of Shankaracharya which united Hindus spread over the entire length and breadth of India under its *maths*. Shankaracharya assimilated several features of Buddhism in his zeal to reform the Hindu order and played a primordial role in re-establishing Hindu hegemony in the subcontinent. This made some scholars comment that Shankaracharya was 'almost a Buddhist in disguise'.

The encounter between the Vedic philosophy and the Buddhist precepts is a highly interesting dialogue of great value in understanding the Indian mind. The fact that Buddha was a Hindu and died a Hindu is significant. It is equally important to know that Buddhism attained its highest expression in India, both in terms of literature and institutions such as monasteries and universities. The Buddhist world view generated introspection among the Hindu elite. As a response, a revitalized Hindu society, on the one hand, decried the increasing role of rituals and rigidity of caste structures and, on the other, incorporated Buddha into its pantheon by treating him as an incarnation of Vishnu. Buddhism is anti-caste but allows divisions according to occupation. Hinduism, by adding several occupational categories to already existing castes, assimilated the economic structure of Buddhism without destroying its own. This made Hinduism retain the caste system and also acquire a certain degree of immunity from Buddhism.

However, Buddhism was to continue elsewhere. It spread to India's neighbours as a part of the general expansion of Indian civilization. The spread of Indian culture carried Buddhism to Nepal, Tibet, Bhutan, Sikkim, Sri Lanka, Vietnam, Cambodia, Java, Myanmar, and Thailand. Buddhism also spread to Central Asia, China, Korea, Japan—areas that had strong spiritual traditions of their own. In such countries, Buddhism had a different kind of relationship than to Indian culture. It became domesticated, adapting itself to indigenous traditions and ideas.

It is not clear why the 'other worldliness' of Buddhism was greatly emphasized in India and not in other countries that accepted Buddhism. This could perhaps be ascribed to the fact that the traditional class of priests wanted to dissuade people from embracing Buddhism and used the argument of the 'other worldliness' of Buddhism. It may be mentioned that in China too the followers of Confucius decried Lao Tze's philosophy as too occupied with nature and other worldliness, and of little relevance to common people and their problems.

Scholars have been re-examining the history of the Buddhist doctrine in the light of modern ideas. Buddha has been considered a rationalist, an empiricist, and a social prophet, and the dharma an ideology for a new age. Modernists feel strongly about the social role religion should be expected to play. In India, for example, a crusade was initiated in 1958 against the caste theory of untouchability. The solution was presented in the form of a return to Buddhism.

Many aspects of the Buddha's quest will appeal to the modern ethos. As S. Radhakrishnan says:

He is one of those rare spirits who bring to me a realisation of their own divinity and make the spiritual life seem adventurous and attractive, so that they may go forth into the world with a new interest and a new joy at heart.[39]

Buddha's scrupulous empiricism, his demand for intellectual and personal independence, his belief in dialogue, his insistence on the 'middle path' are useful beacons to solve our present problems. We may not be able to fully practise the method he prescribed or raise ourselves to the level of his conduct but one can certainly move towards building institutions and supporting individuals that make for a truly compassionate political and social architecture as called for in the Bahudhā approach.

GURU NANAK (AD 1469–1539)

Guru Nanak began a significant attempt to achieve harmony among Hindus and Muslims and his efforts culminated in the establishment of a separate religion of Sikhs. Guru Nanak became the founder as the first guru of the Sikh religion.

SOCIAL AND POLITICAL MILIEU

The period of decline that began after the eighth century AD in India created a political vacuum that was filled by the Muslim invasions and eventual Muslim rule in India. Thus commenced the third civilizational encounter: between Islam and the Hindu world view.

Islam in a predominantly Hindu society became the religion of the ruling elite for nearly 600 years till India came under British colonial rule. It inculcated among its believers faith in a single God,[40] a rigid code of worship, and a strict way of living. To its believers, Islam prescribed a dietary system, dress, language, music, codes of marriage and divorce, architecture, and spirituality. Unlike Mahavira and Buddha, Muhammad would not and could not be accommodated into the Hindu pantheon. The economic and social principles of Islam, insofar as they dealt with property and inheritance, marriage and divorce, also came in the way of harmonization with Hindu marriage and property codes.

There were, however, significant attempts to find a *modus vivendi* between Islam and Hinduism. It meant that India had to devise a means by which Hindus and Muslims could live together in a society based on different spiritual and social conceptions. In fact, Islam gradually lost its Arabic and Persian identity and absorbed many Hindu folk traditions. The influences from Persia and Central Asia gradually began to coexist with indigenous traditions in languages, styles of dress, music, and the cuisine of South Asia. The creative genius of the Indian people—both Hindus and Muslims—found unique expression in Sufism and Bhakti literature, in music and painting, in the birth of the Urdu language and the enrichment of other Indian languages, and in architecture and urban centres.

Islam came to South Asia first as a religion and then as a political force. The peripheral Arab conquest of Sind (beginning AD 711) was a significant beginning. The century following the Arab conquest of Sind saw the sharing of knowledge between Indian and Arab scholars. For example, the scientific study of astronomy in Islam commenced under the influence of an Indian work, the *Siddhanta*, which had been brought to Baghdad in about 771 and translated. The Hindu numerical system entered the Muslim world about the same time. Later, in the ninth century, India contributed the decimal system to Arab mathematics.

Muslim mysticism in India, like Muslim scholastic theology in India, entered the country in a well-developed form. During the twelfth and fifteenth centuries, three great Sufi orders had migrated from Iraq and Persia into northern India: the Chishti, the Suhrawardi, and the Firdausi.[41]

A bhakti movement already flourished among the Hindus, particularly in the south. This was based on the teachings of the Alvar[42] sants of Tamil Nadu. The bhakti tradition in India, just like the Sufis, taught that God is the one and only reality. The best way to serve God is by absolute submission to his will. The best way to approach God is by meditating and singing hymns of love and praise.

The Sufi poems and Hindu devotional songs produced an amalgam that greatly facilitated social intercourse among Hindus and Muslims and created harmony among them in villages and cities. The two most outstanding poets of this fusion were Ramananda (1400–1470) and his disciple Kabir (1440–1518).[43] The fifteenth and sixteenth centuries saw the spread of the Bhakti movement throughout India: Sankardev and Madhavdev in Assam, Chaitanya in Bengal; Jnaneshwar, Namdev, and Tukaram in Maharashtra; Mirabai in Rajasthan; Sadhana in Sindh; and Tulsidas and Surdas in Uttar Pradesh.

It was in this social and political milieu that Guru Nanak was born in April 1469, in Talwandi, a village north-west of Lahore (now in Pakistan). He was the son of a revenue official and belonged to the Kshatriya caste. He received his elementary education in Sanskrit, Persian, and Punjabi, was married at the age of thirteen years and was later blessed with two sons. Nanak began his career as an accountant in the nawab of Sultanpur's office. It was here that he came into contact with a Muslim colleague called Mardana. The two began to organize community meetings where hymns written by Nanak and set to music by Mardana were sung.

At the age of twenty-nine years, Nanak had a mystical experience that became the turning point in his life. This was a revelation from God which made him declare that there is no Hindu or Muslim. Abandoning worldly pursuits, Nanak undertook four long voyages in four separate directions. First, he went eastward as far as Assam. Then he moved towards the south and visited Tamil Nadu as well as Sri Lanka. His third journey was to the northern regions of the Himalayas. His fourth journey was towards the west to Mecca, Medina, and as far as Basra and Baghdad. These travels facilitated the consolidation of Hindu–Muslim ideas of accommodation and syncretism in his mind.[44]

Nam Japo (the recital of all that is true), *Kirat Karo* (dignity of labour as the true manifestation of service), and *Wand Chhako* (the voluntary sharing of honest earnings among all) constituted Guru Nanak's vision for the evolution of an egalitarian society, a society, where the barriers of caste, creed, religion, colour, and of high and low had no place.

The Sikh religion deals more with the way in which life has to be lived rather than its wider philosophy. It is based on faith, but a faith rooted in rational conviction. Truth is an illumination of the soul, an intuitive realization, and it is termed *naam*.

Before Guru Nanak, Kabir had redirected the popular fervour of Bhakti and Sufi devotionalism towards a supreme transcendental godhead that subsumed both Allah of Islam and Brahman of Hinduism. Through his songs and preachings, he brought a rare kind of understanding among Hindus and Muslims, rich and poor.

Kabir believed in the divinity of the creation and also in the existence of a creator, God. His vision, however, was that of unity between approaches to God, between Hinduism and Islam. He claimed that he was the son of both Allah and Ram and he used to ridicule the institutions of both the mosque and the temple.

If God is in the mosque, to whom does this world belong?. . .If Ram is in the image that you worship, who can know what happens outside?. . .Kabir is the son of Allah and of Ram. He is my guru, he is my pir.' (*Guru* and *pir* are the Hindu and Sufi words respectively for a spiritual teacher.)[45]

His verses constitute the folk wisdom of the common people. Both Hindus and Muslims claim him and revere his poetry for its intense devotionalism and remarkable vigour and directness. Because of his rejection of caste, his biting criticism of the prejudices of Hindus and Muslims, and his insistence on inner devotion as opposed to outward observance, he has been hailed in modern India by leaders like Rabindranath Tagore and Mahatma Gandhi as the authentic voice of the Indian people. Kabir usually referred to God as 'Ram' or 'Hari', which are the names of Vishnu, but it is clear that he did not use these names in a sectarian way. He regards God as the *satguru*, the true guru who enlightens human beings with an inner light.[46]

Like Kabir, Guru Nanak insisted on the unity of the godhead and on the equality of all believers regardless of community or caste. The Hindu priests and the Muslim ulema had developed a vested interest in promoting disharmony and division among Hindus and Muslims. They virtually wanted to take God into their hands and took full advantage of dividing God's followers into Muslims and Hindus, Shia and Sunni, Vaishnava and Shaiva. Guru Nanak wanted people to look beyond religious divisions and to concentrate on His name and on His word as revealed to the Guru, and pay full attention to righteous conduct and truth. It is only while traversing this road that one can obtain divine grace to overcome karma and attain salvation. Many people from Punjab's trading and cultivating classes were drawn to this creed and formed a brotherhood (*panth*) under the nine gurus who succeeded Guru Nanak.

The Sikhs believe in ten gurus and the Granth Sahib. Among the gurus, special mention may be made of two, namely the fifth, Guru

Arjan Dev (1563–1606), and the tenth, Guru Gobind Singh (1675–1708).

It was Guru Arjan Dev, the fifth guru, who succeeded in the compilation of the Adi Granth (original Book) which later became Guru Granth Sahib. Adi Granth or the Granth Sahib has in the beginning *Japji*—nearly 1000 hymns, composed by Guru Nanak, which Sikhs recite at dawn each day. This great monument of the Sikhs is the collection of the writings of the first five gurus and the works of Hindu and Muslim saints from all over India, including Kabir. Guru Arjan Dev installed the Granth Sahib as the sacred scripture of the Sikhs, a step that had significant consequences. The Sikhs, not very proficient either in Sanskrit or Arabic, found in the hymns of the Granth Sahib, couched in a native language intelligible to them, a source of great inspiration and contentment.

It was the genius of the tenth guru, Guru Gobind Singh, that the *khalsa*—the brotherhood of all true Sikh believers—was created. It was a great institutional innovation that brought unity and cohesion among the Sikhs. The tenth guru also gave the Sikhs a separate identity—an identity that gave male Sikhs a distinct physical appearance as compared to a Hindu or a Muslim. The male believers in the khalsa were meant to wear five conspicuous symbols, popularly known as the five Ks: uncut hair (*kesh*), a comb (*kangha*), shorts (*kach*), a steel bracelet (*kara*) and a steel dagger (*kirpan*). Another great contribution made by the tenth guru was the conversion of the Adi Granth, into a guru. The intention was not to worship the book but to put it at the heart of Sikh prayers and temples, and this act was performed by placing it at the centre of each gurdwara. The blessing of the Granth Sahib is particularly taken during marriage ceremonies.

The Sikhs have a distinct personality and constitute an enduring religious community separate from both Hindus and Muslims, but always in close social contact with them. Kabir and Guru Nanak, in particular, by putting *sabad*, the revelation of God through the spoken word and his emphasis on recitation of the name (nam) of God, did bring about a new way of looking at religious systems. The role of the guru or the teacher who gives knowledge of the word or name was another distinctive contribution of Sikhism to Indian spirituality.

Though later there were conflicts between Sikhs and Muslims on the one hand, and Hindus and Muslims on the other, Sikhism has shown a way in which rapprochement is possible between these communities if we travel on the path of trust and accommodation.

Sikhism displays an accommodating attitude by adopting the doctrine of karma and avatara of God from the Hindu tradition and by accepting the emphasis on the oneness of God, on congregational worship, rejection of the caste system, and the worship of idols from Islam. It is true that the entire vocabulary and philosophic terminology of the Sikh faith stems from Hindu sources and its major hymns are expressions of loving devotion to Ram and Krishna. At another level, the Sufis of the Islamic tradition had a profound influence on the Sikhs, and the fact that both the Sikhs and the Sufis addressed Hindus and Muslims for harmonious living at the personal level. The message of love and harmony had widespread acceptance and influence.

It may be mentioned that all these mystic poets, whether Hindu, Muslim or Sikh, wrote and sang in the vernacular language, not in Sanskrit, Persian, or Arabic. Kabir was of Muslim origin while Nanak was a Hindu. Together they professed deism in order to emphasize the need for uniting Hinduism and Islam. Kabir, in particular, indiscriminately called his God by its Islamic as well as Hindu name: Allah or Ram. Unfortunately, this powerful movement of popular devotion was not emulated by philosophers or theologians, nor by the politicians of the two religions. Accordingly, this movement never turned into the new religion or the new politics. It is sad that the Bhakti movement that might have provided a basis for the union of the two communities of Hindus and Muslims, and thus the birth of a new India, was never realized. The non-acceptance of teachings of Nanak and Kabir in our social and political processes contributed four centuries later in the partition of India, in 1947, on religious lines.

LORD MAHAVIRA, LORD BUDDHA, AND GURU NANAK

Lord Mahavira, Lord Buddha, and Guru Nanak each showed us 'how to live' based on what they had experienced. The trail blazed by them has guided in a substantive manner succeeding generations of Indians as well as people of several countries in Asia and the world. Their personal examples and philosophies of life enlarged and enriched India's civilizational strength. Each one rebelled against caste discrimination, rituals and priest craft, image worship and irrationality in every form. It is a strange coincidence that in the Indian social order marked by the caste system, each one of these spiritual leaders was born in a Kshatriya family, and not in the traditional caste of priests and scholars, that is, the Brahmins.

Buddha discovered the fundamental truths of his religion through his personal work and experience. Jainism had, however, existed even before Lord Mahavira. There is growing evidence that his predecessor, Parsva, who had lived in India 250 years before him, had taught the principles of Jainism and so had several Tirthankars before him. And yet at the same time, Lord Mahavira became the outstanding and authoritative voice of Jainism and a pathfinder in the true sense of the term. Guru Nanak strove to forge unity among the followers of Hinduism and Islam and received inspiration from devotional songs and later composed several such *bhajans* (songs). He was a product of the Bhakti movement as well as of Sufism.

All three pathfinders were concerned with prevailing conditions in their societies, and took a great interest in the affairs of the State despite their status as monks or gurus. It is no wonder, therefore, that many years after the death of Buddha, the path shown by him, as enshrined in the Buddhist philosophy, became the religion of the state under Ashoka. Similarly, Jainism influenced the Maurya and Gupta kings. A very late tradition maintains that Chandragupta Maurya converted to Jainism towards the end of his reign, renounced the throne in favour of his son, and went to south India, ending his life there by deliberate starvation in the orthodox Jain manner.[47] Sikhism also became the religion of small kingdoms in the Punjab and later of a larger territory in north India under the leadership of Maharaja Ranjit Singh.

Each one of them believed in the Bahudhā approach of the middle way, of creating an understanding among different points of view, and in the case of Guru Nanak, especially, among the two dominant religions—Hinduism and Islam. The theory of anekantavada of Jainism and madhyam nikai of Buddhism directly attacked the exclusivist position in religious and social affairs. Like his contemporary Kabir, Guru Nanak ridiculed rituals as well as the traditional forms of worship of both Hindus and Muslims and believed that his God was both Ram and Rahim.

Each one of them wanted to reach and appeal to the people and not confine themselves to scholars, priests, and the erudite. Hence each one used the *boli* (dialect) of the common people as against the *bhasha* (language) of the scholars.

Each one advocated non-violence with varying degrees of emphasis. In the case of Lord Mahavira, belief in non-violence was absolute. He enjoined his colleagues and followers to observe extreme carefulness in order not to disturb any living being, not even an insect, however troublesome. It therefore flows naturally that the Jains will be strict vegetarians. There were no such prescriptions from Lord Buddha or by Guru Nanak about food.

The religions of the world can be broadly categorized among those that emphasize the object and those that insist on experience. All those paths that emphasize the object call for conduct directed to a superior authority as in Judaism, Christianity, and Islam. The Hindus, Buddhists, Jains, and Sikhs attach importance to experience. *Bodhi*, or enlightenment, which Buddha attained and his followers aim at, is an experience. So is what Mahavira attained through *sadhna* (perseverance) or Nanak through Japji (devotional songs). The possibility of obtaining the experience guides a person to move on a path where a *nirmal* (pure) mind, and love and compassion are essential prerequisites. Experience obtained by journeying on such a path facilitates the realization of harmonious living.

The story of Gautama has particular relevance in our times. We too are living in a period of transition and change, as was north India during the sixth and fifth centuries BC. Like the people of north India then, we find that the traditional ways of experiencing the sacred, and discovering an ultimate meaning in our lives, are either difficult or impossible. As a result, a void has become an essential part of the modern experience. Like Gautama, we live in an age of political violence and have had terrifying glimpses of man's inhumanity to man. In our society too there is widespread malaise, urban despair and anomie, and we are sometimes fearful of the new world order that is emerging.

The Buddhist approach of the middle path, of non-violence, of love and compassion, influences people of a large number of countries in the world. The Buddhist approach of rational self-enquiry also enables a person to achieve a higher state of discipline and harmony beyond narrow sectarian and national prejudices. All these become axiomatic when seen in the light of the well-known Buddhist maxim: 'Be a lamp unto yourself' (*Appa Deepo Bhav*).

NOTES

1. The dialogue between Buddha and his principal disciple Ananda as well as *Dhammapada,* the holy book of Buddhism, refer to this powerful rational thought. The relevant portions are reproduced below:

   (i) *Appa Dipo bhav or so karohi dipmatno.*
       (Be ye lamps unto yourselves)

Therefore, O Ananda, be ye lamps unto yourselves. Be ye a refuge to yourselves. Betake yourselves to no external refuge. Hold fast to the Truth as a lamp. Hold fast as a refuge to the Truth. Look not for refuge to any one besides yourselves. And how, Ananda, is a brother to be a lamp unto himself, a refuge to himself, betaking himself to no external refuge, holding fast to the Truth as a lamp, holding fast as a refuge to the Truth, looking not for refuge to any one besides himself?

And whosoever, Ananda, either now or after I am dead, shall be a lamp unto themselves, and a refuge unto themselves, shall betake themselves to no external refuge, but holding fast to the Truth as their lamp. . . . shall not look for refuge to any one besides themselves. . . . it is they. . . . who shall reach the very top most height! But they must be anxious to learn.

(*Mahaparinibbana-sutta*, in *Sacred Books of the Buddhists*, translated by various oriental scholars and edited by T. W. Rhys Davids, Vol. III, The Pali Text Society, London, 1977, pp. 108–9.)

(ii) *so karohi dipmatno, khippne bvayam pandito bhav*
So strive quickly and wisely to make yourself an island. (a secure place safe from the ocean of samsara).

(*Dhammapada*, Verse 236, the above translation by Rhys Davids. The word 'Dipa' in Pali has two connotations: one is Rhys Davids' version where it has been translated as 'lamp'. Some of the scholars have criticized Rhys Davids' translation preferring 'island', which is based on the interpretation in the *Atakatha*s.)

2. Wislawa Szymborska Exclusive Poetry @ PAN, translated from Polish by Joanna Maria Trzeciak at *http://www.pan.net/trzeciak/*. in November 2004.

3. The ten avataras of Lord Vishnu are:
    Matsyavatara (the fish), Koorma (the tortoise), Varaaha (the boar), Narasimha (the man lion), Vaamana (the dwarf), Parsurama (the angry man), Ram (the perfect human), Balarama and Krishna (the divine statesman), and Kalki (yet to appear).

4. An avatara is a personal form of the Supreme Being. When a personal form of God descends from the higher dimensional realm to the material world, He (or She) is known as an incarnation, or avatara. Although the avataras appear in different forms at different times, places, and circumstances, their purpose is one: to reveal the Absolute Truth in this world.

5. यदा यदा हि धर्मस्य ग्लानिर्भवति भारत।
    अभ्युत्थानमधर्मस्य तदात्मानं सृजाम्यहम्।
    (Bhagavad Gita 4.7–8), Dr. (Mrs.) Vedwati Vaidik, Richa Prakashan, New Delhi, 1997, p. 179–80.

6. Mahatma Gandhi's views on Buddha have been compiled as introductory pages to the book *The Way of the Buddha*, Publications Division, Government of India, New Delhi, 1995. The book opens with the essay entitled 'Gandhi on Buddha', n.p.

7. R. Garbe, 'Lokayata', *Encyclopedia of Religion and Ethics,* edited by James Hastings, Vol. VIII, T&T Clark, Edinburgh, 1958, p. 138. 'There are clear indications of the presence in India, as early as pre-Buddhistic times, of teachers of a pure materialism; and undoubtedly these theories have had numerous adherents in India from that period onwards to the present day'.

8. Jainism is an independent ancient school of thought.

9. The historicity of tirthankars previous to Lord Mahavira is in doubt. However, the historicity of Tirthankar Parsva who preceded Lord Mahavira by 250 years is being increasingly accepted.

10. Indian culture consists of two main trends: Sramanic and Brahmanic. The Vedic tradition comes under the Brahmanic trend. The Sramanic school covers the Jain, Buddhist, and similar other ascetic traditions. The Brahmanic schools accept the authority of the Vedas and Vedic literature. The Jains and Buddhists have their own canons and canonical literature.

11. Y. J. Padmarajiah, *A Comparative Study of the Jaina Theories of Reality and Knowledge,* Motilal Banarsidass, New Delhi, 1963. This book makes an incisive analysis of anekantavada as enunciated by Lord Mahavira and his followers and also its criticism.

12. S. Radhakrishnan, *Occasional Speeches and Writings: October 1952–January 1956,* The Publications Division, Government of India, Delhi, 1956, p. 224.

13. Hiriyanna, by no means an unsympathetic exponent even of Jainism, observes: 'The half-hearted character of the Jaina enquiry is reflected in the seven-fold mode of predication (*sapta-bhangi*), which stops at giving us the several partial views together, without attempting to overcome the opposition in them by a proper synthesis. It is all right so far as it cautions us against one-sided conclusions but it leaves us in the end ... with little more than one-sided solutions. The reason for it, if it is not prejudice against absolutism, is the desire to keep close to common beliefs'. (Padmarajiah, *A Comparative Study of the Jaina Theories of Reality and Knowledge,* p. 364).

14. Lord Mahavira never entertained any doubt about non-violence and instead set a very high level of abstinence in movement, food to be consumed so that no harm is done to animals and insects. In fact, never before in history, and ever since, has such an extreme emphasis on non-violence been either advocated and/or practised both as a philosophy or as a way of life.

15. The *sramans* such as the Buddha or Mahavira, the founder of Jainism, dropped ritual altogether and focused exclusively on the inner 'self'.

The ego is a problem to itself. It is always aware of its partiality and always assumed the whole beyond itself. Only when it aspires to reach beyond itself does it become transcendental.

16. This is illustrated by a classical incident/exchange between Akbar and Birbal:

One day the Mughal emperor Akbar asked his courtier, Birbal, 'What is the sweetest thing in the world?' Birbal replied: 'My lord, words are the sweetest and words are the bitterest'. Akbar did not believe this. How can words be sweet or bitter, he thought and dismissed the idea. A few days later to prove his point, Birbal invited the empress for dinner at his house. When she was leaving his house, after a sumptuous dinner, Birbal instructed his servants to clean up after the queen, using swear words and inappropriate language. The empress overheard the words of insult and was shocked to learn that Birbal thought of her in such a negative way. She felt deeply wounded. When she returned to her palace she complained to the emperor about the incident. This was very hard for the emperor to believe. The next day, he summoned the prime minister. When Birbal arrived, Akbar asked him: 'How dare you insult my wife using swear words?' Birbal replied: 'My Lord, you said words are neither sweet nor bitter, so how can they cause harm or discomfort? How can words hurt the empress?'

17. Now this, O monks, is the noble truth of pain: birth is painful, old age is painful, sickness is painful, death is painful. Contact with unpleasant things is painful, separation from pleasant things is painful and not getting what one wishes is also painful. In short, the five *khandha*s of grasping are painful.

Now this, O monks, is the noble truth of the cause of pain: that craving, which leads to rebirth, combined with pleasure and lust, finding pleasure here and there, namely, the craving for passion, the craving for existence, the craving for non-existence.

Now this, O monks, is the noble truth of the cessation of pain: the cessation without a remainder of that craving, abandonment, forsaking, release, non-attachment.

Now this, O monks, is the noble truth of the way that leads to the cessation of pain: this is the noble Eightfold Path, namely, right views, right intention, right speech, right action, right livelihood, right effort, right mindfulness, right concentration.

(*Dhammacakkappavattana-katha*, Mahavagga, Part I, Bombay University Edition, Bombay, 1944, pp. 15–16).

18. The name of Gautama, by which the future Buddha was known, is perhaps derived from that of Gotama, the ancient rsi, or seer, to whom are ascribed some of the hymns of the *Rig Veda*. He becomes Buddha, or Buddha, the 'enlightened' or 'wise', only after his attainment of perfect wisdom under the Bo-tree. Other titles given to him are

Sakyamuni, 'the sage of the Sakyas'; Siddhartha, 'he who has accomplished his aim'; and Tathagata, 'he who has arrived at the truth'. (*The Encyclopedia on Religion and Ethics*, edited by James Hastings, Vol. 2, T&T Clark, Edinburgh, 1981, p. 881.)

19. B. P. Singh, *India's Culture: The State, the Arts and Beyond*, Oxford University Press, New Delhi, 1998, p. 19.

20. *The Way of the Buddha*, Publications Division, Government of India, New Delhi, 1995.

21. *Young India*, 15 December 1927.

22. *With Gandhiji in Ceylon*, p. 138.

23. Lao Tze was born in the year 604 and in his 80th year he set out for the western border of China (Tibet) but it is not known when he died. The essential teaching of Lao Tze is the *Tao*, or Way, to ultimate reality— the way of the universe exemplified in Nature. The harmony of opposites (*T'ai Ch'ai*) is achieved through a blend of the *Yin* (feminine force) and the *Yang* (masculine force); this harmony can be cultivated through creative quietude (*wu wei*), an effortless action whose power (*te*) maintains equanimity and balance.
    (See *Grolier International Encyclopedia Vol. 12*, Grolier Incorporated, Danbury, Connecticut, 1991, p. 202.)

24. Jay L. Garfield, *The Fundamental Wisdom of the Middle Way: Nagarjuna's Mulamadhyamakakarika*, Oxford University Press, New York, 1995. The book provides a clear and eminently readable translation of Nagarjuna's seminal work.
    The middle path at philosophical level could best be described through the following words:

    Whatever is dependently co-arisen
    That is explained to be emptiness.
    That, being a dependent designation,
    Is itself the middle way.

25. The growth of the essentials of Dharma is possible in many ways. But its root lies in restraint to speech, which means that there would be no extolment of one's own sect or disparagement of other sects on inappropriate occasions and that it should be moderate in every case even on appropriate occasions. On the contrary, other sects should be duly honoured in every way on all occasions. If a person acts in this way, he not only promotes his own sect but also benefits other sects. But, if a person acts otherwise, he not only injures his own sect but also harms other sects. Truly, if a person extols his own sect and disparages other sects with a view to glorifying his sect owing merely to his attachment to it, he injures his own sect, very severely by acting in that way. Therefore restraint in regard to speech is commendable. (See *Asoka's Rock Edict No. XII*, Girnar as translated by Radha Kumud

Mookerji in his book. *Asoka*, Motilal Banarsidass, New Delhi, 2002, pp. 158–61 and as paraphrased by the author.

26. The Dalai Lama, His Holiness Tenzin Gyatso, *Kindness, Clarity, and Insight* translated and edited, Jeffrey Hopkins, co-edited, Elizabeth Napper, Motilal Banarsidass, New Delhi, 1997, p. 29.

27. The Dalai Lama, *Awakening the Mind, Lightening the Heart*, Thorsons (HarperCollins), London, 1997, p. xiv.

28. The Dalai Lama, *A Policy of Kindness: An Anthology of Writings By and About the Dalai Lama*, Snow Lion Publications, New York, 1990, p. 60.

29. Karen Armstrong, *Buddha*, Viking Penguin, New York, 2001, pp. 150–1.

30. 'The word dhamma denotes not only what *is,* but what *should* be. The Buddha's dhamma was a diagnosis of the problem of life and a prescription for cure, which must be followed exactly. Each of the Truths had three components in his sermon. First, he made the bhikkus see the Truth. Next, he explained what had to be done about it: suffering had to be "fully known"; Craving, the Cause of Suffering, had to be "given up"; Nibbana, the Cessation of Suffering, had to "become a reality" in the heart of the Arahant; and the Eightfold Path must be "followed". Finally, the Buddha explained what he *had* achieved: he *had* understood *dukkha* "directly"; he *had* abandoned craving; he *had* experienced Nibbana; he *had* followed the Path to its conclusion. It was, he explained, when he had proved to himself that his Dhamma really worked and that he had actually completed the programme, that his enlightenment had been complete: "I have achieved the final release!" he had cried triumphantly. He had indeed been liberated from *samsara*, he knew that the Middle Way was the true Path, and his own life and person proved it.' See Armstrong, *Buddha*, p. 104.

31. *The Way of the Buddha*, Publications Division. *Digha-nikaya*, Part II, *Mahaparinibbana-sutta*, Bombay University Edition, 1936, p. 123.

32. S. Radhakrishnan, *Eastern Religions and Western Thought*, Oxford University Press, New Delhi, 1985 (Sixth impression), p. 67.

33. Satish Kumar, *The Buddha and the Terrorist: The Story of Angulimala*, The Viveka Foundation: A Centre for Alternative Perspectives, New Delhi, 2004.

34. In several scriptures he was a Brahmin by caste. For our purpose, it is significant that he was a terrorist.

35. Jawaharlal Nehru, *The Discovery of India*, Jawaharlal Nehru Memorial Fund, New Delhi, 1982, p. 178.

36. *Young India,* 24 November 1927. Mahatma Gandhi's views on Buddha have been compiled as introductory pages to the book *The Way of the Buddha*.

37. A.L. Basham, *The Wonder That Was India: A Survey of the Culture of the Indian Subcontinent Before the Coming of the Muslims*, Grove Press Inc., New York, 1954, pp. 265–6.

38. I cannot more properly commence the native accounts concerning this avatar of Buddha than by inserting the subsequent extract relating to him from the Asiatic Researches. It is part of a translation by Sir John Shore of an inscription on a silver plate found in a cave near Islamabad, the first sentence of which reads as follows:

     God sent into the world Buddha—Avatar to instruct and direct the steps of angels and of men.

     Thomas Maurice, *The History of Hindostan: Its Arts, and Its Sciences*, W. Bulmer and Co., London, 1795, p. 485.

39. S. Radhakrishnan, *Gautama: The Buddha*, Hind Kitabs, Bombay, 1945, pp. 64–5.

40. The belief is that there had been authentic prophets of God before Muhammad, the founder of Islam (570–632), but that he was their culmination; it is said that no valid prophet would follow him. Muhammad was hence 'The Seal of the Prophets'. For further details, see Houston Smith's *Islam*, New York, HarperCollins, San Francisco, 2001.

41. The Chisti was the largest and most popular. Ibid., p. 450.

42. The poets who sang the praise of Vishnu as their Lord in Tamil are known as the Alvars. Poihai of Kanchipuram, Bhutam of Mahabalipuram, and Pey of Mylapore, Madras were the first three Alvars.

43. There is some uncertainty about the year of Kabir's birth. The Wikipedia's website records as follows: born in 1398 according to some accounts'.

44. Consolidation of ideas about various methods of worship that people practised and that at the proper level there is need to have respect for each faith.

45. Octavio Paz, *In Light of India*, Harcourt Brace and Company, New York, 1995, p. 44.

46. Ainslie T. Embree (ed.), *Sources of Indian Tradition: From the Beginning to 1800*, Vol. I, Penguin, New Delhi, 1991, p. 373.

47. Arthur Cotterell, *The Penguin Encyclopedia of Classical Civilisations*, Penguin, Hong Kong, 1995, p. 196.

5
The Builders

We must be the change we wish to see in the world[1]
Every reform in the world has been initiated by the efforts of one man[2]

—Mahatma Gandhi

It may be recalled that the fusion of the Aryans and the Dravidians in different parts of India in varying proportions (more Aryans in the north and more Dravidians in the south) settled the demographic composition of India. Later armed bands of Sakas and Hunas and the armies of invading chiefs from Central Asia, professing different faiths and speaking different languages, planted themselves within India. The Aryan elements are equated with the Vedic and Puranic culture of the north and the pre-Aryan with the Dravidian and Tamil culture of the south. The Vedic texts of 1500 BC have several Munda, Dravidian, and other non-Sanskritic terms. These denote intermingling of ideas and even spoken words.[3]

The invasions, conquests, and eventual establishment of Muslim rule in India enormously affected the Indian mind. Over the years Islam was greatly influenced and was in turn influenced by the prevailing Indian way of looking at things. The new bhakti approach as revived by Ramananda, Jayadeva, Ekanath, Tukaram, Sankardev, Chaitanya, Mirabai, and Tulsidas revived values of a cosmopolitan and inclusive society based on love and equality beyond the restrictions of caste and gender. Simultaneously, poets and gurus, such as Kabir and Nanak, created a fusion between Hindu and Muslim ideas. It became commonplace for Hindus and Muslims to visit Sufi shrines for prayers, a tradition that continues to this day.

At the political level this amalgamation produced an emperor like Akbar who felt that truth was not the exclusive possession of any one religion and the sacred books of all religions taught similar truths. He built, at Fatehpur Sikri, the famous House of Worship, Ibadat Khana, where Muslims, Hindus, Jains, Zoroastrians, and Christians could sit and enter into dialogue. He promulgated a new creed, Din-i-Ilahi, which was an amalgam of different religions—an expression of the Indian experience of tolerance and mutual accommodation. That this new faith and order did not take off illustrates the fact that the world is not yet prepared to discard its myriad experiences and accept a single faith.

The establishment of British rule over India by the end of the eighteenth century brought India in direct contact with Christianity, although Christianity was known to Indians from the time of its origin. The impact of Christianity and English education brought about a fresh awakening among Hindus. Raja Rammohan Roy (1772–1833) was the first to see the fundamental unity of spirit in the Hindu, Christian, and Muslim religions. In 1828, he founded the Brahmo Samaj (Society of believers in God), and admitted men of all creeds, classes, and castes into this organization. This message was carried further by his colleagues in Bengal. In the western part of India, the Arya Samaj founded by Dayananda Saraswati (1824–83) proclaimed that it was necessary to unify all sections of human society for the greater good. As S. Radhakrishnan puts it:

India strove throughout her history for the freedom of spirit and the union of hearts. She does not destroy differences but discovers their underlying affinities. India did not treat other peoples who came to settle as aliens, did not ridicule their customs as incongruous but recognised and accepted them all. She has entered into the lives of others and assimilated elements from outside. When new ideas arise, old traditions are not discarded but are treated with respect and introduced by way of interpretation. She did not crave for uniformity. There is a famous passage in the Prthivi Sukta, of the Atharva Veda which refers to the earth as a mother that bears various peoples, speaking different languages, practising different religious rites according to their various places of abode and nourishes them all with milk with equal affection.[4]

There is ample evidence to establish the kind of dialogue that took place between Buddhist monks and *arhat*s and the Hindu *acharya*s and gurus. Much later, there was also dialogue between Christian missionaries and Hindu leaders. The Christian influence on India, however, went deeper and led to the revival of Indian cultural attainments of the past. During the Mughal rule those who refused to accept Islam were free to preserve the symbols and folklore of the past.

It is significant that conflicts among different religious faiths such as the violent conflicts between the Christian crusaders and Islam did not occur in India. There was, no doubt, desecration and destruction of Buddhist sanghas and libraries and of Hindu temples and places of worship by the invading Muslim militia, but it did not degenerate into the kind of religious war that characterized the conflict that took place between Christians and Muslims. Another significant feature was that a large number of invading armies stayed back and settled down in India, were absorbed in Indian society, and in turn made India their home.

In the nineteenth and twentieth centuries, the emergence of great rational minds and an enormous urge for freedom characterized the Indian scene. The era, which, in historical terms, commenced with Raja Rammohan Roy of Bengal, heralded a major attitudinal change among the people of India. The unequal society that had been built in India over the ages needed to be changed in favour of equality and giving people a greater say in religious, political, and economic systems. The contribution of three leaders is indeed of great historical value: Rabindranath Tagore (1861–1941); Swami Vivekananda (1863–1902); and Mahatma Gandhi (1869–1948). Each one grew to become a formidable figure in his sphere of human activity: Gurudev Tagore in literature, Swami Vivekananda in religion, and Mahatma Gandhi in politics.

SWAMI VIVEKANANDA (1863–1902)

The first leader to make a major impact on the Indian consciousness, in his time and thereafter, was Swami Vivekananda. Narendranath Dutt (Swami Vivekananda) was born into an upper middle-class Kayastha (high caste Hindu) family on 12 January 1863 in Calcutta. During his short life span of thirty-nine years he gave new meaning to the Hindu philosophy of tolerance. It was he who built the Ramakrishna Order to propagate the values of the Vedanta philosophy and to work for the spread of quality education and health care throughout the length and breadth of India.

In what could well be an exposition of the Bahudhā philosophy, Swami Vivekananda explained that the Vedanta philosophy was not Brahmanic or Buddhist, Christian, or Muslim, but the sum total of all these. In his historic address to the Parliament of Religions in Chicago on 11 September 1893, Swami Vivekananda clarified:

The Christian is not to become a Hindu or a Buddhist, nor a Hindu or a Buddhist to become a Christian. But each must assimilate the spirit of the others and yet preserve his individuality and grow according to his own law of growth. If the Parliament of Religions has shown anything to the world it is this: it has proved to the world that holiness, purity and charity are not the exclusive possessions of any church in the world, and that every system has produced men and women of the most exalted character. In the face of this evidence, if anybody dreams of the exclusive survival of his own religion and the destruction of others, I pity him from the bottom of my heart, and point out to him that upon the banner of every religion will soon be written, in spite of resistance: 'Help and not Fight', 'Assimilation and not Destruction', 'Harmony and Peace and not Dissension'.[5]

In one of his speeches in Chicago during the Parliament of Religions meeting, the Swami emphasized the Bahudhā philosophy in the following words:

Do I wish that the Christian would become Hindu? God forbid. Do I wish that the Hindu or Buddhist would become Christian? God forbid.[6]

The Indian idea was to make man find the best that he could in his environment, and live up to it in all sincerity. The Hindu conception has been what was described by Paramahansa Ramakrishna in the form of an aphorism: *Jato mat, tato path*, that is, 'As many opinions, so many ways'. He greatly valued plurality of approach in human affairs and spoke against uniformity. He was in favour of harmony among religious beliefs and against one religion for all. As Swami Vivekananda records:

The greatest misfortune to befall the world would be if all mankind were to recognise and accept but one religion, one universal form of worship, one standard of morality. This would be the death-blow to all religious and spiritual progress. Instead of trying to hasten this disastrous event by inducing persons, through good or evil methods, to conform to our own highest ideal of truth, we ought rather to endeavour to remove all obstacles which prevent men from developing in accordance with their own highest ideals, and thus make their attempt vain to establish one universal religion.[7]

The freedom movement against foreign rule in India drew strength from the life and works of Swami Vivekananda. He believed that if India was to be free, it could not be a land exclusively of Hinduism or of Islam. It must be a united land of different religious communities inspired by the ideal of nationalism. Without this concept of harmony of religions and tolerance of all creeds, the spirit of national consciousness could not have been built up in a land full of diversities.

Swami Vivekananda carried forward Shri Ramakrishna Paramahansa's preachings about unity of all religions and the need for the cessation of inter-religious strife. In a highly imaginative dialogue, Shri Ramakrishna taught him that pity is not enough.

Man is a living God. Do we ever think of showing pity to God? No, on the contrary, we feel blessed to be able to serve and worship Him. Therefore, 'pity' is not the right expression. The right kind of attitude should be to serve 'jiva' as 'Shiva', to serve humanity as the manifestation of Divinity. No one should be hated, for even the sinner is essentially God. The same *Narayana* (God) is present in the guise of the thief or the person lacking in culture, as well as in the righteous and refined.[8]

It has been often stated that the relationship between Ramakrishna and Vivekananda was similar to that between Jesus Christ and Saint Paul. Vivekananda can be fully understood only in the light of Ramakrishna Paramahansa. As Subhas Chandra Bose reflected:

. . . I also regard Ramakrishna and Vivekananda as two aspects of one indivisible personality.[9]

Swami Vivekananda was also greatly influenced by Lord Buddha. He saw great merit in Buddha not calling himself or being addressed as a man who had attained enlightenment. Swami Vivekananda hailed Buddha as follows:

Buddha was the great preacher of equality. Every man and woman has the same right to attain spirituality – that was his teaching. The difference between the priests and the other castes he abolished. Even the lowest were entitled to the highest attainments; he opened the door of Nirvana to one and all.[10]

Vivekananda was also very fond of narrating how Buddha accepted a barber as one of his colleagues.[11]

Like Buddha, Swami Vivekananda highlighted the rule of rationality in human conduct. He believed that whatever we do must be justified and supported by reason. Otherwise our beliefs will be reduced to wishful thinking. Man must learn to live with a religion which commends itself to his intellectual conscience, to the spirit of rationality. Besides, religion should be the sustaining faith that insists on the intellectual and spiritual development of every human being irrespective of his caste, creed, community, or race. Any religion that divides man from man, or supports privileges, exploitation, and wars, cannot commend itself.

Very few thinkers in history have seen religion in terms of human suffering, social discrimination, and poverty removal, as Vivekananda did. He declared:

It is a man-making religion that we want . . . Give up these weakening mysticisms, and be strong . . . let all other, vain gods disappear from our minds. This is the only God that is awake, our own race, everywhere His hands, everywhere His feet, everywhere His ears; He covers everything . . . The first of all worship is the worship of those all around us . . . These are all our gods—men and animals; and the first gods we have to worship are our own countrymen.[12]

Vivekananda maintained that service to God should mean service to the poor. This was neither a sermon relating to a particular ritual nor a narrow injunction to be imposed on one's external life. Discarding monks and pundits, temples and mosques, churches and *satras*, which were traditionally the centres for religious dialogues that enjoined on the participants the need to pursue higher values of renunciation and *moksha*, Vivekananda emphasized something new, and that was to help the poor man realize that his essential divinity is the objective of religion. Vivekananda coined a new word *Daridra-Narayana*—'God in the poor and the lowly'—as a religious axiom aimed at removal of poverty. Daridra-Narayana brought in an element of the sense of duty which was enjoined on men to serve the poor if they wanted to serve God.

The level of social discrimination in Indian society in the nineteenth century was both rampant and deep-seated, and marked by untouchability and casteism. Vivekananda was a sworn enemy of the caste system. Untouchability was something he abhorred because it meant humiliation of man and was inconsistent with the great principle that the Divine is in every being. The *antar-jyoti* in everyone must be allowed to help man in uniting him with the Divine and in this goal there could be no room for untouchability.

Vivekananda went beyond religion and social reform and laid the foundations for the national movement for freedom, progress, and harmony. As Jawaharlal Nehru wrote:

He kept away from politics and disapproved of the politicians of his day. But again and again he laid stress on the necessity for liberty and equality and the raising of the masses. Liberty of thought and action is the only condition of life, of growth and well-being. Where it does not exist, the man, the race, the nation must go. The only hope of India is from the masses. The upper classes are physically and morally dead. He wanted to combine Western progress with India's spiritual background: Make a European society with India's religion. . . .Become an occidental of occidentals in your spirit of equality, freedom, work and energy, and at the same time a Hindu to the very backbone in religious culture and instincts.[13]

Nehru used to hail Vivekananda as one of the great founders of the national modern movement of India for a great number of people who took more or less an active part in that movement at a later date drew their inspiration from Swami Vivekananda. Men like Rama-krishna Paramahansa, men like Swami Vivekananda and men like Mahatma Gandhi were great unifying forces, great constructive geniuses of the world not only in regard to the particular teachings that they taught, but their approach to the world and their conscious and unconscious influence on it is of the most vital importance.[14]

In many ways, Vivekananda went beyond the Bahudhā approach of one truth, many interpretations. For the first time he stated that every religion must serve the poor and should aim at the removal of poverty, ignorance, and disease among the downtrodden people of the society. He further emphasized that in this task there could be no discrimination between man and woman, between one sect and another, between one profession and another. He, in fact, raised service to the poor to the level of worship, and at that level, harmony among different faiths automatically became a pre-condition. Such an environment demands reconciliation among human beings. In order to overcome enemies and animosity we need to renounce hatred and cultivate love and compassion for all.

RABINDRANATH TAGORE (1861–1941)

Rabindranath Tagore was born in May 1861 in Calcutta into a large and rich family. The family's aristocratic features, besides wealth, included a cosmopolitan outlook and the presence of talented young persons in the realm of art and literature, commerce, and services.[15] Rabindranath did not complete his school education as he found the school regimen very boring, but continued with self-education and the pursuit of learning.[16] He started writing poetry at the age of thirteen years and had mystical experiences and visions of beauty, joy, and light at the youthful age of seventeen or eighteen years.[17] He was deeply influenced by the Upanishads, Buddhist religious writings, and mystical Baul songs.[18]

Starting from the Upanishads, he studied the different stages in the evolution of a universal Indian culture, influenced in turn by Buddhism, classical Sanskrit literature, and the mystic tradition of the medieval saint-poets like Kabir, Nanak, and Chaitanya. Tagore edited a book entitled *Hundred Poems of Kabir*.[19] He took keen interest in western literature and philosophy, and wrote a large number of books and essays in elegant prose and magical poetry in Bengali. Finally, he found in the West's ideas of humanism a link to his vision of India's ancient history and ideals.

Tagore's creative genius found expression in poetry, novels, short stories, plays, songs, paintings, and essays. His works, including the *Gitanjali,* have greatly influenced the Indian mind and are invaluable in understanding the Bahudhā philosophy. It was Tagore who described his Bengali family as the product of 'a confluence of three cultures: Hindu, Muslim and British'.[20]

Rabindranath describes God as *sivam, santam, advaitam*— perfection, peace, and nonduality. God is both personal and super-personal. He is immanent and transcendent.

To me religion is too concrete a thing, though I have no right to speak about it. But if ever I have somehow come to realise God, or if the vision of God has ever been granted to me, I must have received the vision through this world, through men, through trees and birds and beasts, the dust and the soil.[21]

The idea of a direct relationship with God found expression in many of Tagore's writings. He believed in one god—the god of love. He abhorred social injustice, superstitious beliefs and practices, the caste system, rituals, and untouchability. He extolled the virtues of forgiveness, purity, compassion, and equality. He puts it forcefully in describing his new religion:

Leave this chanting and singing and telling of beads! Whom dost thou worship in this lonely dark corner of a temple with doors all shut? Just open thine eyes and see thy god is not before thee!

He is there where the tiller is tilling the hard ground and where the path-maker is breaking stones. He is with them in sun and in shower and his garment is covered with dust. Put off thy holy mantle and even like him come down on the dusty soil![22]

There were different stages in the development of humanism in Tagore's mental make-up. For example, *Naivedya* ('Offerings', 1901) was as much a prayer to god as it was for people in general. In his book *The Religion of Man* (1932), Tagore traces the growth of the idea of God from primitive notions to universality. Today, he says, all barriers are down and 'The God of humanity has arrived at the gates of the ruined temple of the tribe'. This was also reflected in his earlier conversation with Albert Einstein in 1926 where Einstein had asked him: 'Truth, then, or Beauty, is not independent of Man?' Rabindranath's answer was,

Truth is realised through man. . . .We individuals approach it through our own mistakes and blunders, through our accumulated experience, through our illumined consciousness. . . .[23]

In another dialogue with Einstein, Tagore advocated that science must serve society and humanity.

Tagore insisted that science, which he studied and wrote about from an early age, must, in its application to society, serve society, and not vice versa. This was a conviction with a philosophical basis. In 1930, talking to Einstein, Tagore told him: 'This world is a human world—the scientific view of it is also that of the scientific man.' Though Einstein did not agree, some distinguished scientists now see Tagore's point. One of them, Ilya Prigogine, a Nobel laureate in chemistry, claimed in 1984: 'Curiously enough, the present evolution of science is running in the direction stated by the great Indian poet.'[24]

All these experiences made Rabindranath develop a unique religious sensibility. As he reflects:

I had found my religion at last, the religion of Man, in which the infinite became defined in humanity and came close to me so as to need my love and cooperation.[25]

It is not so much that Rabindranath tried to produce a synthesis of the different religions, either in his life or in his poetry or novels, but that it went into the making of his personality in a natural manner both as a result of the environment in which he grew up and the knowledge that he imbibed from Indian as well as western sources. In his novel, *Ghare-Baire* ('The Home and the World'), the character, who is really the author, declares:

It was Buddha who conquered the world, not Alexander—this is untrue when stated in dry prose—oh when shall we be able to sing it? When shall all these most intimate truths of the universe overflow the pages of printed books and leap out in a sacred stream like the Ganges from the Gangotri?[26]

Tagore was never lacking in judgement or in resolution in siding with the forces of peace and harmony, spirituality and freedom against religious discrimination, nationalistic arrogance, terrorism, and social discrimination. He wanted Indians to learn about how other people lived, what they believed in and so on, while remaining interested and involved in their own culture and heritage. It was in this context, that he emphasized freedom of the mind. A poem in *Gitanjali* catches the Upanishadic philosophy in its totality:

Where the mind is without fear and the head is held high;
Where knowledge is free;
Where the world has not been broken up into fragments by narrow domestic walls;
Where words come out from the depth of truth;
Where tireless striving stretches its arms towards perfection;
Where the clear stream of reason has not lost its way into the dreary desert sand of dead habit;
Where the mind is led forward by thee into ever-widening thought and action—
Into that heaven of freedom, my Father, let my country awake.[27]

The Bahudhā philosophy found powerful expression in Tagore's writings. He had forcefully argued that India and cultural separatism were antithetical to each other. The Indian spirit is inclusiveness of all points of view, and in fact human creativity. He writes:

Whatever we understand and enjoy in human products instantly becomes ours, wherever they might have their origin. I am proud of my humanity when I can acknowledge the poets and artists of other countries as my own. Let me feel with unalloyed gladness that all the great glories of man are mine. Therefore it hurts me deeply when the cry of rejection rings loud against the West in my country with the clamour that Western education can only injure us.[28]

In *Gora*, a novel published in 1910, Tagore carries the Bahudhā approach further towards the end of the novel with Gora, saying:

Today, I am, above all, an Indian. In me there is no conflict of communities —Hindu, Muslim or Christian. Today every caste in India is my caste, the bread of everyone is my bread. . . . At last I have escaped from all futile efforts to adorn my country in false colours.[29]

Rabindranath worked for one supreme cause, the union of all sections of humanity in sympathy and understanding, in truth and love. He raised Visva-Bharati as an international university aimed at assisting students realize the true character of our interlinked humanity and deeper unities of our civilisation in the West and the East.[30] Tagore was a rationalist and he criticized Mahatma Gandhi when the latter announced that the devastating earthquake that struck Bihar in 1934 was 'a divine chastisement sent by God for our sins' and for his statement that 'there is a vital connection between the Bihar calamity and the untouchability campaign'.[31] Tagore, who was equally critical of untouchability, called Gandhi's interpretation irrational and felt that it was necessary to rid people of this kind of unscientific view of natural phenomenon.

Tagore was a great advocate of human brotherhood. Although there was a deep struggle going on in India for the attainment of national independence, Tagore felt that nationalism had its limitations and that excessive nationalism could come in the way of human freedom. It is for this reason that Tagore stood aloof from radical nationalist movements.

Believers in the Bahudhā approach can draw strength from the remarkable fact that Rabindranath Tagore is the author of the national anthems of 'Hindu' India (*Jana, Gana, Mana, Adhinayaka*—which means 'the leader of people's minds') as well as of 'Muslim' Bangladesh (*Amar Sonar Bangla*—which means 'my golden Bengal'). Rabindranath often acknowledged that in India, circumstances had almost compelled us to learn English, and this lucky accident gave Indians the opportunity to access into the richest of all poetical literatures of the world.

Rabindranath Tagore was opposed to every kind of religious fundamentalism and cultural separatism, in keeping with what the Bahudhā approach enjoins[32]: Almost in the vein of a modern Kabir, he wrote:

While God waits for his temple
to be built of love
men bring stones.[33]

The temple of love is yet to be raised.

MAHATMA GANDHI (1869–1948)

Mohandas Karamchand Gandhi was born at Porbandar in Gujarat on 2 October 1869 into a family belonging to the Vaishnava sect. His father encouraged Jains, Muslims, and Parsis to frequent their house and to hold religious discussions. Tolerance of and respect for all religions by a devout Hindu was an article of faith for Mohandas Gandhi. This conviction on his part was based not merely because of family inheritance but, in his own language, on account of 'his experiments with truth'.

On the seventh or eighth day after his arrival in South Africa at the age of twenty-four years, the experience of being ordered to move from a first class compartment to the van compartment on a train from Durban to Pretoria, and then being pushed out of the train on a bitterly cold night, had a profound impact on the young Gandhi. In fact that night a new Gandhi was born. A kind of enlightenment came to Mohandas Karamchand Gandhi on that bitter cold night in a waiting room of Maritzburg railway station. From 1893 till his return to India in 1915, Gandhi was deeply absorbed in the struggle for survival and human rights of the Indian community in South Africa. B.R. Nanda, writes:

What Gandhi did to South Africa was, however, less important than what South Africa did to him. . . . In Bombay, as a young lawyer, he had a nervous breakdown while cross-examining witnesses in a petty civil suit; in South Africa he had founded a new political organisation with the sure touch of a seasoned politician. . . . When he founded the Natal Indian Congress at the age of twenty-five he was writing on a tabula rasa; he could try out ideals which in an established political organisation would have been laughed out of court. What had truth and vows to do with politics?[34]

When Gandhi emerged on the Indian scene in 1915, the nationalist movement under the leadership of the Indian National Congress had already secured a foothold among the educated and professional classes of the country. On a visit to Champaran district in Bihar to assess and intervene in conflicts between indigo planters and peasants, Gandhi was issued orders to quit the district 'by the next available train' as his presence was considered a danger to public peace. He refused to comply and his testimony before the magistrate in April 1917 reveals a significant mindset. Gandhi declared:

I have disregarded the order served on me, not for want of respect for lawful authority, but in obedience to the higher law of our being—the voice of conscience.[35]

The perseverance by Gandhi and his men forced the then Governor of Bihar, Edward Gait, and the Government of India to appoint a Commission of Inquiry styled as the Champaran Agrarian Committee and that, in turn, led to a series of reform measures, including the abolition of the oppressive *tinkarthia* system, and of the illegal exactions under which the tenants groaned.

A bigger success was in store for Gandhi in his home state, Gujarat. In a conflict between a textile mill owner and the workers over pay increase in Ahmedabad, Gandhi decided not only to side with the labour but also to put his life at stake when he declared he would go on a fast-unto-death. The actual decision to fast had come unannounced: 'The words came to my lips', Gandhi later reported. Gandhi rejected the plea of many labourers to fast alongside him. The fast secured the desired results and the workers secured a pay-rise. This was Gandhi's first fast for a public cause. It amply demonstrated not only the viability of satyagraha as a means of peaceful solution acceptable to all concerned, but also demanded strict discipline and self-improvement among the participants and created an ambience of moral authority and pressure. The efficacy of satyagraha was to be seen later more vividly also when Gandhi led a group of satyagrahis in breach of the salt laws at Dandi.

Gandhi united politics and religion in a unique way. The Gandhian approach characterized non-violence and harmony with all religious communities, particularly the Muslims. This reformed version of religion, accompanied by his personal conduct, established deep roots among the people and demonstrated that tolerance and non-violence are not incompatible with perseverance and effectiveness.

It was Tagore who was the first to hail Gandhi as 'Mahatma'. Tagore's critique of Gandhi in his article entitled 'The Call of Truth', published in *Modern Review* in 1921, also describes Gandhi's arrival on the public scene in both moving and realistic terms.

Then at the critical moment, Mahatma Gandhi came and stood at the door of India's destitute millions, clad as one of themselves, speaking to them in their own language. It was a real happening, not a tale on the printed page. That is why he has been so aptly named Mahatma, Great Soul. Who else has so unreservedly accepted the vast masses of the Indian people as his own flesh and blood? At the touch of truth the pent-up forces of the spirit are set free. As soon as love stood at India's door, it flew open. All inward niggardliness was gone. Truth awakened truth.

This, indeed, is the birth of freedom, nothing less. . . . It has little to do with the alien occupation of India. This love is pure affirmation.[36]

In the aftermath of the partition and in the ensuing violence between Hindus and Muslims, Gandhi undertook a fast-unto-death twice for restoration of religious harmony in independent India (in a span of less than six months). Gandhi did not participate in the national celebrations of independence on 15 August 1947 and, instead, chose to walk barefoot through the mud and swamps of Noakhali (now in Bangladesh) preaching the message of non-violence and communal harmony. It was, however, in Calcutta that he had to resort to a fast to stop the Hindu and Muslim communities from attacking each other. The fast was a great success. Mountbatten called it a 'one-man boundary force' that stopped the massacre. His second and last fast began on 13 January 1948, in New Delhi. This again ended when Hindu, Muslim, and Sikh leaders pledged to Gandhi that they would try to make their people live with each other amicably.

In his death, Mahatma Gandhi became both universal and immortal. He became a symbol of peace and harmony among people as against hatred and conflict. Through satyagraha, truth, and non-violence, Mahatma Gandhi set forth a new methodology of conflict resolution, similar to that of the Bahudhā culture.

Some of the finest expressions of the Bahudhā philosophy in the life and works of Mahatma Gandhi can be seen in the context of the supremacy of truth and non-violence, generation of love and compassion, and harmony among religions.

TRUTH AND NON-VIOLENCE

Gandhi's thought process as well as programmes of action were guided by *satya* (truth) with ahimsa (non-violence) as the means.

Gandhi's concept of truth with non-violence was behind his doctrine of satyagraha. In this sense, satyagraha connotes the luminous truth directed towards removal of injustices, and promotion of greater public good. It was in this light that Gandhi wanted a satyagrahi never to deviate from the path of truth or non-violence, because in doing so he could expose the injustice around him, and without harming anyone.

Gandhi believed that the earth had enough resources to provide for human need but not for human greed. He held, therefore, that every man, woman, and child could be given adequate food, clothing, and shelter if there were a greater sharing of wealth in all parts of the world. The constructive programme that included individual and collective efforts to bring religious harmony to remove social abuses such as untouchability, and to promote work relating to education, decentralization of production, and distribution and improvement of health and sanitation among the people had to be based on truth and non-violence for effective implementation. As he reflected:

Thirty-four years of continuous experience in experimenting in truth and non-violence have convinced me that non-violence cannot be sustained unless it is linked to body-labour and finds expression in our daily contacts with our neighbours. This is the Constructive Programme.[37]

Each proposal—political, economic or social—therefore, had to be cast in relation to the principles of satya or truth and the means of attaining it by ahimsa or non-violence. Any deviation from truth or non-violence was not acceptable to Gandhi.

Gandhian satyagraha emerged as a non-violent conflict resolution mechanism in terms of the Bahudhā approach of a dialogic process inviting negotiation and agreement. There are scholars who hold the view that the effectiveness of *satyagraha* as a conflict resolution mechanism would require an opponent with a 'moral conscience' and that this technique, however, will not work against unprincipled totalitarian regimes. Although his technique of non-violent conflict resolution was not used in Germany nor used by the Jews in the face of Nazi atrocities, Gandhi had addressed this question and had felt that this would work with the Nazis as well. David Hardiman has mentioned a brief but successful non-violent campaign waged against the Nazis in 1943.

In Berlin the non-Jewish spouses of some two thousand Jewish males arrested by the Gestapo protested peacefully outside the prison for a week, finally winning the release of their husbands when the Nazis feared the effect of their demonstration on the remaining non-Jewish populace.[38]

This non-violent conflict resolution mechanism has since been successfully applied by various leaders such as Martin Luther King Jr. in the United States, Nelson Mandela in South Africa, and several Gandhian workers in dealing with local situations in South Asia.

It must, however, be said that Gandhi's faith in non-violence did not denote lack of courage or support cowardice. From a historical perspective it has to be appreciated that Gandhi was aware of violence and conflict in the evolution of human society. He wanted truth and non-violence, which are the ideals of a civilized society, to be increasingly realized. But when a choice was to be made between cowardice and use of force, Gandhi permitted the use of force. As he reflected:

If one has not the courage, I want him to cultivate the art of killing and being killed, rather than in a cowardly manner flee from danger.[39]

Again he observed:

The world is not entirely governed by logic. Life itself involves some kind of violence and we have to choose the path of least violence.[40]

Gandhi was the greatest exponent of ahimsa in our times. This was in conformity with India's past wherein ahimsa was the cornerstone of the Hindu, Jain, and Buddhist philosophies. It was Gandhi's genius that he transformed it into a tool of social and political action, in which a large number of Indians participated. He politicized individual courage.

After his death, Gandhi's methods have been applied with a measure of success against racism, foreign rule, and social inequalities and in dealing with conflicts within countries and between countries. In the United States, the movement for civil rights and racial equality bore a strong impress of Gandhi's ideas. Martin Luther King Jr., the renowned leader of this movement, wrote:

Jesus Christ gave me the motivation and Gandhi showed the method. . . Gandhi was probably the first person in history to lift the love ethic of Jesus above mere interaction between individuals to a powerful and effective social force on a large scale.[41]

Today the importance of Gandhi's doctrine of non-violence is even greater. Though the Cold War is over the world has been witnessing increasingly bitter ethnic, regional, and religious antagonisms.

Gandhi was aware of the difficulties of translating his non-violent dream into the world of reality. However, he refused to compromise on what he held to be fundamentals. To the last, he affirmed that even good ends do not justify dubious means. In his view, the family norms of truth, love, and charity are also relevant to groups, communities, and nations. Gandhi believed in non-violence as the law of our species and violence as the law of the brute.

LOVE AND COMPASSION

Gandhi believed that hatred can only be defeated by love and compassion. He was painfully aware that injuries to self-respect from humiliation tended to erupt in violence. The conflict and violence, from the Mahabharata wars to the Second World War, had revealed to Gandhi that the culture of violence always works in crushing and beating others into submission. But violence does not create a stable society, nor does it transform evil into good. It is the courage of love, of compassion, of non-violence, of dialogue that can create a harmonious society. This is at the centre of the Bahudhā approach too: the courage to listen rather than not to hear, the courage to restrain the desire for vengeance and be guided by a vision that would lead to conflict resolution. It is only through the process of dialogue that mutual understanding is born, based on which a peaceful society can be reconstructed.

To those who are persuaded by despair that there is no remedy against the violence of the modern world other than to escape or destroy it, Gandhi offers an alternate way within reach of us all, namely the principle of love. Love is the law of human life, its' natural necessity. The world is approaching a state when this necessity will be manifest, for human life would become impossible if men were to evade and disobey this principle. We have wars simply because we are not sufficiently selfless for a life which does not need wars. The battle for peace must be fought in the heart of the individual. The spirit in him must break the power of pride and selfishness, lust and fear. A new way of life must become the foundation of national life as well as of world order, a way of life which will conserve and foster the true interests of all classes, races, and nations.[42]

RELIGIOUS HARMONY

It is significant to note that in India the historical agents of unity were religious reformers and their disciples, religious bodies, sects, and monks as well as institutions of temples, sanghas, and satras. They always sought and received support from the ruling elite, whether it was a tribal chief or a caste leader, a dynasty or a group of merchants. Tensions between Hindus and Buddhists, and more particularly between Buddhists and the Muslims and between Hindus and Muslims for religious as well as political supremacy did lead to conflict but it never established a unitary or monotheistic approach.

The original Brahmanic religion underwent several changes under the influence of Buddhism and subsequently under the influence of Islam and Christianity. India owes to Islam admirable works of architecture, painting, music, and landscaping, apart from political architecture such as the creation of the Mughal empire. Nevertheless, rivalry between Hinduism and Islam has been a perennial feature of Indian civilizational endeavours. The clash of civilizations in the Indian context was between the pluralism or polytheism of the natives versus the monotheism of the invaders. Both Islam and Christianity believed in one god, one scripture. This also explains why it was difficult for Islam and Christianity to accept plurality of faiths, images, and forms of worship which were the distinctive feature of Indian society over the millennia.

The spirit of tolerance is based on a wisdom which emanates from the profound insight of the dharma. Buddhism refers to this as the wisdom of dependent origination, the wisdom to perceive the truth that all things in the universe are interdependent and interrelated, that they interact and reach fulfilment within a delicate and mysterious matrix of harmony in diversity. The eternal and universal dharma lives within all things, forming the phenomenal world with its dynamic harmonization in interdependence and interrelationship. This, the true aspect of phenomena, is expressed as dependent origination.

As early as August 1905, in an article in his weekly paper, *Indian Opinion* (August 1905), Gandhi argued that the time had passed when the followers of one religion could 'stand and say, ours is the only true religion and all others are false'. The various religions to him were different roads converging upon the same point. What does it matter if we take different roads, so long as we reach the same goal?[43] God, Allah, Ram, Narayan, Ishwar, Khuda were descriptions of the same Being. Gandhiji was very fond of referring to the analogy of the Gujarati saint Narsimha: to the effect that the different shapes into which gold was beaten gave rise to different names and forms; but ultimately it was all gold. So are the religions. In reality, there are as many religions as there are individuals.

Mahatma Gandhi saw and stressed the underlying unity in the teachings of all religions. As early as in 1905 he said: 'All religions teach that we should all live together in love and mutual kindness'.[44] To him God's grace and revelation are not the monopoly of any race or nation; they descend equally upon all who wait upon God. He regarded all the principal faiths of the world as divinely inspired but felt they were imperfect because they had come down to us through imperfect human instrumentality. As Gandhi wrote:

I believe that all the great religions of the world are true more or less. I say 'more or less' because I believe that everything that the human hand touches, by reason of the very fact that human beings are imperfect, becomes imperfect. Perfection is the exclusive attribute of God and it is indescribable, untranslatable. I do believe that it is possible for every human being to become perfect even as God is perfect. It is necessary for us all to aspire after perfection, but when that blessed state is attained, it becomes indescribable, indefinable. And, I, therefore, admit, in all humility, that even the Vedas, the Koran and the Bible are the imperfect word of God and, imperfect beings that we are, swayed to and fro by a multitude of passions, it is impossible for us even to understand this word of God in its fullness.[45]

Gandhi also stressed the need for tolerance for other viewpoints and respect for other faiths. Tolerance did not mean indifference towards one's own faith but a more intelligent and purer love for it.

The need of the moment, he wrote, 'is not one religion, but mutual respect and tolerance of the devotees of different religions. No religion was absolutely perfect; but by the best it produced. In Gandhi's words, 'if only we could all of us read the scriptures of the different faiths from the standpoint of the followers of those faiths, we should find that they were at the bottom all one and were all helpful to one another'.[46]

Gandhi saw the same God in every religion. He reflected:

The Allah of Islam is the same as the God of the Christians and the Isvara of the Hindus. Even as there are numerous names of God in Hinduism, there are many names of God in Islam. The names do not indicate individuality but attributes, and the little man has tried in his humble way to describe mighty God by giving Him attributes, though He is above all attributes, Indescribable, Immeasurable. Living faith in this God means equal respect for all religions. It would be the height of intolerance—and intolerance is a species of violence—to believe that your religion is superior to other religions and that you would be justified in wanting others to change over to your faith.[47]

Gandhi was concerned about the popular notion of the role of violent methods and its place in Islam. To quote:

I do regard Islam to be a religion of peace in the same sense as Christianity, Buddhism and Hinduism are. No doubt there are differences in degrees, but the object of these religions is peace.

I have given my opinion that the followers of Islam are too free with the sword. But that is not due to the teaching of the Koran. This is due, in my opinion, to the environment in which Islam was born. Christianity has a bloody record against it not because Jesus was found wanting, but because the environment in which it spread was not responsive to his lofty teaching.[48]

The Indian secular approach to harmonious living owes greatly to Gandhi's genius and the pluralist approach of the Indian people. Deeply religious as he was, he said that he would have opposed any proposal for a state religion even if the whole population of India had professed the same religion. The resolution on fundamental rights passed by the Karachi Congress in 1931 with Gandhi's approval, affirmed the principle of religious freedom and declared that 'the State shall observe neutrality in regard to all religions'. This doctrine was embodied in the Constitution of independent India even after the Muslim League waged and won the campaign for the partition of the country on the basis of religion. Gandhi considered religion to be a personal matter. He told a missionary:

The State would look after your secular welfare, health, communications, currency and so on, but not your or my religion. That is everybody's personal concern.[49]

Asked as to what he would do when there were conflicting counsels from different religions, Gandhi replied:

Truth is superior to everything, and I reject what conflicts with it. Similarly that which is in conflict with non-violence should be rejected. And on matters which can be reasoned out, that which conflicted with reason must also be rejected.[50]

To him, God was not inseparable from truth or away from human beings. He wrote:

I recognise no God except the God that is to be found in the hearts of the dumb millions. They do not recognise His presence; I do. And I worship the God that is Truth, or Truth which is God, through the service of these millions.[51]

Gandhi's prayer meetings were held not in temples or mosques, but under the open sky, and his prayers were recitations from Hindu, Muslim, Christian, Sikh, Zoroastrian, and Buddhist texts. After the prayers and hymns were sung, Gandhi spoke on the secular issues and concerns which faced the country. During 1944–8, years of bitter religious tension in India, his prayer meetings continued to be attended in large numbers, as if to become a defiant symbol of tolerance and harmonious living.

The freedom struggle under Mahatma Gandhi's leadership expressed the cultural ethos of pluralism through the medium of *prabhat ferris*, morning and evening prayers drawn from scriptures of all major religions practised in India, and work on the spinning wheel, and popularization of cottage and village industries. Everyone who was an active participant in the war for independence under the Gandhian banner took part in these activities. Under the new creed maintenance of communal harmony and removal of untouchability acquired great significance.

VIVEKANANDA, TAGORE, AND GANDHI

Vivekananda, Tagore, and Gandhi were all creators in their respective ways and fearless in denouncing what they considered evil—untouchability, indifference towards the poor, and irrationality. Each one of them was attached to truth. Each one of them wanted us to serve the poor. Each one denounced superstition and ritual, even though they attached the greatest importance to our inheritance from the past and sought to build upon it in the present. All three achieved a rare feat of excellence in their own areas of strength: Vivekananda in religion, Tagore in literature, and Gandhi in politics.

All three drew from the depth of Indian religious inheritance as well as from the context of the new worldwide understanding between religions. Each one of them brought the Indian people and society closer to the best elements of Hinduism, Buddhism, Christianity, and Islam. This was virtually in terms of the Rigvedic axiom 'May He unite us in the relationship of goodwill.' Jawaharlal Nehru acknowledged Swami Vivekananda for his role in laying the foundation for the future nationalist movement in the country. Talking of Tagore and Gandhi, Nehru stated:

Tagore was primarily the man of thought, Gandhi of concentrated and ceaseless activity. Both, in their different ways, had a world outlook, and both were at the same time wholly Indian. They seemed to represent different but harmonious aspects of India and to complement each other.[52]

All of them were fully conscious of the modern world and reacted to it in different ways, but were guided by the spiritual traditions of India. They laid stress on the life of the spirit as well as concrete action on the ground towards building a more equitable and humane society. Vivekananda set up the Ramakrishna Mission to bring about an attitudinal change among the Hindus and to serve the poor and the needy in education, health care, and spirituality. In 1901, Tagore, the great poet and educator, set up Shantiniketan (Abode of Peace) where he sought to blend the best in Indian and Western traditions. Gandhi carried this forward.

Swami Vivekananda was the first to bring service to the poor at the centre of religion. He emphasized social service and established Ramakrishna Missions in different parts of India and abroad. Tagore, too, was solely guided by the need to educate all sections of society so that one could help to improve one's intellectual and economic capacity. Tagore referred to 'the unfortunate people who have lost the harvest of their past, who have lost the present age', and spoke about them as one of the 'disinherited peoples of the world'. He wanted to educate, empower, and move them on the path of rationality. Tagore called his faith the Religion of Man. Gandhi carried the dialogue further. Service to the poor was central to his religion, politics, and writings. Laying stress on India's past treasures of the mind and spirit, Gandhi enjoined the people not to close their doors and windows to the winds that blew in from different parts of the world; and also to not be uprooted or blown away by these winds.

Alone among these creators, Gandhi initiated a movement that could make sense to every individual irrespective of his or her religion or belief, level of education, or skill. He created a new human narrative and tried to convince both the British rulers and his compatriots about the need for freedom and equality. It is another matter that he failed to prevent the partition of India and the accompanying violence. Notwithstanding this, he provided a new way of looking at things in order that all people, including those on the margins of history, could have a say. This inclusiveness under Gandhi's leadership was a major breakthrough that came to be a guiding spirit in any dialogue process among conflicting viewpoints in the twentieth century.

The teachings and the Ramakrishna order of Swami Vivekananda, the poetry and institution of learning (Visva-Bharati) of Rabindranath Tagore, and the politics and the constructive programmes of Mahatma Gandhi helped create an atmosphere that enabled the new Indian republic to choose its path: the road of democracy and secularism, of human rights and social empowerment, and of a plural society. The fact that the works of these great minds were largely in the domain of people like students, teachers, freedom fighters, and social, political and religious workers has been of enduring value in guiding the evolution of society as well as the formation of state apparatus.

CONCLUSION

The religious and social philosophers that developed during the Vedic and Buddhist periods was further embellished by a succession of gurus and acharyas. Shankara and his followers stressed the divine and super-personal aspects of the Upanishads while Vaishnava teachers such as Ramanuja, Madhvacharya, and Vallabhacharya explained the aspects of love, compassion, and worship in the Indian cultural experience. This has consistently held the supremacy of dharma and truth over individuals, however, exalted they may be. The *Brhadaranyaka Upanishad* significantly mentions:

Law (dharma) is the king over the king. There is nothing above Law. Wherefore the weak takes hope against the strong through Law as through the king. Similarly Law is the Truth (satya) of the universe. Therefore they say that one who speaks Truth speaks Law, and one who speaks Law speaks Truth. For both are identical.[53]

The emphasis over truth and non-violence receives even greater support and emphasis in Buddhism, Jainism, and the Gandhian approach to conflict resolution.

The limitations of knowledge and the need for a human approach through love and detachment was another aspect that has characterized the Indian quest. As Rabindranath Tagore expresses it:

This lesson was duly emphasised by the Bhagavad Gita, which finally expounded the harmony between diverse approaches to the Reality that is one, through knowledge, through love, through righteous and detached living, and developed the thesis, that any means that helped the individual to rise above the demands of the ego to his identity with the Supreme Self that is in all being, were the truly legitimate means of that individual's spiritual fulfilment. Thus was rounded up the entire range of Indian spiritual and philosophic speculation and practice, and were reconciled the paths of dispassionate contemplation of the impersonal, of ecstatic devotion to the personal, of disinterested living in the world of the actual. Sacrifice of desire and not of the object, renunciation of the Self, not of the world, were made the keynote of this harmony of spiritual endeavours.[54]

Like many other civilizations, India too had periods of discord and conflict in various domains including that of society and culture but there was always a continuity in cultural change. In each period, notwithstanding wounds inflicted by invasions accompanied by great decline in values, there was a remarkable recovery of spirits through India's own power of self-renewal. The seers of the Upanishads, the Buddha, Mahavira, Kabir, and Nanak, and rulers like Ashoka, Akbar, and Nehru, in their own periods worked for the fundamental spiritual truths and helped us move on to accept the Bahudhā approach of harmony and peaceful living. The way the Bahudhā approach became an integral part of statecraft in times of rulers like Ashoka, Akbar, and Jawaharlal Nehru in particular is discussed in the next chapter.

NOTES

1. An oft-quoted statement that has become part of the twentieth-century political legend. In some western countries, pendants (silver as well as gold) with this utterance of Mahatma Gandhi are sold.
2. *Navajivan*, 14 March 1926.
3. Rabindranath Tagore explains this phenomenon in the following words:

   In the Vedic verses, we find constant mention of conflicts between the original inhabitants of Ancient India and the colonists. There we find the expression of a spirit that was one of mutual distrust, and a struggle in which was sought either wholesale slavery or extermination for the opponents, carried on in the manner of animals who live in the narrow segregation imposed upon them by their limited imagination and imperfect sympathy. This spirit would have continued in all its ferocious vigour of savagery had men failed to find the opportunity for the discovery that man's highest truth was in the union of cooperation and love.

   Rabindranath Tagore, *The Religion of Man*, Unwin Books, London, 1961, p. 100.
4. S. Radhakrishnan, *Fellowship of the Spirit*, The Centre for the Study of World Religions, Harvard University Press, Massachusetts, 1961, p. 24.
5. Swami Vivekananda, *My India: The India Eternal*, Ramakrishna Mission Institute of Culture, Calcutta, 1993, p. 98.
6. Swami Lokeswarananda (compiled and edited), *The Perennial Vivekananda: A Selection*, Sahitya Akademi, Calcutta, 1992 (reprint), p. 6. This is quoted from Swami Vivekananda's address at the final session of the Parliament of Religions at Chicago on 27 September 1893. It reads as follows:

   Much has been said of the common ground of religious unity. I am not going just now to venture my own theory. But if any one here hopes that this unity will come by the triumph of any one of the religions and the destruction of the others, to him I say, 'Brother, yours is an impossible hope.' Do I wish that the Christian would become Hindu? God forbid. Do I wish that the Hindu or Buddhist would become Christian? God forbid.

7. Vivekananda, *My India*, p. 97.
8. Ibid., p. 157. The first encounter between Shri Ramakrishna Parama-hansa and Swami Vivekananda was indeed very interesting. Like other young people Vivekananda wanted to hear him and then had a dialogue with him which in his own language is as follows:

I heard of this man, and I went to hear him. He looked just like an ordinary man, with nothing remarkable about him. He used the most simple language, and I thought,—'Can this man be a great teacher?'—crept near to him and asked him the question which I had been asking others all my life: 'Do you believe in God, Sir?' 'Yes,' he replied. 'Can you prove it, Sir?' 'Yes.' 'How?' 'Because I see him just as I see you here, only in a much intenser sense.' That impressed me at once. For the first time I found a man who dared to say that he saw God, that religion was a reality, to be felt, to be sensed in an infinitely more intense way than we can sense the world. I began to go to that man, day after day, and I actually saw that religion could be given. One touch, one glance, can change a whole life. . . . When I myself saw this man, all scepticism was brushed aside.

Ibid., pp. 137–38.
9. Ibid., p. 209.
10. Ibid., p. 130.
11. The Barber's story is as follows:

Or what could be more beautiful than the Barber's story?
The Blessed One passed by my house, *my* house—the Barber's!
I ran, but He turned and awaited me. Awaited *me*—the Barber!
I said, 'May I speak, O Lord, with Thee?'
And He said 'Yes!' 'Yes!' to *me*— the Barber!
And I said 'Is Nirvana for such as I?'
And He said 'Yes!'. Even for *me* —the Barber!
And I said 'May I follow after Thee!'
And He said 'Oh yes!' *Even* I—the Barber!
And I said 'May I stay, O Lord, near Thee?'
And He said 'Thou mayest!' Even to *me*—the poor Barber!

(Quoted in Sister Nivedita, *The Master As I Saw Him*, Udbodhan Office, Calcutta, 1972, pp. 260–1.)
12. Vivekananda, *My India: The India Eternal*, pp. 216–17. (*The Story of Civilisation: Our Oriental Heritage*, Vol. I, Simon & Schuster, New York, 1954, p. 618.)

148

13. Jawaharlal Nehru, *Discovery of India*, Oxford University Press, New Delhi, 1981, p. 338.
14. Ibid.
15. An elder brother, Satyendranath, was the first Indian to be admitted to the Indian Civil Service (ICS).
16. Rabindranath Tagore's essay 'A Poet's School', first published in the Visva-Bharati Quarterly in October 1926, gives a vivid portrayal of his school life. Tagore reflects:

    In the usual course I was sent to school, but possibly my suffering was unusual, greater than that of most other children. The non-civilised in me was sensitive: it had the great thirst for colour, for music, for movement of life. Our city-built education took no heed of that living fact. . . .The non-civilised triumphed in me only too soon and drove me away from my school when I had just entered my teens. I rely solely upon my own instincts to build up my education from the very beginning.

    The essay has been included in *Vision of India*, Indian Council for Cultural Relations, New Delhi, 2005, p. 25.
17. When I was eighteen, a sudden spring breeze of religious experience for the first time came to my life and passed away leaving in my memory a direct message of spiritual reality. One day while I stood watching at early dawn the sun sending out its rays from behind the trees, I suddenly felt as if some ancient mist had in a moment lifted from my sight, and the morning light on the face of the world revealed an inner radiance of joy. The invisible screen of the commonplace was removed from all things and all men, and their ultimate significance was intensified in my mind; and this is the definition of beauty. That which was memorable in this experience was its human message, the sudden expansion of my consciousness in the super-personal world of man. The poem I wrote on the first day of my surprise was named 'The Awakening of the Waterfall'. The waterfall, whose spirit lay dormant in its ice-bound isolation, was touched by the sun and, bursting in a cataract of freedom, it found its finality in an unending sacrifice, in a continual union with the sea. After four days the vision passed away, and the lid hung down upon my inner sight. In the dark, the world once again put on its disguise of the obscurity of an ordinary fact.

    Tagore, *The Religion of Man*, p. 58.
18. Tagore, *The Religion of Man*, p. 12.
    He writes:

    I mention in connection with my personal experience some songs which I have often heard from wandering village singers, belonging to a popular sect of Bengal, called Bauls, who have no images, temples, scriptures, or ceremonials, who declare in their songs the divinity of Man, and express for him an intense feeling of love. Coming from men who are unsophisticated, living a simple life in obscurity, it gives us a clue to the inner meaning of all religions. For it suggests that these religions are never about a God of cosmic force, but rather about the God of human personality.

19. *The Hundred Poems of Kabir* was published by The Indian Society, London in 1914.
20. Tagore writes:

I was born in what was then the metropolis of British India. Our ancestors came floating to Calcutta upon the earliest tide of the fluctuating fortune of the East India Company. The conventional code of life for our family thereupon became a confluence of three cultures, the Hindu, the Muslim and the British.

(See *Vision of India*, p. 23.)

21. Quoted in *Rabindranath Tagore: A Centenary Volume 1861–1961*, Sahitya Akademi, New Delhi, 1987, p. xix.
22. From *Gitanjali*. Poem No. 11, Rabindranath Tagore, Rabindra Bhavan, Calcutta, 1987, p. 37.
23. Tagore, *The Religion of Man*, Unwin Books, London, 1961.
24. Krishna Dutta and Andrew Robinson (eds), *Rabindranath Tagore: An Anthology*, Picador, London, 1997, p. 7. It may be recalled that Tagore and Einstein met in 1926 and in 1930. The entire dialogue between Tagore and Einstein could be seen in Appendix 1 of the following book Krishna Dutta and Andrew Robinson (eds), *Selected Letters of Rabindranath Tagore*, Cambridge University Press, Cambridge, 1997, pp. 527–36.
25. Tagore, *The Religion of Man*, p. 60.
26. Dutta and Robinson (eds), *Rabindranath Tagore*, p. 1.
27. From *Gitanjali*, Poem No. 35, p. 87.
28. B. P. Singh, 'Bahudhā and the Post-9/11 World', *Social Change: Journal of the Council for Social Development*, December 2004, Vol. 34, No. 4, New Delhi, p. 11.
29. Uma Das Gupta, *Rabindranath Tagore: A Biography*, Oxford University Press, New Delhi, 2004, p. 5.
30. For a detailed analysis see Chapter IX entitled Visva-Bharati: a World University of Uma Das Gupta's book, *Rabindranath Tagore: A Biography*, Oxford University Press, Delhi, 2004, pp. 66–72.
31. See Rabindranath Tagore's letter to Mahatma Gandhi dated 28 January 1934 in Dutta and Robinson (eds), *Selected Letters of Rabindranath Tagore*, p. 434.

32. Rabindranath Tagore wrote:

   The God of Humanity has arrived at the gates of the ruined temple of the tribe. Though he has not yet found his altar, I ask the men of simple faith, wherever they may be in the world, to bring their offering of sacrifice to him, and to believe that it is far better to be wise and worshipful than to be clever and supercilious. I ask them to claim the right of manhood to be friends of men, and not the right of a particular proud race or nation which may boast of the fatal quality of being the rulers of men. We should know for certain that such rulers will no longer be tolerated in the new world, as it basks in the open sunlight of the mind and breathes life's free air.

   (*Mainstream*, Annual 2004 Issue, 25 December 2004, cover page.)

33. Dutta and Robinson (eds), *Rabindranath Tagore*, p. 381.
34. B.R. Nanda, *Mahatma Gandhi*, Oxford University Press, New Delhi, 1989, p. 81.
35. Ibid., p. 100.
36. *Rabindranath Tagore: A Centenary Volume 1861–1961*, p. xiv.
37. Raghavan Iyer, B.R. Nanda, Glenn D. Paige, Daisaku Ikeda, Chaiwat Satha-Anand, B.N. Pande, *Gandhi and Global Nonviolent Transformation*, Gandhi Smriti and Darshan Samiti, New Delhi, 1994, p. 12.
38. David Hardiman, *Gandhi in His Time and Ours: The Global Legacy of His Ideas*, Columbia University Press, New York, 2003, p. xiii.
39. *Harijan*, 15 January 1938, p. 418.
40. *Harijan*, 28 September 1934, p. 259.
41. B.R. Nanda's twelfth Convocation Address at the Central Institute of Higher Tibetan Studies, Sarnath, Varanasi, on 18 February 2005.
42. While a few individuals at random tried to use the method of love in their personal lives, it is Gandhi's supreme achievement to have adopted it as a plan for social and political liberation. Under his leadership organized groups in South Africa and India used it on a large scale for the redress of grievances.
43. R.K. Prabhu and U.R. Rao (compiled by), *The Mind of Mahatma Gandhi*, Oxford University Press, London, 1945, p. 85.
44. *Indian Opinion*, 15 April 1905.
45. *Young India*, 22 September 1927.
46. *Harijan*, 16 February 1934.
47. *Harijan*, 14 May 1938.
48. *Young India*, 20 January 1927.
49. B.R. Nanda (ed.), *Mahatma Gandhi: 125 Years*, Indian Council for Cultural Relations and New Age International, New Delhi, 1995, pp. 146–7. (*Harijan*, 22 September 1946).
50. Ibid., p. 139 (*Young India*, 20 February 1980).

51. *Harijan*, 11 March 1939.
52. *Rabindranath Tagore: A Centenary Volume 1861–1961*, p. 401.
53. Ibid., p. 374.
54. Dutta and Robinson (eds), *Rabindranath Tagore*, p. 247.

6
The Rulers

He who is at the head of a government and is bent upon gathering wealth is forced to use petty persons in office. He may want to do good, but the petty officials rule the country and bring disaster to the state, and all his good intentions are to no purpose. That is why it is said that 'the material prosperity of a nation does not consist in its material prosperity, but in righteousness'.[1]

—Confucius

Both the Greek and Indian civilizations have concerned themselves with statecraft from early times. Plato (427–347 BC), Aristotle (384–22 BC), and several of their European successors reflected in great detail on the origins of the State, the ideal form of government and the basis of laws in politics. Indian civilizational accomplishments in the realm of cosmic forces and dharma overshadowed its legends and literature concerning statecraft and the role of leadership in a state. Kautilya's *Arthashastra*, the first comprehensive work on statecraft and the qualities of an ideal ruler, elaborates, in detail, on the duties of a king and the methods available at his command for practising statecraft, as well as for ensuring the welfare of the people. The book is a storehouse of information about communication by land and sea, agriculture and irrigation, ores and mining, plants and medicines, mechanical contrivances to be used for war, as well as implements for use in agriculture, architecture, and mining. Kautilya also went on to prescribe both righteous and non-righteous methods that could be employed by the king for the governance of the country, the maintenance of its sovereignty, and the conduct of diplomacy.

The great epics, namely the Ramayana and the Mahabharata, also deal with the political philosophy of the ideal State. The ideals of ram-rajya are enumerated in some detail in the Ramayana. Similarly, the Shanti Parva, the twelfth book of the Mahabharata, has several passages on statecraft and human conduct.[2] The myths and legends of *dandniti* (the administration of force) and *rajniti*, (the conduct of kings) have supported the image and ideals of kingship. Similarly, the myth of the *Chakravartin* has fuelled the ambitions of several rulers in India to build a large empire over the Indian subcontinent. In the long history of governance in India, three outstanding rulers who made meaningful contributions to the Bahudhā approach are Ashoka (304–232 BC), Akbar (1542–1605), and Jawaharlal Nehru (1889–1964).

ASHOKA

Among the kings, chieftains, and rulers of early Indian history, Ashoka (304–232 BC) stands out as an outstanding gifted ruler who both propounded and successfully implemented the Bahudhā approach of harmony by laying down some unique conflict resolution mechanisms in the political, social, and religious arenas.

The Indian adventure of Alexander the Great (356–23 BC) and his subsequent withdrawal had many facets. The growing contact between the ruling elites of India and Greece and the exchange of ideas among them made a significant contribution in terms of culture as well as statecraft in both countries.[3] It was during the Mauryan rule of Chandragupta, Bindusara, and Ashoka—for nearly nine decades—that the concept of cakravartin became a reality.[4]

Bindusara had successfully launched a military campaign in the Deccan and extended his rule as far south as Mysore. The Tamil land too cooperated, although no formal rule was extended to this area. At the time of Bindusara's death in 272 BC, practically the whole subcontinent was under Mauryan suzerainty except Kalinga. Kashmir was also included in the Mauryan empire.[5] The Mauryan rule had expanded up to Khotan in Central Asia and Kandhar in Afghanistan. In the neighbourhood, the Mauryas had extremely close and influential relations with Ceylon (present-day Sri Lanka). Nepal too maintained specially friendly relations and the foothills were directly within Mauryan orbit.

Ashoka was born in 304 BC into the Mauryan royal family. His father, Bindusara, was the king and his mother, Subhadrangi the Queen, was the daughter of a Brahman of Campa. Ashoka was the grandson of the legendary king Chandragupta Maurya who founded the Maurya dynasty, consolidated and ruled for twenty-two years over large parts of the Indian subcontinent with the help of Kautilya, the famous philosopher and strategist as his Prime Minister. In the varna system, Chandragupta belonged to the Vaisya varna and not to the traditional one of the ruling elite—the Kshatriyas.

Ashoka grew up in an environment where members of his family took a lively interest in the ideas of their time. Chandragupta Maurya had not only set up a new empire but in his later years accepted Jainism. There was also the influence of the Greeks. As Romila Thapar writes:

Jainism was not, however, the only influence at the court of Chandragupta. A foreign element which may have supported some degree of eclectic thinking, was that of the few Greeks who were undoubtedly present at the court. Some European sources have stated that Chandragupta actually met Alexander, though this event has been doubted by at least one modern historian of the period. We know that Megasthenes came as a friend of Seleucus and lived at the court of Pataliputra for a while. He must certainly have been questioned at length about the thought and institutions of Greece and Asia Minor with which he was familiar. That he must have responded with enthusiasm seems obvious since it appears from his accounts of India that he was a man of lively observation and intelligence.[6]

Bindusara too was greatly interested in new ideas. It is well known both in Indian and Greek literature that Bindusara made a request among other things that a sophist be sent to him as a present from Greece. Besides Patliputra, Taxila in the west had already developed as a cosmopolitan and vibrant city that entertained Vedic, Buddhist, and Greek thought and ways of living. Such an environment and such diverse ideas and influences must have contributed to the building of Ashoka's personality in the formative years and later might have shaped his attitudes towards plurality of faiths and harmonious living.

At an early age, Ashoka came to be associated with state affairs. His first appointment seems to have been to Taxila. At the age of eighteen years, Ashoka was appointed viceroy to Ujjain by his father, Bindusara. Ashoka was crowned king four years after his father's death in 270 BC.

The most significant turn in Ashoka's life came in 262 BC which was a kind of 'enlightenment' that historians have variously described as a 'turning point', 'change of heart', etc. Eight years after his enthronement, Ashoka undertook the annexation of Kalinga (Orissa) and conquered it. The conquest is recorded in some detail in the thirteenth Major Rock Edict. It graphically details the human suffering involved: 100,000 slain, 'many times that number perished' (presumably later from wounds and famine), and 150,000 deported, and more famously, Ashoka's reaction to the horrors of war.

The conquest of Kalinga marked a dramatic transformation in Ashoka's world view. Although Ashoka was born a Hindu, he turned in later life to the teachings of Buddhism. He vowed to maintain his rule by dhamma, and not by force, and in international relations, not to launch military expeditions to subjugate another country by war. By renouncing violence, abjuring war, and advocating the admirable concept of dhamma, Ashoka directly inducted the Bahudhā approach into statecraft. The famous thirteenth Major Rock Edict gives the most vivid description of this new approach:

On conquering Kalinga the Beloved of the Gods felt remorse, for, when an independent country is conquered, the slaughter, death and deportation of the people is extremely grievous to the Beloved of the Gods, and weighs heavily on his mind. . . .Even those who are fortunate to have escaped, and whose love is undiminished, suffer from the misfortunes of their friends, acquaintances, colleagues and relatives. . . .Today if a hundredth or a thousandth part of those people who were killed or died or were deported when Kalinga was annexed were to suffer similarly, it would weigh heavily on the mind of the Beloved of the Gods. . . .

This inscription of dhamma has been engraved so that any sons or great-grandsons that I may have should not think of gaining new conquests, and in whatever victories they may gain should be satisfied with patience and light punishment. They should only consider conquest by Dhamma to be a true conquest, and delight in Dhamma should be their whole delight, for this is of value in both this world and the next.[7]

In more than one way, Kautilya's *Arthashastra* was Ashoka's inheritance, closely associated as its author was with his grandfather. The ideas of this treatise and Kautilya's personage had enormously influenced thinkers and military minds of Ashoka's and his father's generation. The *Arthashastra* makes the conquest of neighbouring territories one of the king's sacred duties. It lists several kinds of war, goes into immense logistical detail on armies and battle plans, and even provides hints on the conquest of the world. In this context, Ashoka's 'change of heart' and new approach to statecraft was indeed both a novelty and revolutionary act. However, after conquest, Ashoka seems to have followed the advice in treating the people of Kalinga as prescribed in the *Arthashastra*:

Having acquired new territory the conqueror shall substitute his virtues for the enemy's vices and where the enemy was good, he shall be twice as good. He shall follow policies that are pleasing and beneficial by acting according to his dharma and by granting favours and exemptions, giving gifts and bestowing honours.[8]

As a ruler, Ashoka went on to strengthen his state system in many significant ways. He raised and maintained a large army. He also set up a fine civil service. He was a great builder of roads and hospitals for men and animals, and initiated a programme of planting of roadside trees and groves, digging of wells and construction of watering wells and rest houses. He is believed to have built no fewer than 8400 Buddhist temples and erected several pillars, some of which still survive.

During Ashoka's reign the Indian political system acquired a pan-subcontinental personality co-terminus with a civilizational character which had existed for a long time. This was achieved by forging unity among diverse elements of the people, by maintaining a strong army, and by running the administration based on the principles of dhamma. All these created among the elite an imperial vision that has been a part of Indian political thought processes for very long.

DHAMMA AS AN INSTRUMENT OF STATE POLICY

Ashoka adopted dhamma as an instrument of state policy and renounced warfare. He approached the question of effecting harmony among people and coordinating relations with neighbouring countries and beyond, in accordance with dhamma. This was the first time that any king anywhere in the world had done so and Ashoka went on to practise it in the remaining three decades of his rule over India.

The Concept of Dhamma

The essence of dhamma was to create an attitude of mind in which social behaviour—was determined in terms of tolerance for another person's point of view and in recognition of an individual's worth. The policy of dhamma was also based on pragmatic considerations inasmuch as Mauryan society in India was a multicultural society as people spoke several languages and dialects and owed allegiance to different clans and sects. People were at different levels of development in intellectual and material terms, with economic, social, and religious forces counteracting each other. A peaceful environment was greatly needed to facilitate the movement of goods and services since the economy was expanding during that period of time. Dhamma was, therefore, consciously developed as a public policy of harmony in society.

Ashoka's concept of dhamma drew heavily from Buddhism but was not synonymous with the Buddhist belief system. Ashoka did not want to make Buddhism the state religion in spite of his personal preferences in the matter. Secondly, dhamma had all the essential attributes of the concept of dharma that were developed during the Vedic period. In fact, the principle of dhamma contained the common elements of harmonious principles of Brahmanism, Buddhism, Jainism, and various other sects that were followed in the country. It was Ashoka's genius that he defined dhamma in terms of good conduct, with stress on tolerance, and did not prescribe rules and regulations for its observance. In terms of Buddhist and Jain traditions, non-violence became the fundamental principle of dhamma. In Ashoka's time, non-violence specifically came to mean renunciation of war and conquest by violence. He also put restraints on the killing of animals. But he did not go so far as to dismantle his army or to abjure military expeditions to control troublesome tribal groups and others.

Keeping in view the comprehensive framework for dhamma that Ashoka had provided, it would be prudent to conclude that dhamma, though inspired by Hinduism and Buddhism, was Ashoka's own invention. Dhamma in many respects was the middle position between ritualistic religion and abstract metaphysics. Dhamma accepted the Buddhist critique of the Hindu order as several malpractices had crept into its rituals, and its thought processes in the hands of priests were marked by irrationality. It also rejected asceticism or self-denial that was a characteristic feature of both Buddhism and Jainism. Dhamma was not an escape from the world but a social construct based on rational thinking.

Although it is difficult to find a single word in English denoting the Pali expression dhamma or the Sanskrit expression dharma, several words are used to denote their meaning such as 'justice', 'piety', 'duty', 'good conduct', 'mercy', 'charity', 'truthfulness', 'purity', or 'decency'. Ashoka conceptualized dhamma, delineated its principal attributes in great detail, preached and practised it, and had it placed on inscriptions and edicts for the people of his land and beyond for guidance. He wanted dhamma to be the bedrock of peace and stability in India as well as in distant lands. As the Seventh Pillar Edict declares:

so that among my sons and great grandsons and as long as the sun and moon endure, men may follow Dhamma.[9]

Purely from the angle of governance, Ashoka's genius lies in making dhamma amenable to implementation in day-to-day life. An elaborate administrative machinery was created. Ashoka introduced the officer of dhamma known as the dhamma-mahamattas in the fourteenth year of his rule.[10] The Fifth Rock Edict clearly provides that 'dhamma-mahamattas have been employed among all sects for the establishment and growth of dhamma and for the good and happiness of those devoted to religion' in all parts of his kingdom. It adds that the dhamma will also be applicable to the soldiers and their chiefs, Brahmanical ascetics and householders, the destitute, and the infirm because of age, for the good and happiness, and freedom from molestation of those who have applied themselves to dhamma.[11] Officials were also given authority to arrest, try, and award punishment to those who violated the explicit orders of the State. The Edict concludes:

These dhamma-mahamattas are employed among those devoted to Dharma in all places within my dominions, whether one is eager for Dharma or established in Dharma or properly devoted to charity.

For this purpose has this religious edict been inscribed that it may be everlasting and that my descendants may follow in this path.[12]

Ashoka carefully chose the appointment of dhamma-mahamattas and they reported to him directly, with freedom to see him anytime during the day or night. He expressed his views passionately in the Sixth Major Rock Edict, which reads as follows:

Thus speaks the Beloved of the Gods, the King Piyadassi: In the past the quick dispatch of business and the receipt of reports did not take place at all times. But I have arranged it thus. At all times, whether I am eating, or am in the women's apartments, or in my inner apartments, or at the cattle-shed, or in my carriage, or in my gardens—wherever I may be, my informants should keep me in touch with public business. Thus everywhere I transact public business. . . .[13]

One of the responsibilities of dhamma was to attend to the welfare of all people including the lower castes and the less fortunate members of the community. The Second Rock Edict identifies certain measures of social welfare that form part of the working of dhamma. These include medical centres for men and animals, the construction of roads supplied with wells and lined with shady trees, and the planting of medicinal herbs. Ashoka wanted good roads and free movement of goods and services. This not only facilitated trade and commerce but also helped in the spread of his ideas more widely.

In the entire scheme of things of virtuous behaviour, the family occupied a very significant place in Ashoka's scheme of things. The family was the unit where it was easy to be guided at different stages in one's life to make a distinction between virtuous and unvirtuous behaviour. The caste system and its emphasis on ties of kinship made it easier to spread and stress such behaviour.

Ashoka also visualized (first separate Rock Edict) that the officers of dhamma must discharge their responsibilities in a manner which would secure the affection of the people as though they were his children. This paternal relationship was again an attitudinal change in the traditional interaction between rulers and subjects.

Ashoka must have been well aware of the history of sectarian conflicts in the country. These would not only impair social harmony but would also, Ashoka believed strongly, greatly undermine both the influence and spread of dhamma. All edicts and inscriptions meticulously mentioned both Brahmins and *sramanas*—an indicator that in Ashoka's scheme of things equality among sects was paramount. Royal edicts and inscriptions encouraged communities and sects to mingle together. Ashoka perceived long ago the need to facilitate dialogue among people as a key element in preventing the growth of sectarianism in politics or religion.

Another important area of concern to Ashoka was tolerance—tolerance of religious sects by the administration, and by one religious sect for the other. Tolerance, therefore, was considered to be one of the goals of life—virtuous life in terms of dhamma. The Seventh Rock Edict categorically pleads for tolerance among all sects. It reads:

His Sacred and Gracious Majesty desires that in all places should reside people of diverse sects. For they all desire restraint of passions and purity of heart. But men are of various inclinations and of various passions. They may thus perform the whole or a part (of their duties). But of his whose liberality is, too, not great, restraint of passion, inner purity, gratitude and constancy of devotion should be indispensable and commendable.[14]

DHAMMA AND COMMON PEOPLE

Ashoka's principal concern, in an era of rudimentary communication systems, was to reach the maximum number of people with his message of dhamma. Accordingly, the rock edicts, the pillar edicts, and cave and pillar inscriptions were in the local language and in a script that could be easily read by the people. Most of the inscriptions and edicts are in Prakrit and in the Brahmi script. Special care was taken to provide special treatment in areas where the Brahmi script was not prevalent. For example, in Kandhar it was inscribed in Greek and Aramaic and at Mansehra and Shahbazgarhi in Kharosthi.

Ashoka's dhamma, therefore, emerges as a way of life in which the Bahudhā approach of 'one truth, many interpretations' is duly incorporated. Besides, Ashoka's personal commitment to dhamma, his insistence on non-violence, according importance to family relationships, and the absence of a set of dos and don'ts were principal factors that ensured good governance. Individual freedom was guaranteed in the interpretation of principles which were enshrined in the dhamma way of life, and yet at the same time any sharp violation of dhamma norms either in relation to human behaviour or ecology attracted the wrath of the officers of dhamma and of Ashoka himself.

External Relations

The officers of dhamma were also employed for external relations. Under the new policy dispensation, the conquest of foreign countries was no longer in terms of war and violence but in terms of dhamma. By conquest, Ashoka did not mean actual control over affairs of a foreign territory. The use of the term conquest only implied that he and his appointed officers would influence the decision-making process in a foreign country in a manner that the principles of dhamma were followed by that country. Towards this, he included the Greek kingdoms of Syria, Egypt, Cyrene, Macedonia, and Epirus, as also the neighbouring territories of Ceylon and Nepal in area of influence through dhamma.

A CONCLUDING NOTE

Ashoka's successors could not hold the Mauryan Empire intact. Their inept leadership combined with their lack of vision and weak character led to the dissolution of the pan-Indian empire so assiduously built by the triumvirate—Chandragupta, Bindusara, and Ashoka—and the emergence of several principalities all over the country. Dhamma by itself failed to hold the empire together. As John Keay aptly puts it:

Yet a policy that failed became an intimation that endured. The Asokan legacy of an empire which stretched from sea to sea and from the mountains to the peninsula was promptly mislaid and would remain so for a couple of millennia. Likewise Ashoka's historicity. But tradition cherished his memory; Indian historians insist that the ideal of a pan-Indian empire was never forgotten; and nor, more certainly, was the spirit of humanity embodied in his Edicts. The innovation which he pioneered of appealing across the barriers of sect, caste and kin to the community of India would be revived by a host of other reformers, not least Guru Nanak of the Sikhs and eventually Mahatma Gandhi.[15]

Ashoka was a statesman who in his person developed an admirable combination of the elements of idealism and realism.[16] He lived in a world where military conquest by ambitious rulers, duly supported by their powerful armies, was common. He was well aware of the violation of Indian territory by Alexander the Great (356 BC) and later by one of his successors Seleucus (312–281 BC). He, therefore, did not disband his army even though he abjured violence. Nor did he divert the attention of the army from its basic responsibilities by asking them to engage in economically productive pursuits of that time even though peace reigned.

Ashoka, with a remarkable sense of history, also indicated how he would like to be remembered: as a king who built a vast Indian empire by giving it a marked territory from ocean to ocean, from peninsula to peninsula; or as a king who for the first time in history made dhamma an instrument of state policy. The instrumentality of dhamma was not a mantra or gospel but a way of life in order to enable his people to live harmoniously, to allow adherents of every religion to follow their own lights, as there would be no state religion. It also meant the beginning of an era in which there would be no military conquest of countries in the neighbourhood and beyond, and that dhamma would ensure peaceful relationships between nations based on mutual respect. The Eleventh major Rock Edict categorically reveals Ashoka's choice between these two approaches:

Thus speaks the Beloved of the Gods, the King Piyadassi: There is no gift comparable to the gift of dhamma, the praise of dhamma, the sharing of dhamma, fellowship in dhamma. And this is: good behaviour towards slaves and servants, obedience to mother and father, generosity towards friends, acquaintances and relatives, and towards sramanas and Brahmans, and abstention from killing living beings. Father, son, brother, master, friend, acquaintance, relative and neighbour should say, 'this is good, this we should do.' By doing so, there is gain in this world, and in the next there is infinite merit, through the gift of dhamma.[17]

Ashoka, as the rock edicts indicate, wanted himself to be called *Devanampiya Piyadassi*. He was indeed both, *Devanampiya* (The Beloved of the Gods) and *Piyadassi* (gracious of mien). Ashoka was loved and honoured by the people of the land and they continue to do so.

AKBAR

Jalaluddin Muhammad Akbar (1542–1605), popularly referred to as Akbar the Great (*Akbar-e-Azam*), was crowned the third emperor of the Mughal Empire in January 1556 at the age of twelve on death of his father, Humayun. The two principal elements of statecraft that Akbar inherited related to the management of administration of occupied territory and the role of Islam. Firstly, the Afghan system of administration was based on the system of governing by means of large camps, each commanded by a general. The second was the dominance of Islam, the religion of conquerors, in religious affairs. All other religions and every other form of worship was considered inferior to Islam and Islamic practices and was to be looked down upon with scorn and contempt.

Akbar, who was endowed with a spirit of enquiry, soon found this set of values to be grossly inadequate and even undesirable. His reflective mind was unwilling to accept the traditional conqueror's approach to hold and exploit India by maintaining a strong armed presence spread over different parts of the country. He was not willing to ignore the feelings, traditions, longings and aspirations of the people of India. His mind was, therefore, preoccupied with establishing a system that would be based on a union of interests of the ruling elite and the subject population. Similarly, in the religious domain, Akbar soon found that Hinduism, the dominant faith of the Indian people, was over three millennia old while Islam was a new religion. He also realized that an enduring empire must lay down a system of administration based on mutual respect and trust. Differences of race, religion and tradition, were to be accorded due recognition, for securing unity of mind among people of different backgrounds, so that they could repose their confidence in his rule. He worked ceaselessly towards that goal. He showed tremendous discrimination and perception in choosing the right people, in trusting them fully, and in enjoying their company.

In the initial years of his rule, Akbar's main occupation was to annex new territories and to consolidate his empire. He moved from one area to the other as far away as Kabul to assert his authority and control. To attain his objectives, Akbar relied as much on negotiations and diplomacy as on force. His Timurid ancestry was a great asset, but Akbar went beyond, befriending the Islamic nobility. More significant was Akbar's recruitment of Hindu Rajput leaders as members of his empire. He went on to confer high rank, pay, and perquisites to Rajput *rajas*. By 1580, as many as forty-three members of the Mughal nobility belonged to this group. In return for imperial rank and privileges, the rajas acknowledged Akbar's authority over their area. This bond was further cemented by several Rajput rajas offering their daughters in marriage to the Emperor, and Akbar, in turn, accepting them. This seems to have been subsequently rationalized. In accepting Akbar's service, the Rajput rajas accepted him and Akbar, by accepting Hindu wives, had the benefit of cordial relations as also of having an additional support base among those noble families.

Akbar not only built a strong army that was respected by his subjects and feared by his enemies but also a well-knit centralized civil administration. He divided the empire into twelve *subahs* or provinces, which later grew to eighteen. He had a strong cadre of centrally appointed bureaucrats with a clear division of responsibilities between revenue collection and law and order. The revenue officer's job was to ensure that the cultivated land was recorded, the value of the crops assessed, and the share of the government fixed in respect of each owner. The magisterial cadre had to maintain law and order and peace.

SPIRITUAL QUEST

By the time Akbar became king, India had developed two mystic movements: the Bhakti movement by the Hindus and the Sufi movement by the Muslims. It is a sheer historical coincidence that the Bhakti movement began in the Tamil land in the seventh century and the Sufi movement at the same time in Basra (Iraq). The mystics among the Hindus and the Muslims were engaged in knowing the Creator and establishing a relationship with God, not through rituals or even by means of rational enquiries but through love and devotion. The Hindu mystics were known as gurus, *sannyasis*, *jogis*, and *gosains*, and the Muslims of this genre, as *pirs*, *dervishes*, and *faqirs*. Both religious orders spoke in the language of the people, and the mystics of Hinduism and Islam living in different parts of India, sought to create a belief, among the people they came into contact with, that the Creator was one and the same and that Hindu–Muslim differences were artificial. For example, Kabir, born a Muslim, believed in the unity of Ram and Rahim and so did Nanak, a Hindu. Both Hindus and Muslims claimed Kabir and Nanak as their own. Others such as Daud Dayal (1544–1603) shared devotional beliefs and practices with sympathetic Sufis. In folk culture there was a substantial sharing of customs, ceremonies, and beliefs between ordinary Muslims and Hindus.[18]

Alongside these mystics, Islam and Hinduism had their own fundamentalists and diehards. The historian of the orthodox Sunni, Mulla Abdul Qadir Badauni (1540–1615), who hated both Sufism and the Shia cult, bitterly resented Akbar's policy of tolerance. But fortunately, Badauni was a recorder of events and not its maker. The man who was making history was Akbar and he was mostly guided by Mubarak and his two sons, Abul Fazl and Faizi. Shaikh Mubarak hailed from Yemen and migrated to Rel in Sind and finally in 1543 to Agra where he became a teacher. The historians of the period testify to the fact that Mubarak had offended the orthodox Sunnis (being a Sunni himself) by his broadmindedness and his reverence for Sufism. The Sunnis accused him of behaving like a seer. Shaikh Abul Faiz, the eldest son of Shaikh Mubarak rose to become a poet of great eminence whom Akbar appointed Poet Laureate of his court in 1588. Mubarak's second and most celebrated son, Abul Fazl, was a child prodigy who rose to become a military commander. He wrote the *Akbarnama*,[19] which is the authentic history of Akbar's reign. Akbar liked his company because Abul Fazl's views and expressions were above religious biases and were close to Akbar's own basic inclination towards a spiritual quest.[20]

The *Akbarnama* reveals that during the year 1561–2, Akbar continually 'made the pain of seeking after God'. In this quest, he consulted the learned men of different religions. By 1575, he had reached a high pitch of inner turmoil and the *Akbarnama* informs us that 'he spent whole nights in praising God' and relentlessly engaged himself in prayer and meditation. It was in 1575 that he decided to raise the 'Ibadat Khana' or 'House of Worship' in the garden of the royal palace in Fatehpur Sikri.

Ibadat Khana

The Ibadat Khana gradually emerged as the principal centre for interfaith dialogue. Initially the attendance at the meetings of the Ibadat Khana were confined only to issues of Islamic theology and to prominent Muslims—saiyids, ulema, shaikhs, and nobles. It was only later that it was opened to men of all faiths—Muslims, Hindus, Jains, Christians, Jews, Zoroastrians, and others. The sessions usually began on Thursday evenings and Akbar personally conducted its proceedings. The discussions among the religious leaders used to be so intense that at times they continued even beyond midday of Friday. Whenever the language of debate among these men of religion became acrimonious it pained Akbar. As a result of this continuing dialogue, Akbar found some good in every religion and praised that aspect openly. He advocated a policy of 'Peace with all' and sought to concern himself with both the spiritual and material care of every individual in his kingdom.

Akbar recognized that it was necessary to take the best from every faith. The British historian G. B. Melleson, rightly observes:

There is good in every creed; let us adopt what is good, and discard the remainder. Such was his motto. He recognized this feature in the mild and benevolent working of Hinduism, in the care for the family inculcated by it, in the absence of the spirit of proselytism. He recognized it in the simple creed of the followers of Zoroaster. He recognized it in Christianity. There was good in all. He believed, likewise, that there was good in all men. Hence his great forbearance, his unwillingness to punish so long as there was hope of reform, his love of pardoning. 'Go and sin no more' was a precept that constituted the very essence of his conduct.[21]

ABOLITION OF *JIZYA*

The year 711 heralded the beginning of the unequal relationship between the Muslim minority and the Hindu majority in India. In that year, Muhammad ibn al-Qasim succeeded in converting a part of the Indian subcontinent, now Pakistan, to Islam. During his rule, he introduced a discriminatory policy under which all non-Muslims including Hindus, Buddhists, Christians, and Jews would belong to the 'protected people category' referred to as *dhimmi*. Non-Muslims would be required to pay the *jizya*, a poll tax. As Muslim rule expanded to other parts of India, the arena of operation of jizya, the poll tax, also expanded.

Akbar became the first among the Mughal rulers to order a certain degree of equality of treatment among believers of all faiths. Akbar repealed the jizya in 1564, the year of his first pilgrimage to Muinuddin Chishti's shrine in Ajmer.

Din-i-Ilahi

In 1582, Akbar summoned a General Council to which he invited all masters of learning and military commanders. It was here that he announced Din-i-Ilahi, literally making himself the founder and head of a new religion. Din-i-Ilahi contained all the good features of Islam, Hinduism, and Christianity that ensured harmonious living. During the course of his address, he openly confessed that the enmity between the followers of different religions disturbed him greatly. The Din-i-Ilahi in many ways was an expression of what he had acquired in his personal search for enlightenment.

Akbar was very clear in his mind that those alone could be admitted into the Din-i-Ilahi who had 'earnestness of purpose' and the spirit of rational enquiry. Accordingly, the Din-i-Ilahi did not have an independent place of worship. It prescribed no book. Its success lay in establishing among people at the highest level of governance an attitude of mind that harmonized different points of view.

The Din-i-Ilahi, not surprisingly, was viewed by the Muslim clerics as blasphemy. A question that is often raised is whether joining the Din-i-Ilahi order was tantamount to renouncing Islam. This does not seem to be so. Akbar, the founder of the Din-i-Ilahi as, well as Mubarak and members of the Din-i-Ilahi, Abul Fazl and Faizi, always regarded themselves as Muslims. The only Hindu member of this new religious order was Birbal.

Akbar, notwithstanding the authorship of the new path of Din-i-Ilahi, never renounced Islam. He was born a Muslim and died a Muslim. In 1601, five years before his death, Akbar in a letter addressed to the Portuguese Viceroy at Goa, called himself 'the great Lord of the law of Mahomet'.[22] It needs to be emphasized that the funeral rites performed following Akbar's death were those prescribed by Islam and there is no claim that his burial ceremony was not in conformity with his expressed wishes or intentions. However, several of Akbar's attitudes and practices were at variance with the Islamic faith. There is enough evidence to show that from 1580, Akbar had openly started worshipping the sun. According to Badauni, the Emperor had started sun worship under the influence of the Zoroastrians, his Rajput wives, and Birbal.[23] We learn from Abul Fazl that Akbar celebrated the Hindu festival of Diwali with great regularity. Akbar had such a regard for the feelings of the Hindus that when Dusehra happened to fall on the day after his mother's death, he suspended mourning for that day and celebrated the festival as usual.

Akbar at the same time used to celebrate the anniversary of the Prophet's birth with great fervour.[24]

By the late 1580s, Akbar's rule over the Indian subcontinent was firmly established. The era of social conflict and bitterness between Hindus and Muslims was gradually yielding place to better appreciation by both sides of each other's systems of belief. Several mystics, scholars, intellectuals, and common people, both Hindus and Muslims, actively developed an attitude of harmony and understanding, and even of synthesis, among world views of the two religions.

It needs to be emphasized that the ruling nobility among the Muslims had always looked down on other religions. Although Akbar was born in that environment, it was through the spirit of learning from other religions that he had found not only shortcomings in his own religion but also good points in other religions. Once the leading elites of different religions and sects in his kingdom saw in Akbar a person who had the power to rise above narrow and sectarian considerations for the welfare of the people, they started confiding in him. The way he announced rewards and punishment, it became very clear that he recognized merit and public service and disdained wicked and conceited people, and of all areas of conceit, the conceit of learning was most deplorable in Akbar's eyes.

AKBAR AND BAHUDHĀ

Akbar's mental journey on the path of developing a public policy that ensured harmony and goodwill among Hindus and Muslims reveals all the essential ingredients of the Bahudhā approach. He was a devout Muslim and yet when he began to develop an interest in the world around him, he displayed enormous patience to examine whether the other person's point of view and system of belief could be right.

There are several important features of Akbar's approach towards religious harmony. Firstly, in accordance with the Sufi belief system that God is the only reality and all else is illusion, Akbar devoted himself to one God, and again in conformity with Sufi tradition, he did not impose his God upon others.[25] Secondly, like Ashoka, Akbar advocated tolerance for different faiths. He believed that every religion contained a measure of truth. 'It is my duty', he declared 'to be in good understanding with all men. If they walk in the way of God's will, interference with them would be in itself reprehensible: and if otherwise, they are under the malady of ignorance and deserve my compassion.'[26] Akbar went further and in a letter to the Shah of Iran, he defined the responsibility of kingship as follows:

Divine mercy attaches itself to every form of creed, and supreme exertions must be made to bring oneself into the ever vernal flower-garden of 'Peace with all' . . . the eternal God is bounteous to all souls and conditions of men. Hence it is fitting that kings, who are the shadow of Divinity, should not cast away this principle.[27]

Another aspect of Akbar's religious practice lies in his respect for holy men and ascetics irrespective of the religion they professed. He, however, entertained contempt for those who claimed to be men of God but hankered after riches and even misused their position to acquire wealth.

He wanted the scriptures of different religions to be translated so that the components of major religions could be widely shared. Abul Fazl records:

Being aware of the fanatical hatred between Hindus and Muslims, and being convinced that this arose out of mutual ignorance, the enlightened ruler sought to dispel this ignorance by making the books of each religion accessible to the other. He chose the Mahabharata to begin with, as this is the most comprehensive and enjoys the highest authority, and arranged for it to be translated by competent men from both religions. In this way he wished to demonstrate to the Hindus that a few of their erroneous practices and superstitions had no basis in their classics, and also to convince the Muslims that it was absurd to ascribe a mere 7,000 years of existence to the world.[28]

Akbar's great spiritual experiment made a deep impact on Islam itself. Two dominant attitudes among the Muslims became discernible. One was India-oriented and the other looked towards the roots of the Islamic faith beyond India in the Arab lands. This division became sharper during the reign of Akbar's grandson, Aurangzeb. As Annemarie Schimmel observes:

The dual nature of Indian Islam is clearly manifested in Shah Jahan's sons, Dara Shikoh, the mystic, and Aurangzeb, who would be regarded as a fundamentalist today. Aurangzeb wanted to make India a truly Islamic nation. He would only permit those forms of punishment and taxation which were sanctioned by Islamic law.[29]

It was no wonder, therefore, that Aurangzeb reinstated the jizya in 1679.

AKBAR AND THE ARTS

Akbar was intensely involved with the arts. He demanded the highest level of accomplishment from the artists working under him. Despite his inability to read, Akbar enjoyed the literary and historic texts he had read to him regularly and, through a comprehensive plan of selection and illustration, he saw to it that manuscripts produced by the artists reflected his philosophical and religious principles in new and creative ways.

The principal features of the expression of various forms of art during Akbar's domain were beauty and tolerance. He wanted painting in particular to impart among the viewers a kind of peace and almost in the great Hindu tradition, homage to the creator. As Michael Brand and Glenn D. Lowry record:

Akbar demanded that equal attention be paid to both a subject's inner essence and its outer form. His determination that any given form should lead the viewer to a deeper, esoteric meaning is one of the main factors that makes Mughal painting from Akbar's reign so visually and emotionally satisfying. Some of these new powers of artistic expression had a decidedly practical use, allowing Akbar to gauge, for example, the true character of a courtier through his portrait and also strengthened the didactic possibilities of painting. On a metaphysical level, the search of the inner essence behind a given outer form was ultimately seen to bring both patron and artist to a fuller awareness of the Divine, and the power of God the creator.[30]

AKBAR: THE 'REAL INDIAN FOUNDER' OF THE MUGHAL EMPIRE

Akbar was a multifaceted genius. While very young, he established himself as a brilliant warrior, conqueror and administrator. However, Akbar's interests extended far beyond military and civil affairs. Proud of his descent from Timur and Chingiz Khan, he viewed himself as a near-divine figure, responsible for the spiritual and intellectual life of his subjects, as well as for their social life.

Akbar can be rightly called the 'real Indian founder' of the Mughal empire. Babur and Humayun, though men of enormous talent, did not make much impact on statecraft and administration. They remained conquerers.

Akbar's success as a ruler lies primarily in his being a capable administrator. He was endowed with an incisive intellect and vision, a great thirst for knowledge, immense physical strength and courage, and a phenomenal personality. This, coupled with his sincerity, hard work and the strong desire to do what was right, enabled him to build a vast empire. He raised a fine state-system and society that valued unity and harmony more than purity of religion and its practices. The fact that he ruled not merely the land but the hearts of his people has given him a prominent place in history.

JAWAHARLAL NEHRU (1889–1964)

Jawaharlal Nehru was born on 14 November 1889 at Allahabad. His father Motilal Nehru and mother Swarup Rani Nehru were Brahmins from the state of Kashmir who had migrated to Uttar Pradesh, India's most populous state.

The young Nehru had tremendous admiration for the senior Nehru as Motilal seemed to him to be 'the embodiment of strength and courage and cleverness, far above all the other men I saw, and I treasured the hope that when I grew up, I would be rather like him'.[31] Jawaharlal was a lonely child in his father's mansion at Allahabad and was raised by European governesses and tutors, and not by *pandits* and *maulvis* of primary schools that was the lot of children of his age in Allahabad. He was sent to Harrow, in England, in 1905 for his school education. Subsequently, Jawaharlal went to Trinity College, Cambridge where he did his tripos in Natural Science with chemistry, geology, and botany and then to the Inner Temple to study law, being called to the Bar in 1912.

During his stay at Cambridge, Jawaharlal did not join the student politics of the university. Nor did he participate in the union meetings though he was a member and used the club rooms. However, Jawaharlal was interested in political thought and more particularly in the socialist ideas of the Fabians. His attitude was greatly influenced by the British and he himself confessed:

I had imbibed most of the prejudices of Harrow and Cambridge and in my likes and dislikes, I was perhaps more an Englishman than an Indian.[32]

Transformation of Nehru

Three events during 1919–20 transformed Jawaharlal from a young and methodical lawyer of the Allahabad High Court to a rebel and leader of India's freedom struggle and a close follower of Mahatma Gandhi.

The first event related to the introduction of the Rowlatt Bills which sought to empower the authorities, even in peace times, to arrest a person without a warrant, try him quickly, and sentence him.

Explaining Gandhi's distress over these developments, Nehru writes in his autobiography:

Gandhiji has passed through a serious illness early in 1919. Almost from his sick bed he begged the Viceroy not to give his consent to the Rowlatt Bills. That appeal was ignored as others had been and then, almost against his will, Gandhiji took the leadership in his first all India agitation. He started the Satyagraha Sabha, the members of which were pledged to disobey the Rowlatt Act, . . .were to court gaol openly and deliberately.[33]

Jawaharlal wanted to join the Satyagraha Sabha immediately but his father was much against this idea. It was only at Gandhiji's intervention that Nehru did not join the Satyagraha Sabha.

The second event, the Jallianwala Bagh tragedy, followed soon thereafter. M. J. Akbar summarizes the sequence of events as follows:

Ramnavami (the celebration of the birth of Ram) was on April 9 that year. In Amritsar it passed off amid great scenes of communal harmony, but on April 10 the British arrested two local leaders, Dr. Saifuddin Kitchlew and Dr. Satyapal, under the Defence of India Rules. As news spread, a procession formed, demanding their release. The police stopped the crowd at a railway crossing and opened fire. Many died. In anger, the mob retaliated; half a dozen Englishmen sitting in their offices were seized and killed. On April 11, Brigadier-General R.E.H. Dyer arrived to take charge. On April 12, the satyagrahis announced that they would hold a meeting the next day at 4:30 in the afternoon, a few hundred yards away from the Golden Temple, in a park called Jallianwala Bagh. That Sunday was also the day of Baisakhi, a joyous spring celebration that is accompanied by a colourful mela. The Jallianwala Bagh was crowded with more than satyagrahis; there were at least 10,000 people in that walled space with only a single narrow lane to serve as an outlet. General Dyer decided to teach the natives a lesson in the might of British power. With no provocation whatsoever, his troops fired a non-stop fusillade of 1,650 rounds within ten impossible minutes that afternoon, killing, by the official count, 379 people and leaving 200 gasping for life on the ground. That evening the provincial government requested the Viceroy to establish martial law in Punjab; the request was granted on April 15. Censorship cloaked all news of the Jallianwala tragedy from India.[34]

The report of the ghastly massacre of innocent civilians at Jallianwala Bagh spread slowly within the country. The All India Congress Committee formed a committee to conduct an enquiry into the atrocities in the Punjab and Nehru was given the task to assist the committee. Further, the attitude of the British government before their official commission of enquiry was not one of remorse. Instead, it justified these brutal killings. This upset him as much as the reaction of the Englishmen to these events. Nehru wrote many years later that

this cold-blooded approval of that deed shocked me greatly. It seemed absolutely immoral, indecent; to use public school language, it was the height of bad form. I realised then, more vividly than I had ever done before, how brutal and immoral imperialism was and how it had eaten into the souls of the British upper classes.[35]

Jawaharlal's resolution to fight against this 'brutal and immoral imperialism' grew firmer. This tragedy clarified his mind and provided a line of action.

The third event related to Jawaharlal's distress at the exploitative mechanisms that the British had set up to extract money in the name of land revenue from the peasants (*kisans*) of Uttar Pradesh. This had impoverished the peasants. Back at Allahabad, Nehru got entangled in the kisan movement. As Nehru records in his auto-biography: 'That entanglement grew in later years and influenced my mental outlook greatly'.[36] Jawaharlal encouraged the kisans to fight for their rights against the landlords and the zamindars. The kisans reciprocated by giving Jawaharlal their love and trust.

GANDHI AND NEHRU

Gandhi's first impact on young Nehru was strong indeed. Jawaharlal was, in his own words, 'simply bowled over by Gandhi straight off'.[37] It was the Gandhian influence that changed the Nehrus' lifestyle and provided the father and son another way of looking at events taking place around them. Simple living came to Jawaharlal and, in fact, to his entire household. Jawaharlal learnt fast how to spin, moved away from western clothes to khadi attire, and began to read the Bhagavad Gita regularly, 'not from a philosophical or theological point of view', but because 'it had numerous parts which had a powerful effect upon me'.[38] By late 1921, both father and son had experienced their first jail sentences.

It was in Amritsar that Jawaharlal first heard of Gandhi's slogan of *Hindu–Musalman ki jai*. The Hindu–Muslim unity gradually became an integral part of Nehru's political philosophy. As early as in 1921, Jawaharlal records enthusiastically:

It was remarkable how Gandhiji seemed to cast a spell on all classes and groups of people and drew them into one motley crowd struggling in one direction. He became, indeed (to use a phrase which has been applied to another leader), 'a symbolic expression of the confused desires of the people'.[39]

For the next twenty-seven years, Gandhi was Nehru's leader and mentor, and harmony among Hindus and Muslims a basic feature of Nehru's political philosophy. The bond between Gandhi and Nehru lasted for more than a quarter century and deeply influenced the policies and programmes of the Congress party, of the freedom struggle, and also similar struggles for independence against colonial rule in other parts of the world.

Gandhi's concept of non-cooperation and satyagraha greatly impressed Nehru. He was also attracted to Gandhi's ability to harmonize moral principles of truth and non-violence with street techniques of civil disobedience. As a traveller, on the path of a struggle for freedom based on Gandhian principles of truth and non-violence, Nehru found a new meaning to his life.

As Prime Minister of an independent India, Nehru strengthened the institutions of parliamentary democracy and worked strenuously to give India institutions of governance, and also to guarantee their independence and impartial functioning. He launched massive community development programmes and wanted the minorities, the Scheduled Castes, the Scheduled Tribes, and women to play a major role in national reconstruction. He was the father of the Non-Aligned Movement (NAM) and acquired an impressive and unique stature in world affairs.

Bahudhā Approach

Nehru in his own impressive style contributed meaningfully to the Bahudhā approach of 'one truth, many interpretations' and strove earnestly as prime minister and leader of independent India to strengthen the dialogue process and involve the common people of the land in decision-making. He also worked ceaselessly to arrive at the middle path in order that everyone was benefited. Towards this end, he wanted the right means to be followed. He concluded his address to the General Assembly of the United Nations in 1960 with the following words:

I am equally convinced that if we aim at right ends, right means must be employed. Good will not emerge out of evil methods. That was the lesson which our great leader Gandhi taught us, and though we in India have failed in many ways in following his advice, something of his message still

clings to our minds and hearts. In ages long past a great son of India, the
Buddha, said that the only real victory was the one in which all were equally
victorious and there was defeat for no one. In the world today that is the
only practical victory. Any other way will lead to disaster.[40]

Nehru engaged himself in the task of conceptualizing and
implementing some of the core principles of the new Indian nation-
hood: democracy, secularism, socialism, a mixed economy, and non-
alignment. He had implicit faith in dialogue and democratic methods
for achieving harmony among different sections of society as well as
in conflict resolution. This was visible in some of the most significant
areas of social and political concerns: religion, communal harmony,
and secularism, foreign policy, and internal policies in areas of conflict
such as Nagaland.

Religion

There is complete dissonance in the views of Jawaharlal Nehru and
Mahatma Gandhi regarding religion. In his *Autobiography*, Nehru
quoted some of Mahatma Gandhi's writings on religion. Mahatma
Gandhi had categorically said that 'no one can live without religion.'
In another observation, Gandhi linked religion with truth. According
to Gandhi:

My devotion to truth has drawn me into the field of politics; and I can say
without the slightest hesitation, and yet in all humility, that those who say
that religion has nothing to do with politics do not know what religion
means.[41]

Commenting on Gandhi's views on religion, Nehru observed:

Perhaps it would have been more correct if he had said that most of those
people who want to exclude religion from life and politics mean by that
word 'religion' something very different from what he means. It is obvious
that he is using it in a sense—probably moral and ethical more than any
other—different from that of the critics of religion.[42]

Nehru was well aware of the highest and spiritual type of religious
leaders and had enormous respect for them. But organized religion
never appealed to him. For he believed:

'organized religion invariably becomes a vested interest and thus inevitably
a reactionary force opposing change and progress'.[43]

Nehru, however, had developed a fascination for theosophy, the
advaita philosophy of the Vedanta, the Bhagavad Gita, and the River

Ganga, and took enormous pride in the cultural heritage of India. Nehru, however, always dissociated himself from organized religion because rationally he equated it with obscurantism. He was a passionate believer in the separation of religion and politics and an upholder of a secular approach in social relations and in the political processes of decision-making.

Nehru's vision of secularism had four integrated aspects. First, he felt there should be complete segregation of religion from the political, economic, and social aspects of life; religion must be treated as a purely personal matter. Secondly, the State should dissociate itself from religion. Thirdly, there should be full freedom for all religions, and tolerance should be the guiding principle in inter-faith dialogue and contacts. Fourthly, both society and the State should provide equal opportunities for followers of all religions to grow and prosper.

Secularism was, from the beginning, made a basic constituent of the nationalist ideology and the national movement's conception of the independent Indian State. Moreover, at every stage the movement actively opposed communalism. In this respect the transition in Gandhi's thoughts over the years seems very interesting. For years he had emphasized the close connection between religion and politics, but then by religion he meant the common code of morality (dharma) which underlies all religions. But when he saw that communalists were using religion in the doctrinal or sectarian sense to attract people to their politics, he categorically stated in 1942 that religion is the personal affair of each individual. It must not be mixed with politics or national affairs.[44] Similarly, Nehru argued that secularism could form the only basis for national unity in a multi-religious society. Bhagat Singh, the great martyr, declared in the 1920s that communalism was as avowed an enemy of the Indian people as was colonialism.

It is true that the national movement failed to successfully combat communal forces and ideology and the country underwent partition in 1947. But the strength of the movement's deep commitment to secularism was demonstrated when despite partition and the attendant communal violence, independent India made secularism a basic pillar of its Constitution as also of the State and society.

Several scholars have discerned a change in Nehru's attitude towards religion and ethical values as he grew old. R. K. Karanjia writes:

Nehru spoke to him of ethical and spiritual solutions. 'What you say,' Karanjia said, 'raises the vision of Mr. Nehru in search of God in the evening of his life.' 'Yes', said Nehru, 'I have changed. . .the old Hindu idea that there is a divine essence in the world, that every individual possesses something of it, and can develop it appeals to me.[45]

Notwithstanding these statements, Nehru remained an agnostic. Nehru was always too concerned about the life of the present, about rationality, and possibly did not realize 'the divine harmony within him'. It is another matter that after his death his family decided to cremate him in accordance with traditional Hindu rites and it would be appropriate to conclude that it was not against Nehru's wishes.

Religion is both a private and collective affair in India and in other countries of South Asia. We cannot, therefore, think of India in terms of secularism in its elitist sense with its anti-religious and atheist overtones. At the same time, Nehru's emphasis on keeping the State free from taking sides in religious matters is a very sound approach. There is need to evolve an Indian model of secularism within the Gandhi–Nehru framework.

Communal Harmony

From the beginning of his political career in the early 1920s, Jawaharlal Nehru was totally opposed to communalism. Nehru forcefully supported the 'Hindu–Muslim Bhai–Bhai' approach for he realized, like other leaders of the freedom struggle, that Hindu–Muslim unity was necessary for winning independence. Nehru believed that communalism did not represent the Indian social reality and the real problems that affected the country and the people. He could see clearly that although Hindus, Muslims and Sikhs did not share a common religion, they had common social, economic, and political interests. He condemned both Muslim communal organizations and their Hindu counterparts. He saw that the communal card was being played for securing jobs in government offices or seats in legislatures. Accordingly, it was patronized by the upper middle classes, princes, landlords, and zamindars.

Nehru believed that communalism was the Indian version of fascism. Nehru's commitment to a secular democratic social order took deeper root as he moved around the entire country and talked to common people as well as their local leaders. Nehru could clearly see that religion was not at the root of communalism and, though India had many religions, religious differences were not the cause of communalism. Communal conflict, he wrote in *The Discovery of India* 'had nothing to do with religion though religion often masked the issue'.[46]

His total opposition to communalism also meant his total commitment to secularism. Immediately after independence and the partition of India there were voices within the country, duly supported by some quarters within the Congress, that demanded that India should do to Muslims in India what Pakistan was doing to the Hindus across the border. Nehru condemned this attitude and declared that India should be willing 'to stand or fall' by its commitment to secular values. He carried out a massive private and public campaign against communalism and in favour of secular values through speeches, radio broadcasts, interventions in Parliament, and letters to Congressmen as well as to chief ministers of states. Nehru was so passionate a critic of communalism that in October 1951 he declared:

If any person raises his hand to strike down another on the ground of religion, I shall fight him till the last breath of my life, both as the head of the Government and from outside.[47]

On 2 October 1947, Nehru condemned the demand of the Hindu Mahasabha and Jan Sangh in very strong words while addressing the Delhi Pradesh Congress Committee, 'The demand for a Hindu State is not only stupid and medieval but also fascist in nature. Those who put forth such ideas will meet the same fate as Hitler and Mussolini.'

Nehru played a major role in the Constituent Assembly to ensure that the Constitution fully embodied secular ideas. Nehru was more liberal towards the Muslims as they were backward and more disadvantaged, and also because he wanted to allay their fears so that they could be reassured about their equal status within the Indian Union. Nehru rightly observed:

Our Constitution lays down that we are a secular state, but it must be admitted that this is not wholly reflected in our mass living and thinking. In a country like England, the state is, under the Constitution, allied to one particular religion, the Church of England, which is a sect of Christianity. Nevertheless, the state and the people there largely function in a secular way. Society, therefore, in England is more advanced in this respect than in India, even though our Constitution may be, in this matter, more advanced.[48]

According to Y. D. Gundevia, in late 1963, Nehru had joined one of the Friday morning meetings at the foreign office where all the members of the Indian Foreign Service had gathered for a general free-for-all. Taking advantage of Nehru's presence the topic shifted to the professed neutrality of the services. Gundevia asked:

Well, sir, this being the case, what happens if tomorrow, shall we say, the Communists come into power? We have had a Communist government in Kerala. But what happens to the services if the Communists are elected to power, tomorrow, at the Centre, here in Delhi?

Nehru pondered before answering, 'Communists, Communists, Communists! Why are all of you so obsessed with Communists and Communism? What is it that Communists can do that we cannot do and have not done for the country? Why do you imagine the Communists will ever be voted into power at the Centre!' A pause, and then the words came slowly and deliberately: 'The danger to India, mark you, is not communism. It is Hindu right-wing communalism'.[49]

Before the meeting closed, Jawaharlal Nehru repeated those two sentences. The message against communalism was loud and clear.

Foreign Policy

Jawaharlal Nehru was an irrepressible idealist both in national affairs and in foreign policy. He could visualize the impermanence of the post-Second World War arrangements of the world divided into two power blocs. The Non-Aligned Movement established by Nehru along with Sukarno (1901–70) of Indonesia, Marshal Josip Broz Tito (1892–1980) of Yugoslavia and Colonel Gamal Abdel Nasser (1918–70) of Egypt provided a middle path and gave rights to the newly independent countries to take a stand on global issues of peace and development on merit. In this middle path, the dignity of people long subjected to external domination and neglect was asserted.

Nehru never saw foreign policy exclusively in terms of the interests of India. In his view it was a means to promote peace and harmony in the whole world. He always associated Indian interests with the larger interests of mankind. This was in line with his approach as a freedom fighter. This policy brought India at the centre-stage of global affairs and earned him enormous respect.

Nehru consistently spoke against the use of nuclear energy for military purposes. As a pacifist he went on to pledge that India would not make nuclear weapons. At the same time, he was against any discriminatory regime in respect of nuclear weapons. It is in this spirit that he rejected the Non-Proliferation Treaty which provided that the five privileged nuclear weapons powers—USA, USSR, UK, France, and China—were free to proliferate nuclear weapons while other countries like India and were denied the right to manufacture them.

From the very beginning, Nehru followed a policy of peace and friendship towards China. His principled approach to politics found expression in the 1954 agreement between India and China enunciating the five principles of Panchsheel: respect for sovereignty, non-aggression, non-interference in internal affairs, equality and peaceful coexistence. Later the same year, the Joint Declaration issued by Nehru, at the end of the eighteen-day State visit of Yugoslav leader Josip Broz Tito to India, reiterated the five principles or Panchsheel. Nehru wanted them to be followed in world affairs.

Nehru's idealism suffered grievously in relation to China, which launched a military offensive against India in 1962. Nehru admitted soon after the Chinese invasion that he was living in a world of unreality. On 3 September 1963, he informed the Rajya Sabha that

we had thought in terms of carrying the banner of peace everywhere and we were betrayed. China has betrayed us; the world has betrayed us. Our efforts to follow the path of peace have been knocked on the head. We are forced to prepare for a defensive war, much against our will.[50]

Nehru had realized that China could not be trusted. Yet he decided to adhere to his policy of conciliation with regard to China. As a follower of Mahatma Gandhi, he was firm in his resolve that he would not compromise on basic issues of security and the territorial integrity of the country, and there was no room for fear. However, he emphasized a middle path between war mongering and panic. He was firm on seeking a peaceful settlement with China despite what they had done. Nehru's successors have also followed this approach in relations with China and it is slowly yielding results.

Naga Policy

Jawaharlal Nehru was a great admirer of the tribal way of life. He was fascinated by the spontaneity of tribals and their capacity for joy and heroism. At the same time, he was aware of their appalling poverty, destitution, and ignorance. To him, the protection of tribals from exploiters and the safeguarding of what was beautiful, free, and enchanting in their societies and culture were important tasks. In his thinking, one of the signs of a civilized, democratic society was that the state system must be sensitive to the tribal way of life. An effort was necessary to protect the tribal languages and prevent the loss of their oral literatures and identity. The process of modernization, according to him, must not force a sudden break with their past but help them to build upon it. People should be allowed to develop along the lines of their own genius and nothing should be imposed on them, and their traditional arts and culture must be encouraged.[51]

The policy of large-heartedness and magnanimity that Nehru advocated towards the tribes was put to severe test in his lifetime in dealing with the Nagas.[52] Soon after Independence, a demand was made by certain groups of Nagas for an independent country.

In the first general elections in February 1952, the electoral process could not take place in the Naga Hills as, at the instance of Zapu Phizo, the Nagas did not seek election either to the State Assembly or the Lok Sabha and none voted although arrangements were made by the Election Commission to hold elections.[53] The fate of the first elections to the newly-formed district councils was similar.

On 22 March 1956, the Naga National Council (NNC) proclaimed the independent Naga Federal Government under the leadership of Zapu Phizo, and insurgency commenced in an organized manner. This necessitated deployment of armed forces in Nagaland, but Nehru persevered with his policy of willingness to discuss the aspirations of the Naga people if the Naga leadership decided to abjure violence and thoughts of sovereignty. Nehru was concerned about evolving possible ways to make the Nagas feel at home in India and was in favour of according a favoured treatment to the Nagas. Violence from Nagaland always disturbed him. On 22 January 1957, in a communication to S. Fazl Ali, the then Governor of Assam, Nehru wrote:

About the Nagas, I am much worried. This worry is not due so much to the military or other situations but rather to a feeling of psychological defeat. Why should we not be able to win them over? I do not like being pushed into repressive measures anywhere in India ... this long-drawn out business has a bad effect, both internationally and nationally, and, if I may say so, personally on me. I am, therefore, prepared to consider any reasonable approach to this problem which promises a settlement.[54]

The army succeeded in controlling the insurgency. Phizo fled to Europe. The moderates among the Nagas started getting primacy over those who advocated violent methods of secession.

Nehru was very clear that the demand of the Nagas for giving them the Tuensang frontier division, which was then part of North-East Frontier Agency (NEFA), could be considered by amending the

Constitution. Notwithstanding the opposition of Bishnu Ram Medhi, the Chief Minister of Assam, Nehru announced that he would be willing to, in consultation with Naga opinion, amend the Constitution so as to grant the maximum autonomy to the Nagas and help them on the path of self-development rather than attempt any imposition of reforms. Accordingly, on 1 December 1957, Tuensang district came to be a part of the Naga Hills. It was because of Nehru's farsightedness that the state of Nagaland was inaugurated on 2 December 1963.

Fortunately, the process of dialogue, as a means for the resolution of conflict in Nagaland, has been continued by Nehru's successors. In keeping with Nehru's legacy there should be sincere and imaginative efforts to accord the people of Nagaland powers that should be given to a federating unit within the constitutional and parliamentary framework of empowerment. The Nagas have a great sense of realism, and once it is clear to them that the Government of India is willing to give them all that it can within the framework of the Constitution and powers of Parliament, it should not be difficult for them to conclude an agreement to end this long period of strife and uncertainty. The empowerment of the Naga people and their democratic institutions of governance would lead to peace and amity among the tribes and their neighbourhood, as also unprecedented economic and cultural progress.

Nehru had great affection for the tribals and the tribals had faith in him. Verrier Elwin, Nehru's friend and a person dedicated to the cause of the tribals, perhaps expressed Nehru's contribution to the tribal philosophy meaningfully when he wrote:

Into our thinking about the tribes he has brought science, humanity and respect; and I liked the man who once remarked to me that 'the whole of the Prime Minister's tribal policy can be summed up in one word—humility'![55]

CONCLUDING REMARKS

Nehru was committed to the persuasive powers of dialogue with even one's bitterest enemies and therefore, despite the Chinese perfidy, did not put India on a permanent path of confrontation with that country. He was a firm believer in deliberative forums like legislatures and the parliament, and international political institutions like the Commonwealth and the United Nations. His commitment to democracy was matched equally by his belief in the plurality of Indian culture, which over the millennia had acquired several beautiful patterns. It was against this background that Nehru did not either accept or reject Western or Indian ideas and practices in their totality, but subjected them to rational evaluation and the need of the hour. This was in conformity with the values that were propagated by the builders of the Indian nation such as Swami Vivekananda, Mahatma Gandhi, and Rabindranath Tagore.

ASHOKA, AKBAR, AND NEHRU

Ashoka was born and brought up a Hindu. It was later that he was attracted to, and adopted, Buddhism, and popularized it within and outside India. He, however, neither formally renounced Hinduism nor adorned the garb of a bhikku.

Akbar, too, was born and brought up a Muslim. It was only through dialogue with believers of other faiths that he saw merit in them. His rational enquiry convinced him that every religion had some element of truth, and that there was need for having a new religious and ethical order that combined the positive points of all faiths. In many ways, Akbar was the first to make a comparative study of religions and in this task he was assisted by learned men of different faiths of his time: Islam, Hinduism, Christianity, and Zoroastrianism.

Nehru was born a Hindu but was brought up in a secular environment. He did not go to any school in Allahabad and teachers who taught him at his father's mansion in Allahabad were Christians. His father was not a practising Hindu. The only traditional Hindu influence upon Jawaharlal as a child was that of his mother, Swarup Rani, who was deeply religious. Two of Jawaharlal's aunts in the family home at Allahabad too were also devout Hindus. As a child, Jawaharlal was more attracted towards and thus was more influenced by his father, Motilal. His subsequent seven-year stint in England for studies kept him away from Hindu religious environs. It was, therefore, no surprise that in 1912, on his return from England, Nehru described himself as 'more an Englishman than an Indian'.

After the conquest of Kalinga, Ashoka had adopted the way of the Buddha. He renounced war as an instrument of national policy. Equally significant is his positive approach in looking at harmony among people and conducting relations with neighbouring countries and beyond in accordance with dharma. Never before in history were officials appointed with the unique title of dhamma-mahamattas, and more importantly, they delivered service. In the remaining approximately four decades of rule, Ashoka never deviated from the path of dhamma and non-violence and dedicated himself solely to the task of welfare of the entire people.

It may be recalled that although Akbar was born in India (in Sind, now in Pakistan), he had Turkish, Mongol, and Persian ancestors. On his father's side he was the seventh generation in descent from Timur (1336–1405), and through the mother of Babur he was a descendant from Chingiz Khan (1162–1227). Both Chingiz and Timur were outstanding generals and their military strategy had greatly influenced Akbar. Notwithstanding this martial background, a transformation took place in Akbar as he moved to administer the country, mingle with the common people in courts and incognito in bazaars, and engaged in learned discourses with leaders of different faiths. Akbar soon developed a strong desire not only to acquire an imperial halo for himself but also to be genuinely respected by the Hindus and Muslims of India, and to have a place of honour in history.

In many ways, Akbar carried forward in his Din-i-Ilahi the essence of the synergetic approach enunciated by Kabir and Nanak, but it failed. Din-i-Ilahi could not become a substitute for Hinduism, Islam or Christianity despite Akbar's patronage. Perhaps rulers are ill suited to be pathfinders of religious or spiritual orders. And Akbar could never become a Confucius or a religious leader.

There is nothing to show that Akbar was aware of Ashoka and his achievements. Although separated by a distance in time of 1800 years, both Ashoka and Akbar, had similar ideas about India and its territorial boundaries. Ashoka's conquest of Kalinga and Akbar's annexation of Kashmir, Orissa, Sind, and the Deccan kingdoms were at a conceptual level attempts at bringing far-flung territories of India within its ambit.

Ashoka, Akbar, and Nehru had different beginnings in terms of the leadership of India. Ashoka began his rule over India with some of the finest armies and set up his empire over the major part of the Indian subcontinent. He became a pacifist towards the end of his rule but never reduced the armed strength of the empire. Similarly, Akbar began as a conqueror and gradually built a strong military, and it was only after his kingdom was firmly established that he developed policies of peace and religious fraternity in the country. Again like Ashoka, he never reduced his military strength. Nehru, contrary to both Ashoka and Akbar, began his life as a freedom fighter and a believer in truth, non-violence, and peace under Mahatma

Gandhi's leadership. He did not attach much importance to strengthening the armed forces as the prime minister. It was not that he was not conscious of the need for a strong army or its relevance, but he attached primacy to peace and development over the military might of the country.

It is evident that for the maintenance of peace and the rule of law, as well as for a harmonious quality of life, political leadership and the presence of credible armed forces are essential. The Bahudhā approach flourishes in such an environment and also helps to provide society sustainable peace and development.

Nehru had enormous respect for Ashoka and his contribution to the building of the great Indian empire. In his *The Discovery of India*, Nehru ends his essay on Ashoka quoting approvingly the following words of the famous novelist and historian H. G. Wells:

Amidst the tens of thousands of names of monarchs that crowd the columns of history, their majesties and graciousnesses and serenities and royal highnesses and the like, the name of Ashoka shines, and shines almost alone, a star. From the Volga to Japan his name is still honoured. China, Tibet, and even India, though it has left his doctrine, preserve the tradition of his greatness. More living men cherish his memory today than have ever heard the names of Constantine or Charlemagne.[56]

It was Nehru who moved a resolution in the Constituent Assembly to make Ashoka's lion the seal of the Republic, which was unanimously adopted. Nehru had an immense admiration for Akbar as well and particularly what Akbar achieved in his task of strengthening the common culture in India and also in centralizing its administrative structure. However, in his view, Akbar failed on two counts. Firstly, as Nehru writes:

With all his great prestige as the Great Mughal and the strength of his empire as a land power, he was powerless at sea. Vasco da Gama had reached Calicut, via the Cape, in 1498; Albuquerque had seized Malacca in 1511 and established Portuguese sea power in the Indian Ocean. Goa on the western coast of India had become a Portuguese possession.[57]

Secondly, Nehru felt that:

Akbar might have laid the foundations of social change if his eager, inquisitive mind had turned in that direction and sought to find out what was happening in other parts of the world.[58]

It is true that Akbar did not build the navy, nor did he take advantage of the progress in science and industry that the western countries were making in his time. But Nehru too erred. Some historians would blame Nehru for neglecting the task of modernization of the armed forces and some others for his limited achievement in the area of universalization of primary education. And yet Nehru fashioned not only the office and role of prime minister but also deeply influenced the working of other political and constitutional offices through his personal guidance and example. He initiated a deep and wide-ranging dialogue about tradition and modernity and directly talked to the people. He succeeded hugely in modernizing Indian society through his emphasis on rational enquiry and scientific temper.[59]

Jawaharlal Nehru was a great exponent of the Bahudhā approach of dialogue and ceaselessly emphasized the need for harmony in social affairs. The Executive Board of UNESCO brilliantly summed up Nehru's role in this regard in its resolution which reads:

Jawaharlal Nehru has radiated over the world like a beacon of tolerance and understanding among the peoples. This is because, all his life long, he never ceased to believe in the supremacy of the spirit in history and because never, not even while in prison and not even while holding power—which is also a prison in many respects—did he allow the call of human brotherhood and the demands of individual and national freedom to become separate spiritual aspirations.[60]

The Nehruvian ideals of socialism within the country and non-alignment as a policy in international relations may have little relevance today but Nehru is still being admired as the person who, along with Gandhi, became the most visible embodiment of India's struggle for freedom, working tirelessly and imaginatively as prime minister in building modern India in the seventeen years of his stewardship of the national government of the world's largest democracy. While assessing Nehru's rank in the pantheon of twentieth century leaders, Ralph Buultjens rightly observes:

. . .by criteria that combine intellect, humanity and enlightened leadership with scale of endeavour, Nehru makes it to the top rung of modern political giants—probably the only non-Western head of government to do so.[61]

All three—Ashoka, Akbar, and Nehru—attempted to rethink and mould society anew, according to the vision and principles of good government as they perceived it. In their perception they thought ahead of their time. Each of them had great personal charm, brilliance of mind and sense of dedication, and looked upon themselves as men of destiny. Each one left a remarkable legacy that has profoundly enriched both Bahudhā philosophy and history. All three are legendary figures and the lore and fables of the Mauryas, the Mughals, Mahatma Gandhi, and Jawaharlal Nehru, and other participants in the epic struggle for freedom constitute the common heritage of the people of India and the world.

NOTES

1. Confucius (551–478 BC) also prescribes duties for public servants. He further goes on to write:

   To see men of worth and not recommend them to office, or to fail to be the first to do so—that is being disrespectful or negligent of one's duty toward his ruler. To see bad men and not be able to remove them from office and to fail to remove them as far away as possible—that is weakness.

   Further he remarks: 'The life of the moral man is an exemplification of the universal moral order. The life of the vulgar person, on the other hand, is a contradiction of the universal moral order.'

   Please see *www.confucius.org* for this and other quotations.

2. A.L. Basham, *The Wonder that was India: A Survey of the Culture of the Indian Subcontinent before the Coming of the Muslims*, Grove Press, New York, 1954, p. 80. Basham writes:

   From the Gupta period and the Middle Ages a number of political texts survive, the most important of which are the Nitisara ('Essence of Politics') of Kamandaka, perhaps written during the Gupta period, the Nitivakyamrta ('Nectar of Aphorisms on Politics') of Somadeva Suri, a Jaina writer of the 10th century, and the Nitisastra ('Treatise on Politics') attributed to the ancient sage Sukra, but evidently of later medieval origin. These repeat much that has been said before, but here and there contain original ideas. Besides sources specifically dealing with political life and thought, ancient Indian literature as a whole, from the *Rg Veda* onwards, yields much information, and inscriptions of one kind and another are extremely valuable in this connexion.

3. It is possible that one of Seleucus' daughters came to the Mauryan court at Pataliputra, in which case a number of Greek women would have accompanied her. Seleucus' ambassador Megasthenes lived for many years at Pataliputra and travelled extensively in India. There was a regular exchange of envoys between the Mauryas and the Seleucids, accompanied by an exchange of gifts (which included many potent aphrodisiacs!). That foreigners were welcome to Pataliputra seems

evident from the statement that the municipality in the city had a special committee to look after the welfare of foreigners. See Romila Thapar, *A History of India,* Vol. 1, Penguin, Middlesex, 1966, p. 71.

4. In Buddhist literature cakravartin is described as universal emperor whose dominions included the whole of Jambudvipa—from ocean to ocean. For further details see Romila Thapar, *Asoka and the Decline of the Mauryas,* Oxford University Press, New Delhi, 1997, p. 146.
5. There are legends that it was Ashoka who had built the city of Srinagar.
6. Thapar, *Asoka and the Decline of the Mauryas,* 1997, pp. 138–9.
7. Ibid., pp. 255–7.
8. Kautilya (ed. and trans. L.N. Rangarajan, etc.,) *The Arthashastra,* p. 741. Quoted in John Keay, *India: A History,* Grove Press, New York, 2000, p. 92.
9. Thapar, *Asoka and the Decline of the Mauryas,* p. 266.
10. The Fifth Rock Edict clearly stipulates both the fact that there were no dhamma-mahamattas previously and that they have only now been created.
11. Radhakumud Mookerji, *Asoka,* Motilal Banarsidass, New Delhi, 2002 (reprint), pp. 139–42.
12. Ibid., p. 144.
13. Thapar, *Asoka and the Decline of the Mauryas,* pp. 252–3.
14. Mookerji, *Asoka,* pp. 149–50.
15. Keay, *India,* p. 100.
16. The famous author Radhakumud Mookerji opens his pioneering work, *Asoka,* with the following words:

In the annals of kingship there is scarcely any record comparable to that of Ashoka, both as a man and as a ruler. ... To bring out the chief features of his greatness, historians have instituted comparisons between him and other distinguished monarchs in history, eastern and western, ancient and modern, pagan, Moslem, and Christian. In his efforts to establish a kingdom of righteousness after the highest ideals of a theocracy, he has been likened to David and Solomon of Israel in the days of its greatest glory; in his patronage of Buddhism, which helped to transform a local religion into a world religion, he has been compared to Constantine in relation to Christianity; in his philosophy and piety he recalls Marcus Aurelius, he was a Charlemagne in the extent of his empire and, to some extent, in the methods of his administration, too, while his Edicts, 'rugged, uncouth, involved, full of repetitions,' read like the speeches of Oliver Cromwell in their mannerisms [Rhys Davids]. Lastly, he has been compared to Khalif Omar and Emperor Akbar, whom also he resembles in certain respects.

See Mookerji, *Asoka,* p. 1.
17. Thapar, *Asoka and the Decline of the Mauryas,* pp. 254–5.

18. John F. Richards, *The New Cambridge History of India: The Mughal Empire*, Cambridge University Press, Cambridge, 1993, p. 34.

19. The three volumes of *Akbarnama* by Abul Fazl contain the most comprehensive information about the organization of the Empire and the army, down to the number of employees in the fruit storerooms, and the food that was given to the best hunting leopards (cheetahs). *Ain-i-Akbari* is an incomparable guide to Mughal administration.

20. The following record would testify this:

    Abul Fazl was much distressed by discord between different faiths. 'I became acquainted with the tenets of all creeds', he states in almost the same terms as Akbar, 'and my spirit was weary of their multitude.' The following extract, from the inscription composed by him for a temple in Kashmir, expresses his philosophy:

    If it be a mosque, people murmur the holy prayer, and if it be a Christian church, people ring the bell from love to thee. Sometimes I frequent the Christian cloister, and sometimes the mosque, But it is Thou whom I search from temple to temple.

    He embarked on an exposition of Hindu religion and philosophy 'in order that hostility towards them [the Hindus] might abate and the temporal sword be stayed awhile from the shedding of blood'. He rationalised idol worship by explaining that images 'are fashioned as aids to fix the mind and keep the thoughts from wandering, while the worship of God alone is required as indispensable'. He had married Hindu, Kashmiri and Irani wives who were all 'occasions of great joy' to him.

    See S.M. Burke, *Akbar: The Greatest Mogul*, Munshiram Manoharlal, New Delhi, 1989, pp. 101–2.

21. G.B. Malleson, *Rulers of India: Akbar*, Clarendon Press, Oxford, 1890, p. 199.

22. Burke, *Akbar: The Greatest Mogul*, p. 122.

23. Both Akbar and Abul Fazl are emphatic that worship of the sun was not meant to be 'a deification of the sun' but a means of worshipping God. 'A special grace proceeds from the sun in favour of kings', argued Akbar, 'and for this reason they pray and consider it a worship of the Almighty.' According to Abul Fazl, 'the fire of the sun is the torch of God's sovereignty' and 'if light and fire did not exist, we would be destitute of food and medicines; the power of sight would be of no avail to the eyes.' And it is in respect for the sun 'the light of all lights' that 'actuates His Majesty to venerate fire and reverence lamps.' To worship fire and light was 'a religious duty and divine praise'; only the ignorant considered this to be forgetfulness of the Almighty and fire-worship'. A fire was kept alive perpetually in the royal palace in a fire-pot (*agingir*). In the evening the entire court had to rise respectfully

when the lamps and candles were lighted. See Burke, *Akbar: The Greatest Mogul,* pp. 122–3.

24. Burke, *Akbar: The Greatest Mogul,* p. 122.

25. The Emperor's obsession with God is evident from the fact that he named his cult Din-i-Ilahi, his calendar Ilahi Era, his unit of measurement Ilahi Gaz, and his gentlemen troopers Ahadis (*ahad,* one, emphasizing the unity of God). A paraphrase Burke, *Akbar: The Greatest Mogul,* p. 126.

26. Burke, *Akbar: The Greatest Mogul,* p. 127.

27. Ibid.

28. Annemarie Schimmel, *The Empire of the Great Mughals,* Oxford University Press, New Delhi, 2004, p. 113.

29. Ibid., p. 109.

30. Michael Brand and Glenn D. Lowry, *Akbar's India: Art from the Mughal City of Victory,* The Asia Society Galleries, New York (Distributed by Sotheby Publications, London), 1985, p. 128.

31. *Jawaharlal Nehru: An Autobiography,* Oxford University Press, New Delhi, 1988 (sixth impression), p. 7.

32. S. Gopal, *Jawaharlal Nehru: A Biography,* Volume 1, Oxford University Press, New Delhi, 1975, p. 28.

33. John Lane, *Jawaharlal Nehru, An Autobiography,* The Podly Head, London, 1936, p. 41.

34. M.J. Akbar, *Nehru: The Making of India,* Viking, London, 1988, pp. 117–18.

35. See Jawaharlal Nehru's article on the Quetta earthquake written in August 1935 and reprinted in Jawaharlal Nehru *India and the World,* George Allen & Unwin, London, 1936, p. 147 (available with Nehru Memorial Museum and Library, New Delhi).

36. Nehru, *An Autobiography,* p. 51.

37. Tibor Mende, *Conversations with Mr. Nehru,* Secker & Warburg, London, 1956, p. 23.

38. Ibid., pp. 24–31.

39. Ibid., p. 75.

40. Quoted from B.R. Nanda (ed.), *Mahatma Gandhi: 125 years,* Indian Council for Cultural Relations and New Age International Publishers, New Delhi, 1995, pp. 118–19. (Jawaharlal Nehru, speech to the UN General Assembly, New York, 3 October 1960).

41. Nehru, *An Autobiography,* p. 377.

42. Ibid., p. 380.

43. Ibid., p. 377.

44. Bipan Chandra, 'The Legacy of India's Freedom Struggle', Nalini Menon (ed.), *The Indian Experience,* Media Transasia, Bangkok, 1997, p. 16.

45. R. K. Karanjia, *The Mind of Mr. Nehru,* George Allen & Unwin, London, 1960, pp. 32–3.

46. Jawaharlal Nehru, *The Discovery of India*, Oxford University Press, New Delhi, p. 343.
47. Mani Shankar Aiyar, *Confessions of a Secular Fundamentalist*, Penguin, New Delhi, 2004.
48. S. Gopal (ed.), *Jawaharlal Nehru: An Anthology*, Oxford University Press, New Delhi, 1980, pp. 330–1.
49. Akbar, *Nehru: The Making of India*, p. 580.
50. *Jawaharlal Nehru Centenary Volume*, Oxford University Press, New Delhi, 1989, p. 600.
51. Ibid., pp. 585–6.
    The finest expression of Nehru's tribal philosophy is recorded in his preface to Verrier Elwin's treatise *A Philosophy for NEFA*. Quoted in Balmiki Prasad Singh's article Nehru's Tribal Philosophy in Jawaharlal Nehru Centenary Volume, Oxford University Press, Delhi, 1989, p. 586.
52. The origins of the word 'naga' or 'nagas' is shrouded in mystery. But its popularization is certainly a 19th century phenomenon. For a very long time, the Assamese plains' people have called them 'noga'. The appellation 'nagas' has acquired a generic form that includes more than 30 tribes that live in Nagaland and the neighbouring states of Assam, Arunachal Pradesh, and Manipur and the bordering nation-state of Myanmar.

    The Nagas migrated into the Naga Hills from southeast China and Burma over a long period of time. The Naga legends make us believe that all the Naga tribes migrated from Burma across the Somra tracts and reached a place called Khezekenoma just across the border of Manipur. The name Naga was given to them by outsiders. The Nagas resented the name for long, till political expediency caused it to be accepted. The different Naga tribes never lived as one group. Each tribe lived in one village or more which belonged to them exclusively. Each village was self-sufficient as demands were limited and by and large maintained its independent character. Any interference, trespassing or encroachment by members of other villages (which invariably meant another tribe) in its territorial jurisdiction usually provoked inter-village war leading at times to head-hunting.
53. Democratic processes have since taken root in Nagaland. The idea that power can be turned to utilitarian goals in a democracy is well accepted. This has been possible in great measure because the policies enunciated by Nehru were pursued by successive prime ministers.
54. Gopal, *Jawaharlal Nehru: A Biography*, Vol. 3, p. 29.
55. *Jawaharlal Nehru Centenary Volume*, p. 591.
56. Nehru, *The Discovery of India*, p. 135.
57. Ibid., p. 260.
58. Ibid., p. 264.

59. Judith M. Brown, *Nehru: A Political Life*, Oxford University Press, New Delhi, 2003, pp. 338–45.
60. *Nehru and the Modern World*, Indian National Commission for Cooperation with UNESCO, New Delhi, 1967, p. 7.
61. Ralph Buultjens, *India: Statesmen for All Seasons*, Asian Review, Hong Kong, October 2005, pp. 19–41.

7
Among People

Blessed are the meek, for they will inherit the earth. . .
Blessed are the peacemakers, for they will be called children of God.[1]

—The Bible

India's chequered political history and the intertwining of religion into the socio-political fabric of the country has imparted a typical temper and personality to the Indian people that sets them apart from people elsewhere in the world. Ancient scriptures like the Ramayana, the Mahabharata, and the Bhagavad Gita are as much part of the Indian subconscious as other scriptures and writings. Different religious or ethnic groups such as Buddhists, Jains, Muslims, Christians, and Parsis, and many more, have added beliefs and expressions from their rich heritage to this commonality of expression.

Jawaharlal Nehru captures the pluralist ethos of India admirably when he writes in *The Discovery of India*:

India with all her infinite charm and variety began to grow upon me more and more, and yet the more I saw of her, the more I realised how very difficult it was for me or for anyone else to grasp the ideas she had embodied. It was not her wide spaces that eluded me, or even her diversity, but some depth of soul which I could not fathom, though I had occasional and tantalising glimpses of it. She was like some ancient palimpsest on which layer upon layer of thought and reverie had been inscribed, and yet no succeeding layer had completely hidden or erased what had been written previously. All of these existed in our conscious or subconscious selves, though we may not have been aware of them, and they had gone to build up the complex and mysterious personality of India. That sphinx-like face with its elusive and sometimes mocking smile was to be seen throughout the length and breadth of the land. Though outwardly there was diversity and infinite variety among our people, everywhere there was that tremendous impress of oneness, which had held all of us together for ages

past, whatever political fate or misfortune had befallen us. The unity of
India was no longer merely an intellectual conception for me: it was an
emotional experience which overpowered me. That essential unity had
been so powerful that no political division, no disaster or catastrophe, had
been able to overcome it.[2]

The struggle for freedom led to the discovery of a new Indian
identity. The travels of freedom fighters from one city to another led
them to the sacred centres of different religions and also enriched
their understanding of how different communities had come into India
and made it their home. Accordingly, there was a greater understanding of different methods of conflict resolution and new streams
of thought. The famous civil servant and scholar, J. H. Hutton, has
rightly observed:

It cannot be denied that society in India is still largely organised on a basis
of caste and religion, and social conduct is much influenced by practices
which may not be in themselves religious but which are subject to religious
sanctions.[3]

The People of India Project (1984–6) identified 4,694 different
communities in India, comprising people of different faiths and castes,
tribes, and ethnic groups. Of these, 2,204 were main communities,
589 were segments, and the remaining 1,900 territorial units. There
were 324 languages/dialects and 25 scripts.[4]

One must bear in mind that out of a total population of over a
billion people residing in India over 80 per cent are Hindus followed
by Muslims, Christians, Sikhs, Buddhists, Jains and others such as
tribals, Zoroastrians, and Jews.[5] Hinduism itself has a great variety of
sects and is indeed, in sociological and religious terms, a federation
of faiths. As T.N. Madan observes:

The plurality of religions in India is often obscured by the fact that Hinduism
is generally regarded as both the demographically dominant and the
culturally characteristic—even hegemonic—religion of the country not only
in popular imagination but also by official reckoning – four out of five
Indians are Hindus, and they inhabit the length and breadth of the land.
From the cultural perspective, anthropologists and sociologists have
provided details of the many components of culture and aspects of social
structure of the so-called non-Hindu communities that have either been
borrowed from the Hindus, or are survivals from their pre-conversion Hindu
past, with or without significant alterations.

The foregoing popular view of the cultural scene in India, buttressed by official statistics, needs to be qualified in several respects. Unlike the other religions of India, Hinduism is a federation of faiths which has a horizontal as well as vertical distribution, rather than a single homogeneous religion. Not only do the religious beliefs and practices of Hindus vary from one cultural region of the country to another (say, between Bengal and Maharashtra), Hindu castes in each area are also characterised by similar differences.[6]

There has been tremendous sharing of social, economic and cultural traits across communities. For instance, if one takes the communities grouped into religious categories, one finds that the Hindus share a very high percentage of traits with the Muslims (96.77 per cent), Buddhists (91.19 per cent), Sikhs (88.99 per cent), and Jains (77.46 per cent). The Muslims–Sikhs also share a high percentage of traits (89.95 per cent), as do Muslims–Buddhists (91.18 per cent), and Jains–Buddhists (81.34 per cent).[7]

Another important factor in understanding Indian society from the standpoint of social harmony is caste. The maintenance of harmony among castes and sub-castes is a major social as well as political challenge. The Constitution of India treats all communities equally without any distinction on grounds of caste, creed, religion, or language. And yet, at the same time, it has to be understood that each community has its own world view and a strong sense of solidarity with certain practices. Above all, there are realities of social and economic inequality and thereby of exploitation and dominance. It is important to identify and understand the links between the past and present in order to understand the complexities of Indian character.

The people of India are located within the frameworks of civilization that they have built. They enjoy a distinct Weltanschauung. There is also a common literary vocabulary cutting across language barriers. All ethnographers who have written about castes have discerned this underlying unity. As Jawaharlal Nehru says, India is a cultural unity amidst diversity, a bundle of contradictions held together by strong but invisible threads. These threads are the traits, thoughts and feelings that we share.[8]

There is an all-pervasive sense of Indianness amidst all the distinct personalities of different communities. Rabindranath Tagore has expressed it well when he says:

Here the Arya, here the Anarya,
Here the Dravida and the Chin
Saka, Hun, Pathan, Moghul,
All merged to form one body.[9]

I wanted to test the Bahudhā approach within this broad civil-izational framework of the Indian people. Accordingly, a forty-day field visit was made with effect from 4 January 2005 to 12 February 2005. Keeping the cultural and geographical habitats in mind the visit covered Calicut in Kerala; Kenduli village in Birbhum, West Bengal; Khuntitoli village in Simdega, Jharkhand; Sarisab-pahi village in Madhubani, Bihar; and Hajo in Kamrup, Assam. This opportunity was utilized to interact with religious preachers, artists, school teachers, ritualists, tourists, pilgrims, government officials, and common men and women.

The basic objective of this visit was to bring out how the common people in India retain the essence of harmonious living and manage crises and conflicts of various categories in everyday life in their respective habitats. People, mainly the villagers in India, since time immemorial have been known for their deep sense of spiritual power, dignity, and humanity. A truthful narration of the discussions along with a few reflections are outlined in this chapter.

KERALA

Kerala has a long history of cultural unity. The people of Kerala are mostly Hindus, Christians, and Muslims. Shankaracharya, the noted Indian philosopher, was a native of Kerala. The first Indian converts to Christianity were made in Kerala by St. Thomas, the Apostle of Christ, in the first century AD. Today their descendants form a flourishing Syrian Christian community. Similarly, the first Indian Muslims were the Moplas of Malabar, hailing from Arab traders who married local women, settled down in Kerala, and later moved elsewhere. Some of the earliest Jews in the world were also in Kerala. In spite of this religious medley, the people have developed a homogeneous character. They speak the same language, wear mostly the same white dress, follow the same customs and manners, and are proud of their inheritance. For instance, Onam, the great Malabar festival, during which the mythological king, Mahabali, is supposed to descend to the earth to see how his people are faring is observed with equal enthusiasm by Hindus, Christians, and Muslims.[10]

Calicut—a famous port town—is the headquarters of the Kozhikode district of Kerala. The Kerala District Gazetteer records the following about its origin and history:

According to the Keralolpathi it was part of the Cheraman Perumal's territory and became the Zamorin's possession following the departure of the Perumal for Mecca. The Chinese were the first to establish commercial contact with Calicut. They brought gold, silver, copper, spikenard and clothes of silk and gold, and exchanged them for pepper, cinnamon, ginger, nuts and textile products. When Ibn Batuta of Tangiers visited Calicut during the period 1342–47 the Moors were the predominant trading class. By the beginning of the 15th century they had broken the Chinese monopoly of trade. Ibn Batuta is said to have come to Calicut no less than six times and stayed there for three months on his first visit. To him Calicut was one of the chief harbours of the country of Malabar, where people from China, Sumatra (Jawa), Ceylon (Saylan), the Maldive islands (Mahal), Yemen and Fars come and here gather merchants from all quarters of the globe and the harbour of Calicut is one of the largest in the world.[11]

In May 1498, Vasco da Gama landed at Kappad, sixteen kilometres north of Kozhikode and was received by the Zamorin himself. Kozhikode attained a position of pre-eminence in the trade of pepper and other spices. Kozhikode port was favoured by the Arab and Chinese merchants because of its efficiency, cosmopolitan environment and security of person and property.

The Portuguese, Arab traders and Christian missionaries settled in Calicut. The English and French were permitted by the Zamorin to settle there in 1667 and 1703 respectively. The Calicut municipality was established as early as in 1865. Today there are a large number of temples, mosques, and churches in the city.

Hindus constitute the majority of the population followed by the Muslim and Christian communities respectively. The Hindu community is organized on the basis of caste and sub-castes as elsewhere in the state. They worship all the major gods and goddesses of the Hindu pantheon, Vishnu and Shiva being the major ones. The Muslims are known as Mappilas. A great majority of them are Sunnis noted for their piety. Christians of different denominations are to be found in Calicut.

There is a widely held view that Kerala has always maintained harmony among the believers of the three major faiths: Hinduism, Islam, and Christianity. Is it true? M. Ramakrishna, Programme Officer, Calicut University, replied, 'It is not that conflict never occurred in

Kerala. Earlier, the low caste people were not allowed to enter temples. This was, however, countered by several revolutionaries and social reformers. One such great personality was Narayana Guru (1854–1928),[12] a great social reformer. He relentlessly fought against Brahmin domination and assiduously worked for the spread of education in the state. In spite of belonging to a lower caste, he installed the Shiva idol at Aravipuram in 1888. The Aravipuram *Pratistha* was a unique event of historical importance because a person of a lower caste, forbidden from entering the temple, had been able to consecrate the Shiva image in a temple. On the wall of the temple he inscribed the following words: "Devoid of dividing walls of caste, of race, the hatred, the rival faiths, we all live here in brotherhood". For millions of people, Narayan Guru was a saint, seer, philosopher, poet, and social reformer. He held that the essence of all religions is one and the same, and advocated the comparative study of all faiths. The centenary of the Aravipuram *Pratistha* was celebrated on Shivaratri day in 1988.'

Kerala has rich traditions of different art forms: decorative arts, performing arts, and utilitarian crafts and architecture.

Usually *Teyyam* performances—an outstanding folk ritual and theatrical dance-form of north Kerala—are given by the 'so-called lower castes', but during the ritual, the performer goes into a trance-like state and is possessed by the deity to be transformed into a medium between the audience and the gods. In a trance he is treated as an incarnation of the deity, and as a result, everybody—from low caste to a very high graded Brahmin—gets his blessings. This is the time when the caste structure of high and low gets liquidated into an extraordinary form of cultural and social harmony. Muslims and Christians also come to them with the same respect and get their blessings.

K.M. Mohammed of the Department of Arabic of Calicut University observed that 'at the very outset it should be understood that Islam is a complete way of life, which gives importance to religious and secular education. The Prophet asked his companions to "seek knowledge even if it is from China" and it was obeyed in letter and spirit. There are many Quranic verses asking man to strengthen his faith by understanding the varied creations in the world.'

He continued, 'The Ulema of Kerala were learned in different disciplines. Makhdum Ahmad Zaynuddin (died 1028 AH) has the credit of being the author of *Tuhfatul Mujahidin*, the first authentic history of Kerala, written by a Keralite. You know William Logan had made

significant remarks about the scholars of Ponnani? He walked to his
neatly maintained bookshelf and took out *A Manual of Malabar Vol.
I.* (Madras, 1951.) written by William Logan to quote exactly what
the author said. He opened the appropriate page and read, 'Genuine
Arabs of whom many families of pure Arab blood are settled on the
coast, despise learning and impart knowledge, are themselves highly
educated in the Arab sense. Their knowledge of their own books of
science and history are very often profound and to a sympathetic
listener who knows Malayalam they love to discourse on such
subjects. They have a great reverence for truth, and on their finer
feelings their approach is nearer to the standard of the English
gentleman than any class of person in Malabar.'

Finally he concluded, 'what is needed is that outsiders and also
teachers and students of traditional Islamic institutions understand
the value of a rational and secular education within the boundary of
religious education. There cannot be a secular education without a
religious background.'

WEST BENGAL

The civilizational encounters between Hinduism and Christianity
found their most creative expression in the renaissance movement in
Bengal in the nineteenth century. This was both caused and facilitated
by English education, Christianity, and the integration of the Indian
market with the overseas markets. Being the capital of British India,
Calcutta became the centre not only of administration but also of
trade and commerce. In the process, a class of Bengali elite—
popularly known as *bhadralok*—developed and interacted with
the ruling British elite. This Bengali bhadralok became the harbinger
of change. Raja Rammohan Roy (1772–1833) was the initiator of
this renaissance movement. His personality and intellect greatly
influenced the direction of Bengali thought, and later of the rest of
India. Raja Rammohan Roy's efforts were carried forward by several
personalities including Keshab Chandra Sen (1838–84), Bankim
Chandra Chattopadhyay (1838–94), Kedarnath Datta Bhaktivinoda
(1838–1914), and Michael Madhusudhan Dutt (1824–73). The
establishment of Hindu College in Kolkata with English as the prime
medium of instruction brought Western sciences, philosophy,
literature, and grammar close to the Indian mind.

This enlightenment released the creative energies of the Indian
people. The new Indian elite, however, firmly held the view that
they did not want Indian society to be a copy of British or European

society but to rebuild India in terms of its own civilizational genius and they greatly succeeded in their endeavours.

To learn about the Bahudhā approach of harmony and dialogue in a prominent village of West Bengal, Kenduli village, was chosen for enquiry.

KENDULI, BIRBHUM, WEST BENGAL

Kenduli is a roadside village in Birbhum district of West Bengal. It is believed that Jaidev[13]—the celebrated author of the *Geetagobinda*—was born in Kenduli, and wrote his famous book by the side of the river Ajay in the village. Every year, on *Paush Sankranti* (14 January), a week-long fair takes place in this village. More than 500,000 people, mainly from West Bengal and a fraction of them from the neighbouring states of Jharkhand and Orissa, attend this *mela*. The Kenduli mela is the only place where thousands of Bauls from all corners of the country congregate. It is also known as *Bauler Bagan* (Bauls' orchard).

Kenduli mela is a rare symbol of communal harmony. It is the meeting ground for Bauls[14] as well as believers of the various sects of Hinduism: Shaiva, Shakta, Tantra, and Vaishnava. The Muslims also come to the mela to participate. Visitors enjoy every minute of their stay there without any communal, religious, or sect bias. The mela has its own history and numerous legends and stories are woven around it.

According to one dominant legend, on the instructions of Lord Jagannatha, Pandit Ramdeb Mishra came to Kenduli from Puri with his wise and beautiful daughter and solemnized her marriage with Jaidev. In one of the meetings at Kenduli village, Arun Chakrabarty, a Bengali poet said, 'Jaidev was initially a believer of Shiva and involved in deep penance to get complete maturity in the science of Tantra. A minor incident changed his world view. One fine morning when he was in profound meditation, he saw that Shiva and Kali appeared together in front of him. He was delighted to see them. There was no end to his ultimate pleasure. All of a sudden, Shiva's face converted into Radha and Krishna appeared from the face of Kali. This was sufficient for Jaidev to think in terms of unity among the sects of Hinduism. From that day, he became an ardent devotee of Vishnu too. Inspired by this episode, Jaidev created his magnum opus *Geetagobinda*. It is an example of harmony.'

We might wonder how the legend associated with Puri and Lord Jagannathaa helps to maintain harmony among the sects of Hinduism and also among the believers of various faiths. To this Mahendra

Mishra, a scholar of folklore from Orissa, who has been visiting the mela for the last fourteen years, replied, 'Jagannathaa has multiform manifestations. He is Shiva or Bhairava and goddess Vimala is Bhairavi. Shaivism and Shaktism are fused in him. Jagannatha is further identified with Buddha. His iconographic representation without hands and feet approximates to the meditating Buddha. The triad of Jagannathaa, Balbhadra and Subhadra is depicted as Buddha, Dharma and Sangha—the three gems of Buddhism; some Buddhists even find a discernible affinity of the car-festival with Buddhist festivals. Buddha's tooth-relic is supposedly inside the images of the triad and is known as *brahma-padartha*, divine-matter.'

Mahendra Mishra continued, 'Muslims also regard Puri *kshetra* as a central place of brotherhood. The initial animosity and ignorance of the Muslims had seen many attempts at desecration of the Jagannathaa temple during the early period of Muslim rule. A gradual moderation in the fastidious Muslim outlook persuaded them to be reconciled with the Jagannathaa cult. Muslims even broke through Islamic shackles to visit the temple and partake of the *mahaprasad* (food-offerings to the triad) with the Hindus jointly. The mahaprasad brotherhood continued for a long time and this tradition transcends religious barriers. . . . Salabega, a Muslim of Orissa, consecrated his life to the devotion of the triad, and his mystic yearnings and pleas before Jagannatha still reverberate. His tomb on the path of the car-festival bears testimony to it. Tradition has it that Kabir visited Puri and was enamoured with the triad of Jagannatha, Balbhadra and Subhadra. A monastery which was set up by him at Puri is still called Kabir-Chaura. Hindus and Muslims visiting Puri must go there first and jointly consume food and drink (*torani*) there. The inter-religious fusion is more than just a tradition. Religious distinctions cannot vitiate the human race. This is the supreme message of spiritualism.'

Mahendra Mishra also talked of the story of harmony in Puri between Hindus and Sikhs and said: The tradition of '*guru ka langar*' is similar at Bauli and Mangu monasteries set up to commemorate Guru Nanak's visit to Puri. A universal mode of spirituality and religious tradition irrespective of time, clime and country, being craved for by Nanak, was at last found by him in the Jagannatha Dharma during his visit to Puri. This tradition of the founder of Sikhism was so rich that devout Sikhs continue to adore the triad. Even Maharaja Ranjit Singh wanted to present the Koh-i-noor diamond to Jagannatha.

Baul's World View and Harmony

In response to a question about the basic philosophy of the Bauls, Dindayal Baul sang two couplets:

I have made the world my home
And my home the world,
I have made 'others' my own people,
And my own people 'others'.

Once the song was over, he said, 'A Baul is a Baul because he is Baul. He sees the world as his home. In people's pleasure he feels his pleasure; and in people's pain, his pain. He does not care what others think about him. He does not wait for a teacher to come and guide him on how to worship, when to worship. He sings when he feels like singing; dances when he wants to dance; weeps when pained; cries when emotionally charged. He worships whenever he wants to worship; eats when he is hungry; sleeps when willing to sleep; eats—vegetarian and non-vegetarian foods—depending on his taste, desire, and the availability of the food. For a Baul every human being is equal: neither low nor high.'

Dindayal Baul sang another two lines to confirm his statement:

As long as you judge in terms of high and low you are deluded;
All are the same to one who knows reality. . .

When asked about his source of inspiration to compose songs and sing, Dindayal responded, 'It is emotional music about all the five elements of Nature: Earth, Sky, Air, Fire and Water. Our music, Baul's music, is about God's power, the power of music we play for God and all those who believe in him. Our inspiration comes from the elements, Nature, a bird's chirping or songs, the sound of spring water and the leaves in the wind. It also comes from different cultural practices. Sometimes inspiration comes directly from God. In that sense, God is our writer and director and this world is His stage. We are just actors playing our role in His direction.'

When asked, 'What is God? Who is he?' Dindayal responded, 'God is the source of power. Through duty, deep spiritual knowledge, virtue, merit and meditation, one can find Him. In this world there are many paths and every man is free to choose his own path. Everyone has a different idea of what is right and what is wrong. We all have different tastes but music is the one art that everyone loves.

If the music contains some deep knowledge the people can gain this while listening. This is the reason a Baul cannot live without music. Bauls are musical people. Music and songs are like husband and wife. United they give good things to the world.'

The message of a Baul is simple. 'None by reason of birth, poverty, age or sex will be debarred from divine blessing or at times the presence of his god. The way is but one—that of bhakti.'

JHARKHAND

Jharkhand is traditionally home to a number of tribal communities. It has thirty-two primitive tribal groups. Some districts have a predominantly tribal population. The demographic profile has, however, changed in the wake of modernization, making tribals a minority population in the state. Today (in terms of 2001 Census), the population consists of twenty-eight per cent tribals, twelve per cent Scheduled Castes, and sixty per cent others.

Etymologically speaking, Jharkhand means the land of jungles, forests and *jhari*s (bushes). Some of its charmed beauty has since disappeared due to increased human intervention by way of modernization and industrialization. Jharkhand has unparalleled mineral wealth and forestry products that has attracted people from different parts of India to pursue economic activities such as mining of coal, iron ore, copper, bauxite, uranium, gold and silver. Industrial centres like Ranchi—the capital of Jharkhand—Jamshedpur, Bokaro, and Dhanbad have become large urban centres.

The relationship between the tribals and outsiders soured because of the transfer of land owned by tribals to Bihari Hindus, popularly referred to as Dikus. The transfer occurred at a very rapid pace. In recent years the land situation, in Simdega and other parts of Jharkhand, has by all accounts grown worse. The region's tribal rural population is increasingly becoming landless labourers or at best, owners of small holdings.

The modernization process has alienated the indigenous population as they have been unable to participate in and thus cope with the pace of change. They have a tendency to blame outsiders for everything that has gone wrong. The attitude of the village tribals towards tribal leaders and businessmen, or other middle-class gentry, is also far from cordial. Several of the tribals have now joined the Naxalite movement.[15] Efforts are being made at the national level to contain this movement.

The loss of jobs to outsiders and the lack of correct and updated land records, and exploitation by landlords and moneylenders, have alienated an important section of tribal society from mainstream democratic politics. The persistence of social conflicts has further prevented the spread of education and health care facilities in the rural areas. The democratic dialogue process has very limited application in many parts of the state and elements of disparity, instability and unrest are becoming conspicuous, calling for immediate intervention. It is against this background that an attempt was made to find out about the Bahudhā approach in the Simdega area.[16]

SIMDEGA, JHARKHAND

Simdega is a small town—now a district headquarters—in the extreme south of Jharkhand. The boundaries of Simdega touch the Indian states of Orissa and Chhattisgarh.

On being told about the attempt to understand the Bahudhā approach in relation to social harmony, a popular leader's widow, Mrs Tigga in one of the meetings responded, 'The initiative is simply superb. Jharkand is an extraordinary example of harmony between people and their cultural practices. Plurality in cultural practices, race and linguistics are the strength of Jharkhand. From ancient times, Jharkhand received people who migrated into the area. Major Adivasi groups like the Santhals, Mundas, Oraons, and the Hos and other early settlers reached Jharkhand after a series of migrations. Today Jharkhand is the abode of thirty-one tribes. . . . Besides these, many ethnic castes such as the Kurmi, Ghatwal, Mudi, Banik, and Muslims have lived with them since time immemorial. They use the term *Sadan* for the old immigrants of Jharkhand.'

On being asked why many of the districts were affected by the Naxalites and why did the tribals and non-tribals, early settlers, and late settlers fight amongst themselves, a local leader Nirmal Minz replied, 'There is a continuous history of exploitation behind it. The people of North Bihar came here to get some job opportunities. Those people were mainly Teli, Suri, Bania, and fractions of Muslims. They got small pieces of land to construct their houses and begin their business. They were very smart and shrewd people and contributed financially to the innocent tribes for a specific purpose. Their rate of interest was, and is, exorbitant. Within a limited span of time they became major landlords. They bought all cultivable lands and ornaments from many innocent tribal families by allurement, deceit, and occasionally force. Now after the spread of education and awareness drive by NGOs, social animators and government agencies, many youngsters have come to know the reality of these people. As a result, they show their revulsion for them. The tribals of this region want to retrieve their land and respect from these people. Ironically, the tribes whose extensive land these outsiders took have been working as bonded labourers in their own land for outsiders. Later some unemployed youths joined hands with the Naxalites. Now their connection is very deep. The women are also involved in Naxalite activities.'

Later Nirmal Minz spoke about a song composed in the late 1970s by an urban Adivasi intellectual in the hope that 'one day it might become Jharkhand's anthem'. It illustrates how other ethnic groups have also been included and considered as Jharkhandis or Jharkhand communities. Unity and consensus are the dominant themes. Some of the song's lines read:

They speak the same language. . .
in a united Jharkhand. . .
Hindus and Muslims
Adi-dharmi, and Christians,
Sikhs, Jains and those of other faiths,
they can all live here
in a united Jharkhand. . . .
Mundas, Oraons, Santhals,
Let them go forward together.
Kharias, Hos, Paharias,
together with the Sadans
in a united Jharkhand. . . .
All are pained in one pain.
All are happy in one happiness.
For us any one destiny is written by the ordainer
in a united Jharkhand. . . .

'In the text of the above song', said Nirmal Minz, 'nobody is excluded from the Jharkhand communities on the basis of language, religion or ethnic ascription. The scope of the Jharkhand community described in the song seems to respond to the political need to surpass a narrow tribal conception of Jharkhand by including the Sadans. The Sadans are the old dikus (outsiders). Jharkhandis that have not been catalogued as Scheduled Tribes and who immigrated into the region in early times such as the Sandan, Mandal, Mahto, Kurmi, and Ghatwal are basically treated by the tribes of the state as Sadans. The artisan castes like the Kumars (potters), the Telis (oilmen), the Kamras (blacksmiths), the Gowalas (milkmen), as well as the Momins (Muslim weavers), etc., have developed a close association with the tribes through the ages.'

He concluded, 'May his dream come true.'

BIHAR

From early times, Bihar has occupied an important place in Indian history both as the principal seat of imperial power and as the main centre of Indian civilization. It was in Bihar that Lord Buddha—the founder of Buddhism—and Lord Mahavira—the founder of Jainism, were born. Earlier during the Vedic period, the Mithila region was a prominent place for Vedic scholars. Mithila was associated with the legendary King Janak of Videh whose daughter Sita had married Lord Ram of Ayodhya. Another legend describes Bihar's Champaran as the home of Maharshi Valmiki, author of the Ramayana. Kautilya, the celebrated author of *Arthashastra*, lived in Pataliputra, modern day Patna. Bihar was also the place where the tenth and the last guru of the Sikhs, Guru Gobind Singh, was born and attained sainthood. It was in Vaishali in Bihar where the rule of the Lichhavis, contemporaries of Lord Buddha, flourished. Bihar has impressive credentials in the field of traditional scholarship and wisdom of the people. Nalanda and Vikramshila universities were world class learning centres. After their destruction in the thirteenth century, Bihar has not seen any educational centre of world repute.

In recent years, Bihar has maintained a high level of harmony among religious communities. A major village of Mithila region, Sarisab-pahi, has the following story to narrate.

SARISAB-PAHI, MADHUBANI, BIHAR

Sarisab-pahi is a very famous village in the heart of the Mithila region in north Bihar. It has a thousand years of history of scholarship, initially in Sanskrit and now, for the last 125 years, in modern English, science, and management. It is also famous for maintaining harmony among people of various caste-groups and Hindu–Muslim unity. Ayachi Mishra was an outstanding product of this village. He was an extraordinary scholar of his time, in the early thirteenth century AD, and known for his honesty, and non-attachment to worldly matters.

Even today, people go there to touch the sacred land of Ayachi Mishra in Sarisab-pahi to be blessed in scholarship.

We spoke to four people in the village. Kedar Thakur, seventy-six, a goldsmith; Thakai Mandal, sixty-five, a dhanukh from the labour class; Kedar Safe, forty-five, a dhobi or washerman; Idrish Mian, fifty-seven, a mason belonging to the Muslim community.

Thakai Mandal began, 'Sir, we are very poor people. We have no land to construct our houses in the village. The population has grown in the village but the land is in the hands of a few Shrotriya families. We are jobless people. Our children have gone to Delhi, Patna, Punjab, Kolkata, Mumbai and Assam to earn their livelihood. We are ready to buy the land to construct our houses but the rich people do not want to sell their lands.'

Kedar Thakur said, 'It is a great village. Initially the Shrotriya Brahmans came here and constructed their houses. Later, they needed other technical people and gave free land to all castes to construct their houses to live in the village. Today it is represented by all castes and a few households of Muslim.'

People of all the castes in Sarisab-pahi practise agriculture directly or indirectly. Shrotriyas give their agricultural lands on *batai*, sharing basis. In the batai system, the needy person takes a piece of land from the landowner, cultivates it and shares the cost and the produce with him on a fifty-fifty basis. Normally in order to feed the family members the lower caste and landless people practise batai cultivation. Batai is also resorted to by absentee landowners. Such families visit the village once a year, check the accounts of the whole year, collect their share and return to the places of their current residence.

About forty families of *Julaha*s or weavers, reside in Julahatohi in Sarisab-pahi. The village women mostly spin cotton on the *takuri* or charkha and prepare fine yarn, which is used to prepare *janeu*, sacred thread, and khadi yarn for domestic consumption only. Every house has a charkha and takuri. Nowadays this practice is gradually declining.

The system of *Jajmani* is in practice in the village. At the time of death or other rituals and occasions the *Mahapatra*, *Doma*, and *Musahar* go to their Jajmans, render their services and, in return, get cash, grains, and gifts like dhotis.

The few communities falling under the Jajmani system are the Mahapatra (performers of *shraddha*, death rites and rituals), the Doma (bamboo weaver), the *Laheri* (bangle makers and sellers), the *Hazam* (barber), and the *Chamar* (cobbler). The Purohit is also a part of Jajmani. Besides there are certain specialized artisan communities such as *Sarota* makers, *Pankha* makers, *Sikki* item makers, and the *Halwai*s. A few people are specialists in thatching houses and some others as masons in building *kuccha* as well as *pucca* houses. The villagers consult them during the course of their planning. They are paid if their services are used.

Residents of Sarisab-pahi work at various places not only in Bihar but also in different parts of the country. Some of them are residents abroad and work in various capacities as engineers, professors, doctors, factory workers, rickshaw-pullers, and in other skilled and unskilled jobs. Some of them are engaged in business. Most of them live with their families. More than ten people lead retired lives in the village along with their families. They receive regular pensions through the bank and the post office.

Traditionally, the Brahmins including the Shrotriyas are a land-owning community. Some of them own large tracts of land. Communities like the Keot, Dhanuk, Musahar, Dom, and Chamar, have to work for the other communities for their livelihood. The Bania, Sonar, and Halwai are independent communities. The dependent communities receive remuneration for their services. Some of them practise batai cultivation of their masters' lands to meet unusual expenses. Earlier at the time of death and marriage, etc., they used to mortgage their expensive items to the Bania, Sonar or any other moneylender, on an interest basis. This old system has been changing slowly. Most of the youngsters are not interested in agriculture or allied occupations and perform several jobs in towns and cities to earn their livelihood. Consequently, there is a scarcity of support services in the village. Those available in the village either demand high remuneration or prefer employment of their choice.

Almost every caste maintains its caste council. In case of minor offences the caste council mediates and settles the matter. Such caste councils exist among the Keot, Dhanuk, Musahar, Chamar, and the Dom. Major offences are dealt with by the Panchayat, which has four to five well-recognized people. Their opinions are considered as judgements. Normally the offender accepts his mistake. If fined, he pays without any hesitation. Major offences are hardly committed but offences like cattle grazing on the cultivated land or fishing in someone else's pond often take place. Such cases are resolved orally.

Among Shrotriyas and Brahmianas the most respected senior person of the village presides over the meeting to settle the dispute.

HARMONY IN EVERYDAY LIFE IN THE VILLAGE

Sarisab-pahi is in the centre of the villages in the area. It has been a village of intellectuals for some time. Because of the village's huge population, all major political parties always treat it as a vote-bank. All the major communities of the village are extremely conscious of their interests and expect their leaders to provide them with a better standard of living. Of late, caste politics has started gaining ground.

The law and order situation in the village is normal. Incidents of minor theft are reported but there has been no major incident of robbery, murder, suicide, sexual offence, drug abuse, transgression of human rights, and communal riots in the past fifteen years.

The Hindus and Muslims of the village live in harmony and never experienced any communal conflict. Muslims also work on the Jajmani system. The Hindus treat the Muslims as part of the village and want the latter's religion to be respected. The villagers are proud of being born in this village that has produced a galaxy of scholars in Sanskrit.

Simple living and high thinking is the basic ideal of the people, mainly the elders. The villagers live in thatched houses or huts and wear simple dhotis, and kurtas. Those who can afford a better standard of living do not spend. Among all groups, ceremonial friendship is prevalent within the village and outside. These friends are invited on ritual occasions and at functions.

In household matters, women are at liberty to take independent decisions. Normally, they do not indulge in any work outside their households. Women do not go to agricultural fields, though women among the lower castes participate in agricultural and allied work with their male partners. Once the produce comes to the house it is the entire responsibility of the women to manage it. Children are taught to give due respect to their mothers, grandmothers, and elders. Women play a very active role in the decision-making process of the family especially in matters like marriage.

Different communities offer worship in different forms. The Mallahs, for example, worship Koilabeer, the Dusadhs worship Raja Salhesh and Alha-udal and organize dances and songs with full preparation. A few villagers tell the story of Lorik and Dinabhadri and organize *pooja*.

Senior citizens, usually, hold the view that a good life means leading a simple and honest life and performing one's duties. Living peacefully and doing the assigned job within the house and getting support and encouragement from their husbands, is, for most of the village women, synonymous with a good life. For young people modern amenities with luxurious life and stable jobs are the essentials of a good and prosperous life. With violence only terror can be created, but with non-violence one can win anybody's heart. Freedom is necessary to present one's view and understand the problems of others. Equality among various sections of society is the demand of the times for the growth of society. A peaceful and harmonious society, according to them, opens new paths of development and desired goals can be achieved.

Due to the spread of modern education the villagers are enlightened enough to understand the importance of communication and modern media. Most of the villagers read the newspaper daily and discuss the important issues relating to politics, sports, etc. The constitutional provision of reservation in jobs to the Backward Classes has certainly changed their socio-economic conditions. Politically, every villager is aware of his own interest and also the interests of their own community. Whenever an MLA or MP holds a meeting in the village, the villagers assemble and raise their problems.

Sarisab-pahi is a unique combination of the old and new values of life. The villagers have adopted new innovative ideas that have developed with the passage of time. Simultaneously, they respect and want to retain old values, which they have gained from their traditional culture. Old, experienced, and educated people of the village feel that the new political and administrative system is not so efficient as to take charge of a large population. They argue that the rise in crime is only due to loose administration and believe that dirty politics cannot create clean and good administration. Thus a clean and transparent democracy is required.

LEGEND OF AYACHI AND AN EXAMPLE OF HARMONY

There are numerous legends and anecdotes in Mithila that centre around the life and attainments of Mahamahopadhyaya Bhavanatha alias Ayachi Mishra and his son, Shankara Mishra. Ayachi was famous in the locality for *ayachiness*.[17] A labourer was once digging the land adjacent to his hut and found a pitcher full of gold coins. The labourer wanted to hand it over to Ayachi, but the latter did not touch it. He escorted the labourers carrying the pitcher to be presented to the king. The king did not want to store the coins in his treasury and repeatedly requested Ayachi to accept the pitcher. However, in spite of repeated requests to accept the coins, Ayachi handed them over to the king of Mithila. For Ayachi, according to the Dharmashastra, the fortune buried underground belonged to the head of the State.

ASSAM

Major changes have occurred in all regions of India since the country attained independence in 1947. However, given its comparatively cloistered existence until then, the transformation in north-east India has disturbed its traditional societies more radically than elsewhere. The political and administrative arrangements in the region have also altered more drastically than in other areas: once synonymous with the state of Assam, the north-east now contains seven states created out of the same territory. The ethnic variety and range of the area is the most complex in India—there are over 200 Scheduled Tribes here, and its non-tribal population, too, contains a rich variety of ethnic groups.

North-east India offers a fascinating story of the entry of different faiths among the local people. The number of believers in tribal animistic faiths declined, particularly since the beginning of the twentieth century, having embraced the more developed religions of Hinduism and Christianity.

In north-east India the Brahmaputra Valley became the centre of the Ramayana and Mahabharata tradition. It was in Assam that the interaction between tribal animism and Hinduism led to the birth of the Tantric form of Hinduism.[18]

The Ahoms, a branch of the Tai or Shan race, came into the Brahmaputra Valley and ruled over Assam for six hundred years, from 1228. They gradually accepted Hinduism. The most significant feature for our purpose is the Vaishnavite movement led by Sankardev (1449– 1569) in the Brahmaputra Valley. Sankardev's movement contributed to the community life, congregational gatherings, art forms, music and dances of both the tribals and the plains' people.

Buddhism did not come to Assam from Bihar, (as was the case with Brahminism), but from across the borders of the country—from Tibet via Arunachal Pradesh and from Burma via Mizoram and then to other parts of north-east India.

Historically, the impact of Islam in Assam began in 1205–6 with the unsuccessful endeavours of the Turko-Afghan ruler of Bengal, Bakhtiar Khilji to conquer Assam. The Ahom rulers patronized Muslim saints with sizeable land grants and exemption from forced labour.

Azan Fakir, the Muslim preacher, patronized by the Ahom king Gadhadhar Singh (1681–96), helped him settle in the state permanently. Muslim religious preachers were attached to Ahom courts. The Ahom's tolerant social outlook and the teaching of Hindu reformers such as Sankardev and Madhavdev in the sixteenth century brought Hindus and Muslims in Assam closer to one another.

Christianity first came to the region in 1837. The spread of new ideas by Christian missionaries began in the Brahmaputra valley and in the neighbouring hills with the publication in 1846 of *Arunodoya*, a Baptist monthly in Assamese, the translation of the Bible into Assamese, which rendered the tribal languages into the Roman script, and the setting up of schools and colleges for boys and girls, culminating in the establishment of Cotton College at Gauhati in 1901.

Of late, Assam[19] has been in the news. Today the entire Brahmaputra Valley has been engulfed by two terrorist movements: one led by United Liberation Front of Assam (ULFA) demanding cessation of Assam from India; and the Bodo insurgent groups demanding creation of a separate state for the Bodos (a prominent plains tribal community). There are strained relationships between the Assamese caste Hindus and Bodos on account of disputes over paddy lands and forests, language and script and the Bodos' ambition to have a separate political personality which is resisted by the Assamese elite. The ULFA, on the other hand, wants a separate homeland for Assam and often comes into violent conflict not only with the security forces but also with their own people who do not believe in the separation of Assam from India.

The forces of democracy, dialogue, peace, and development are at loggerheads with the exclusivist approaches of the ULFA and the Bodo insurgent outfits. The insurgency is drawing strength from illicit arms, illegal money gained through extortion from tea estates, oil establishments and the market, and unemployed youth.

In this ongoing battle between the forces of democracy and the forces of violence, it is interesting to look at the prevalence of social harmony among the religious and tribal groups at Hajo, a highly place significant in the Brahmaputra Valley.

Hajo, Assam

Hajo is a large village centre and has been for quite some time the headquarters of a revenue circle, a development block, and a major police station in Kamrup District of Assam. Hajo is a multi-caste and multi-religious village with a sizeable Muslim population. It is a great centre of culture and learning. Paddy is the principal crop grown in the area. Paddy fields lie mostly around the village settlement area. The settlements are usually in the form of hamlets.

Harmony in the Religious and Sectarian Diversity

Hajo has great ethnic and religious variety. Assamese caste Hindus, Bodos, and Muslims live together. Despite several variations in terms of caste, sect, and religion, the people of Hajo are integrated into one single village community. In matters of activities relating to the development of the village, the caste, sect and religious distinctions among the people become secondary. Under the influence of Sankardev's Vaishnavism, the caste restrictions had lost ground. Vaishnavism not only diminished the rigidity of the caste system but also brought tribes under the pan-Assamese social fold. Nowadays, there is proportional representation of different castes and religious sections of the people in village level corporate bodies and institutions.

However, a form of social segregation also exists. In Hajo, the villagers live in several subahs, clusters or hamlets. Each subah is basically a caste or religion-based concentration. This indicates the presence of a clear sense of caste or religious sentiment among the people. In spite of this inter-caste and inter-religious relations have become easier with the weakening of untouchability practices. Hindu–Muslim relations have become closer. Many Muslims express their positive feelings towards this unity. A Muslim youth stated, 'Hindus are nowadays changing with regard to their observances of untouchability. In the earlier days, Muslims were not allowed to even enter Hindu residential quarters, particularly in the case of Brahmins. At the same time, a Hindu never used to visit a Muslim home. Whenever a Muslim had to visit a Hindu home to meet someone, he was required to wait in the courtyard. He was never allowed to sit on chairs used by the inmates of the house. If tea was offered, it was served in separate utensils kept reserved for such a visitor. In fact, the visitor himself was required to wash the utensils after their use. The Hindus have changed considerably. Nowadays, they do not act in this fashion.'

The religious life of the Hindus of Assam cannot be understood without knowing two important institutions: the *Namghar* and the *Satra*. These two institutions have come into being under the influence of Sankardev's teachings of Vaishnavism and have virtually become symbols of Assamese culture.

The Namghar is a community prayer hall. The hall has a rectangular ground plan that is divided into two compartments. The inner one (sanctum sanctorum), which is comparatively smaller, is called *mandir* and the outer one is *sabhaghar*. In the mandir part, *thapana* (seat) as a symbol of the presiding deity is installed. The raised plinth upon which the thapana is laid is called *mandap*. In the sabhaghar, the devotees gather as a congregation to sing nam, devotional songs, or for scripture reading sessions in front of the thapana.

The people, through Namghar Samiti (elected body), manage the Namghar. The Namghar Samiti is always a single caste organization. A man who is assigned the duty of maintenance and upkeep of the Namghar is called *Namghariah*.

The Satra is another important religious institution. It is a highly organized Namghar where the head or the preacher stays permanently. The activities of a Satra are quite elaborate. The head of the Satra is designated Goswami, Satradhikar or Gosain. Such a person is held in high esteem by the followers. In a Satra, the *Satria* dance, Nam (devotional singing), scripture reading and many other religious acts are performed. It is a centre for the cultivation of devotional art and culture. This way, a Satra is a religious and cultural centre for the people. The followers of Sankardev (1449–1569) and Madhabdev are opposed to Brahminical rituals.

In Hajo, both Hindus and Muslims live as members of the same village community. There is no history of major Hindu–Muslim conflict in the village. Occasional minor clashes have, however, been reported between the two groups of people, particularly the youth. In such cases, sensible village elders settle disputes and appropriate punishments are imposed upon the wrong doers.

Tirtha Kshetra Hajo: Harmony in Pilgrim Centres of Three Religions

Hajo is famous for the *Panchtirtha*s (five pilgrim centres) in Assam: the temple of Hayagriba-Madhab, the temple of Kedareshwara (or Kedara Shiva), the temple of Kamaleshwara, the temple of Kameshwara, the temple of Ganesha. The Hayagriba-Madhab temple is also considered to be the Chaitya of Mahamuni Buddha. A small and beautiful *majar* of Giyasuddin, a Muslim saint, is located in Hajo on a hillock opposite Manikuta. It is called Poa Mecca. The believers of Islam in the neighbouring locality visit this place with respect and

offer their prayers. All these shrines or religious structures make Hajo
an extraordinary place in Assam.

The Hayagriba–Madhab temple, however, figures more prominently in the religious history of Assam. The Hayagriba–Madhab
temple is situated at the top of Manikuta, a hillock. It has a beautiful
building—exhibiting the wonderful specimen of architecture and
sculpture—which was constructed by the Koch King Raghudeva-
narayana in AD 1583. However, the original temple was constructed,
in all probability, in the sixth or seventh century AD. A portion of the
original temple still exists in the present building. Many scholars
maintain that the original building of the Hayagriba–Madhab temple
belonged to a Buddhist Chaitya. Certain motifs of the original work,
particularly a row of caparisoned elephants in high relief encircling
the building appear to be specimens of Buddhist architecture. The
elephant motifs are identical to the decorative style of the cave temple
at Ellora in Maharashtra. In winter, a number of Buddhist pilgrims
from different parts of the world flock to Hajo. They claim the image
of the temple's Bura Madhab to be that of the Buddha and call it
Mahamuni. People offer prayers in the temple according to their own
beliefs, rites and customs. This presents the most congenial
atmosphere among believers of two religions. The Hindu priest of
the temple observed, 'Yes, we know that the Buddhists come here to
offer their prayers thinking that it is the temple of their God, Mahamuni
Buddha. We have no problem with them. They worship the God
according to their beliefs, rites and customs and we worship according
to Hindu beliefs, rites and customs. Why should there be any conflict
among pilgrims of two faiths? Everything here runs smoothly. We
honour their sentiments and they honour Hindu sentiments. That's
all. There is complete harmony between us.'

POA MECCA

The lofty Garurachala Hill beside the Kedar Hill contains a holy shrine
of Muslims. It is known as Poa Mecca and contains a mosque and the
grave of a Muslim saint, probably a Sufi, Giyasuddin Auliya. A Persian
epigraph at this site shows that the old mosque, which no longer
exists, was built during the reign of the Mughal Emperor Shah Jahan
in AD 1657.

It is widely believed that Giyasuddin Auliya arrived in the sixteenth
century to preach Islam in this region. According to legend, Auliya
brought a lump of earth from Mecca and enshrined it at a spot where

a mosque was subsequently built and his devotees also buried him at this site. There is a strong belief that Poa Mecca blesses a Muslim pilgrim with one-fourth of piety, which can be achieved by a pilgrimage to Mecca.

There are different myths associated with Giyasuddin Auliya. A section of scholars has argued that through him the Sufi movement spread to the whole of the north-eastern part of India. People like Hazrat Azan Faqir, originally known as Shah Miran, is considered to be a spiritual descendant of Giyasuddin Auliya. According to Mohammad Yaha Tamizi, 'The Sufi had to travel a long way before coming to eastern India. The number of Sufis in this region is not small. The whole of eastern India hummed with Sufistic activities during the thirteenth and fourteenth centuries AD. It should be noted that Sufi monasteries which developed as institutions, were private. They were patronised by the Sultans, no doubt, as they were highly educated and religious-minded people. But they exercised no control over the institutions of the Sufis.'

The Khadim of Poa Mecca stated that, 'Poa Mecca does not belong to any religion. It belongs to humanity. It belongs to the people who love humanity, peaceful living and those who respect non-violence. It is open for people of all religions. People suffering from pain or trouble visit this place in expectation of some miraculous treatment. And they are also treated. You can see how many Hindu boys and girls move freely in the campus.'

The Khadim believed that there is a very close relationship between Hindus and Muslims of this locality. 'Many Muslim villages, such as Kalitakushi, Bamanbari, Heerajani and Dolaitalla, retain their Hindu names. It is an indication that the ancestors of these villagers were Hindus. They changed their religion, but did not change the name of their villages. That way, both Hindus and Muslims believe they are brothers or sons and daughters of the same ancestors. This helps us to maintain harmony in the area. In this locality, as a result, we have not faced any major clash between followers of the two religions.'

The Khadim projected the arrival of Muslims in India in the context of his understanding of the historical role of Islam. The Khadim portrayed a romantic and idealistic picture of much of the history of Muslim presence in India. The Muslims who came to India from abroad settled down in the country for good, thus making it their home. Thus, it was under Muslim rule that most of India was unified into one administrative unit and the country was brought into contact with the outside world. Muslims helped develop new and rich styles of architecture, art, dress, language and literature, as well as promote trade, agriculture and industry. More importantly, Islam provided Indians with the concept of divine unity, bitterly critiquing polytheism, priesthood, idolatry and various superstitious beliefs and practices. Its message of social equality and women's rights, too, had a profound impact, and many Hindu reformist sects owed their inspiration to this Islamic influence. In more recent times, Muslims also played a leading role in the struggle against British imperialism and for the cause of Indian freedom.'

On being asked about his opinion about Osama bin Laden, he replied, 'He is a terrorist. He has ruined the innocent people of Afghanistan and many parts of the Muslim world. If a Muslim constructs a mosque from Osama's money, I will refuse to offer my prayers there. Because God said to Muhammad: "You must not pray in a mosque built by terrorists." Real Muslims are not terrorists, because Islam is the most tolerant of religions. When Hitler killed Europe's Jews, the Jews were safe in Muslim countries. It is a historical fact. A Muslim historian of repute has told me this fact. Terrorists are false Muslims!'

Hajo presents an extraordinary picture of parallel existence of multiple religions, all existing according to their own way of life without hurting the sentiments of others. Dipen Bhagawati, a local *panda* (priest) says, 'Hajo is a *Triveni-sangam* of three religions: Hinduism, Buddhism and Islam. Every religion flourishes without disturbing the flow of others.'

CONCLUSION

Attitudes, values, and beliefs that are sometimes collectively referred to as culture are changing in rural areas in the face of modernization and are providing new methods of dealing with old flash points in human relations related to religion and caste on the one hand, and factors of production like land, money, and labour on the other. We have noticed that cultural factors, profoundly influenced by religion, continue to exercise considerable influence in traditional societies like Sarisab-pahi in Bihar, Hajo in Assam, and Kenduli village in West Bengal. The modern educational system has not made effective inroads into these villages, notwithstanding the influence of one or two individuals. Yet, at the same time, things are changing and boys and girls are seeking opportunities to improve themselves economically.

The Bahudhā approach to conflict resolution is contributing significantly to maintenance of peace and harmony among different castes and religions in Sarisab-pahi, Kenduli, and Hajo, but its inadequacies are too glaring in Simdega in Jharkhand in the face of the Naxalite movement. Here the dialogue process has completely disintegrated and needs to be revived. There is enough justification for hoping that an effective intervention by the state, both in terms of law and order and strengthening of the education and health care infrastructure, coupled with land reforms would positively contribute towards restoration of the traditional methods of conflict resolution. The slow pace of economic progress cannot be merely ascribed to local cultural attitudes but is largely due to the absence of gainful employment in the area, as market institutions are undeveloped and the state system is not yet an effective instrument in the creation of opportunities in the arena of education, livelihood, and even maintenance of peace. The low priority given to education of girls has been a countervailing factor in all these states except Kerala.

The general notion that madrasa education is not conducive to secularism as it teaches orthodoxy and conformity is not borne out by facts prevailing in Kerala. Believers of Islam are well aware of the historical context as Islam was a progressive force for several hundred years after it was founded by Prophet Muhammad in early seventh century. So long as madrasas accept the education curriculum prescribed by a secular state, allow and inculcate in their students an enquiring mind by encouraging questions and even dissent, it can be as good an institution as its counterparts run by Christian missionaries or the Ramakrishna Mission.

It was also seen, both among the people of Hajo as well as Calicut, that the understanding of Islam at the grassroots level is not one of Islam being a rigid religion. Its Sufi tradition has allowed its believers to entertain people of other faiths at its dargahs and also to facilitate them to seek the blessings of their pirs.

It was interesting that in Hajo there is a single shrine for the Hindus and the Buddhists and that Muslim villages have Hindu names. In fact, villagers often go and offer flowers to Lord Shiva's temple and later go to Namghar for kirtan. In this act they do not see any conflict in simultaneously observing Brahminic rituals while in Shiva's temple and participating in kirtans in namghar—an institution opposed to Brahminic rituals. Hajo is a symbol of great religious harmony among Buddhists, Hindus, and Muslims.

Sarisab-pahi has another lesson to impart, namely, that scholarship could be autonomous and yet flourish. The Ayachi system of 'each one teaching ten' when operated under the guidance of an effective leader can impart learning at any given point of time to as many as a thousand people. But while scholarship can meaningfully contribute to the tradition of dialogue and harmony and thus ensure social and economic progress, the presence of Naxalite armed intervention goes to prove that effective state intervention is a prerequisite for the Bahudhā approach to flourish in such areas.

The Bauls' world view is at best a specimen of a society yearning for happiness and in the process a group of men and women transcending the narrow confines of caste and religion and other divisions of society. Kenduli has also shown that both mundane activities and music of the Bauls can coexist in a society ruled by the leftists continuously for nearly four decades.

One notices that despite religious and caste divisions a psychological unity, based on years of communitarian living in villages and towns, has contributed significantly to united action and the oneness of the Indian people. It is heartening to see in Nirmal Minz's national anthem for Jharkhand a place for everyone and in Khadim of Hajo's, a denunciation of Osama as a terrorist and threat to peace.

Unfortunately one saw ignorance among the villagers about other lands particularly about Latin America and Africa. As we seek harmonious living at the global level, one should know more and more about other people and their faiths. It should become as normal for an American or a European to be familiar with the civilizations of the East—the Chinese, the Japanese, and the Indian—as he is now with the Greek, Roman, and Jewish cultures. Similarly the Chinese, the Indian, the Japanese, the Indonesian, and the Egyptian should know about Christianity and Western values and about people living there.

One of the widespread feelings among the rural folks is that the composite Indian heritage of dialogue and coexistence, the message of 'live and let live', and the insistence on tolerant understanding and accommodation were critically embattled during the partition of India. However, the spirit of pluralism and anekantavada, which is deeply embedded in the intellectual and spiritual spirit of India, re-emerged in free India under secular democratic order.

Lack of basic facilities—like toilets, safe drinking water, undeveloped schools, and scanty healthcare systems—characterize villages in several parts of the country. However, there is an explosion in consciousness and an emergence of unfettered minds that see enormous benefits in social harmony and good governance. But injustices and inequities of centuries are creating rebellious crowds and support for insurgency and naxal movements. Democracy and the rule of law have asserted themselves in several areas and provided economic opportunities and livelihood. There is both considerable promise and genuine uneasiness at its slow pace of actualization.

The unifying role of politics and democracy is getting greatly subdued as politicians are influencing the wide network of caste, ethnic, economic, and religious ties for their narrow ends of winning elections or securing contracts for their relations and favourites. And yet one gladly notices that democratic culture is widespread and permanent and is strengthened by mutual interdependence and culture.

Attitudes and beliefs of people everywhere are changing. Reforms, however, are called for in the institutional system operating in these societies in order that the dialogue process is not inhibited, and concerned citizens and civil society institutions are strengthened. A continuous process of dialogue between the individual and the State is important but dialogue among individuals needs to be kept in the forefront not only for national consolidation but also for harmony.

NOTES

1. Matthew 5:3–11.
2. Jawaharlal Nehru, *The Discovery of India*, Oxford University Press, New Delhi, 1988, pp. 58–9.
3. J.H. Hutton, Census of India, Government of India Publication, New Delhi, 1931, p. 379. Anthropological Survey of India, Calcutta, 1992.
4. K.S. Singh, *People of India: An Introduction*, Anthropological Survey of India, Calcutta, 1992, pp. 57, 68–70.
5. According to the 2001 Census, the percentage of population by religion in India is as follows: Hindus: 80.5 per cent; Muslims: 13.4 per cent; Christians: 2.3 per cent; Sikhs: 1.9 per cent; Buddhists: 0.8 per cent; Jains: 0.4 per cent; and Others: 0.6 per cent. See *Statistical Outline of India 2004–5*, Tata Services Limited, Mumbai, January 2005, p. 34.
6. T.N. Madan, 'Religions of India: Plurality and Pluralism', Veena Das (ed.), *The Oxford India Companion to Sociology and Social Anthropology*, Vol. I, Oxford University Press, New Delhi, 2003, p. 775.
7. Ibid., pp. 775–801.
8. Nalini Menon (ed.), *The Indian Experience*, Media Transasia Limited, Bangkok, 1997, p. 40.

9. Quoted in the opening page of Ramdhari Singh Dinkar's book *Bhartiya Sanskriti Ke Char Adhyaya*, Udayanchal Press, Patna, 1956. Originally from Rabindranath Tagore, *Sanchyata*, Poem entitled *Bharat Tirtha*. The original Bengali transcript reads as follows:

   हेथाय आर्य, हेया अनार्य हेथाय द्रविड़-चीन,
   शक-हूण-दल पाठन-मोगल एक देहे होलो लीन।

10. K.P.S. Menon, *Many Worlds: An Autobiography*, Oxford University Press, London, 1965, p. 1.

11. A. Sreedhara Menon, *Kerala District Gazetteers: Kozhikode*, Government Press, Trivandrum, 1962, p. 752.

12. Born on 20 August 1854, Narayana Guru preached brotherhood for all including untouchables. A champion of the humble and downtrodden, he gave the watchwords: 'One People, One Dharma, One God for all men'. He died on 20 September 1928.

13. Jaidev's actual date of birth is not known. But scholars suggest that he composed his *magnum opus Geetagobinda* some time during the twelfth and thirteenth centuries.

14. K.M. Sen, *Hinduism*, Penguin Books, London, 1961, pp. 103–4. In chapter 19 of the book Sen captures the story of the Bauls as follows:

   The religious life of India has produced few more interesting phenomena than the *Bauls* of Bengal. They provide a most moving example of the 'simple' (*sahaj*) man's search for 'the Man of my heart' (*moner manush*) i.e. God. Baul means madcap and is probably derived from the Sanskrit word *vayu* (wind) in its sense of nerve currents. Another derivation connects it with the regulated breathing exercises which are practised by some cults. The religious tradition grew on the ruins of Buddhism, *Tantra*, and Vaishnavism. Ever on the move, removed from all traditional ties, the Bauls are free as the wind.

   The Bauls accept no divisions of society, such as caste or class, no special deity, nor any temple or mosque. They sometimes congregate during religious festivals, mainly those of the Vaishnavas, but they do not take part in worship. Their ideal is to be sahaj and they avoid and criticize the external forms of religious worship. The Baul devotees come from the lowest social strata of the Hindu and the Muslim fold. The Bauls learn their customs from their gurus, and in fact this is how their traditions are maintained.

15. The Naxalite movement began as an armed peasant struggle in the late 1960s in the Naxalbari subdivision of the Siliguri district of West Bengal and spread to Andhra Pradesh, Orissa, Madhya Pradesh, Maharashtra and Jharkhand among several states. At present the Naxalite movement is considered to be active in 102 districts in thirteen states with an estimated armed cadre of about 18,000 people.

16. The headquarters of Simdega district was earlier created as a subdivision of Ranchi district in 1915. The Bihar District Gazetteers of Ranchi records:

> The origin of the name of Simdega is not definite. Some say it consists of two words, namely, *sim* meaning hen and *dega* meaning step. Others suggest that it means watershed of the hills which girdle it. None appears to be convincing.

See N. Kumar, *Bihar District Gazetteers: Ranchi*, Government of Bihar, Revenue Department, Patna, 1970, p. 607.

17. Not accepting anything from anybody.
18. The Manipuris or the Meiteis were Hinduized in the fifteenth century. So were the Kalais and Rupinis of Tripura.
19. According to the 2001 Census, the total population of Assam is 26.6 million.

III

Bahudhā as an Instrument of Public Policy for Harmony

8

The Culture of Bahudhā

That since wars begin in the minds of men, it is in the minds of men that the defenses of peace must be constructed.[1]

—Constitution of the United Nations Educational,
Scientific and Cultural Organization (UNESCO)

Arnold Toynbee, author of the celebrated *A Study of History,* observed:

Danger, even when it is as extreme as ours is today, is never a sufficient stimulus in itself to make men do what is necessary for their salvation. It is a poor stimulus because it is a negative one. A cold-blooded calculation of expediency will not inspire us with the spiritual power to save ourselves. This power can come only from the disinterested pursuit of a positive aim that will outrange the negative one of trying to avoid self-destruction; and this positive aim can be given to men by nothing but love.[2]

Today, people are increasingly viewing their identity not only in terms of nation-states to which they belong, but also as members of their religious, racial, and ethnic groups. Such consciousness of one's heritage and a sense of pride in it gives satisfaction at the personal level. Yet, at the same time, a lack of understanding with other members of society in respect of economic opportunities, political rights, and religious sensibilities provides grounds for discord and often degenerates into violence. It also frequently leads to the formation of certain negative images and opinions that guide individual and group actions for a long time to come. Tragic examples of violence range from school shootings to suicide bomb attacks. The terrorist attacks in the United States on 11 September 2001, and subsequent retaliatory measures, have resulted in armed conflicts and loss of property and precious lives.

Terrorism, including human bombs, is the latest instrument in violent conflicts that are being sanctioned in the name of redressal of religious and ethnic grievances. The story of the Al-Qaeda as a terrorist organization is 'the story of eccentric and violent ideas sprouting in the fertile ground of political and social turmoil'.[3] The moot question is: how can one stop this cycle of violence leading to more violence and suffering?

In this context, the need for belief in 'one truth, many inter-pretations' has acquired great relevance in terms of formulation of a widely shared public policy of harmony. The culture of Bahudhā is deeply rooted in the inculcation of a special attitude from an early age. In the process of dialogue it is essential to have a state of mind where one can strongly believe in one's own way of looking at issues while simultaneously accommodating another's point of view. It is a mental discipline that makes one willing to consider the validity of other person's viewpoint. If the principles of non-violence and truth can guide the affairs of each individual and society, this approach can be further strengthened.

NATURE OF CONFLICTS

Conflict and violence are integral features of human affairs. The varied causes of conflict and violence have been analysed by scholars. Several perspectives have been offered, ranging from individual rivalry to conflict along religious, ethnic, and ideological lines. Armed conflicts as well as the Cold War among nation-states are too well known. After the end of the Cold War several scholars led by Samuel P. Huntington of the United States have described the conflict between civilizations as the latest phase in the evolution of conflict in the modern world. People use politics and their democratic freedoms not only to promote themselves but also to give their groups an identity on the lines of ethnicity, caste, language, and religion.

During 1945–89, some thirty-two ethnic and religious conflicts occurred between the Arabs and Israelis, Indians and Pakistanis, Sudanese Muslims and Christians, Sri Lankan Buddhists and Tamils, and Lebanese Shi'ites and Maronites. The conflicts between Serbs and Croats in the former Yugoslavia, and between Buddhists and Hindus in Sri Lanka, became extremely violent.

The world is witnessing a revival of religions as never before. There is a revivalist movement among believers in Islam, Christianity, Buddhism, Hinduism, Shinto, and Judaism. There are signs that many Chinese and Russians are returning to religion. Fundamentalist Islam is asserting itself even among the westernized middle classes of Turkey and Egypt. The main cause for concern is the reiteration of an earlier belief pattern that religious scriptures contain necessary and sufficient information to guide the conduct of *all* human affairs. Such religious reaffirmations are retrograde in nature. They stifle innovation of new approaches that are required to deal with fresh economic, technical, and social issues. They do not encourage people to take advantage of new instruments of information and communication technology in the solution of problems. Such movements support an exclusivist position in which contact and dialogue with believers of other faiths, and even learning of new education skills, have minimal value or relevance.

Religious resurgence is primarily a reaction to the loss of personal identity and group stability produced by the process of social, economic, and cultural modernization that swept across the world in the second half of the twentieth century. In the second half of the twentieth century 'economic and social modernisation became global in scope and at the same time a global revival of religion occurred'.[4] With traditional systems of authority becoming disrupted, people tend to get separated from their roots in a bewildering maze of new rules and expectations. Such people need new sources of identity, new forms of stable community, and new sets of moral precepts to provide them with a sense of meaning and purpose. Organized religious groups, both mainstream and fundamentalist, are growing today precisely to meet these needs. It has pervaded 'every continent, every civilisation, and virtually every country.'[5]

Another important feature of conflicts relates to rivalry among religions. Christian and Islamic fundamentalism has had a long period of violent confrontation in history. Similarly, the clash of civilizations between Hinduism and Islam, and between Buddhism and Islam has also degenerated into violence periodically and more particularly when Islam made expansionist inroads into the Indian subcontinent. The massive killing of people on account of religious wars in Bosnia and Herzegovina during 1992–5 has ended, thanks to international intervention under the aegis of the United Nations. During 1984–2004, India witnessed violent conflicts of an unprecedented nature. The killing of innocent Sikhs in 1984, the destruction of the Babri Masjid at Ayodhya in 1992 and the subsequent violence in Mumbai, and the massacre of Muslims in Gujarat in 2002, are reminders that while the state system was found wanting in the prevention of such conflicts, the pluralist secular ethos of India also needs to continually reassert itself. Observers of South Asian society and religion view these recent outbursts of religion-based violence, and political developments related thereto, with great alarm. The opportunistic use of religion by political leaders and groups and of politics by religious leaders and groups, have increasingly contributed to rise in intolerance and suffering. There is need to generate an environment of mutual understanding and compassion and for the redressal of hatred and suffering.

Equally significant is the conflict within religions. The history of Christianity has innumerable instances of the persecution of heretics. The conflicts between Shias and Sunnis in different parts of the world leading to the destruction of property and loss of lives is a continuing feature of Islam. The Hindu order is characterized by caste wars and periodic ethnic conflicts. Buddhist fundamentalism also brought about the schism between Hinayana and Mahayana Buddhism. The religion, which started with the principle that by reaching Dharma one is freed from all natural and social evils and the human misery arising from them, became divided on the issue of interpreting the method of reaching Dharma.

Conflicts between groups often arise and continue not only because of the differences between them, but also because of their similarities. People everywhere have developed traits to demonize others and to be loyal to their own group or clan. Such persons entertain a strong belief that they themselves, and those they identify with, are virtuous while others are wicked. They remember and fantasize past wrongs committed against them and/or their group and make plans in order to seek revenge. Sadly, human beings everywhere share the capacity to hate and kill each other, including their own family members and neighbours.[6]

Ideological conflict still continues though it is no longer as sharp as it was after the Russian Revolution of 1917 when it was between the ideology of communism, on the one hand, and that of capitalism and democracy, on the other. Fortunately, the fascist and Nazi ideologies as instruments of state policy were relegated to history after the Second World War. The period of the Cold War between 1945–91, which was dominated by the slogan of democracy versus communism, has also ended. In fact, after the political collapse of the Soviet Union and subsequent changes in the East European countries, the integration of the market has taken place, leading to a massive expansion in the ideology of globalization and democracy.

Conflict also arises from the growing economic inequality in the world. It is true that the economic progress the world has accomplished during the last fifty years is higher than any in previous periods in history. We are living in a world where the global economy generates over thirty-one trillion dollars a year. And yet, nearly one billion people in developing countries live on less than one dollar a day. In this inequitable world, less than twenty per cent of the people control eighty per cent of the income and resources of the globe. This inequality is likely to increase in view of demographic expansion. Five hundred years ago, the population of the world was about 500 million. Today, it is 6.4 billion. By 2050, the world's population will increase to 9.1 billion people, and virtually all the population growth will be in the developing world, especially in the fifty poorest countries.[7] During 1995–2005, sixteen of the twenty poorest countries suffered a civil war. Along with this inequity and poor governance in conflict-ridden societies, the electronic media and internet technology have fuelled human aspirations for material benefits as never before.

According to Samuel P. Huntington, conflict between civilizations is the latest phase in the evolution of conflict in the modern world.[8] He perceives this clash of civilizations as being caused by a variety of factors. First, differences among civilizations are not only real but also basic. Cultural characteristics and differences are less mutable, and hence less easily compromised and resolved than political and economic ones. Secondly, as the world is becoming a smaller place, the interaction between peoples of different civilizations is increasing. This increasing interaction intensifies consciousness and awareness of differences and commonalities between civilizations and within civilizations. This cultural basis is what can provide a ground for political and economic operation and cooperation. Therefore, civilizational identity will be increasingly important in the future, and the world will be shaped in large measure by the interaction among seven or eight major civilizations.[9]

BAHUDHĀ AND MAJOR CIVILIZATIONS

Civilization is a broad cultural grouping of people. In this sense, a civilization contains several cultures, nation-states, and several other identities that are integral to the formation of groups. Although civilizations, like other human creations, are mortal, they also evolve and survive in the form of enduring ideas and values. The four prominent civilizations which cover an overwhelmingly large segment of the global population are: Indian or Indic, Chinese, Islamic, and Western.[10] The Bahudhā approach of 'one truth, many interpretations' has been an important feature of every civilization.

INDIC

The Indic civilization[11] is polytheistic in the broadest sense of the term. From the very beginning it has included different world views and has undergone many changes. The most significant initial change was due to the fusion between the Dravidian and the Aryan cultures. The Brahminic religion that is associated with the Vedas flourished around 1500 BC and underwent many changes, primarily under the influence of Buddhism and Jainism. The Indian subcontinent subsequently saw a major civilizational encounter with Islam and later with followers of Christianity. The clash between the polytheism of the Indians and the monotheism of Islam, and Christianity has been significant. It is important to note that India never accepted the monotheistic approach of one God, one Book, and one ruler of Islam and Christianity. And yet she has integrated the people of different faiths within the folds of her plural and polytheistic culture.

The major changes brought about in the Hindu world view as a result of interactions with Buddhism and Jainism, and later with Islam, Sikhism, and Christianity broadened the character of the Indian civilization. Today, India as a civilization and as a history of people is far larger than Hinduism *per se*. The basic pluralistic character of Indian civilization from time immemorial has remained unaltered. The Republic of India as inaugurated on 26 January 1950, in terms of its Constitution, has laid a strong foundation for a secular pluralistic constitutional system. The working of the state despite its short-comings and failures has further strengthened the ethos of pluralism and secular values in the country.

The maxims of ancient Hindu scriptures *Vasudhaiva kutumbakam* (The world is one family) and *Ano bhadraha kratava yantu vishwataha* (Let noble thoughts come to us from all sides) continue to make their impact on the government as well as civil society institutions.

SINIC

The Chinese civilization[12] is another monotheistic civilization. Confucianism, Taoism, and Buddhism, despite their differing world views at the time of their origins, have flourished in China. Classical China recognized a multiplicity of divinities and spirits. Before the unification of China in 221 BC, the emperor was expected to be the chief worshipper of the principal powers. The Han empire, however, was also an age of religious synthesis, when many diverse ancient cults were amalgamated in accordance with an elaborate cosmology.[13]

The Buddhist tradition, originating in India, encompasses largely the Hindu spirit of pluralism. The Confucian attempt to repress and if possible, eradicate Mahayana Buddhism did not succeed. Buddhism was supported by Taoist scholars, who saw in Mahayana doctrines a reflection of their own concerns: 'Hatred of violence, and the avoidance of excess'. Accordingly, Mahayana Buddhism came to be accepted as a living force in the Sinic world. The philosophies of Taoism and Mahayana Buddhism succeeded in forging a close relationship in China. Over the years, China came to have a good blend of the rigid Confucian social norms and the tolerance of Taoism duly supported by the compassion and pluralistic Buddhist tradition. But eclecticism was born as much from the circumstances of the arrival of Buddhism from India as from the ability of the Chinese mind to hold a number of different propositions simultaneously without apparent distress.

The Te-Tao Ching (The Way of Virtue) attributed to Lao-Tse, who was born in 604 BC, is one of the most sacred texts of Taoism. It talks of experiencing the oneness in all things—fulfilling life by affecting harmony with nature as well as the inner self. The life and works of Confucius (551–479 BC) brought order and good governance to China. He invoked the example of a more stable part of China in his teachings about the proper way to live. Gentlemen, he said, ought to maintain good relations with the spirits by acting with decorum both in private life and as officials of the government. The followers of Confucius were convinced that the Taoists were entirely misguided in their concentration on Nature, and they marvelled that they could waste time on the study of apparently worthless things. In particular, Confucianism brought in order and obedience to respect for learning. Several sayings of Confucius became famous not only in China but all over the world. For example: 'Virtue is not left to stand alone. He who practices it will have' and 'To be able under all circumstances to practice five things constitutes perfect virtue: these five things are gravity, generosity of soul, sincerity, earnestness and kindness'. His teachings were codified, and knowledge of his works became the mark of an educated man and a qualification for holding office. The classical teachings of Confucius have influenced succeeding generations of Chinese in significant ways and greatly enriched Chinese civilization as well as the state system.

Chinese civilizational strength, based on Taoism, Confucianism, and Buddhism, found manifold expression in literature and the arts, philosophy, and science. The induction of the communist philosophy in China in 1949, and the Constitution of the Chinese People's Republic based on that philosophy, has not disturbed harmony at the social level in any significant way. The Bahudhā approach of harmony and dialogue among people have severely suffered at the civilizational level in Tibet and also in the suppression of the pro-democracy movement in Tiananmen Square in 1989.

The rapid advances in science, technology, and trade by China since the 1980s have helped China emerge as a civilizational centre for people of Chinese origin, not only those living within China but also elsewhere in the world. The people of Chinese origin play an important role in western countries including the United States, and see mainland China as a core state of the Sinic civilization.

Islamic

Like Judaism and Christianity, Islam[14] is strongly monotheistic. Its most basic belief, prayer, or mantra is known as the *shahaada*: 'There is no God but Allah, and Muhammad is his prophet'.[15]

Muslims are enjoined to defend Christian churches and Jewish temples while regarding the Bible's Old Testament as a sacred work, though not on the same level as the Quran, with its accompanying interpretive narrative, the *hadith*. Moses and Jesus are both venerated as major prophetic figures, though neither is the son of God in the same singular sense as Muhammad. The Quran enjoins upon all Muslims to respect all of God's creations, regardless of their religion or method of worship. In Surah Kafirun, verse 109, the Quran says: 'Tell the disbelievers I do not worship what you worship nor do you worship what I worship. I will not worship what you worship, nor will you worship what I worship. To you: your religion, and to me: mine'.

Unity of thought is a strong feature of Islam and the Ummah (the religious wing of the Muslim community) has an important role to play. The concept of equality, promotion of social peace, and piety are its essential features. Islamic civilization not only contributed to the state system but also enriched art and architecture, literature and law.

Notwithstanding emancipation from colonial rule, Islamic countries are yet to be united. In cultural terms too they are divided. Most Muslims in the world no longer understand Arabic. There are political as well as social and economic differences and difficulties, like the problem of Palestine left behind by the collapse of the Ottoman Empire which is still to be resolved. Many believers in Islam look back to their golden era not simply in terms of empire building but also in terms of the development of philosophy and the arts, science, and architecture. But there is a perceptive yearning for change and modernization as seen in western countries.

WESTERN

During the last four centuries western civilization has made rapid strides in the sciences and arts, language and literature. The major change was brought about during 1275–1475. The Reformation movement in Europe weakened the hold of the Catholic Church and helped in the emergence of the Renaissance movement.

The great civilizational strength of the western world is derived from the Christian faith. Historically, after the crucifixion of Jesus, Christianity began to spread through the Roman Empire. Christianity began as a Jewish sect, and inherited the Jewish scriptures and traditions, along with the New Testament, which recorded and interpreted Jesus' life and teachings. Later the Church also blended Greek and Jewish heritages. Christian churches created a new identity and community for the poor and oppressed of the Roman world, and extended its influence in Mesopotamia and India. Judaism and Christianity both greatly supported the Bahudhā approach by putting love and compassion, peace and non-violence as paramount goals of civilization.

The Old Testament (Isaiah, 2:4) which is appropriately written on a plaque in front of the United Nations building in New York reads:

And He will certainly render judgement among the nations and set matters straight respecting many peoples. And they will have to beat their swords into ploughshares and their spears into pruning shears. Nation will not lift up sword against nation, neither will they learn war anymore.

Western civilization, since the seventeenth century, has made an enormous impact on all other civilizations in terms of science and technology. Several inventions leading to massive industrialization originated in western countries and had a worldwide impact. As a result of these developments, people in other parts of the world have attempted to catch up with the West in wealth and modernity.

Civilizations have a long history of dialogue among themselves. Today the rapid strides in information and communications technology have enormously facilitated this dialogue process. There is a growing realization that we cannot and must not promote the universal features of one civilization even if it be in terms of science and technology. In a multi-civilizational and multi-religious world there is no need to look for a universal civilization or a common faith but to accept diversities and to respect them.

RELIGIONS

Religion is a central feature of each major civilization. The Indian, Chinese, Islamic, and Western civilizations draw their strength from Hinduism, Confucianism, Islam, and Christianity respectively. Cultures give religions their mode of expression: forms of worship, dialects, and other intangibles. Religion offers ultimate meaning to each culture, including its principal attributes: painting, sculpture, dance, and poetry. When we recognize pluralism and respect diversity, creativity is at its best. When we strive for harmony, we resolve to build the very core of peace. The irony is that while religions have contributed to the peace of the world, they have also led to division, hatred, and war. Religious leaders have, on several occasions in the past as well as in contemporary history, betrayed the high ideals they themselves have preached.

When believers in a religious faith accord their religion a monopoly of the truth, they tend to look upon other competing faiths as heresies, falsehoods, or wrongs. They mobilize powerful philosophical arguments for the fundamental doctrines of their world views. This belief impels them to ostracize or suppress other faiths for the sake of the truth they hold. Most often, such people behave as religious zealots or fanatics who will not be moved by any appeal to reason. This is at the root of violence. This mentality is called a 'crusading spirit', or 'crusader mentality'. Fortunately, there is considerable promise in all faiths as people are gradually and increasingly seeing the futility of the 'crusader mentality'. For example, among adherents of Islam, there is a strong group of reformists who are open to influence as against radicals who have a closed mind. The Bahudhā approach would facilitate not only a dialogue among believers of Islam but also with other faiths. It would also facilitate the formulation of policies and approaches on the part of ruling elites of western countries where a large number of Muslims live.[16]

Religions have no physical boundaries, notwithstanding their origins in a particular country. In fact, a religion can and should be used by any group of people or person who finds it beneficial. What is important for each seeker is to choose a religion that is most suitable to himself or herself. But, the embracing of a particular religion does not mean the rejection of another religion or of one's own community. The world is becoming smaller and smaller—and more and more interdependent—as a result of rapid technological advances and international trade as well as increasing transnational relations. Today we are mutually independent. The value of religion, accordingly, lies in the promotion of a fellowship of spirit and service rather than in exclusiveness or emphasis over differences in approach.

The term 'religious harmony' is itself in a sense self-contradictory, because no true religion can lead to disharmony. If any tradition of thought or belief leads to disharmony, then it cannot be spiritual or religious. Any 'ism' that leads to unethical or immoral action cannot be the outcome of spirituality. It is only by misusing religion that disharmony is perpetrated.

Dialogue and cooperation among religions is required to tackle urgent global problems as these can be most effectively tackled, not by each religion separately, but by the joint efforts of all religions and all societies. John Locke rightly says:

The toleration of those who hold different opinions on matters of religions is so agreeable to the Gospel and to reason, that it seems monstrous for men to be blind in so clear a light.[17]

TOLERANCE

The source of conflict is not the diversity of religions but the lack of tolerance. Tolerance teaches us open-mindedness. We may follow different roads but our goal is the same. Believers in different religions must treat one another as spiritual brethren. This perspective of tolerance should be carried forward in most religious beliefs as well as rituals. In two of the largest countries in the world, China and India, and also in several others, there are no State religions.

History shows that our tolerance levels have continued to increase despite conflicts and wars. The Bahudhā approach implies the act of listening carefully to the thoughts of others, admitting the diversity and differences based on a commitment to protect the universal principles of liberty, justice, human dignity, and peace. It is contrary to authoritarian approaches, politics, and social systems. Authoritarian personalities and politics can neither admit nor tolerate personal, political, and social opinions, groups or systems that differ from their own. In social matters too, respecting differences and improving relations is antithetical to authoritarianism.

Violence and aggression are coercive and imprecise instruments. Everywhere they create undying animosities that frequently blow back on the perpetrators of violence.

UNESCO'S EFFORTS

In the aftermath of the Second World War, political and intellectual leaders from around the world founded UNESCO and gave the organization the unique mandate of building the defences of peace in the minds of men and women. It is not enough, they argued, to base peace upon economic and political agreements. It must be founded upon the intellectual and moral solidarity of humanity.[18]

Over the years, UNESCO has concerned itself actively with issues of building as well as strengthening constructive and enduring peace. Towards this, it has relentlessly emphasized the need for individuals and institutions to act in a spirit of solidarity and cooperation. It was in pursuance of this that it took the lead in promoting a culture of peace by launching a massive programme in February 1994. This was in realization of the fact that:

the old way of looking at the world, seeing others as enemies, spending our resources on armaments, is an obstacle to the global cooperation and solidarity needed to face new threats to security. Increasingly, it is recognized that we can and must transform society from the dominant culture of war to a culture of peace. The goal of a culture of peace, reflecting the movement which brings it about, is a world in which the rich diversity of cultures is cause for appreciation and cooperation.[19]

Unfortunately the culture of peace movement did not take off at the expected levels. It is, therefore, necessary to see what fresh approaches can be made. It is in this connection that the Bahudhā approach, which exclusively focuses on attitudes and temper, needs to be looked at in the post 9/11 world.

BAHUDHĀ APPROACH

Each one of us wants to avoid suffering and achieve happiness. Unfortunately, several individuals in their quest for happiness use different methods, including those that are cruel and repellent. This becomes self-defeating. As the fourteenth Dalai Lama observes:

When we take into account a longer perspective, the fact that all wish to gain happiness and avoid suffering, and keep in mind our relative unimportance in relation to countless others. We can conclude that it is worthwhile to share our possessions with others, When you train yourself in this sort of outlook a true sense—of compassion—a true sense of love and respect for others—becomes possible. Individual happiness ceases to be a conscious self-seeking effort; it becomes an automatic and far superior by-product of the whole process of loving and serving others.[20]

Love and compassion are not only individually or socially beneficial virtues but they also constitute the moral fabric of world peace.

There is a growing body of shared values in respect of development, free flow of information, and on the full participation and empowerment of women. The need is to take it to deprived people and societies. While the Bahudhā approach does not deny the conflicts that arise from diversity, it nevertheless calls for non-violent solutions based on dialogue.

The Bahudhā approach is not only relevant to the affairs of state but also to civil society, and in the everyday life of citizens.

One of the finest expressions of the Bahudhā philosophy in India's foreign relations was the philosophy of Panchsheel. On 29 April 1954, India and China arrived at an Agreement on Trade and Intercourse between the Tibet Region of China and India, where it was enunciated that the Agreement was based on the following five principles:

(i) mutual respect for each other's territorial integrity and sovereignty;
(ii) mutual non-aggression;
(iii) mutual non-interference in each other's internal affairs;
(iv) equality and mutual benefit; and
(v) peaceful coexistence.[21]

Jawaharlal Nehru, with his great sense of idealism in global affairs, felt that the Panchsheel Agreement provided the principles for governing relations among nations and ushering in an era of peace. The principles enshrined in the Panchsheel were to guide relations not only between India and China but also between China and Burma (Myanmar), India and Burma (Myanmar), and with Indonesia. This was also to eventually become the cornerstone of the relationship of Vietnam with Laos and Cambodia.[22] At the State banquet given in honour of the Chinese Premier at New Delhi, Nehru *inter-alia* declared:

These principles are not only good for our two countries but for others as well. . . . If these principles can be recognised in wider spheres, then the fear of war would disappear and the spirit of cooperation between nations would develop.[23]

Unfortunately, the Panchsheel policy which is largely based on the Bahudhā approach, collapsed when China, without resorting to any dialogue process, introduced the Communist ideology on the Tibetan plateau—a Buddhist land—and later followed highly repressive policies there. China also militarily crushed the uprising of the Tibetan people in March 1959. The subsequent Chinese armed invasion of India in October–November 1962 buried the Panchsheel principle.

It was John Locke who in his celebrated book *Essay Concerning Human Understanding* (1689) used the famous phrase 'the pursuit of happiness'. This has since been incorporated in the Constitution of the United States and has influenced the writings of a large number of political scientists and economists. Public institutions, including the government, are expected to create an environment in order to promote 'the pursuit of happiness' for its citizens.

Most people of the world, whatever society, culture, civilization, or religion they revere or feel part of, simply want to live—and let others live—in peace and harmony. To achieve this, all of us must realize that the human community is inescapably bound together. More and more, whatever affects one sooner or later affects all.

The Bahudhā culture is not a complete philosophy of life, but in its application to any given situation it emphasizes a certain kind of discipline. It does not call for any dilution in one's family, ethnic, religious, or national identity. Instead, these plural identities and their relevance are emphasized and that the conflict resolution mechanisms have to be based on a dialogue process and at every stage of that dialogue and follow-up action, non-violence will be the key factor.

The culture of Bahudhā is not the absence of conflict, it recognizes the fact that in a diverse world with so many races, languages, and religions and competing claims over limited economic and educational opportunities, conflict will continue to be a part of the life process among individuals and nations.

The Bahudhā approach only helps in resolution of the conflicts in an innovative and creative fashion so that in any given situation the maximum win–win position for all concerned can be accomplished.

The philosophy of 'one truth, many expressions' would help people engage themselves in the light of their common heritage, which is full of love and compassion. They will be able to see clearly the need to abstain from terrorism and violence, war and destruction, and enter into an era of mutual respect and understanding, peace and development. Such a process can be determined by massive participation of the people and not guided by the domination of a few. A revolutionary transformation is possible and Bahudhā is an attitude to further that process.

In the Bahudhā philosophy, everyone counts. People do hold different views, and once a person or a group believes that his religion or politics has the absolute truth and/or is superior to others, everyone else would cease to count. The fundamentalist dictum that his version of truth being perfect gives him or his group the authority to impose it on others is not suited to solving the problems that people face today either in the domain of religion, or of politics and economy.

Fortunately, claims such as 'my country is always right', 'my people are the greatest in history', and 'my faith is the superior faith' are being increasingly discarded as a result of rational enquiries. Such enquiries are encouraging people to study and examine the essence of their own faith, culture, and civilization, and those of others in a world that is being seen as becoming increasingly interdependent.

The Bahudhā culture offers an environment in which, over time, people and nations can learn to respect different points of view and eschew fear and hatred. It can help institute the dialogue process and consolidate the gains. Bahudhā goes beyond the moral realm, and, in practical terms, it is the cornerstone of plural society and liberal democracy.

Ours is a highly diverse world. Over six billion people pursue a wide range of occupations and speak different languages and dialects, worship different gods and goddesses under myriad forms of worship with distinct ways of cultural expression. Pluralism in such a multi-lingual, multicultural, multi-ethnic, and multi-religious society is to be understood both in terms of competition, and also in terms of complementarity and convergence through free communication and living. The different visions of God and their varied expression through music, print and visual media such as photography, cinema, radio, television, as well as scientific inventions enrich the world we live in. Some individuals and some nations contribute more than others and there are always fears of cultural domination, which are not always unfounded. However, once civil society develops a regime of pluralism, the differences become negotiable because no one truth or reality falsifies another. Similarly, conflict resolution mechanisms are developed and mediation takes place, creating at times harmony, and equality with differences on another occasion.

BAHUDHĀ AND DEMOCRACY

The Bahudhā approach can be regarded as a prerequisite of democracy, harmony, integration, and peace. The true spirit of Bahudhā is an attitude of persevering, and attempting to solve problems according to the principles of peace, rather than by resorting to aggression or repression, even if one side crosses the limits of tolerance. In other words, the psychological and intellectual attitude that recognizes differences and diversity solicits harmonious and peaceful coexistence among incompatibles.

The ability to listen to another point of view can be cultivated through education. In addition, the recognition of existing social and cultural diversity and differences cultivates the Bahudhā spirit. These in turn form the foundation for democracy. Paradoxically, diversity and differences are harmoniously recognized in a democratic order. Therefore, both Bahudhā and democracy are in a mutually complementary relationship. The democratic political environment thus determines the Bahudhā temper and is in turn shaped by the Bahudhā spirit.

BAHUDHĀ AND LAW

Every country has a legal regime that contains provisions—varying in length as well as emphasis—which outline the fundamental duties of the citizens of the land to build a peaceful and harmonious society. Such an approach also guides the United Nations Charter. The Preamble of the UN Charter (1945) requires, 'the peoples of the United Nations . . . to practise tolerance and live together in peace with one another as good neighbours, and to unite our strength to maintain international peace and security.'

The Charter goes on to define the 'fundamental obligations' of member-states to 'pursue . . . a policy of eliminating racial discrimination . . . and promoting understanding among all races'. The United Nations General Assembly in its Declaration of 25 November 1981, declared that 'it is essential to promote understanding, tolerance and respect in matters relating to freedom of religion and belief', because such freedom 'should also contribute to the attainment of the goals of world peace, social justice and friendship among peoples and to the elimination of ideologies or practices of colonialism and racial discrimination'.

IMPERATIVES FOR ACTION

The following measures are required to be taken for the generation of the Bahudhā approach:

- New emphasis to be laid in dialogues of all faiths that actions based on love and compassion bring real victory as well as provide protection to one's own religion.
- A fresh approach for establishing harmony among various faiths could be by looking at differences among them and then learning to respect those dissimilarities.
- Religious leaders of various traditions should meet each other at local, state, and national levels in order to develop personal relationships with a view to remove misunderstandings and to set good examples for their followers.
- Inter-faith dialogue, inter-religious prayers, and pilgrimages to various holy places by each other should be encouraged.
- Religious leaders should be alert and resist exploitation by politicians in the name of religion, particularly by creating groups or vote banks.
- Attempts should be made to eradicate the gap between religious doctrine and the daily conduct of its followers.
- Inter-faith understanding must lead to a functional degree of amity among all religions without disturbing the uniqueness of each tradition.
- To recognize that religions and beliefs of the world have a vital role in the promotion of tolerance.
- Mass media and others providing information services should judiciously adhere to standards of objectivity in their work.
- To work for setting up a pluralistic and independent media to ensure the free flow of ideas essential for inculcation of the Bahudhā approach, particularly among the youth.
- Action should be taken to involve young people in experiencing the task of building a harmonious society, by imparting education that ensures respect for human rights and fundamental freedoms of all people.

- To identify leaders who have managed to preserve their humanity, and to treat them as role models for instilling in society a hope that there are ways out of the vicious circle.

In sheer pragmatic terms, problems can only be successfully resolved with a calm and clear mind. On the other hand, we lose our sense of judgement when we are guided or moved by hatred, selfishness, jealousy, and anger. At the level of presidents and prime ministers, when decisions are required to be taken concerning rights or claims of sovereign nation-states, a mindset guided by hatred and anger can lead to decisions that may degenerate into armed conflicts. The Bahudhā approach of dialogue and discrimination is useful to all, especially to those responsible for running national affairs.

The Bahudhā philosophy always believes that there are many ways of perceiving truth and in determining the relationship between God, nature, and human beings. It recognizes the role of religion in human affairs. While we may pursue different faiths and regulate our affairs in various ways, the objective remains the same—human happiness. This unites us all with the bond of goodwill. The Bahudhā approach thus could provide an enduring framework for a global public policy for harmony among different peoples and societies in the post-9/11 world.

The future of Bahudhā is closely linked to the nature of challenges and the responses to them that human society would make in the coming years.

THE WAY AHEAD

The world is undergoing a gloomy period in its history. There is something coarse, and at times extremely cruel, in our behaviour towards each other. Social and religious resentment accompanied by economic inequality and the exploitation of deprived individuals and backward nations has the propensity to create lasting disturbance in the world. Above all, the problem of terrorism and the ecology crisis call for augmentation of our dialogue processes and enhancement of cooperation skills. The forces of spirituality, democracy, and ecology need to join hands to eliminate the fundamental causes of conflicts and violence. Inter-faith global cooperation is one way that people of different civilizations can find common cause. Another approach relates to global environmental cooperation seeking to maintain and enhance the earth's life-sustaining capacities. Disparities in income need to be tackled at local, national, and global levels. An integrated market will not solve this crisis unless guided and controlled public action is undertaken by concerned citizens as well as democratic institutions. Democracies teach us that everywhere in the world we have a stake in working for the freedom and welfare of future generations, not least because the future of our own children and grandchildren is at stake.[24]

Human nature will continue to be a union of opposites: love and hatred, peace and violence, truth and falsehood, unselfishness and self-centredness, saintliness and sinfulness, and the spiritual and the physical. In fact, these opposite traits are inseparable from one another. The greatness of the human mind lies in building a system that is inclusive and judicious and one that ensures dialogue among persons, groups, and nations. Towards this end, religion and spirituality, education and culture, and global political and economic institutions have major roles to play.

NOTES

1. The UNESCO Constitution, adopted on 16 November 1945, goes on to explain this concept further as follows:

   That ignorance of each other's ways and lives has been a common cause, throughout the history of mankind, of that suspicion and mistrust between the peoples of the world through which their differences have all too often broken into war;

   That the great and terrible war which has now ended was a war made possible by the denial of the democratic principles of the dignity, equality and mutual respect of men, and by the propagation, in their place, through ignorance and prejudice, of the doctrine of the inequality of men and races;

   That the wide diffusion of culture, and the education of humanity for justice and liberty and peace are indispensable to the dignity of man and constitute a sacred duty which all the nations must fulfil in a spirit of mutual assistance and concern;

   That a peace based exclusively upon the political and economic arrangements of governments would not be a peace which could secure the unanimous, lasting and sincere support of the peoples of the world, and that the peace must therefore be founded, if it is not to fail, upon the intellectual and moral solidarity of mankind.

   (Quoted from the Constitution of the UNESCO).

2. Arnold Toynbee, *A Study of History*, the first abridged one-volume edition, Strand Book Stall, Bombay and Bangalore, 1995, p. 47.

3. *The 9/11 Commission Report: Final Report of the National Commission on Terrorist Attacks upon the United States*, W.W. Norton & Company, New York, 2004, p. 48.
4. Samuel P. Huntington, *The Clash of Civilizations and the Remaking of World Order*, Simon & Schuster, New York, 1996, p. 95.
5. Ibid., pp. 95–6.
6. Wendell Bell, 'Humanity's Common Values Seeking a Positive Future', *The Futurist*, Bethesda, September–October 2004, pp. 30–6.
7. See World Development Report, 2003 entitled Sustainable Development in a Dynamic World: Transforming Institutions, Growth and Quality of Life, The World Bank, Washington DC, 2003, pp. 1–9 (Chapter I: Achievements and Challenges).
8. Huntington, *The Clash of Civilizations*, p. 28.
9. Ibid., p. 45.
10. Ibid., Huntington says:

    The identity of the major civilizations is not contested. 'Reasonable agreement,' as Melko concludes after reviewing the literature, exists on at least twelve major civilizations, seven of which no longer exist (Mesopotamian, Egyptian, Cretan, Classical, Byzantine, Middle American, Andean) and five which do (Chinese, Japanese, Indian, Islamic, and Western). Several scholars also add Orthodox Russian civilization as a separate civilization distinct from its parent Byzantine civilization and from Western Christian civilization. To these six civilizations it is useful for our purposes in the contemporary world to add Latin American and, possibly African civilization.

11. This is one of the oldest living civilizations that has existed on the Indian subcontinent for the past 5000 years. This is generally referred to as Indian or Hindu civilization.
12. This is popularly known as the Chinese civilization. The term Sinic, however, describes the common culture of China and the Chinese communities in Southeast Asia and elsewhere. Like Indic civilization, Sinic civilization is also 5000 years old.
13. Arthur Cotterell (ed.), *The Penguin Encyclopedia of Classical Civilisations*, Penguin Books, Middlesex, England, 1995.
14. The Islamic civilization is a major civilization that originated in the Arabian peninsula in the seventh century AD and is now a significant force in Central Asia, Southeast Asia, and the Indian subcontinent, besides North Africa. The Islamic civilization includes Arab, Turkic, Persian, and Malaysian cultures. There is considerable Muslim presence in the West too (see n. 16 below.)
15. See *http://www.submission.org/muhammed/shahada.html* dated 14 October 2007. The relevant portion reads:

    The 'Shahada' which is the first cornerstone of Islam is twofold and reads: 'I bear witness that there is no God but Allah and that Muhammad is His servant and messenger.' In the first place 'God bears witness that there is no god but Him and so do the angels and those possessed of knowledge. In justice, there is no god but Him, He is the exalted, the wise.' As for '. . . and Muhammad is His servant and His messenger.' This is a statement of absolute fact. Anyone refusing to accept Muhammad as a messenger of God and the seal of His prophets falls outside the pale of Islam. The correct answer to the question 'is Muhammad a messenger of God and the last of the prophets?' is 'with certitude he is!'. It is not part of the confession of faith as dictated by God, but merely a statement of fact.

See also D.S. Margolionth's contribution entitled Muhammad in James Hastings (ed.), *Encyclopaedia of Religion and Ethics*, Vol. VIII, T&T Clark, Edinburgh, 1958, pp. 871–80.

16. Jocelyne Cesari, *When Islam and Democracy Meet: Muslims in Europe and in the United States*, Palgrave Macmillan, New York, 2004. It is estimated that nearly 12 million Muslims live in Western Europe (mostly in France, Germany, Italy, Netherlands, and the United Kingdom) and almost six million in America. The Muslims have emerged as a significant minority group in several Western democracies.

17. John Locke, *A Letter on Toleration*, Clarendon Press, Oxford, 1968, pp. 168–9.

18. Quoted from *UNESCO and a Culture of Peace: Promoting a Global Movement*, UNESCO Culture of Peace Programme, France, 1995, p. 3.

19. Ibid., pp. 10–11.

20. *The Spirit of Tibet: Universal Heritage—Selected Speeches and Writings of His Holiness the Dalai Lama XIV*, Allied Publishers, New Delhi, 1995, p. 263.

21. Claude Arpi, *Born in Sin: The Panchsheel Agreement—The Sacrifice of Tibet*, Mittal Publications, New Delhi, 2004, p. 215.

22. *International Herald Tribune*, 19 October 1954.

   Indian Prime Minister Jawaharlal Nehru flew to Peking today (October 18) with a promise from the Viet Minh leader Ho Chi-minh that he would respect the sovereignty of Laos and Cambodia and refrain from attacking them. An official communiqué said Ho told Mr. Nehru that he believed fully in the five principles which had been agreed upon between the Prime Ministers of China and India, and wished to apply them in the relations of Viet Nam with Laos and Cambodia, as well as with other countries.

23. Arpi, *Born in Sin*, p. 139.

24. Wendell Bell, 'Humanity's Common Values Seeking a Positive Future', *The Futurist*, September–October 2004, Bethesda, pp. 30–6.

IV

The Global Imperatives of Bahudhā

9

Religion for All Beings

Tell the disbelievers I do not worship what you worship nor do you worship
what I worship. I will not worship what you worship, nor will you worship
what I worship. To you: your religion, and to me: mine.[1]

—Quran

SETTING AND ARGUMENT

Towards the end of the nineteenth century, the famous German
thinker Friedrich Nietzsche (1844–1900) made an astounding
statement declaring the 'death of God'. The conception behind this
declaration was that the traditional idea of God as creator of the
universe and omnipresent is no longer relevant. In the *Genealogy of
Morals*, Nietzsche wrote:

There is no 'being' the doing, acting, becoming; the 'doer' has simply been
added to the deed by imagination—the doing is everything. . . . our science
is still the dupe of linguistic habits; it has never yet got rid of those
changelings called 'subjects.[2]

Subsequent thinkers and writers went on to highlight the fact that
people were no longer as interested in God as they were earlier. It
was felt that faith could not guide worldly affairs as it had done in the
past and, more importantly, its relevance was dependent on whether
faiths were prepared to be affected by that world to which they spoke
and sought to influence. It was propounded that secularism and
rationality were guiding human affairs more decisively than religious
beliefs in various parts of the world.

Advances in science and technology gave human beings new
powers of control over the forces of nature and that, in turn, led
several writers and thinkers to declare their independence from God.
The Age of Reason had dawned and started asserting itself. Ludwig
Feuerback, Karl Marx, Charles Darwin, Friedrich Nietzsche, and
Sigmund Freud hammered out philosophies and scientific interpretations of reality in which God had no place.

By the end of the twentieth century, however, religion began to re-assert itself and began to influence world events. The break-up of the Soviet Union also meant the rapid rejection of the official philosophy of atheism practised in that country. Church buildings in Moscow and elsewhere in the erstwhile communist world began to be renovated suddenly. In several other western countries, people began taking a keen interest in religion. This was true of the rest of the world as well. Politicians, journalists, and scholars started realizing the extremely powerful value of the religious motives of citizens and the need to use their beliefs in the promotion of development, peace and happiness in society.

Simultaneously, religions also witnessed the rise of fundamentalist groups in their midst. Jewish fundamentalists, Hindu radicals, angry Buddhist monks, Christian rightists, and Muslim fundamentalists started catching news headlines. The rise of Islamist elements among believers of Islam, in particular, received extraordinary notice in the West and people began expressing their world views in terms of a clash between Islam and Christianity. The re-assertion of religion in public affairs also came to mean a revival of the traditional belief that 'my religion is the best'. The fact that identifying religion with dogmas and beliefs had led to several wars in the past and inflicted sufferings on fellow citizens began receding in human consciousness. The famous saying of the Presbyterian elder who concluded his argument with a Jesuit by saying, 'We must agree to differ. We are both trying to serve the same God—you in your way and I in His',[3] suddenly became a subject of retrieval.

It is a sad fact of human history that religion has been a source of discord, conflict and wars. Faiths differ from each other rather sharply in terms of dogmas, beliefs, and rituals. This itself can cause conflict and discord. But when, to this is added, human ingenuity of a more sinister variety to use religion as a factor in the promotion of the economic and geopolitical interests of a nation-state and/or a group of people, the situation becomes violent/explosive.

All religions are human constructs and therefore, full of short-comings and infirmities. But, at the same time, all religions have also been creative and, have in fact, enabled men and women to attain a certain degree of meaning in their lives. Today, there is need to stress the age-old truth that religion is a significant human endeavour to comprehend truth. Dogmas, beliefs, and rituals are only instruments which seek to arouse a spiritual quest in order that we can realize new possibilities in life. True religion means a wholehearted commitment and dedication to a transcendent reality, as in moments of devotion and prayer, when we surrender ourselves completely. Such religious experiences unite rather than divide.

Major religions and their world views are intimately linked to contemporary political, social, economic, and moral issues. Several questions are being asked: What is the political role of religion? How does it affect state policy? What is our religious experience? What challenges does it pose to world peace and what challenges does it face? What positive role religion can play towards global peace and formulation of public policy for social harmony? Is secularization of the state the answer? What help the Bahudhā approach can render in this context?

RELIGION, POLITICS AND STATE

The role of religion as an important force in social and political affairs is engaging the fresh attention of politicians, journalists, and scholars, and of course, religious leaders these days. Assessments about religion's newly acquired position in public affairs, however, vary from scholar to scholar and also from country to country. There are many who would tend to underestimate religion's influence, while some others overestimate it. Finding and holding a middle point is not always an easy task.

The importance of religion in politics in many countries is directly linked to national prestige and/or ethnic identity concerns. At another level, modernization processes have generated insecurity among the minds of various segments of society, and to safeguard their identity and interests, they have been drawn to religious fundamentalism and political conservatism. Religious fundamentalists are also concerned that the development of society is not proceeding along the lines of their belief. Instead, the pace of change accelerated by globalization and market forces, mass media and technology have challenged traditional belief patterns. These people also entertain a common fear that their religiously oriented way of life is under threat from Western and American influences.

It may be mentioned that fundamentalists are not only an exclusive Islamic phenomenon but are also to be found among believers in Christianity, Judaism, Hinduism, and Buddhism. Fundamentalists in every religion feel their identity is being threatened by the rapid pace of modernization and secularization, and they would like to return to their old ways, in fact even to their narrow religious or ethnic cocoons. Another significant feature relates to the fact that while religious fundamentalists in Judaism, Christianity, and Islam invariably fall back upon their scriptures to express their opposition to secular politics, believers in Hinduism and Buddhism, on the other hand, draw strength more from national pride and ethnic identity and their past traditions than from their religious scriptures.

Religious violence and its impact on political affairs is also well known. Examples such as the Sikhs under Jarnail Singh Bhindranwale in India's Punjab, Egypt's Islamic group under Sheikh Omar Abdel-Rahman, or Thailand's right wing 'Kill-a-Commie-for-Buddha' monk do provide lessons for formulation of corrective policy measures. We also need to understand that religion has even motivated people to eliminate top political leaders. The assassinations of Mahatma Gandhi and Indira Gandhi were solely motivated by religious fanaticism. Similarly Anwar Sadat of Egypt and Yitzhak Rabin of Israel were consumed by religious flames.

Religion commands both symbolic and emotional power. Age-old animosities between followers of different religions and sects living within a geographic area have often caused violence and influenced political behaviour. Hindu–Muslim and Hindu–Sikh violence in India, the Catholic–Protestant impasse in northern Ireland, and the bloody Muslim–Jewish stand-off in Israel have made an impact on the politics, and even the history, of their respective countries.

Meanwhile, contemporary history, especially after 9/11, has shown the growing association of religion with violence as well as politics. Religious conflicts escalate quickly and disappear slowly, more so when politicized. Leaders whose charisma is on the decline also get tempted to raise a religious banner to secure votes and increase their following.

There is a close and somewhat inseparable relationship between politics and state. A complete separation of church and state is still to be fully achieved. One cannot keep politics open to religion and ethnicity and keep the state closed from their influence. If religious visions can become political agenda and vice-versa within the state, policies cannot remain secular.

In the complex relationship between religion, politics, and the state, one sees curious combinations of secular states and secular politics, religious states and religious politics, secular states and religious politics, and religious states and secular politics. A country cannot be permanently labelled as belonging to a single category. As politics stands today, we find that several of the European countries like Germany, France, the UK, as also countries like China, Russia, and the USA, could be put into the category of secular states that pursue secular politics. Similarly, Iran, Israel, Pakistan, and Bangladesh would belong to the category of religious states that also pursue religious politics. Indonesia is a significant country which is a religious state but it pursues secular politics. Japan, India, and Poland are secular states, where religion plays a significant role in their politics. Religion is not likely to leave politics in these countries even when they get rapidly modernized.

RELIGION, INTERNATIONAL RELATIONS AND WORLD PEACE

The criss-crossing of religion and international relations has become an important area of analysis and speculation. The conflict-enhancing potential of religion is borne out by history. In recent years, the major powers and the United Nations have worked hard at peace-making efforts in the wake of religion-based social and political strife in various parts of the world, ranging from Cambodia to South Africa and more particularly in Rwanda, northern Ireland, Mozambique, and Bosnia. In the tumult of these happenings, it has almost been forgotten that religion can also be an instrument of conflict resolution. After all, religions advocate peace and exhort their followers to work towards attaining it.

The recent war on terrorism has clearly established that there is loss of confidence among the people in the Islamic world towards the West. This state of affairs has arisen both because of terrorist attacks in the USA and in Europe and a breakdown in communications, particularly between the Western and Islamic countries.

Everyone agrees that the terrorist attacks in the name of religion and political grievances have heightened tensions between the Western countries and the Arab world and also between Muslims and the rest of the population living in Western countries. Several scholars also believe that the political role that religion has assumed in recent years would have an impact upon the nature of polity management. The radical Islamists feel that power must be accompanied by moral purpose of good governance in terms of Quranic wisdom. The principle of nationalism gets another orientation when these Islamic radicals support the use of violent means for achieving its objectives in Palestine, Chechnya, Bosnia, Kashmir, Xiajiang, and the Philippines, unmindful of geographical boundaries and the sovereignty of nation-states.

Islam was born in an Arab land and gradually moved to Asia, Africa, Europe, and the United States. At the level of allegiance to Islam, therefore, there is a distinction between the Arabs and the rest. Many scholars tend to divide the believers of Islam into two groups, that is those who are Arabs and thus fall in the category of natural or original Muslims, and the rest who are converts to Islam.

Religions can see each other in two different ways—by emphasizing their commonalities or by highlighting their differences. In the context of Islam, Graham E. Fuller advocates the need for understanding the political, religious, and psychological aspects of Muslim society as a whole. He writes:

Indeed, the vehicle of political Islam might be one of the very best ways to understand the politics of Muslim world in general, far more revealing than to follow. . ., socialist, nationalist or even democratic politics of Muslim societies. The reason is simple; Islam pervades the daily life of Islamic society and political culture more profoundly than any other single ideological or conceptual force.[4]

Incidentally the word 'fundamentalists' came into currency in the 1920s[5] in the US referring to a group of conservative Protestants. These Christian fundamentalists believed in the basic tenets of religion as presented in *The Fundamentals,* a series of twelve pamphlets published in the US from 1910–15, giving in detail features of a biblically based moral code.

When speaking of Islamic fundamentalism, however, we are talking of an altogether different situation. It was Ayatoullah Khomeini, the leader of Iran's Islamic revolution of 1978–9, who forcefully argued for Islam and Islamic fundamentalism. In his perception, when Muslims obeyed God's commandments, He enabled them to create great empires and civilizations and when Muslims cease to obey divine law, they become weak and subservient to the US and other Western countries. Osama bin Laden has carried forward this philosophy and has resented Western domination over the Muslim world and also the idea of modern secular states.

Religious ideas, issues and concerns have received renewed emphasis in the Muslim world since the Iranian revolution in 1979. This was followed by religious fundamentalism guiding politics and the state in Sudan and Afghanistan. Political Islam, with its age-old instrument of Jihad[6], was further strengthened by radical Islamist groups by adopting terrorism as an instrument of political domination. Powerful and effective use of terror has been applied not only against the US and European countries but also in such countries as Algeria,

Egypt, Palestine, Lebanon, Pakistan, India, Iran, the Philippines, Saudi Arabia, Somalia, Yemen, Chechnya, and Uzbekistan.

The presence of a sizeable Muslim population in Europe and their rising numbers are becoming matters of growing concern to analysts and administrators. It may be recalled that after 1945 labour force was imported from developing countries for reconstruction of war-ravaged Europe. A significant number of them were Muslim migrants who subsequently settled in Europe and made it their home. Unfortunately, they have not been fully integrated into Western society and polity. As a consequence, Muslim offspring feel left out and increasingly resent their status. The recent terrorist attacks in the US, Madrid, and London and even in some parts of Asia have shown that the Western-educated Muslim youth find terrorist activities attractive.[7]

In the Western world, too, Christianity is finding a renewal and a new meaning in terms of both a moral code and a distinctive mark in the post 9/11 era. Samuel P. Huntington in his work, 'Who Are We?' talks of preservation of American religious identities. He puts it in very categorical terms:

September 11 dramatically symbolized the end of the 20th century of ideology and ideological conflict and the beginning of a new era in which people define this is primarily in terms of culture and religion. The real and potential enemies of the US now are religiously driven militant Islam and entirely non-ideological Chinese nationalism. For America, the religious component of their identity takes on new relevance in this environment.[8]

Religion has emerged as a major factor in the West also because of the restoration of the old belief in the public mind that the moral decline that characterizes industrial society could be reversed only through religion.

Earlier in 1985, Chief Justice William Rehnquist of the United States clearly mentioned the importance of religion in public life when he pronounced:

The wall of separation between Church and state is a metaphor based on bad history. Its individual expressions of faith by federal employees. Christians will be able to keep Bibles on their desks. Muslim women will be able to wear headscarves. Jewish workers who want to honour their high holy days will have to be accommodated as much as possible. No one will be able to stop a federal worker from talking about or arguing about religion during coffee breaks and lunch.[9]

The United States is the most religious among countries in the industrialized world and yet fully committed to separation of religion and state. The basic values of American society and politics do not relate to religious dogmas or rituals but to democracy, civil rights, non-discrimination, and the rule of law. This has greatly contributed to making the US the most advanced country in the world and also a superpower. Fears are being expressed that these features of American society and politics may undergo change with the emergence of religion and ethnicity as important factors in American identities.

THE RELIGIOUS EXPERIENCE

THE INDIAN SCENE

Every nation has its own unique history. Although religion has been given a role in its political affairs it is being gradually realized by everyone that religion should be kept outside the state apparatus rather than within it. Even people living in Islamic countries such as Egypt, Turkey, Pakistan, Bangladesh, and Indonesia find that scriptures alone cannot provide answers or solutions to their problems. All these countries are under the intense pressure of the forces of globalization and modernization and also of Islamization.

India occupies a special position in the history of religions. It is the birthplace of Hinduism, Jainism, Buddhism, and Sikhism— popularly referred to as Indic religions. Christianity, Judaism, Zoroastrianism, Islam, and the Bahai faith have come to India from abroad at different points of time and have taken deep root.[10]

One of the principal features of Indian history has been the tradition of dialectical arguments (*sastrartha*) among pandits and scholars along with sermons by the pathfinders and gurus. It was Buddha more than anybody else who started the practice of dialogue in Sanghas and of preaching at urban centres and in villages. His sermons at Sarnath are well known. This tradition was followed by his followers who held the 'Buddhist Councils'. This dialogue among monks and scholars from different places, belonging to different schools of thought, had commenced shortly after Buddha's death. The first of the four Buddhist Councils was held at Rajgir and a century later in Vaishali. There is no unanimity among historians about the date(s) of the meeting of Buddhist Councils held on four occasions. The first Council was held in Rajgir in the fifth century BC in 487 BC. According to some others it was held in 544 BC. The second Council was held in fourth century BC probably in 387 BC. The third council was held in

Pataliputra in 250 BC or in 326 BC. The fourth Council was held in Kashmir around 100 CE. Ashoka, during his reign, held the third Buddhist Council at Pataliputra (now Patna), the then capital of India. A century later, the fourth Council was held in Kashmir. The deliberations of these councils helped to resolve the differences in religious principles and practices and made social harmony and progress possible. It must also be appreciated that in these deliberations, social and economic issues and interests of common people also figured.

This ancient Indian tradition of dialogue and religious pluralism was later carried forward. During the Mughal period, Akbar in the late sixteenth century chaired meetings involving leaders of different religious faiths including Hindus, Muslims, Christians, Parsis, Jains, Jews, and even atheists. Another strong feature of the Indian experience has been its accommodation, not only of different religions and faiths, but also of different ideas in terms of science and technology, arts and architecture, music and dress. A significant feature of Indian pluralism could be found in a very impressive corpus of religious literature, both in prose and poetry, and in different languages. This literature throws light on conflict resolution through dialogue.[11]

The colonial experience, more particularly of the twentieth century, has a somewhat different story to narrate. During this period, Indian society and polity came to be marked by a sharp division between Hindus and Muslims, culminating in the partition of the country in 1947.

The idea of secularism was made a cardinal principle of governance. After the terrible communal killings in the aftermath of the partition, and its recurrence involving different faiths from time to time, it is axiomatic that the instruments of laws in particular must uphold secular values. The fact that the Indian leadership opted for a secular constitutional arrangement for independent India despite the division of India in the name of religion, speaks eloquently about India's strong traditions of pluralism and secular values. 'We have to build the noble mansion of free India', Jawaharlal Nehru declared in his celebrated midnight speech, 'where all her children may dwell'.[12]

It must also be kept in mind that secularism cannot survive as a value-system only in the glory of its past. It has to be lived. Informed citizens can assist in building an environment for secular values. This requires equal respect for all religions as India is a country which is deeply rooted in religious belief and religion cannot be ignored.

Two religion-related incidents that have adversely influenced the character of Indian polity in recent years relate to the atrocities on the Sikhs following Indira Gandhi's assassination on 31 October 1984; and the destruction of the Babri Masjid in Ayodhya on 6 December 1992.

On 3 June 1984, Prime Minister Indira Gandhi ordered the Indian army to enter the holiest shrine of the Sikhs—the Golden Temple at Amritsar—to flush out Sikh radicals who had made the holy shrine their operational base under the leadership of Jarnail Singh Bhindranwale. The objective of this fundamentalist Sikh preacher was to build a wall of hatred between Hindus and Sikhs in order that an independent homeland for the Sikhs (Khalistan) could be created. The army action, code named 'Operation Blue Star', involved three days and nights of bitter fighting in which army tanks moved inside the shrine. Bhindranwale and several other militants were killed and a part of the Golden Temple complex was severely damaged. Five months later, two of Prime Minister Indira Gandhi's Sikh bodyguards gunned her down in the garden of her official residence.

Indira Gandhi's assassination was followed by the killing of 3,500 Sikhs, most of them in Delhi itself. The massacre of Sikhs fuelled Sikh terrorism in which Hindus were targeted by the Sikh terrorists. Hindu–Sikh polarization began to take place. Thanks to the tradition of dialogue and democracy, the Hindu–Sikh divide did not take root and Sikh terrorism gradually disappeared.

The Sikhs constitute less than two per cent of India's one billion people. On 22 May 2004, a major democratic event took place and almost in a dramatic fashion Manmohan Singh, a Sikh, was sworn in as India's fourteenth Prime minister. This was made possible by Sonia Gandhi, the daughter-in-law of Indira Gandhi who had sent the Indian army into the Golden Temple and the leader of the Indian National Congress and natural claimant to the office of the prime minister. It was one of the finest examples of democracy's healing touch in a multi-religious, multi-ethnic, and multi-lingual country.

Hindu–Muslim unity received a serious setback with the destruction of the Babri Masjid by Hindu radicals on 6 December 1992 in Ayodhya. A masjid was built in Ayodhya in 1528 by a lieutenant of Babur, the Mughal emperor, at a place which the Hindus have all along believed to be the birthplace of Ram. Many historians also subscribe to the view that a Ram temple existed on the site prior to 1528. In 1987, the Bharatiya Janata Party (BJP) in concert with the Bajrang Dal and the Vishwa Hindu Parishad, the two strong Hindu organizations, embarked on a campaign to demolish the structure and erect in its place a grand temple to Ram, the avatar of the Hindu God Vishnu and the hero of the great epic, the Ramayana. For centuries, Ram has been a familiar name to every household in India—Hindus, Muslims, Sikhs, Christians, Parsis, Buddhists, Jains—as a symbol of justice and renunciation, suffering and endurance. An overwhelming majority of Hindus, however, while desirous of having a grand Ram temple at Ayodhya, did not react favourably to the destruction of the disputed structure.

The Economist in a special report on religion and public life sums up the Indian scene as follows:

Today India is a test-tube for religious politics. The birthplace of four big religions (Buddhism, Jainism, Sikhism and Hinduism), it has remained religious even as it has modernised. It was founded in the throes of a religious conflict–partition between Hindu India and Muslim Pakistan. And religion informs three different political conflicts: the external one with Pakistan; an internal one between the Hindu majority and the sizeable Muslim minority; and a rip-roaring debate about religion in the public square.[13]

The tension in Hindu–Muslim[14] relations in contemporary Indian history can be traced back to the early 1980s when incidents of conversion of Dalit communities to Islam took place in Meenakshi-puram in Tamil Nadu in 1981. A chain of events has followed since then. The demolition of the Babri Masjid in Ayodhya in 1992 and the countrywide incidents of violence that followed, more particularly in Mumbai, estranged relations between Hindus and Muslims. The gruesome violence leading to the murder of 2000 Muslims in Gujarat in 2002 following the incident of fire in a train at Godhra in the same state in which nearly five dozen Hindu passengers were burnt. It was widely assumed that Muslim terrorists were responsible for this and have led several scholars to question whether Hindus and Muslims could live together—or are they living separately together?

It must be mentioned that Hindus and Muslims in South Asia have not been living in separate compartments. There have been constant exchanges not only in the market place but also on agricultural lands, in construction of houses, in marriages and in exchange of pleasantries on days of religious festivals. At the social level, there is an under-standing on display that is infinitely richer than what the fundamentalists and radicals in both communities would like us to believe. The forces of harmony are reasserting themselves and one sees that people are joining each other in economic and social pursuits, leaving behind bitter memories of Ayodhya, Mumbai, and Gujarat.

The Indian experience, notwithstanding some aberrations, clearly establishes that the common people of India, irrespective of their individual religious identities, have traditionally respected religious plurality. This pluralist orientation is visible in the markets and in civil society organizations where religious identities do not necessarily come in the way of agreement on secular issues.

Take the case of language. Linguistic diversity is an established way of life in India. This is one vital aspect of pluralism. People in a multi-lingual country develop ways of speaking in which they can maintain their own language and still communicate with speakers of other languages; they become bilingual or multi-lingual. All languages are important but different languages have different roles in society, and have different positions in the education system. That each speaker has access to the other's variety (e.g. Hindi or Urdu) and also to the common variety, that is (Hindustani) underscores the integrative aspect of such variations. Similarly, a Tamil-speaking person has access to English to converse with a Hindi-knowing person and vice-versa. The assertion and acceptance of identities are reciprocal and mutual. In this way, different social groups can maintain their separateness on the one hand, and express their togetherness on the other.

In the realm of religion too, one observes that a good life can be lived by following different paths. This practical knowledge creates a better understanding of other faiths and takes away the archaic approach that 'my religion is superior to yours'. Common schools of boys and girls of different faiths and common political processes help secure pluralist integration. As long as democracy gives adequate space for different faiths to flourish and be part of national identity, a plural society is secure and enriched in many ways.

Pluralist integration is thus different from the 'melting pot' and the segregated variety. The melting pot results in a merger of identity or complete assimilation with the dominant group. Separateness or segregation results in isolation. The pluralist ethos under a democratic framework calls for pluralist integration. This needs to be underlined and promoted and that alone can strengthen the idea of democratic secular India.

The concept of secularism has to be seen exclusively in terms of the presence of mutual respect among the followers of different religions and a non-discriminatory state. Both these features of social and political order have come under severe strain on several occasions but India's pluralist traditions and democratic framework have restored secular values both as a lived social reality and state policy. T. N. Madan highlights this phenomenon in the following words:

The traditional elite of the 19th century were famous with this folk pluralism, but considered it as no more than the ignorance of the unlettered masses. Today's modernised intelligentsia have opted for the ideology of secularism, which seeks to drive religion into the privacy of people's lives if not altogether eliminate it. This ideology envisages a pluralism that is concomitant of structural differentiation in society. Needless to emphasise, two pluralisms—the peoples and the intellectuals—are different in several crucial respects. For example, and most notably, the former is wholly spontaneous—the lived social reality—but the latter is ideological and in that sense self-conscious or constructed; the former is based on a positive attitude towards religion, but the latter is sceptical. Indeed, there is a hiatus between the two pluralisms, but this has not been examined with the seriousness it deserves.[15]

The common people of India acknowledge religious differences as a part of social and experienced reality. They do not consider it in good or bad terms. Social harmony is built on and reflects this difference.

The critics of the Bahudhā approach highlight the fact, that while at the philosophical level the Bahudhā approach has great meaning and relevance, at the social level it has not been operating effectively either in the past or at present. It is argued that in social intercourse, inclusiveness is not entertained in India. It was an extreme idea of exclusiveness, that gave birth to concepts of purity and impurity, and consequentially to the emergence of untouchability and a class of untouchables. The complex nature of the Hindu mind has been tolerant and inclusive in philosophical speculation and religious practices but rigid and exclusive in social life and practices. In contemporary India as well, religious, ethnic, and caste identities have dominated public life. An inclusive social order that democracy demands could not be achieved through religious and caste divisions having a say in the selection of candidates for Parliament and assemblies, and also on the outcome of election results.

Pluralism, however, is deeply embedded in the intellectual and spiritual heritage of India. It is India's primary civilizational value and flows essentially from the ancient Vedic traditions which gave over-riding and intrinsic primacy to the quest of 'truth' and recognized the principle of truth in its many facets. The composite Indian philosophy of dialogue and coexistence, the message of 'live and let live', and the insistence on understanding and accommodation, though critically embattled from time to time, gained strength and a rare resilience in the discourse of India through the ages. It is in that continuing discourse in its long history that India finds cultural, philosophical sustenance for its contemporary creed of secularism.

IS SECULARISM THE ANSWER?

During the nineteenth and twentieth centuries, secularism was developed in social science and literature as a comprehensive public policy for modernization and change. This was viewed as a natural concomitant of the spread of science, education, and technology, all of which advanced the age of reason and rationality. All over the world there was a phenomenal increase in the number of people who came to believe in secularism.[16]

Secularism is not always in conflict with the pursuit of religion, and at times, guarantees it. India's 150 million Muslims have pursued their religious faith while participating in a secular democratic framework. They know secularism is what protects them, their religion, and their freedom.[17]

As a political arrangement, pluralism finds comprehensive expression in secularism. The Constitution of India reflects both the traditional pluralist orientation of the Indians and also some of the finest expressions of the Indian people during the epic freedom struggle.

The Indian experience has shown that religious pluralism flourished even when we had a religiously ordained social order. Ashis Nandy records as follows:

It is not modern India which has tolerated Judaism in India for nearly 2,000 years, Christianity from before the time it went to Europe, and Zoroastrianism for more than 1,200 years; it is traditional India which has shown such tolerance. That is why today, as India gets modernised, religious violence is increasing. . . . The moral of the story is this: the time has come for us to recognise that, instead of trying to build religious tolerance on the good faith or conscience of a small group of de-ethnicised, middle-class politicians, bureaucrats and intellectuals, a far more serious venture would be to explore the philosophy, the symbolism and the theology of tolerance in the faiths of the citizens and hope that the state systems in South Asia may learn something about religious tolerance from everyday Hinduism,

Islam, Buddhism, and Sikhism rather than wish that the ordinary Hindus, Muslims, Buddhists and Sikhs will learn tolerance from the various fashionable secular theories of statecraft'.[18]

It, however, needs to be mentioned in this context that though tolerance was indeed practised in traditional India, it was organized hierarchically, a strong feature of the Vedic system, and not democratically under a secular constitutional framework, as is the case these days.

One of the major shortcomings in the interpretation of religion on the part of several secular leaders lies in the fact that they want religion to be confined only to private quarters as a set of individual beliefs. In fact, several of the advocates of secularization and modernity have taken the concept of separation between the domains of the Church and the state almost literally. They ignore the fact that every major religion is both a private belief as well as a social event. Another flaw lies in looking at religion largely in terms of ideas, doctrines, and metaphysics, and totally neglecting the living practices which have emerged over time based on the interpretation of the respective scriptures and commentaries thereon. This is not to deny that religion is predominantly an encounter with the sacred rather than with the market and that cults, rituals, and sacrifices, however significant and binding, do not represent the core elements of a religion or its quest for the vision of Absolute Reality.

In the past when religion and the state had a close relationship, secularists and modernists believed that a weakening of the hold of religion over the state, and the move towards and creation of secular nation-states would solve major social problems. Today in secular countries and, more particularly, after 9/11, people are demanding renewed political power for religion. It is being argued that nationalism and socialism and the free market alone cannot solve social problems and that religion, ethnicity and caste must be given adequate consideration in policy-making. No wonder that in various countries including democracies, religion, ethnicity, caste, and gender are providing a basis for political mobilization along with ideologies such as socialism, nationalism, and liberalism.

Placed in these contexts, religious fundamentalism is both a revival of a literal interpretation of scriptures and a political mobilization. The religious fundamentalists view secularism as an overpowering threat to their identity and do not treat their religions, including its different elements, that is creed, cult, and code, as outmoded ideas in polity management.

Although we live in an era of renewed religiosity, secularism is not in retreat. Individuals, cultures, nations, and societies still continue to entertain both religious and secular perspectives. Neither the religious nor secular dimensions of modern society are likely to disappear.

It is being increasingly appreciated that European countries have not been successful in making a large number of immigrants, particularly Muslim immigrants, feel at home. There is no such appellation as Indian American or Chinese American in the UK or in France as we see in USA or Canada. It would be disastrous in the long run to be known as Muslim British or Hindu French or Buddhist German. One hopes identities such as Tunisian French, Indian British and so on would gradually emerge. Once the second or third generation immigrants acquire secular identities and constructive engagement is further strengthened in the market as well as in political arenas, the present environment of distrust largely due to religious divides in Europe, will rapidly transform itself into one of accommodation and goodwill.

The 7 July 2005 bombings in downtown London on its metro and bus transport system has again sharpened the conflict between Muslims and Western Europeans. Western society and the state system again views Muslims as suspect and consequently curtail their liberties and opportunities for employment. According to Thomas L. Friedman, the answer lies with the Muslim world. He writes:

It is essential that the Muslim world wake up to the fact that it has a jihadist death cult in its midst. If it does not fight that death cult, that cancer, within its own body politic, it is going to infect Muslim-Western relations everywhere. Only the Muslim world can root out that death cult.[19]

Friedman goes on to lament that the Muslim world

has been derelict in condemning the madness of jihadist attacks. When Salman Rushdie wrote a controversial novel involving the Prophet Muhammad, he was sentenced to death by the leader of Iran. To this day, no major Muslim cleric or religious body has ever issued a *fatwa* condemning Osama bin Laden.[20]

It is possible to paint Islam as the sire of most contemporary wars, as a repository of economic backwardness, and as antipathetic to democracy. But the truth is different. When there are elections in

Muslim countries, most voters reject parties that sympathize with the extremists. Countries that have convinced themselves that elections will bring to power radical Islamists—like Egypt, Algeria, Saudi Arabia, and Jordan—overlook what seems to happen in an open electoral arena: the softening of the edges and the strengthening of the moderates.

Most countries with large numbers of Muslims—including Indonesia (240 million), India (121 million), Bangladesh (114 million) and Turkey (70 million)—are liberal-minded and democratic. All have populations that overwhelmingly reject the terrorist jihad. All find the rigidity of Islamic belief as exhibited in the many smaller countries of the Middle East both archaic and uninformed theologically. For them it is the ballot, not the bullet, that counts.

The secularization of the state needs to be continually emphasized and pursued. At the same time, each religion has its own reservoir of tolerance, good neighbourliness, love and peace, and that too would be required to be adequately stressed. What is likely to emerge is a changing balance between religion and secularism at different periods of time in order that religious and cultural strengths are used for addressing the needs of democracy, ecology, and peace. The challenge before each religion is to accept that there are many paths to God, that one path is not superior to the other, and that there is no need to denigrate the faith held by others.

RELIGION AND THE BAHUDHĀ APPROACH

Every student of the history of religions is deeply aware of the existence of the plurality of traditions and a plurality of variations in each tradition. Every religious path teaches us the ultimate reality and prescribes the way to salvation or liberation. The exclusivist approach creeps in as adherents of each religion start asserting the superiority of his or her path.

Notwithstanding such exclusivist assertions in different religions, the Bahudhā approach or a pluralist orientation too has found significant assertions. In the New Testament, Jesus Christ takes note of the life that lightens every man (John, 1:9). In the enunciation of the Islamic faith, the well- known Sufi poet Maulana Jalaluddin Rumi puts it beautifully when he writes, 'The lamps are different but the light is the same: it comes from beyond'.[21] There are similar expressions in Buddhism and in Hinduism. All these strengthen the logic that there can be salvation outside the church or the synagogue, outside the temple or the sangha, and outside the mosque or the gurudwara. Even under the guidance of the same scripture, different communities have developed different ways of worship and communion with the Creator. This, in turn, has created manifold forms of religious dialogues and forms of worship. All these have loosened the grip of the exclusivist approach of *outside the church no salvation*.[22]

Sikhism and now the Bahai faith advocates oneness of humanity, oneness of religion, and oneness of God. One of the significant features of the Bahai faith is that it sees total agreement between science and religion.

The Bahai faith would like us to view religion not as an independent entity, but as a never-ending process that has guided and spiritually trained humanity. The Bahai holy writings state, 'Divorced from true religion, morals lose their effectiveness and cease to guide and control man's individual and social life'. According to Bahaullah (1817–92), the founder of the Bahai faith: 'Religion is the greatest of all means for the establishment of order in the world and for the peaceful contentment of all that dwell therein'.[23]

Unfortunately, the efforts of Sikhism and the Bahai faith towards unity among religions have not so far succeeded. There are, however, philosophers and saints who believe that the world will give birth to a new faith which will unite mankind. I, however, do not see the emergence of a world religion transcending existing manifestations of faiths. All major religions would continue to hold sway and the level of conversion of people from one religion to the other may perhaps be confined to some unattached people or to a few intellectuals. In the coming years, the scale of conversion is bound to be at a nominal level compared to what happened during the medieval period and, more recently, during the nineteenth and twentieth centuries.

The information and communications technology and the quality of modern scholarship have facilitated the spread of information about different religious traditions available in several languages. Above all, because of cosmopolitan living and long distance travel people are getting opportunities of dialogue and face-to-face familiarity with practitioners of different religions. The fact that some politicians and leaders manipulate religious differences to serve their own purpose is increasingly coming to notice. Historical happenings are being interpreted in terms of modern needs. For example, people now agree that the Crusades and the Inquisition are blemishes on European history; that the Reformation gave rise to the devastating Wars of

Religion and so on. The recent killings in the name of religion in different parts of the globe are driving people to believe that there is no other way to peace and harmony except in the fact that believers of different faiths will have to learn to live together.

The Bahudhā approach assumes great importance in providing a framework for resolution of existing and possible conflicts between Islamic and Christian world views. A world without terrorism can only be built by a non-confrontational attitude. Liberal Muslims have a role to play in putting Islamic society on the path of modernity and not allowing the radicals to hijack Islam to pursue their programmes.

The believers in Islam and their leaders have a great tradition of learning, social equality, attitude of respect to others and peace. The Islam has a tradition of mutual consultation in the tradition of convivencia. The religious attitude of good neighbourliness, its appreciative view about the goodness of creations, its belief in God as the world's inner-most source of love are virtues that properly articulated could strengthen forces of peace and harmony The need is to understand each tradition, to hold consultations and support those organizations which believe in inter-faith dialogue. Karen Armstrong expresses it rightly when she writes:

If Muslims need to understand our Western traditions and institutions more thoroughly today, we in the West need to divest ourselves of some of our old prejudice. Perhaps one place to start is with the figure of Muhammad: a complex, passionate man who sometimes did things that it is difficult for us to accept, but who had genius of a profound order and founded a religion and a cultural tradition that was not based on the sword— despite the Western myth—and whose name 'Islam' signifies peace and reconciliations.[24]

It was through the divine education imparted by illustrious luminaries such as Ram, Krishna, Mahavira, Buddha, Confucius, Laotze, Socrates, Moses, Zoroaster, Jesus Christ, Muhammad, and Nanak that great civilizations and cultured societies came into existence. These noble beings taught their followers to practise forgiveness, generosity, and peacefulness. They made it clear that the sole purpose of religion was to bring people closer together, to guide their spiritual growth and to promote justice. Unfortunately, an insistence upon dogmatic adherence to rituals and traditions and insisting that religious truth can be attained only in this or that special way is at the root of conflict and discord.

It needs to be borne in mind that a continual harping on the theme of Christianity–Islam unity or Hindu–Muslim accord will not by itself bring about harmony or unity. It is necessary to identify points of differences as well as similarities. A public discourse as well as dialogue among faith leaders would help identify points of unity and discord.

Towards this, one will have to move from the message that several popular books and television programmes are transmitting in the West. Titles like Race of Islam, Sword of Islam, or Terror of Islam are being frequently used to describe Islam. Islam is also being dubbed as a faith that is undemocratic and sanctions violence and terrorism. This is a total falsehood. The initial pronouncements of President Bush too used religious terminology in support of the war against terror.[25] It must be appreciated that each conflict when seen in religious terms only supports religious conflicts and facilitates the fundamentalists in interpreting and reinterpreting their scriptures in order to meet the challenges of the day.

FELLOWSHIP OF SPIRIT: RELIGIONS FOR HARMONIOUS LIVING

The whole purpose of religion is to generate love and compassion among human beings and to inculcate in them virtues of tolerance, humility, and forgiveness. Even if we are sincere believers in our own faith, it will not help us if we neglect implementation of these basic qualities in our daily life. Moreover, if the faith leaders are not compassionate and disciplined themselves, how can they expect such an attitude from others? A genuine dialogue based on rationality and guided by a sense of mutual respect between leaders of different religions would go a long way in strengthening the Bahudhā approach.

One view that has gained currency in the post-9/11 world is that the monotheistic character of Judaism, Christianity, and Islam is conducive to conflicts and violence. It is further contended that violent activities will not frequently occur in case of polytheistic religions. At the same time coexistence of gods and goddesses in a religious order contributes immensely to pluralism and coexistence.

A fresh civilizational encounter can be expected to take place between instruments of science—information technologies, mass media, print media, new scientific discoveries in bio-technology and medicine—on the one hand and factors of religion, democracy, and peace on the other. Many scholars see in the present day situation potentialities of the axial age.[26]

Religion as a private affair will continue to be important, sacrosanct, as well as a symbol of identity. The religious stories and symbols will continue to find expression in art and architecture, philosophy and literature, music and dance as has been the case during several creative periods of history. The most significant development, however, is likely to be a better understanding among people professing different faiths. The use of information and communications technology would assist in uniting minds through the transfer of ideas.

The understanding of different religions and their practices could help people respect the contrasting methods of worship and spiritual experiences in various religions. What is required to develop a genuine respect for religious pluralism, in spite of different ways of realization of reality prescribed by each faith tradition? S. Radha-krishnan catches this approach in a masterly fashion when he writes:

In every religion, we have people who do not believe in provincialism, who emphasize religion as experience to be attained by self-conquest and self-transformation, appreciation of other faiths, and a sense of loyalty to the world community. If man is to achieve wholeness for himself and for the world, if he seeks harmonious living he must know other religions. We must set aside differences caused by the existence of geography and history and accept the universal ideas transmitted by a common heritage. It should become as normal for an American or an European student to be familiar with the civilizations of the east, the Chinese, the Japanese and the Indian as he has now with the bases of European civilization, in the Greek, the Roman and the Judaic cultures. The different religions should be regarded as comrades in a joint enterprise in facing the common problems of the peaceful coexistence of the peoples, international welfare and justice, racial equality and political independence of all peoples.[27]

We are slowly moving in the direction of a separation of areas of influence between the state and religion. Several western countries and nation-states like India and Japan have moved a long distance on the path of secularism.

Secularism and, in particular, the separation of religious and temporal domains would help immensely in securing peace and harmony in multi-religious and multi-ethnic societies. It is only through the process of dialogue and by inculcation of the Bahudhā spirit among individuals and communities that we can understand that all the world's major religions are concerned with helping individuals to become good human beings. A good human being would invariably be a good citizen as he would understand and be attracted to the preachings of all religions that emphasize love and compassion, tolerance and forgiveness, humility and patience.

NOTES

1. In Surah Kufiran, verse 109.
2. Lloyd Ridgeon (ed.), *Major World Religions from their Origins to the Present*, Routledge Curzon, London and New York, 2003, p. 299.
3. Quoted in S. Radhakrishnan, *Fellowship of the Spirit*, Harvard University Press, Cambridge, Massachusetts, USA, 1961, p. 5.
4. Graham E. Fuller, The Future of Political Islam, Palgrave Macmillan, New York, 2003, p. xiv.
5. In the US, Conservative Protestants became prominent in the 1920s. That same decade, the Muslim brotherhood was regained in Egypt. The Rashtriya Svayamsevak Sangh (RSS) was founded in 1925.
6. Jihad, translated in English would roughly mean 'striving'. These pertain to both personal and communitarian activities undertaken by Muslims in attempting the path of Allah. At the personal level, the jihad is the individual non-violent striving to live a good Muslim life following God's will. It includes adhering to the five pillars of Islam: (i) Profession of faith; (ii) Regular prayers; (iii) Fasting during Ramadan; (iv) Giving charity; and (v) Performing Haj, a pilgrimage to Mecca. As a member of the community, the Muslims would go for jihad as an application in a world divided into the land of Islam (*dar al-Islam*) and the land of conflict (*dar al-harb*). The Muslim community, the Umma, was required to engage in jihad to expand dar al-Islam throughout the world so that all humankind could benefit from living within a just political and social order. Within Islam, martyrdom is attained when a person dies in jihad.
7. Samuel P. Huntington, 'Who are We?', Simon and Schuster UK Ltd, London, 2004, p. 340.
8. Robert S. Leiken, 'Europes's Angry Muslims', Foreign Affairs, July/ August, 2005, New York, pp. 120–23. The mass immigration of Muslims to Europe was an unintended consequence of post-World War II guest-worker programmes. Today, Muslims constitute the majority of immigrants in most western European countries, including Belgium, France, Germany and the Netherlands, and the largest single component of the immigrant population in the United Kingdom. It is estimated, that between fifteen and twenty million Muslims now call Europe home and make up for up to five per cent of its total population. (Muslims in the United States probably do not exceed three million, accounting for less than two per cent of the total population). France has the largest proportion of Muslims (seven to ten per cent of its total population),

followed by the Netherlands, Germany, Denmark, Sweden, the United Kingdom, and Italy. Given continued immigration and high Muslim fertility rates, the National Intelligence Council projects that Europe's Muslim population will double by 2025.

9. Quoted in Huntington, 'Who are We?', pp. 349–50.

10. Jews came to India shortly after the fall of Jerusalem. Jewish arrivals continued in later waves, in the fifth and sixth centuries from southern Arabia and Persia until the last wave of Baghdadi Jews from Iraq and Syria, mostly to Bombay and Calcutta, in the 18th and 19th centuries. Christians, too, came very early, and by the fourth century there were large Christian communities in what is now Kerala. Parsis started arriving in the late seventh century, as soon as persecution of Zoroastrianism began in Persia. The Bahais were among the last groups to seek refuge in India, in the last century. Over this long period, there were other migrations, including the settlement of Muslim Arab traders, which began on India's western coast in the 8th century, well before the invasions that came from other Muslim countries via the more warlike north-western routes. There were in addition many conversions, especially to Islam. Each religious community managed to retain its identity within India's multi-religious spectrum.

11. As A.C. Bouquet, an accomplished expert on comparative religion, has pointed out: 'India in particular furnishes within its limits examples of every conceivable type of attempt at the solution of the religious problem'. See A.C. Bouquet, *Comparative Religion*, Harmondsworth: Penguin, 5th edn, 1956, p. 112.

12. Jawaharlal Nehru's 'Tryst with Destiny', 14–15 August 1947 speech in Subhash C. Kashyap (ed.), *100 Best Parliamentary Speeches 1947–1997*, HarperCollins, New Delhi, 1998, p. 29.

13. *The Economist*, 3 November 2007, London, p. 259.

14. Several scholarly books and articles have been written on this topic. Mention may be made of the following: (i) Peter Gottschalk, *Beyond Hindus and Muslims: Multiple Identity in Narratives from Village India*, Oxford University Press, New York, 2001; (ii) Jackie Assayag *At the Confluence of Two Rivers: Muslims and Hindus in South India*, Manohar, Delhi, 2004; (iii) Imtiaz Ahmad and Helmut Reifeld (eds), *Lived Islam in South Asia: Adaptation, Accommodation and Conflict*, Social Science Press, Delhi, 2004; and Jamal Malik and Helmut Reifeld (eds), *Religious Pluralism in South Asia and Europe*, Oxford University Press, New York, 2005.

15. T.N. Madan (ed.), 'Religions of India, Plurality and Pluralism', in *India's Religious Perspectives from Sociology and History*, Oxford University Press, New Delhi, 2004, pp. 31–32.

16. Secularism owes its origins to the French word *Seculer* (itself from the Latin *saecularis*). It was, however, only in 19th century that the word

secular became familiar and a group of scholars and leaders formulated the doctrine of secularism stating categorically that religious institutions and values should play no role in the affairs of the nation-state. By the end of the 19th century, 'secularisation', 'secularists' and 'secularism' were used for advocacy of a philosophy that would eliminate the role of the Church and religions in affairs of the state. In 1851, George Holyoake, a radical atheist in England used this word almost as a replacement for expressions like 'atheis', 'infidel', 'freethinkers', 'unbelievers', etc.

17. Salman Rushdie's interview in *Financial Times*, London, 27 September 2005, p. 10 entitled 'Fabulist takes on the Literalists'. Rushdie argues that the Quran is an interpretation itself (as it would be improper to believe that God speaks Arabic), and so further acts of interpretation are also legitimate.

18. Ashis Nandy, 'The Politics of Secularism and the Recovery of Religious Tolerance', in Veena Das (ed.), *Mirrors of Violence*, Oxford University Press, Delhi, 1990, pp. 69–93.

19. Thomas L. Friedman, 'Muslims in Danger', *International Herald Tribune*, Hyderabad, 9 July 2005.

20. Ibid.

21. R.A. Nicholson (trans), *Rumi, Poet and Mystic (1207–1273)*, George Allen & Unwin, London, 1964.

22. *Encyclopedia of Religion and Ethics*, Vol. XII, T&T Clark, Edinburgh, 1958, pp. 331–3.

23. Quoted in 'The Promise of World Peace', Bahai Publishing Trust, New Delhi, 1985, p. 7.

24. Karen Armstrong, *Muhammad: A Western Attempt to Understand Islam*, Victor Gollancz Ltd, London, p. 266.

25. Jonathan Rahan, *The New York Review*, September 2005. He writes: 'On September 11, George W. Bush quoted the 23rd Psalm and spoke of the conflict (though not yet the war) between 'good and evil'. At Harlem gospel choir sang hymns in the ruins of the World Trade Center. On September 16, Bush announced that America was now embarked on a 'crusade'. 'This is a new kind of evil, and we understand, and the American people are now beginning to understand, this crusade, this war on terrorism, is going to take a while.' The greatest military power in history has shackled its deadly hardware to the rhetoric of fundamentalist Christianity, with all its righteously simplistic moralism, in a war of 'good against evil' and 'freedom against fear'.

26. In her book *The Battle for God*, Karen Armstrong, has given a very interesting account of the spiritual needs of the present times. In spiritual terms, she writes, the circumstances we live in today are similar in nature to the Axial Age (4–3 millennia BCE), during which most of the great spiritual traditions emerged, be it the Socratic philosophy of

Greece, the teachings of Hindu sages and the Buddha, Confucianism and Taoism or the Judaic monotheism that further begot Christianity and Islam. People of the Axial Age developed rich internal lives which required a spirituality that 'did not depend entirely on external forms such as the Pagan deities'. Moreover, this type of spirituality also provided an ethical rhetoric to speak against the social injustice which was built into the agrarian socio-economic system. With a belief in the transcendental source of universal sovereignty and the ubiquitous concept of afterlife, the new spirituality also acted as a quasi-solution for the problems of the downtrodden and the suppressed. Karen Armstrong, *The Battle for God*, HarperCollins, London, 2001, pp. xi–xii.

27. S. Radhakrishnan, *Fellowship of the Spirit*, Harvard University Press, Cambridge, Massachusetts, USA, 1961, p. 39. He, however, talks of 'birth of a new faith which will be but the old faith in another form, the faith of all ages. . .'. I, however, do not see that happening.

10
Education for Harmony

If I tell you that this is the greatest good for a human being, to engage every day in arguments about virtue and the other things you have heard me talk about, examining both myself and others, and if I tell you that the unexamined life is not worth living for a human being, you will be even less likely to believe what I am saying. But that's the way it is, gentlemen, as I claim, though it's not easy to convince you of it.[1]

—Socrates

Education is at the centre of both individual development and overall progress in society. From ancient *gurukul* ashrams in India and Egypt's Books of Instruction to modern day institutes of technology, medicine, and management, civilizations have contributed to prosperity and social harmony by educating their youth.

Education enables human beings to develop their capacities so that they can lead fulfilling and dignified lives. From a sociological perspective, schools can help foster a sense of community. These institutions provide a forum for boys and girls from different religions and cultures, from different castes and ethnic backgrounds, to mingle and develop friendships. A good education empowers people to take responsibility for their own lives and for improving the lives of those around them. Modern technology and the forces of globalization have reduced distances and increased connectivity. The content and quality of education have enormous potential to make an important contribution to global peace and stability.

David E. Bloom and Joel E. Cohen have emphasized, among other things, two basic goals of education:

The skills taught should include reading with understanding, writing with clarity, and speaking with confidence. . . . Additional skills worthy of attention include peaceful ways to manage and resolve, where possible, conflicts and differences, within and between a variety of cultural units. The conflicts and the means of resolving them will differ culturally (e.g.

compromise vs consensual discussion vs majority vote vs appeal to tradition) but the skills of dealing peacefully with conflict may have widespread or universal value.

The knowledge to be imparted must focus on both the self and others. In human terms, others might include the family, the local community, other communities and cities, the nation state (if relevant), other countries and cultures, and humankind. In non-human terms, others might include other living species and the major non-living components of the Earth. . . . Also at stake are the inventiveness and civility of the people among whom we will live, and the richness of our own opportunities to learn from them.[2]

In an age where even the educated youth are joining suicide squads and indulging in senseless violence, the moot question is whether the education system can be made sensitive to this challenge.

The very civilization of which science, the Internet, and related sources of knowledge are integral parts is now under threat from fundamentalism and the ignorance that underlines it. It has fuelled helplessness, hopelessness, and a distortion of religious beliefs. Many believe that we have to look beyond science and technology to the learning of religions, history, literature, and the arts.

Democracy depends on the ability to manage conflict constructively. Learning how to deal with conflict in a civil manner is one of the great lessons that schools must teach. In a long span of school and university education of nearly two decades students who have been exposed to tackling controversial issues in a civil manner would perform better in leadership roles than those who have no such experience.

Action is needed in several areas. One, devising a curriculum that encourages respect for diversity and multiculturalism; two, addressing problems of shortages of good teachers; three, providing infrastructure for schools; and four, opportunities for lifelong learning. Diversity of cultures and religions are to be viewed as assets. Our education system can make an enduring contribution to the building of tolerance and mutual respect that can help turn diversity from being a problem to becoming an asset for harmonious living.

EDUCATION FOR ALL

One of the early achievements of the United Nations was to adopt the Declaration of Human Rights in 1948, which, among other things, proclaimed free and compulsory education to be a basic human right.

It was, therefore, not surprising that the heads of state and governments who assembled at New York to finalize the Millennium
Declaration—the major points of which formed part of the Millennium
Development Goals (MDGs)—called upon governments to secure
education for all by the year 2015. Rapid progress has been made in
this direction as the level of illiteracy in the developing world has
fallen from 75 per cent a century ago to less than 25 per cent today.
One of the remarkable features of this phenomenon has been the
spread of literacy among girls.

The goal of universal education, however, has yet to be attained
and there are also serious problems regarding the quality of education.
Rote learning is still being practised in several schools in developing
countries. There is an extreme shortage of well-qualified teachers
and the school infrastructure is still grossly inadequate. To this is
added the unhealthy feature of school drop-outs. Nearly 25 per cent
of boys and girls in developing countries are estimated to be leaving
school before reaching the fifth grade.

Every educational system is built on certain assumptions. One of
them is that a child goes to school at the age of five or six years,
sometimes even seven years. Among the first things that he learns
are what are called the 3Rs—reading, writing, and arithmetic. In the
process, something intangible but very precious also takes shape in
the child's mind—an awareness of the wide world, attitudes, and
habits that ultimately go to build his personality and in fact his whole
character.

A teacher or guru plays a pivotal role in shaping the character of
his student. He is a source of inspiration and a point of reference not
only as a provider of correct answers to questions from textbooks
but also as a guide and role model. As the Persian proverb goes: 'If
the teacher be corrupt, the world will be corrupt'. A teacher must be
a person of integrity and also one who is willing to continuously
learn. Tagore rightly said, 'A lamp can never light another lamp unless
it continues to burn its own flame'.[3]

Classrooms play an important role in the promotion of development and peace. The prosperity, welfare, and security of people are
dependent upon knowledge, proficiency in science and technology,
arts and humanities. Accordingly, the quality of education greatly
determines not only individual prosperity but also the economic
strength of the country and hence the world.

BAHUDHĀ APPROACH AND EDUCATION

Since education shapes the minds of the youth it is essential to monitor the textual content of educational books. Content that can be offensive or detrimental to their understanding and interpretation of the world and society around them must not be allowed a place in school books. In fact, the positive achievements of different religions, cultures and ethnic groups and people must be highlighted. The curriculum should be such as to encourage children to become good and active citizens. It should inculcate a spirit of tolerance and a habit of appreciating the multiplicity of perspectives. All these efforts would empower the students to become responsible adults who can make meaningful contribution in resolving matters of social, economic, religious, and political conflict.

Apart from homes, the neighbourhood and the reports in the mass media, the classrooms are the most vibrant place where one learns how to discriminate between truth and falsehood, and good and evil. The acquisition of knowledge and skills combined with appreciation of moral and spiritual values, will enable students to discharge their responsibilities as citizens and also as members of the community.

In the aftermath of 9/11, liberal scholars in several countries are critically examining school textbooks. There is a demand that textbooks containing disparaging remarks about other countries and civilizations must be expunged. In Saudi Arabia, the *Arab News,* a Saudi English daily, reported as follows:

Our education system, which does not stress tolerance of other faiths—let alone tolerance of followers of other Islamic schools of thought—is one thing that needs to be re-evaluated from top to bottom. Saudi culture itself and the fact that the majority of us do not accept other lifestyles and impose our own on other people is another. And the fact that from the 4th to the 12th grade we do not teach our children that there are other civilizations in the world and that we are part of the global community and only stress the Islamic espiers over and over is also worth re-valuating. And last but certainly not the least, the religious climate in the country must change.[4]

In western countries as well, the issue of imparting instruction about different religions receives serious attention. Many scholars and journalists have indicated the ignorance of students in respect of other religions and faiths. In Germany, people have discovered that Muslim children are taught that:

The Muslim people's existence has been threatened by Jews and Christians since the Crusades, and it is the first duty of every Muslim to prepare to fight against these enemies.[5]

Some terrorists have also physically attacked schools with a long history of secular education. A school set up by a British missionary in 1891 in Jammu and Kashmir state of India was torched in July 2004, in the wake of propaganda that secular education is turning Muslims into infidels. This Islamic school had educated Muslims of Kashmir in secular values for several generations. Fortunately, this school has since been rebuilt.[6]

An effective and self-renewing educational system is fundamental to the creation of social cohesion and also for civilizational progress. Education has to be a pursuit of both truth and beauty. It is only by inculcating values of universal brotherhood that education can enhance the dignity of a human being. While it is necessary to master science and the arts, it is equally essential that schools should inculcate values into young minds that decry pettiness, hatred, enmity, and disharmony.

Almost in conformity with the Bahudhā approach, Nobel Prize laureates in 1999 inter alia suggested in their six-point Manifesto for the Millennium Year, the need to listen, to understand, in order to 'defend freedom of expression and cultural diversity, giving preference always to dialogue and listening without encouraging any fanaticism, defamation and the rejection of others'.[7]

The need to instil a culture of respect and tolerance in schools is essential. Towards this, one must work on different approaches ranging from advocacy (including videos, publications and lectures) to specific support for restructuring the education system itself. Efforts should also be made to focus on resource materials, which teachers then integrate into the curriculum, whilst other approaches concentrate on helping teachers to internalize the values and attitudes associated with peace prior to teaching these to the students.

Education is no longer confined to local or national realities alone. It is becoming increasingly a human concern, fully conscious of global problems that are already with us.

While several scholars have talked about the emergence of a universal culture, one does not see that happening. For, at the global level, one sees the diversity of cultures growing and flourishing, and affording to their adherents a sense of belongingness and rootedness.

The possibilities for participation of people in the cultural life of their communities even in distant lands are on the rise. The identity of groups and nations will be increasingly expressed in their cultural life even as global tasks and organizations grow.

The Industrial Revolution generated material success and monetary profit and also led to the emergence of multinational corporations. All these have fuelled ambitions in the minds of the youth. The educational systems have also been moulded accordingly.

If the present approach towards education of only imparting knowledge of the material world is to continue, there is no reason to expect results that would be different from those that we have obtained in the past. It would mean further progress in science and technology but little in terms of social cohesion and harmony. It is only when we link education with spirituality and human welfare that we can hope to get different results.

Education accommodates the influence exercised by adult generations to arouse and develop in the child a certain degree of curiosity about his environment and culture. Adults are in a position to respond to the curiosities of the young by referring to the knowledge that is preserved in great detail in oral traditions, books, sculptures and instruments of several kinds and their own experiences. Every individual, through the process of dialogue with the youth, contributes in enriching mankind. Education creates in the child a new being.

Educational programmes must aim to reduce prejudice and hostility, the factors that have enormously contributed to escalating hate crimes and violence against social groups. There is a need to develop the potential of the mass media so that it becomes a part of the solution to violence and not a contributor to the problem by giving information that inflames passion. Schools are becoming increasingly aware of the need to train students in peaceful methods of conflict resolution. In order to make this possible, a fresh look is needed at the following areas: school commitment; classroom environment; communication; curriculum; instruction; home environment; and family—school—community partnerships. It is also being realized that if at the end of teaching, graduates are to go into the world as peacemakers then educational institutions must prepare them for this role.

The famous American educationist, Maria Montessori, in one of her public talks in the 1930s said:

Those who want war prepare young people for war; but those who want peace have neglected young children and adolescents so that they are unable to organise them for peace.[8]

There is a growing realization in the world that children should be educated in the art of peaceful living. Towards this, various developing and developed countries have formulated teaching modules and even textbooks that deal with value education and moral education. The need to nurture peace in the hearts of children is being increasingly appreciated. Learning about the virtues of non-violence and peace—what UNESCO calls 'peace education'—is necessary for making today's children tomorrow's good citizens.

The answer to the question of how to live also lies in the art of living together. The author of the 'Learning the Way of Peace: Teacher's Guide to Peace Education' strongly feel that this should be taught. The teachers have put before themselves the following ideas:

Obviously, the world is shrinking into a global village due to the technical advancements, which facilitate travelling, communication and transaction. Yet our present mindsets are unable to accommodate the global unity of mankind. What we really need is to enlarge our minds when the world is becoming small. Only then can we capture the global human brotherhood. Unless we overcome the tribalistic mentality of divisive tendency, we are as a species, doomed to extinction, through destroying each other. By learning to live together, we broaden our vision, gradually move from self-centredness, to community, to nation and from there to the global family. It also means to learn to cooperate and share with each other and accept diversity and live in harmony.[9]

At the social and political levels, a set of fair structures and procedures for peaceful handling of issues that have divided our society in the past is necessary. It is also essential that there is an effective working relationship between the groups involved. A society cannot develop effective working relationships among its different communities if their structures are not fair. Similarly, structures by themselves cannot function effectively, however fair or idealistic these may be, if there is no cooperation among citizens. The Bahudhā approach is necessary for effecting a reconciliation among groups who were divided in the past. It is heartening to note an increasing support for dialogue and discussions aimed at the prevention of violence. There is also support for the inclusion of citizenship education in schools. Several national governments are looking at their textbooks in order that teachers could use the new instruments of advocacy (including videos, radio, and printed literature) that would bring to a student, information about what is happening in society and what needs to be done to construct enduring peace.

SCIENCE AND VALUE EDUCATION

On 15 October 1936, Albert Einstein, in his address at Albany, New York said:

The school has always been the most important means of transferring the wealth of tradition from one generation to the next. This applies today to an even higher degree than before. Through modern development of the economic life, the family as a bearer of tradition and education has weakened. The continuance and health of human society is, therefore, to a still higher degree dependent on the school than formerly.[10]

Every civilization has developed a set of values over the centuries. These are in the religious as well as secular domains of social, economic and scientific experiences. One of the sacred tasks of a teacher, and in fact of the entire educational system, is to make efforts to draw not only from one's own civilizational strengths but also from the traditions of other countries and cultures.

The need to look at the goals of education in the modern context is also necessary for making the right approaches for the inculcation of values in schools. Today the goals of education are confined to the development of literacy, the acquisition of information, and the learning of skills in specific areas. Several scholars have observed that such an aim would naturally give preference to the acquisition of material gains over the values of harmony and happiness. The idealistic view of education demands that schools and colleges must prepare students to become both good individuals and good citizens. There are, however, scholars who feel that it is only through religious instruction that a person can become a good human being.

RELIGION AND EDUCATION

Religions adopt different approaches concerning the development of an individual's soul and about his political aspirations as a good citizen. In Christianity, a clear distinction has been made between temporal and spiritual authority. In Islam, on the other hand, both temporal and spiritual authority is vested in the Caliph. Accordingly, in Christian lands, the Pope and the Prime Minister are different people drawing authority from different sources. In Hinduism, religious instruction aims at establishing a relationship between an individual and God. Confucianism, on the other hand, is a political religion. In his personal life, Confucius moved from court to court and concerned himself with the problems of governance and with the instilling of such virtues in people as well as officials so as to make good governance possible. Buddhism, on the contrary, is essentially non-political. It is, however, another matter that in Tibet, both religious and political authority flow from the Dalai Lama. The recent efforts of the Dalai Lama are to separate religious authority from temporal power.

Over the years, education all over the globe has moved from awakening of the soul to education in citizenship. It is realized that if the youth are to grow into citizens capable of furthering good governance and democracy, then education must prepare them in this task.

Nonetheless, there are scholars who believe that it is only through religion that the higher virtues of love, compassion, and brotherhood can be taught. Religion alone could provide a commonality of approach towards the inculcation of basic values of love and compassion in youth, not only in schools but also in their homes and in society at large. Karl Mannheim in his 'Challenge to Christian Thinkers by a Sociologist' writes:

Only a generation which has been educated through religion, or at least on the religious level, to discriminate between immediate advantage and the lasting issues of life, will be capable of accepting the sacrifice which a properly planned democratic order must continually demand from every single group and individual in the interests of the whole.[11]

The primary threat from traditional religious attitudes to education emanates from its emphasis on blind faith. One of the severest criticisms of religious instruction comes from Bertrand Russell. In his book, *Education and the Social Order*, Russell advocates:

The effect of religious teaching upon morality is bad in various ways. It tends to sap self-reliance, especially when it is associated with the confessional; through teaching the young to lean upon authority, it often makes them incapable of self-direction . . . .Another morally undesirable aspect of religious education is that it underestimates the intellectual virtues. Intellectual impartiality, a most important quality, it regards as positively bad; persistent attempts to understand difficult matters it views, at best, with toleration. The individuals whom it holds up for admiration in the present day are seldom men of first-rate intelligence; when they are, it is because of some folly to which they have given utterance in a foolish moment. Owing to the identification of religion with virtue, together with the fact that the most religious men are not the most intelligent, a religious education gives courage to the stupid to resist the authority of educated men, as has happened, for example, where the teaching of evolution has been made illegal. So far as I can remember, there is not one word in the Gospels in praise of intelligence; and in this respect ministers of religion follow gospel authority more closely than in some others.[12]

Some scholars feel that the religious impulse is a strong and persistent force in human life and should not be ignored. The education of the conscience is a basic need. It helps a student to make a distinction between right and wrong and needs to be cultivated in adolescence in order that as an adult, he could use this sense of discrimination in the discharge of his responsibilities. It is felt that changes in religious approach are also possible. Julian Huxley advocates that religious authorities should

Re-adjust their social and ethical policies in relation to the needs of the new type of society which is in process of being born. If they attempt this with sincerity, it is incumbent upon society to meet them halfway. If this should be accomplished, organized religion in some new and at present unguessable form will come alive again as a social function, and could then rightly claim to have an important place in that other social function that we call education.[13]

Rabindranath Tagore stressed the importance of harnessing all the resources that would instil in the mind of the child a strong desire to know. The goal has to be a synthesis of knowledge and feeling. Learning by doing was also emphasized in order that the idea becomes an act. Accordingly, Rabindranath brought to the students of his education centre prayers and sayings associated with the Buddha, Christ, Mohammad, Chaitanya, and other great men of thought and action. He saw great virtue in the ancient Indian tradition of forest schools (*tapovan*). He wrote appreciatively as follows:

The forest, unlike the desert or rock or sea, is living; it gives shelter and nourishment of life. In such surroundings the ancient forest-dwellers of India realized the spirit of harmony with the universe and emphasized in their minds the monistic aspects of truth. They sought the realization of their soul through union with all.[14]

Religion cannot altogether be banished from value education. What is important is that the primacy of faith over rationality must not be emphasized in what is taught in schools. We live in an age where despair and hopelessness can drive religious zealots to inculcate hatred and violence in the minds of the youth. However, despite centuries of violent happenings, humanity exists because of love, compassion, and mutual needs, and that approach should inform the education curricula for making the youth both good human beings and good citizens.

The tradition of learning by rote, to use quotations as if they are arguments, to cite the scriptures as the last word on the subject associated with religious training need to be replaced by logic and scientific enquiry. It is only through rational enquiry that we would be able to convert the full stops of centuries into question marks. All institutions of learning where new innovations have taken place have been preceded by the application of the reasoning process and techniques involving teachers as well as students. At the same time, the spiritual dimension will have to be accorded a primacy of place in our educational thinking.

There is a clear distinction between 'education about religions' and 'religious education'. An educational institution in a secular state will encourage the study of religions and religious thoughts as these constitute the eternal internal quest of mankind. It will not, however, impart religious education that is largely concerned with the teaching of the tenets and practices of a particular religion. Education about religions, however, must be handled with extreme care. All steps must be taken both by the state and the civil society in advance to ensure that no personal prejudices or narrow-minded perceptions are allowed to distort the real purpose of this venture. Similarly, no rituals, dogmas and superstitions are to be propagated in the name of education about religions. All religions need to be treated with equal respect (*Sarva Dharma Sambhav*) and there has to be no discrimination on the basis of any religion *(panthnirapekshata)*.

It is necessary that the study of religions should be done in a manner that a student understands the basic features of major religions. It is only when one knows about several ways of the divine path that one can practise the Bahudhā approach of 'one truth; many inter-pretations'. It is only through a proper understanding of other faiths that misconceptions about other traditions created through myths and oral traditions, and also through misrepresentation of other faiths in textbooks, can be removed.

Every culture accords education a central place and would like its values to be a sustaining force of its education programmes. There is nothing wrong with that approach so long it is supplemented by logic and rational enquiry.

Modern education also puts considerable emphasis on external objects in terms of acquisition of wealth and position. This approach ignores the need to address the inner world, that is, to be introspective and to be at peace with oneself. It is only by understanding one's own life, of the processes of life, and one's relation with society that one becomes a good citizen and contributes effectively to peace and harmony, both within himself and in the outer world. It is true that nobody is taught to be selfish, greedy, arrogant, jealous, dominating, and so forth, but the overall approach sends a message that contributes to imprinting of these values in the young minds as against the values of being helpful, respectful, tolerant, and truthful.

People want peace, harmony, mutual respect, and understanding in society and these can only be generated through education that inculcates human values in students. Peace at the social level can best be achieved if there is peace within each individual, which again is possible only if the individual develops and cultivates peace in himself or herself. The need is to have this approach in the educational system.

Mention may be made of the traditional Buddhist approach in this context. In this, primary education must teach a student ethics, wisdom, and the power of concentration. It is a cultivation of the path leading to transcendental transformation of the personality that should be an important objective of the educational system. According to Buddhism, love and altruism should be and can be developed, to an unlimited extent, not only as counter-positive forces against the afflictive emotions of ignorance, desire, and hatred but also as a driving force for all sentient beings.

One of the most important values to be imparted in schools is the cultivation of a clear view of one's own dharma. Literally, dharma means something that holds in the midst of change. Dharma is an individual's effort to reach out to the central order of things. Every civilization has developed its essential features of dharma, which can be known by different names. Each individual must work out for himself his own concept of dharma and his commitment to the inner self as well as to the world outside.

The explosion of information that is being facilitated by the information and communications technology revolution, such as the

Internet and the electronic media, is the fountainhead of a new civilizational encounter between different knowledge systems and ways of living. Thanks to the rise of information in society, students in developing countries now have opportunities to learn a great deal about developments in science and technology. The material progress of any society can be secured only by mastery over science and technology and all that goes with it. Science and technology can be used in meeting challenges such as removal of poverty, unemployment, and disease.

It also needs to be appreciated that a knowledge-based world is an open world. When we talk of the fusion of science and spirituality, we are not putting any limitations on the autonomy of either scientific or spiritual endeavour. Any limitation on the objectivity and autonomy of science and any prescription for a singular path of spirituality would come in the way of progress and peace and thus could not be beneficial for the development of a harmonious world. The need is to work for the development of a more cohesive and inclusive world view in which science and spirituality are complementary and mutually reinforcing.

There are people who fear that an emphasis on values in education would push us back to an ancient era. These fears are unfounded. What is true is that religion and spirituality were developed by our ancestors much more than science. What characterizes the past century as well as the present is the phenomenal progress in science. The task of linking spirituality and values with the present day development in science and technology is essential for building a global peaceful order. For it is only through spirituality that forces of greed, hatred, and despondency can be overcome.

Education should continue to constantly focus on the promotion of excellence. However, in the ultimate analysis, education must promote self-discipline and self-control. Such an attitude alone will eschew violence of any kind, in thought, word, or deed. It is the duty of teachers to ensure that educational institutions become centres, both for attaining proficiency in science and the arts and also in the cultivation and enrichment of self-discipline and social and moral values.

There is an old saying that one's education is not complete till one has helped one's neighbour and others. For, as the traditional fable adds, this is the rent that we must pay for living on this beautiful earth.

Education should continue to recognize the ideals of truth, duty, and peace as final and binding for everyone and in all places. Education must be ultimately concerned with values that are independent of time or place. While these enduring values will be given new interpretations in different times and environment, their basic features will remain the same.

A society can survive only if there exists among its members a sufficient degree of homogeneity and cohesion. An educational system reinforces this idea in the child's mind from the beginning. On the other hand, education must not seek to achieve uniformity but must respect diversity as that is necessary for development and progress. As William Boyd and Wyatt Rawson put it:

Static religion pre-supposes that the search for truth is ended, and that its final formulation is contained in one of the holy books— in the Bible, for instance, or the Quran, or the Pali Texts of Buddhism. It demands obedience to precepts and rules of behaviour laid down in past ages for other civilizations, and equates 'salvation' with this unreasoning obedience. It ignores the creative powers of man, including that of love, which can discover ways of helping unknown to the commandment-makers. And, above all, it forgets that the elemental energies that form part of man require an outlet in this world and must be given constructive and more than personal objectives if they are not to turn against us and become destructive in their effects. But religion as a dynamic force is a very different thing, as the spiritual leaders of mankind have always taught. Their gospel was intended to release men's powers, not to circumscribe them, and their message was love, understanding and reconciliation, not the promulgation of any set of moral laws with the self-righteousness and habit of moral judgement that go with them. Their appeal was, therefore, to men of every race and background, and their message universal.[15]

The enormous challenge that the world faces today in terms of the need to develop respect for faiths, languages, traditions, and cultures of others besides their own has imposed enormous responsibility on international organizations such as UNESCO as well as on nation-states to chart out a new approach. These bodies should draw upon the strength and wisdom of scholars, philosophers, and thinkers. It is they who, in terms of their understanding of the past and knowledge of the present, will be able to convert the challenges posed by the distress, violence, and divisiveness into opportunities to prepare a cohesive society that knows how to live together in schools as well as outside. It is only through the Bahudhā approach of developing an inclusive and non-partisan approach that modules of harmony and acceptance of the otherness can be developed.

EDUCATION IN MADRASAS

Since the horrendous events of 11 September 2001, several scholars, politicians, professors, and students have been making enquiries about the mindset of perpetrators of this and subsequent terrorist attacks. Enquiries are also being made about the origins of hatred and exploration of possibilities of building a system under which human minds could be made to travel on a path that would not allow them to entertain such sinister thoughts. The need for improvement of the education system in Muslim countries, and also among Muslims who live in Western countries, is being increasingly emphasized. It is true that most of the terrorists were educated in religious schools. But several prominent ones also received education in Western societies. It is also true that many of them lacked formal religious training and were not living in an oppressive environment. Special attention is being paid to education in madrasas in Muslim countries. Several questions have been posed. What are these schools? What do they teach? How do they teach? What is the source of their funds? What is the quality of the teachers? What do the textbooks contain? What kind of supervision does the state system provide to these educational institutions?

The fountainhead of knowledge in the Islamic tradition is the Quran. The Quran was revealed by the Prophet Muhammad at places of worship. Later these pronouncements were compiled. The mosques became the first schools of Islam. In every traditional Muslim people assemble at the mosque, and debate and improve their knowledge of the Quran. This in essence is not different from the Hindu, Buddhist, and Christian traditions, wherein too, places of worship have been centres of religious learning. Over the years, educational institutions such as *maktabs* and madrasas were established in all Muslim countries and also in Muslim-dominated areas in non-Muslim majority nations.

It is important to understand the difference between maktabs and madrasas. In a maktab, children read and recite the Quran only. It is usually associated with a mosque or the house of teachers of the Quran. Madrasas, however, are organized institutions with classrooms and teachers. Many madrasas offer board and lodging facilities for students free of charge. Most madrasas teach several subjects besides imparting instruction in Islamic religious thought.

The first two madrasas are associated with Egypt and Iraq at the beginning of the eleventh century.[16] The madrasas initially put great emphasis on independent reasoning and were associated with the golden age of advancement in science, technology, and philosophy in Muslim countries and also in countries such as Spain where the Muslims ruled for almost eight hundred years. After the defeat of the Muslim empires by the European colonial powers, the level of learning and scholarship in madrasas declined. The introduction of English and other European languages as the medium of instruction also contributed to a decline in the quality of madrasa education. In its long history, the madrasas have alternated between secular and religious education.[17]

There has been a phenomenal growth in madrasas since the 1970s. In the 1980s, madrasas received enormous funding and political support in Afghanistan and Pakistan as these were viewed as recruiting grounds for anti-Soviet mujahidin (Islamic guerillas) fighters. The US, Saudi Arabia, and several European countries funded these madrasas. The madrasas have traditionally received funds as donations from Muslims only. The induction of fresh funds brought in a sudden change in the standard of living of teachers and also the physical infrastructure of some madrasas. What is more significant is that this fresh money was not spent on providing quality education in science and computers and/or on training of teachers. Instead, the educational institutions were tweaked to create hatred and a Jihadi mentality among its students. The transformed madrasas gradually became centres of geo-politics. It was no wonder that Taliban leaders who ruled over Afghanistan in the 1990s were the products of madrasas in Pakistan.

At least fifty developing and transitional countries have Muslim populations of ten per cent or more. The madrasas provide free education to the poor in these developing countries. The situation varies from country to country.[18]

Our country-wise analysis has revealed the wide reach and deep influence of madrasas in different parts of the world. There are, however, two schools of thought. One sees madrasas as the breeding ground for terrorism and the other treats the phenomenon of terrorism as a political problem.

Many scholars believe that the terrorist attacks in Madrid, Washington, New York, and London clearly reveal that a significant number of terrorists were educated in western countries and were assimilated within its liberal societies. In their view, it would be inappropriate to find answers for questions of terrorism in madrasas.

These terrorists are basically addressing political issues and are guided by political ambitions.

At the political level, the starting point of the quarrel is the collapse of the Ottoman empire and consequently the Caliphate. The defeats of Arab countries against Israel in successive wars of 1948, 1967, and 1973 and also the unresolved issue of Palestine have influenced the minds of these terrorists. Like all revolutionary movements, Islamism propounded by Osama bin Laden and his cohorts provides to their followers a sense of purpose and also a sense of superiority. The basic issue that has to be determined by the Muslims themselves is whether this ideology is representative of Muslims all over the world or not and whether terrorists are correctly interpreting Islam or have merely hijacked it to serve their own purpose.

Questions are also raised about the impact of television, technology, the communication revolution, and all the processes of globalization, on the Muslim society which feels left out and sees no escape from domination of the United States and other Western countries. An opinion is frequently expressed that religious fundamentalism is a symptom of this deeper malice of unequal power sharing and unbalanced access to the world's resources.

Several books and articles have been written to support this thesis that Islamic fundamentalism has replaced communism as the main challenge to the Western world view. This seems to be far from the truth.

The parallel drawn between the dangers of communism and those of Islam gave Washington's strategic planners the illusion that they . . . could simply transpose the conceptual tools designed to apprehend one threat to the very different realities of the other. . .[They] were culturally incapable of grasping an actor that was not, in the final analysis, a state. . . . The strategy of destroying the Afghan base and then annihilating Saddam Hussein's 'rogue state' presented the advantage of being operational: it allowed the Pentagon to use its panoply of high-tech weapons, forged in the confrontation with the USSR. . . . But it missed the intended target. The very intangibility of the Al Qaeda network precluded a traditional military conquest.[19]

On 4 July 2005, 170 Muslim scholars from forty countries assembled in Jordan to have a dialogue on the theme of 'The Reality of Islam and its Role in the Contemporary Societies'. Addressing the issue of terrorism, King Abdullah II of Jordan said that 'the acts of violence and terrorism carried out by certain extremist groups in the name of Islam are contradictory to the principles and ideology of Islam'.[20] He went on to stress that Muslims are obliged to correct the tarnished image of Islam. One of the suggestions before the Conference was to issue a fatwa against Osama bin Laden and declare him an apostate. The final communiqué of the Amman Conference, issued on 6 July, however took a different position when it clarified:

It is not possible to declare as apostates any group of Muslims who believe in Allah the Mighty and Sublime and His Messenger (may Peace and Blessings be upon him) and the pillars of faith, and respects the pillars of Islam and does not deny any necessary article of religion.[21]

The importance of madrasas in the life of a large segment of the Muslim student population cannot be overemphasized. An estimated six million Muslims study in madrasas around the world and twice that number attend maktabs. All madrasas and maktabs are not militant organizations. Some major reforms in the madrasas education system, however, are urgently needed.

First, scientific learning and computer education must be introduced in all madrasas. This would bring to the students and teachers knowledge available at the global level.

Secondly, for changing the mindset of the students, a more innovative approach is called for. Students in madrasas are taught about the superiority of Islam over other religions and the textbooks contain statements that denigrate other faiths and other communities. Madrasas also teach precepts that are antithetical to human rights and rationality—for example, almost all madrasas stress that 'women are not to be trusted and that beardless boys are going to hell'. A fresh look at both the education curricula and textbooks are needed at the political level.

Thirdly, the power structure needs to be revamped through democracy. This would in the long run also reduce the political clout of madrasas. The dependence of poor students on madrasas both for education and for board and lodging needs to be eliminated over the years.

Fourthly, the rate of illiteracy among women in several Muslim countries is as high as ninety per cent. It is, therefore, necessary that special measures are taken to provide free and compulsory education to the girl child. Action taken in this regard by Turkey, and in recent years in Bangladesh, need to be emulated elsewhere.

Fifthly, there is absolutely no denying that the Quran would and should continue to give meaning to the lives of believers in Islam but madrasas must reflect new religious and political realities, including the concerns of women and respect for human rights.

CURRICULUM

In recent years, statesmen, philosophers, teachers and leaders in industry, agriculture and labour have expressed an opinion that the educational curriculum at the elementary school level should be such, that regardless of the family circumstances into which a child is born, he or she should be entitled to the greatest possible opportunity for self-development.

There is broad public support for educational reform as it is felt that something is amiss. People are increasingly concerned about finding wise men and women through whom to communicate across lines of race, religion, ethnicity, and social class in order to forge common purposes. As Diane Ravitch rightly points out

When we as a nation set out to provide universal access to education, our hope was that intelligence and reason would one day prevail and make a better world, that issues would be resolved by thoughtful deliberation. Intelligence and reason, however, cannot be achieved merely by skill-building and immersion in new technologies. Intelligence and reason cannot be developed in absence of knowledge about the judgment that has formed by prolonged and thoughtful study of history, literature and culture, not only that of our own nation, but that of other civilizations. That we have turned away from such studies, that we have limited them to advanced classes in secondary schools, and that they have become electives in higher education are not encouraging. As our common culture becomes constricted, so too does the possibility for informed citizens to adopt the shape of their shared future. What we risk listening is part of the common fund of knowledge needed to sustain a truly democratic society. . . . As scholars, as teachers, as parents, as citizens, we must reclaim our common culture – or risk seeing it disappear.[22]

Any programme for improving the elementary school curriculum must include an analysis of the problems that confront our society. Some social realities that have implications for the curriculum plan are: the dynamic nature of our society; the inter-dependence of our society; the changing status of the home; problems confronting the consumers; and the conservation of natural resources and the nation's health.

A school can inculcate in a student habits of reading. It is important, however, to know what to read and what not to read. Education is learning to grow, learning what to grow towards, learning what is good and bad, learning what is desirable and undesirable, learning what to choose and what to reject.

Historically speaking, educational curriculum underwent change with society's transition from an agricultural to an industrial base. Earlier, the school year followed the old agrarian calendar in order to enable students to help their parents on the farms. Today, all this has changed to conform to weather and religious festivities. However, the basic format of the teacher speaking while the student listens remains intact. The method of teaching by asking questions as practised by Socrates in Athens and Kautilaya in Pataliputra is still operative in our schools. The Industrial Age has enhanced the need for information and skills. The emergence of the Internet and other methods of distance learning technology have changed the curriculum but are not basically conducive to socializing. A sense of community among children can be developed by engaging them in acts of community service, team building, exercises, constructive programmes related to studies and sports. The important role that schools play in offering opportunities to develop socializing skills would need to be retained.

People from different religious, ethnic, racial, and linguistic groups live in close physical proximity in urban centres. But coexistence within a specific geographical area does not automatically mean that they know each other, relate to and care deeply about one another. It is a good thing that the children of these parents go to common schools but the fraternity among them could be strengthened only when the school curriculum includes important information about different religious and ethnic groups. A student needs to understand about his own religion and traditions, of those of the majority community as well as of others in his school or city.

The saga of achievements of different religious, ethnic, and linguistic groups must not be placed in a single book but should be incorporated as achievements and experiences in a wide variety of disciplines—history, economics, sociology, psychology, mathematics, science, literature, art, politics, music, health care, and agriculture. The curriculum must not gloss over social problems and the realities that characterize ethnic and linguistic identities. Multicultural education as a goal of school curriculum is crucial.

COMPLEXITIES AND CHALLENGES

Schools and colleges all over the world are facing a variety of demands that go beyond the traditional responsibility of preparing students for academic excellence. Everyone expects that education will provide something that would help resolve their problems. Political leaders, religious preachers, parents, working or jobless adults, captains of business and industry and those in charge of law and order expect a great deal from educational institutions. It is obvious that education cannot provide a panacea for all our ills. But yet, at the same time, it must enable the youth to meet the challenges of tomorrow with poise and determination.

The biggest challenge faced by the education system relates to its inability to fulfil market and industry expectations. It is true that the education system gets the maximum blame for the mismatch between market supply and demand. Policy-makers and planners are responsible for providing good teachers and make such changes in education curricula that meet the demand of the market. Towards this end, it is the responsibility of the government not only to provide adequate funds but also to create a national consensus on education. In the wake of problems of terrorism and massive unemployment, it is necessary to resort to dialogue among political parties, religious groups, business, and industry. The efficacy of education as a long-term instrument largely depends on the successful relationship that could be built between education and peace, and education and the needs of society. The computer and the Internet, radio and television, cable and satellite broadcasting, audio and video records are making an impact both on the content and the method of learning. The responsibility of the civil society and the state to develop suitable educational software is both urgent and important.

The last century has spoken against totalitarian regimes and paved the way for universalization of democratic principles. It has also clearly established that an inclusive society can provide better education and job opportunities. The minorities in all societies need to be involved in the process of education and social change. The teaching of history in its broadest sense, as the UNESCO report emphasizes:

Should inculcate in the young a spirit of tolerance and dialogue, so that the legitimate aspiration to preserve traditions and retain a collective identity is never seen as incompatible with a spirit of fellowship and solidarity, and so that the maintenance of social cohesion never implies a closed, inward-looking attitude or fundamentalism. Lifelong education is, of course, a safeguard against the most painful form of exclusion—exclusion due to ignorance.[23]

The educational system should constantly strive for celebration of pluralism and for respect for diversity. This would not only generate hope among the minorities but it would also constitute an active principle for the enrichment of the cultural and civil life of societies. It is only through this process that diversity could be converted into a constructive contributory factor of mutual understanding between individuals and groups. Education that teaches tolerance and respect for others' beliefs is good for social harmony, and is indeed a prerequisite for democracy.

We have to see clearly that individuals also learn throughout life from their social environment. While education can contribute to the social environment, it is the responsibility of the concerned citizens to see that the benefits of the educational system do not evaporate in the face of the harsh realities of social order. The potential of communication technology to spread values of a more caring and compassionate social order could be of tremendous support to thwart the designs of fundamentalists.

CONCLUSION

Education is not a magic formula for curing the violence and hatred that characterize the world. But it is certainly one of the principal instruments available to us that can make an effective contribution towards the reduction of poverty, ignorance, and disease, and in the building of an inclusive and democratic society.

It is being increasingly realized that while the death toll in the last World War was at a staggering figure of fifty million, since 1945 too, some twenty million people have died in several ethnic conflicts and wars. It is, therefore, necessary that the objectives of peaceful and harmonious living should be propagated not only at the global level but also at the village, city, and the regional levels.

It is only through an emphasis on the cultural dimensions of education that a person can grasp the individuality of other people, and understand the complexities of human development. It is in this context that self-enquiry is essential.

A knowledge-driven society that is emerging in our midst is bound to make an enormous impact not only upon our lives but also upon what training we are going to impart to our youth. One thing that is clear is that a knowledge-driven society can only flourish in a 'learning' society where education is pursued throughout life well beyond schools and colleges.

One of the major consequences of the information and communications technology revolution relates to the use of technology that provides extensive information to students as well as to adults. This has virtually led to the emergence of an information explosion in our midst. The education system, therefore, has to impart to students a critical spirit so that they can sort out useful information for their work and discard all that is peripheral and useless.

It is important to learn about diversity and the multiple loyalties of every person and group. This diversity and loyalty would range from religion to ethnicity, language to dialects, and folklore to literature. All these which bind an individual to his memories and shared experiences enrich the cultural and civic life of the village or the city in which we live. Education must be sensitive to this aspect of our social experience and in particular devise ways and means that give minority groups a place in the collective scheme of things so that they do not feel ignored or alienated. It is this kind of approach in education that is expected to generate tolerance and social harmony.

The Bahudhā approach would demand that we do not fall prey to a minimalistic form of tolerance that advocates merely putting up with others. This attitude, though harmless, does not help in harmonious living. It is only through dialogue and faith in the 'one truth, many interpretations' philosophy that we can understand and appreciate others. In terms of education, it is a question of helping students to acquire a degree of knowledge and, more significantly, sensitivity towards other languages, faiths, and ways of living. This would give students the ability as they grow into adult citizens, to make the right decisions in life and to solve problems in the social, economic, and religious spheres. The teaching of history, sociology, arts, and philosophy should always have a dimension that respects plurality of views and diverse expressions of human creativity as the heritage of all peoples and societies.

Through education, we are making a deliberate attempt to guide the development of children. Let us not be misunderstood that the child's freedom and his power of choice is being ignored. It is only being acknowledged that the child will inevitably be influenced by the prevailing culture of society, by his textbooks, and by his environment. It is, therefore, necessary that we cultivate in the child, positive virtues of freedom, democracy, and peace.

The task of utilizing education as an instrument of harmony is not an easy affair. The educational curriculum, in particular, has become in several countries an ideological battleground. The interpretation of historical events often excites religious and ethnic groups who start taking positions that are not always rational. Yet, education is the most dependable resource for preparing the youth for initiating dialogue. It is true that in societies marked by a continuing intolerant ethos, in which religious or ethnic groups blindly espouse their narrowest possible perceptions, education can only play a limited role. Patience and time are needed for education to play its expected meaningful role in bringing peace and harmony in the world. The biggest positive factor is that despite all odds youth all over the world are full of hope.

The primary goal should be to produce students who are aware of their ignorance both in terms of their own culture as well as of others. The need, therefore, is to move towards enriching the minds of students about various cultures and practices. The educational system must respect the life of the mind, its freedom, and its diversity. Martha C. Nussbaum puts this ethos correctly when she writes:

We do not fully respect the humanity of our fellow citizens—or cultivate our own—if we do not wish to learn about them, to understand their history, to appreciate the differences between their lives and ours. We must therefore construct a liberal education that is not only Socratic, emphasizing critical thought and respectful argument, but also pluralistic, imparting an understanding of the histories and contributions of groups with whom we interact, both within our nation and in the increasingly international sphere of business and politics.[24]

We have to look beyond the events that have characterized the global scene since 9/11. Two aspects of education would, however, remain paramount. First, education must strive to create in young minds a willingness to tolerate differences of opinion and the desire to understand different points of view. Second, the massive progress in science and technology has tended to stress the intellectual rather than moral and spiritual values. What we need is a synthesis of these values—spiritual and moral as well as intellectual—with the aim of producing a fully integrated human being. Such a person would be both inward looking as well as outward looking, who searches his own mind in order that his nobler self may prevail at all times, and at the same time recognize his obligations to his fellow men and the world around him.

NOTES

1. Socrates, in Plato, *Apology* 38A.
2. David E. Bloom and Joel E. Cohen 'Education for All: An Unfinished Revolution', *Daedalus*, Cambridge MA, Summer 2002, pp. 84–95.
3. Quoted in Muriel Wasi, *The Narrow Corridor, Moments in a Woman's Life*, Promilla & Co., Publishers in association with Bibliophile South Asia, New Delhi and Chicago, 2005, p. 68.
4. Thomas L. Friedman, 'Saudi Schools Foster a Culture of Death', *International Herald Tribune*, Hyderabad, 4 June 2004. Earlier, The Saudi English language daily, *Arab News*, published a series of articles by the liberal Saudi writer Raid Qusti about the need to re-evaluate Saudi education.
5. Richard Bernstein, 'A Thorn for German Schools: Islam', *International Herald Tribune*, Hyderabad, 30 June 2004.
6. Basharat Peer, *The Rediff Special*, 26 July 2004. at *www.rediff.com* or *http://us.rediff.com/news/2004/jul/26/specl.htm*
7. In preparation for the International Year, Nobel Prize laureates in 1999 drafted the following six-point Manifesto:

   • Respect all life: Respect the life and dignity of each human being without discrimination or prejudice;
   • Reject violence: Practise active non-violence, rejecting violence in all its forms: physical, sexual, psychological, economical and social, in particular towards the most deprived and vulnerable such as children and adolescents;
   • Share with others: Share my time and material resources in a spirit of generosity to put an end to exclusion, injustice and political and economic oppression;
   • Listen to understand: Defend freedom of expression and cultural diversity, giving preference always to dialogue and listening without engaging in fanaticism, defamation and the rejection of others;
   • Preserve the planet: Promote consumer behaviour that is responsible and development practices that respect all forms of life and preserve the balance of nature on the planet;
   • Rediscover solidarity: Contribute to the development of my community, with the full participation of women and respect for democratic principles, in order to create together new forms of solidarity.

   Manifesto 2000 is based upon the United Nations resolutions and translates the basic principles of a culture of peace from the language and concerns of international diplomacy into the language and behaviour of everyday life.
   See *http://www.unesco.org/bpi/eng/unescopress/99-38e.htm* (10/15/07), Manifesto 2000 For a Culture of Peace and Non-violence.

8. A.S. Balasooriya, *Learning the Way of Peace: A Teacher's Guide to Peace Education*, UNESCO, New Delhi, p. 34.
9. Ibid., p. 120.
10. Quoted in J. S. Rajput's 'Tradition Lives through Schools', *Pioneer*, New Delhi, 22 July 2005.
11. Quoted in *The Content of Education, Proposals for the Reform of the School Curriculum*, University of London Press, Malham House, Bickley, Kent 1945, p. 77.
12. Bertrand Russell, *Education and the Social Order*, London, Sydney, Wellington, 1932, pp. 72–3.
13. *The Content of Education, Proposals for the Reform of the School Curriculum*, p. 99.
14. Quoted in Uma Das Gupta, *Rabindranath Tagore: A Biography*, Oxford University Press, New Delhi, 2004, p. 17.
15. William Boyd and Wyatt Rawson, *The Story of the New Education*, Heinemann, London, 1965, p. 193.
16. The first known madrasa is said to have been established in 1005 AD by the Fatimid Caliphs in Egypt. This madrasa taught the minority Shi'ite version of Islam. It had a library and teachers for different subjects. Students who were admitted were provided with ink, pens and papers free of charge. A catalogue of inventory of this madrasa prepared in 1045 revealed that it had 6,500 volumes on different subjects, including astronomy, architecture and philosophy. When the Sunni Muslims conquered Egypt, they revamped the Shi'ite version of Islam in this madrasa and replaced it with the Sunni version, destroyed the books and manuscripts that seemed contrary to their version of Islam and preserved the volumes that related to the earthly knowledge. A huge number of books were taken to Baghdad where a Seljuk Vizier called Nizam-ul-Mulk Hassan Bin Al-Tusi, established the first organized madrasa in 1067.

    See Munir Ahmed, 'Islamic Education Prior to the Establishment of Madrassa', *Journal of Islamic Studies*, 1987.
17. Uzma Anzar rightly points out:

    Some madrasas have evolved from the centres of Islamic learning to the centres of secular knowledge acquisition, to the current state of greater emphasis on Islamic teachings only. This is especially true for madrasas in Pakistan and some parts of Indonesia. Others have tried to maintain a balance in teaching both religious and secular subjects (Egypt and Bangladesh). However, increasingly, some Muslim ulema are emphasising that secular knowledge should be taught in light of the knowledge revealed in the Quran.

    See Uzma Anzar, 'Islamic Education: A Brief History of *Madrasas* with Comments on Curricula and Current Pedagogical Practices', March 2003, p. 6 (unpublished).

18. *India*

The 86th Constitutional Amendment, 2002 makes elementary education a fundamental right of every Indian child. India has made remarkable progress in net enrolment of six to ten-year-olds in recent years. Notwithstanding this, India accounts for one-quarter of the world's 104 million out-of school children.

The madrasas have played an important role in bringing education to Muslim children. Since 1857, the Muslim leadership in India followed two different approaches towards modernity and conservation of Islamic culture. The first group led by Sayyid Ahmad Khan (1817–98)—founder of Aligarh Muslim University—supported Western scientific education and learning of the English language by Muslims. The traditional Muslim clergy, however, was opposed to westernization and set up several madrasas, the two famous ones being, (i) Dar al-ulum, Deoband (1866); and (ii) Nadwat al-ulama, Lucknow (1893) or Nadva in short.

Madrasas in India have not justified violence in their schools. There are, however, genuine concerns on the need to provide a modern scientific education to Muslim boys and girls who are lagging behind other religious communities. One way out would be to set up Central school/Navodaya school type of institutions in locations with a concentration of Muslims.

Pakistan

The mission of most madrasas in Pakistan was to prepare students for religious duties. General Zia-ul-Haq's Islamization policies in the 1980s had resulted in a massive expansion in the numbers of madrasas. During this period, militant interpretations of Islam were systemically incorporated into the mainstream public school curriculum. Current national syllabus guidelines required students in Class I–VI, for example to 'recognise the importance of Jihad in every sphere of life' and 'make speeches on Jihad'. At the hands of fundamentalists, Jihad has lost its original meaning, which also included overcoming one's weaknesses. Estimates of the number of students who receive education in madrasas in Pakistan vary from half a million to two million. In a television broadcast in August 2005, President Musharraf acknowledged that over a million students, particularly the poor, were undergoing educational instruction in the madrasas. There are about 14,000 madrasas functioning in different parts of the country. It is well-known that the madrasas run by Jamaat-e-Islam (JEI) and Jamiat Ulema-e-Islam (JUI) have been the production units of jihadis for over the past three decades, the glaring ones being terrorist groups like Hizbul Mujahideens. The direct link between Al-Qaeda and JEI are well known. Most of the Taliban leaders were trained in madrasas run by JEI. Mullah Omar, the ousted leader of Afghanistan, was a student of one such madrasa in Pakistan. The most disturbing feature is that the ulemas (Islamic religious leaders) want students to completely adhere to their version of Islam in which hatred and militancy occupy an important place. Several Islamic scholars in Pakistan continue to resist improvements in the curriculum of madrasas to reflect diversity of faiths and democratic norms, including human rights and the concerns of women.

Bangladesh

Bangladesh has made significant progress in education in the last two decades, especially in regard to enhanced enrolment and gender equality. Despite this progress, critical problems persist. There has been a phenomenal growth in the number of madrasas in Bangladesh, and at the beginning of 2005, there were over 9,000 madrasas. [See ANI report of 6 August 2005 entitled 'Number of Madrasas in Bangladesh rise by 22 percent compared to 10 percent general institutes' from Dhaka@yahoo].

There are two types of madrasas in Bangladesh, i.e. (i) Quomi (also known as Dars-e-Nizami); and (ii) Aliya. Aliya madrasas function under the auspices of the government and teach secular as well as religious subjects. Quomi madrasas teach only Islamic subjects. There has been a significant increase in terrorist activities in Bangladesh since 9/11. There are fears that madrasas may turn out to become centres for the production of terrorists. Fortunately, saner people in Bangladesh recognize the need for scientific education, improvement in labour productivity, economic growth, and the quality of life.

Egypt

In Egypt, most madrasas teach both secular and Islamic subjects to their students. These madrasas are run by the Al-Azhar University education system, a body established in the eleventh century. It maintains separate madrasa facilities for male and female students. It is responsible for education in Islamic values as well as other components of a secular curriculum.

One good feature of madrasas in Egypt is that students who successfully complete four years of secondary religious school can enrol at Al-Azhar University.

The education authorities are conscious of the need to keep schools free from becoming centres that would breed terrorists and a jihadi mindset.

Indonesia

Indonesia, home to the largest number of Muslims in the world, has two types of Islamic schools: Madrasas and 'Pesantrens' or 'Pondok' meaning the bamboo hut. The former is an Islamic day school while the latter is an Islamic boarding school.

Indonesian madrasas provide education at three levels: primary, lower secondary, and upper secondary. These schools teach the national education curriculum and use extended hours in which to teach basic Islamic education and principles. As in Egypt, students who graduate from the Upper Secondary level of accredited madrasas in Indonesia are qualified to enter a regular university.

Recent years have seen a tremendous increase in the number of madrasas in Indonesia. An expanded role for local government in the delivery of educational services is being organized. The World Bank, the Asian Development Bank and other aid agencies are supporting Indonesia's local education capacity building programmes.

Turkey

Turkey is known for its secular educational institutions. In 1997, Turkey adopted a new Basic Education Law, which has extended the duration of compulsory schooling from five years to eight years and has also sought to improve the quality of education. It envisages a role for government as well as private organizations. In rural areas, however, there are about half a million children of basic education age who are not in schools. (See *The World Bank, Project Appraisal Document of Second Basic Education Report,* Turkey, Ankara, 12 June 2002, pp. 3–6, and pp. 86–94.)

The basic education programme has created a new environment for enabling children to improve the quality of their basic education including attaining proficiency in computer education.

19. Max Rodenbeck, 'The Truth About Jihad', 11 August 2005, *The New York Review of Books*, p. 52.
20. Judea Pearl, 'Islam Struggles to Stake Out its Position', *International Herald Tribune*, 20 July 2005.
21. Ibid.
22. Diane Ravitch 'Education after the Culture War', *Daedalus*, Cambridge MA, Summer 2002, pp. 5–21.
23. Jacques Delors, 'Learning: The Treasure Within', p. 212.
24. Martha C. Nussbaum, *Cultivating Humanity, A Classical Defense of Reform in Liberal Education*, Harvard University Press, Cambridge, Massachusetts, London, 1997, p. 295.

11

International Political Architecture
The United Nations

And He will certainly render judgement among the nations and set matters straight respecting many peoples. And they will have to beat their swords into ploughshares and their spears into pruning shears. Nation will not lift up sword against nation, neither will they learn war anymore.[1]

—The Old Testament

All human creations are subject to atrophy, decline, and dissolution. This applies to international organizations as well. The effort to create international organizations has only a limited history. 'Four times in the modern age,' John Keegan, the British historian, records, 'men have sat down to reorder the world—at the Peace of Westphalia in 1648, after the Thirty Years War, at the Congress of Vienna in 1815 after the Napoleonic Wars, in Paris in 1919, after World War I, and in San Francisco in 1945 after World War II.'[2] All previous international arrangements, barring the efforts at the San Francisco Conference establishing the United Nations (UN) with headquarters at New York City, have long become part of history.[3]

THE UNITED NATIONS

The United Nations came into being on 24 October 1945. In the preceding six years had the world witnessed several million deaths and enormous suffering caused by the use of force by nation-states aimed at imperialist conquests. Against this backdrop, the victorious Allies felt the need for an international organization that not only brought nations together but also made sure that the structure of the global political system would leave no loopholes for ambitious leaders to order their armed forces to cross borders and wage devastating wars. Franklin Delano Roosevelt, President of the USA, and his successor Harry Truman, Winston Churchill, Prime Minister of Great Britain, Joseph Stalin of the Soviet Union, and several others who had assembled at San Francisco, were deeply conscious of the fact that a post-war international organization alone could secure the peace, advocate global prosperity, alleviate poverty and un- employment, and promote human rights worldwide. All these leaders had lived through the economic crisis of the 1930s, the rise of fascist aggressive states in Germany, Italy, and Japan, and the horrors of the Second World War. They had seen the collapse of the League of Nations.[4] These statesmen were also actuated by a strong desire that they owed it to their children and grandchildren to set up a new international political architecture that could make things work better for everyone and ensure peace through the rule of law.

The Preamble of the UN Charter accordingly started with a pledge and in the name of 'we the peoples' of the United Nations' with the determination 'to save succeeding generations from the scourge of war' and almost in reiteration of the Bahudhā philosophy went on to add 'to practice and live together in peace with one another as good neighbours', and to 'promote social progress and better standards of life in larger freedom'.

The framers of the UN Charter were deeply conscious of the need to strike a balance between state sovereignty and the power of intervention by the United Nations, a multilateral organization. This delicate balance was achieved under Article 2(4) and Article 2(7) of the UN Charter. Article 2(4) reads as follows:

All members shall refrain in their international relations from the threat or use of force against the territorial integrity or political independence of any state, or in any other manner in consonance with the purposes of the United Nations.

This is an affirmation of the sovereign equality of all members of the UN. Article 2(7) goes on to provide limitations on the power of intervention by the UN except where action is required with respect to threats to peace, breaches of peace and acts of aggression as provided under chapter VII of the Charter. Article 2(7) reads as follows:

Nothing contained in the present Charter shall authorise the United Nations to intervene in matters which are essential within the domestic jurisdiction of any state or shall require the Members to submit such matters to settlement under the present Charter; but this principle shall not prejudice the application of enforcement measures under Chapter VII.

It was clearly understood that states were the most important actors in world politics. Accordingly, it was categorically stated in the Charter that the use of military force against a sovereign state is to be resorted to only by the Security Council in an extreme situation for peace-keeping as well as for peace enforcement purposes. It was also felt that the benefits of a pluralist approach to international politics was far more beneficial to human progress than any form of unilateralism. The United Nations is a symbol of that belief, a faith in the ability and potential of human beings to work together despite diversity in religion, race, and lifestyles. It is this form of faith in multilateralism that has prompted states to join the United Nations and as such its membership steadily grew and stands at 191 today from a meagre fifty-one in 1945. The concepts of pluralism and multilateralism in which the foundations of the United Nations are squarely grounded are also essential tenets of the Bahudhā approach to resolution of conflicts.

In the initial years, the UN played a crucial role in dismantling of the colonial order and in facilitating entry of newly independent states in the international system. Subsequently, the bi-polar power structure and the conflict in ideology between the US and the former Soviet Union cast its shadow on the functioning of the UN. The veto power of the five permanent members of the Security Council contributed to their domination over the decision-making processes. Yet the UN did act as a balancing force in global politics and gave developing countries a voice in an international forum.

The UN Charter incorporated special provisions for international economic and social cooperation and went on to provide for an Economic and Social Council, with fifty-four members elected by the General Assembly with wide-ranging powers to initiate studies and make recommendations under chapter X. In a far-sighted provision it provided for consultation with non-governmental organizations as well. For development, financial stability, and trade a separate set of institutions was visualized by the leaders at the Bretton Woods[5] Conference.

BRETTON WOODS INSTITUTIONS

In the aftermath of the Second World War, the US and other western countries were keen to establish global economic institutions to promote free market economics. Accordingly, the international economic system was redefined by the agreements at Bretton Woods among developed and developing countries. The Bretton Woods system created three separate organizations: IMF, the World Bank, and the General Agreement on Tariffs and Trade (GATT). The IMF was designed to deal with currency exchange and balance of payments problems stemming broadly from international trade. The World Bank was created to assist in the development process of the member states, specifically to arrange for loans including soft loans to facilitate the creation of infrastructure. The GATT was the mechanism by which states could resolve disputes and increase the volume of international trade by lifting restrictions and barriers that sovereign states impose on the movement of goods and services. The negotiating rounds of GATT have recently been formalized, leading to the creation of the WTO.

Today, the IMF, the World Bank, and the WTO are the principal institutions which play a major role in the global economic order. The manner in which these organizations have functioned in the post-Second World War era has generated fierce debate among economists, non-governmental organizations, and political leaders, particularly about their domination over developing countries. In fact, the voice of criticism in recent years has become loud and clear, alleging that these institutions perpetuate the dominance of western countries and their multinational corporations over the global economy.

Another feature of the global economic system is the growth of regional groupings, including regional multilateral banks in Europe, North America, Asia-Pacific, South-East Asia, and other regions. As a result, a series of regional trade agreements coexist with multilateral trade strategies.

The working of global institutions in the areas of politics and economics have come in for criticism in the wake of globalization and the information and communications technology revolution. As Joseph E. Stiglitz puts it:

Globalization, by increasing the interdependence among the people of the world, has enhanced the need for global collective action, and the importance of global public goods. That the global institutions which have been created in response have not worked perfectly is not a surprise; the problems are complex and collective action at any level is difficult.[6]

WORKING OF THE UN AND ITS SHORTCOMINGS

The birth of the United Nations did create a short-term period of euphoria. The founding members including the USSR viewed their own role as liberators in the face of aggression by the Axis powers. One of the great achievements in those very early days was the drafting of the Universal Declaration of Human Rights and its adoption by the General Assembly by a vote of 48:0.[7] The Soviet Union got rapidly transformed from a wartime ally to a major Cold War adversary. As a result, the Security Council was effectively neutralized. Each superpower threatened and in several cases also exercised its right to veto resolutions authorizing military action by the Security Council.

The end of the Cold War demanded, and in substantial measure, secured a new methodology of cooperation among the five permanent members of the Security Council. It showed considerable promise in the early 1990s. The Security Council, enjoying a new era of cooperation, took the lead in ending the long war between two neighbouring Muslim countries, Iraq and Iran. It also successfully repelled the Iraqi invasion of Kuwait. Conflicts in Cambodia and Central America were resolved and Namibia got independence.

Unfortunately the post-Cold War era was accompanied by a resurgence of nationalism, ethnic conflicts, civil wars and the new phenomenon of failed states. One of the consequences was greater demands than ever before on the UN to deal with peace and threats to security as well as to the environment and disease. UN peace-keepers were called on to rebuild Cambodia, Nicaragua and Namibia, to monitor human rights' violations in Yugoslavia, and to oversee humanitarian relief in Bosnia, Uganda, Kosovo, Congo, East Timor, and Afghanistan. The liberation of Kuwait from Iraq's control called for special efforts to rebuild that country under the leadership of the UN. Most of these problems were internal in nature and led to divisive controversy on the limits of national sovereignty.

Very soon it became evident that UN peacekeepers could not function effectively. The UN intervention in Bosnia-Herzegovina, Somalia, Rwanda, and Kosovo in the early 1990s established the abject failure of its peacekeeping operations.[8]

Such inaction by the UN has made many, even within the UN, realize that in order to meet effectively the challenges of both inter-state and intra-state warfare, the UN has to reform not only its approach but also its major decision-making bodies, most importantly, the Security Council. In an exceptional Agenda for Peace, Butros-Butros Ghali had suggested that consent by the host state might not be an invariable requirement of peacekeeping operations. In a way, he was questioning Article 2(7) of the UN Charter that limited UN intervention in the internal affairs of another state.[9]

It is also to be appreciated that the UN is essentially a political body and primarily concerned with the armed conflict involving two member countries or more and not so much with intra-state violence, although this has come to be significant in the context of genocide and terrorism.

The United Nations was powerfully affected by the attacks of 11 September 2001, that took place in New York just as the General Assembly was about to convene for its annual session. It became evident to everyone that these terrorist attacks would require major new efforts and that the UN had to play an effective role. A very aggressive US administration emerged after 9/11, under President George W. Bush, whose message to the world on 20 September 2001 was to state that 'either you are with us or you are with the terrorists'.[10]

Article 51 permits military acts in self-defence by member states to resist an armed attack. The moot question, however, is whether self-defence can be used against a potential armed attack or against the existence of certain weapons of mass destruction within the territory and control of a member state or with a terrorist group operating from the territory of a member state. The UN Charter is explicit against the use of force against an imaginary threat. Article 51 does mention collective action. But collective action against armed attack cannot be extended to mean collective self-defence under Article 51. The Charter, therefore, clearly prohibits arbitrary and unilateral use of force by member states. The location of the primary response for maintenance of world peace and security lies in the Security Council and not with member states. The Security Council was intended to be the apex body of the UN where the big five, with the help of ten temporary members, would make all the major decisions. To function outside this is to deny legitimacy to the UN itself.

The principal weakness, however, of the UN flows from two factors. Firstly, the UN has no power to initiate military interventions without the unanimous approval of the Security Council. Each of the five permanent members of the UN have the right to veto a decision arrived at by the remaining members or a majority of members of the Council. Since each country views developments from its own perspective and plans to act in accordance with its own interests, it is not possible for the Council to pass a clear resolution on each issue. Secondly, we are living in a world where governments of some member states wilfully violate the rights of their citizens. The biggest source of ineffectiveness of the Security Council emanates from its inability to take a unanimous and firm stand to prevent deadly violence. The fact that the UN has no army and armed police of its own is a serious drawback.

It is true that in the changing nature of terrorist-sponsored warfare, a legalistic approach to conflict resolution will not help safeguard the life and property of innocent civilians. It is, therefore, necessary that the Security Council should have at its command, as Winston Churchill had said, 'all constabulary power before which barbaric and atavistic forces will stand in awe'.[11] Towards this, the UN should either be allowed by the member states to have a military capability of its own, or member states themselves from among their own forces earmark sufficient resources to be made immediately available to the Security Council for peacekeeping and peace enforcement responsibilities. This is necessary for achieving the goals set in the noble words of the UN Charter 'to save succeeding generations from the scourge of wars'.[12]

It may be recalled that the Bretton Woods institutions like the IMF and the World Bank, and subsequent organizations like the WTO, have functioned independently of the UN. As a result, the UN does not play any significant role either in the balance-of-payment crisis of a member state or in their development programmes. The UN, however, convened a Millennium Assembly that took place at the United Nations in September 2000, attended by 147 heads of state and government—the largest gathering of world leaders in history. In the Millennium Declaration formulated by them a consensus was reached on the most challenging problems facing the world. Subsequently, these were made into the eight Millennium Development Goals (MDGs). The MDGs rightly identified the goal of halving the number of poor people living on less than one dollar a day; reversing the spread of HIV/AIDS, malaria and other major diseases; and accelerating the reach of elementary education by 2015, as important programmes for action.

There is great inequality between people as well as between nations. In a global economy driven by information technology, the existing unequal relations among nations need to be taken into account. For example, the richest twenty per cent of the population account for over ninety per cent of Internet users, while the poorest twenty per cent account for only 0.2 per cent. This not only explains the existing concentration of wealth and resources in rich western countries but also gives an indication of the continued increase in wealth and prosperity in those countries. Another aspect of this uneven growth can also be witnessed among fairly affluent countries of the Arab region where access to the Internet is extremely low.[13] The participation of 191 member states in the UN decision-making demands a close look at the need for spread of information technology.

There are clear limits to the UN's authority. It is totally dependent on its members for its budgets and assignments. Even if the UN were authorized to undertake peace enforcement tasks in a country, it can only execute the order through armed forces of participating states. The UN has no independent authority and it is certainly not a world government. And yet as President Dwight Eisenhower once said:

With all the defects, with all the failures that we can check up against it, the UN still represents man's best-organised hope to substitute the conference table for the battlefield.[14]

INVASION OF IRAQ AND ITS LESSONS

The events leading to the US invasion of Iraq moved very fast. On 12 September 2002, a year and a day after 9/11, President Bush addressed the General Assembly and declared '. . . our principles and security are challenged today by outlaw groups and regimes that accept no law of morality and have no limit to their violent ambitions'. President Bush went on to announce, 'in one place, one regime, we find all these dangers—Iraq'.[15] On 5 February 2003, Secretary of State Colin Powell made a detailed presentation to the Security Council of US intelligence perceptions of an Iraqi cover-up of Weapons of Mass Destruction (WMD). This was not supported by UN inspectors in their reports to the Security Council on 14 February 2003 and they needed more time for further investigation. Newton R. Bowles writes about subsequent developments leading to the invasion of Iraq as follows:

The line up now was clear: in favour of immediate action were the USA, UK, Spain and a few others; in favour of more time for inspection were France, Germany, Russia, China and many more. Nevertheless, serious efforts continued to avoid an impasse. France and Germany proposed strengthening the UN team. Canada proposed setting specific steps for inspection so as to have a base for assessing progress. All to no avail. Colin Powell floated a draft Security Council resolution authorising immediate invasion. The PERM 5 were split: USA and UK in favour, China, France and Russia opposed. The issue was not so much whether as when. President Bush said now. Leading the opposition moderates, President Chirac said that France would veto. Colin Powell withdrew his draft. The show was over. US and UK forces entered Iraq.[16]

In between, the United States released its National Security Document in September 2002 making inter alia its unilateralist approach in tackling terrorism explicit. A core paragraph reads as follows:

While the United States will constantly strive to enlist the support of the international community, we will not hesitate to act alone, if necessary, to exercise our right of self-defence by acting pre-emptively against such terrorists, to prevent them from doing harm against our people and our country.[17]

A large number of member states of the UN and concerned citizens all over the world opposed the US invasion of Iraq. Strong feelings were expressed that meddling in the affairs of other countries is contrary to the principles enshrined in the UN Charter. It is true that WMDs are not kept on a shelf that can be easily found out. But the inspectors were seeking some more time. Intelligence reports too were not categorical and, as subsequent findings revealed, were in fact exaggerated. In such a confusing environment, the judgement of a particular country can always go wrong. It is, therefore, necessary that as provided under the UN Charter, decision-making should rest with the Security Council.

The UN Charter calls upon member states to attempt to settle disputes peacefully and failing that, to make a reference to the Security Council for appropriate action. The Security Council did not approve the US proposal to undertake military intervention against Iraq. Notwithstanding this, the US went ahead. Those who seek to justify the invasion of Iraq by the US and the UK under Article 51 of the Charter are clearly in the wrong. Article 51 reads as follows:

Nothing in the present Charter shall impair the inherent right of individual or collective self-defence if an armed attack occurs against a Member of the United Nations, until the Security Council has taken measures necessary to maintain international peace and security. Measures taken by Members in the exercise of this right of self-defence shall be immediately reported to the Security Council and shall not in any way affect the authority and response of the Security Council under the present Charter to take at any time such action as it deems necessary in order to maintain or restore international peace and security.[18]

The categorical position emerging out of Article 51 is that states refrain from the use of its military till an armed attack takes place. This has been repeatedly violated.

The theory of pre-emptive or preventive strike enshrined by the National Security Strategy 2002 of the US has added a new dimension when it declares:

Given the goals of rogue states and terrorists, the United States can no longer solely rely on reactive postures as we have in the past. The inability to deter a potential attacker, the immediacy of today's threats, and the magnitude of potential harm that could be caused by our adversaries' choice of weapons, do not permit that option. We cannot let our enemies strike first.[19]

Preventive war has the flawed principle that it is possible to foresee what is to come. It presumes that any member state can acquire all the intelligence. The reality, however, is that one can only make intelligent guesses about arsenals as well as intentions of the enemy.

An emphasis on preventive war would be in negation of the Bahudhā philosophy. For preventive war rules out the route of dialogue, negotiations, and arbitration. The existing system where a state feels threatened by the possible use of WMDs by another country or group should first go to the General Assembly/Security Council. A system based on the rule of law demands that it is the UN that should devise ways and means to control biological, chemical and nuclear weapons in terms of global treaties. If a particular country is unwilling to comply with these regulations, action in terms of sanctions, embargos, seizures of assets abroad, or in extreme cases, military action could be authorized by the Security Council.

Transnational terrorist networks are now using religion and items of economic wealth, like illegal trade in drugs, in pursuit of their objectives. The increasing relevance of warlords in polity manage-ment, the growing number of insurgent outfits, and new mercenary agencies have strengthened terrorist networks and added a new feature to warfare. This is a trend towards a denationalized warfare. The new terrorism has prospered particularly in those countries where law and order has broken down to a considerable extent, for example, in Afghanistan, Sudan, and Somalia, and where religious funda-mentalists have an impact on the education system and considerable say in the state policy formulation mechanisms.

Member states certainly will always have separate ideals and goals to pursue. But these need not be in violent conflict with the UN Charter. In fact, the objects of global peace and the prevention of terrorist activities should easily transcend the ideals and goals of member states. The General Assembly and the Security Council alone can provide that kind of forum for continuous dialogue and arrival of a middle-way in terms of the Bahudhā ideology which is crucial for peace and good governance.

It is true that the framers of the UN Charter had not envisaged the existing nature and complexity of global terrorism and accordingly the Charter makes no mention of terrorism as such. However, once the spectre of terrorism spread, the UN in 1997 passed the International Convention for the Suppression of Terrorist Bombings, and two years later, a convention on the suppression of funding of terrorism. The Security Council also set up a Counter Terrorism Committee. After the 9/11 attacks, the Council has fully committed the entire UN to the battle against the menace of terrorism.

There is a need to look at the Iraq war as an exception rather than a rule. It is an overall strengthening of the UN system's capacity in the realm of crisis prevention and peace operations that will lead to a peaceful world. As Tobias Debiel rightly points out:

Post-9/11, the United Nations finds itself at the cross-roads. Reforms to improve its efficiency are challenged by an era that is obviously characterised by the renaissance of geo-politics. This could result in a rather undesirable outcome—a more efficient world organisation in the context of weakened and ineffective multilateralism. . . . But the present tendency to reduce it to the role of an optional rubber-stamp will lead inexorably to its power—as a universal legal authority and an effectual actor— being undermined. The UN needs to be strengthened as the core element in a system of cooperative security.[20]

The broad undercurrents of international politics and global political and economic realities indicate that without the support of the US, it will not be possible to bring the UN towards the centre of things. UN reforms which should herald a new global political order could, of course, be dominated by the US and its allies, but at the same time it would be sensitive to other countries of the world because without their cooperation global issues cannot be effectively tackled and enduring peace cannot be a feature of the new world order.

The world is facing an entirely unprecedented situation wherein a small group of terrorists in possession of lethal devices, strike at will and attack the very basis of democracy and civilized behaviour. The terror attacks at various places in the world, and the invasion of Iraq by the USA, have brought into focus the fact that the UN cannot sit back and hold the view that time will ease the problem. If the UN is not kept at the centre of things or if it is bypassed, it will not only go the way of the League of Nations but it would also mean a chaotic situation in world affairs. The need, therefore, is to make the UN an effective instrument for maintaining the rule of law in the world.

In view of the special position of the USA—as a country both with the will and the means to back international armed intervention or hold its delivery—it is necessary that it follows the provisions of the UN Charter. The US, in the past, has been guided by the philosophy of restraint as well as multilateralism. This was amply expressed by President Harry Truman when he spoke at the closing session of the 1945 UN Conference in San Francisco:

We all have to recognize—no matter how great our strength—that we must deny ourselves the licence to do always as we please. No one nation, no regional group, can, or should, accept any special privilege which harms any other nation. . . .That is the price that each nation will have to pay for world peace. Unless we are willing to pay that price, no organisation, for world peace, can accomplish its purpose and what a reasonable price that is.[21]

REFORMS IN THE UN

Everyone agrees that the UN needs reforms that will reflect new political, social, and economic realities. The world has changed since 1945 and it is only through major structural reforms that the UN can fulfil its objectives of ensuring a peaceful world. There are divergent perspectives: developed countries want more productivity and efficiency from the UN system and a continuation of their hold over the system; developing countries want greater economic and political equality through redistribution of resources and an enhanced say in decision-making; NGOs want the UN to be more open and accountable to civil society, allowing them participation in its decision-making.

High Level Panel

It is being widely recognized that if the UN is to be the vehicle through which nation-states shall meet the challenges of global peace and prosperity, today as well as tomorrow, then it needs major reforms to strengthen its relevance, effectiveness, and accountability.

In October 2002, in order to streamline the UN Reforms Agenda, the UN Secretary General Kofi Annan set up a High Level Panel on 'Threats, Challenges and Change' under the Chairmanship of Anand

Panyarachun, the former Prime Minister of Thailand. Consisting of fifteen other distinguished panelists from all over the world, the panel's main task was to point out the pitfalls and discrepancies in UN functioning and in doing so, using their own expertise and experience, suggest measures for reforming the UN to meet the challenges of the twenty-first century.

The Report entitled 'A More Secure World: Our Shared Responsibility' was submitted to the Secretary General in December 2004. According to the authors of the Report, there are six clusters of threats with which the world must be concerned in the years to come: (i) war between states; (ii) violence within states, including civil wars, large-scale human rights abuse, and genocide; (iii) poverty, infectious diseases, and environmental degradation; (iv) nuclear, radiological, chemical, and biological weapons; (v) terrorism; and (vi) transnational organized crime.

Terrorist attacks and the possibility of their having access to chemical and biological warfare materials as well as nuclear weapons have added a new dimension to the problem. The language of Article 51 of the Charter is highly restrictive. A threatened state can take action only when the attack takes place or at best a situation has developed where the attack is imminent. It does not cover the fact of possession of nuclear weapons capability or chemical or biological warfare material. Even in the event of a military threat or of its imminence, the Security Council should be approached and any military action must emanate from the Security Council's authority and from that authority alone. It is, therefore, necessary to have a clear understanding among members of the UN that preventive military action is ruled out.

A study of the working of the UN and internal disorders over a period of time suggests that the immense diversity of internal conflicts precludes the development of general rules for treatment of civil strife. The UN may have jurisdiction, including expression of concern, but a crisis need not be postponed merely to give the UN a role or to build its record. In fact, efforts should be made to encourage all parties, whatever their legal status, to negotiate within a regional context or via bilateral processes. The interests of the larger international society and of durable peace could be served in this way.

The High Level Report makes an eminently reasonable proposal when it says that in the world of the twenty-first century, the international community has to be concerned about nightmare scenarios combining terrorists, WMD and irresponsible states. Such situations may conceivably justify the use of force, not just reactively but preventively and before a latent threat becomes imminent. The question is not whether such action can be taken: it can, by the Security Council, if as the international community's collective security voice, at any time, it deems that there is a threat to international peace and security. The Council may well need to be prepared, to be much more pro-active on these issues, taking more decisive action earlier than it has in the past.[22]

The prescription of the High Level Panel report has been a subject of great debate and critical evaluation. In a perceptive article entitled 'Idealism at the UN', Michael J. Glennon argues that although ideals of peace and collective security by the UN occupy an important place in international discourse, the need is to look at their practicality. He writes:

States, like individuals, are driven by preferences that they often call ideals. The point here is twofold: that there is no transcendent reason why those ideals are necessarily shared by every other state or individual on the planet and that, whatever their origin, global ideals cannot be advanced unless idealists confront the practical navigational problems that stand in the way of their realisation.[23]

Two aspects of the UN reforms which are crucial for establishing the primacy of the rule of law in conflict resolution are the following: first, commonality of understanding among member states about the collective security system that was envisaged by the framers of the UN Charter; and second, strengthening of the Security Council, the primary body for maintenance of international peace and security.

Collective Security

The principle of collective security would demand that peace in the international community should be maintained through a pre-determined binding agreement to take collective action to preserve it. The security arrangements of the UN do not constitute a holistic system of collective security. It, however, does envisage that any threat or use of force by one sovereign member of the international community against another would attract the attention of the Security Council; the Council then would initiate appropriate action and, in extreme cases, embark upon military intervention. It was expected that such an authority with the Security Council would thwart a belligerent member state from initiating acts of aggression.

The Security Council of the UN was also intended to exercise a monopoly on the use of force. The Charter envisages that a state, if attacked, would report to the Security Council and that the Council, drawing upon advice provided by member states and in consultation with its own Military Staff Committee, would itself respond to the breach of peace. The victim state, however, was expected to use defence force between the period it sends a report to the Security Council and the Council's response to it. Article 51 of the Charter required states to await actual armed attack before defending themselves militarily. The system, however, was not followed in letter and spirit. In actual operation, collective security throughout the twentieth century has been implemented imperfectly and in the US invasion of Iraq, the UN has been bypassed totally. All these go to establish that the UN is yet to emerge as an effective instrument of collective security that will eliminate military aggression of one state against another.

The prerequisites that could provide an environment for the UN to act effectively get negated in the face of political realities. Unfortunately, the theory of collective security proposes a legal response to issues that are fundamentally political. The political response cannot be provided by an international public servant like the Secretary General but by member states of the Security Council. Regrettably, member states can rarely become impartial judges, as in one way or another, even in the post-Cold War era, there is a convergence of political interests with one country or another involved in the dispute on the part of one member of the Council or the other. The ideal situation demands that the members of the Security Council, and more particularly the P5, must transcend their political interests, first, in determining a derelict, and, later in providing necessary resources in order that the response of the Security Council becomes immediate and effective.

Another dilemma is at the level of implementation. The security forces are invariably drawn from more than one state or a group of states and are expected to act in harmony and impartially as 'blue helmet peacekeepers' under direct UN command. There is no doubt that during the last six decades, the UN peacekeepers have done commendable work and have shown professionalism in their behaviour, transcending political preferences of their country, but it has not always been up to expected levels. Similarly, in respect of economic sanctions a great deal of cooperation is required from member states and private sector actors like multinational corporations. Experience has shown that in the implementation of military tasks as well as economic sanctions much needs to be done to make them effective. Strengthening of regional organizations such as alliances among democracies and economic groups would support the maintenance of peace and security more effectively by the Security Council.

THE SECURITY COUNCIL

There is no denying that the working of the Security Council had generated fresh hopes after the end of the Cold War. But these have evaporated and the UN's public image is that of a weak organization. The High Level Panel has offered suggestions on the enlargement of membership of the Security Council in order to make it more democratic and accountable. It has provided two clearly defined alternatives as models (a) and (b). In model (a) there will be six new permanent members of the Security Council without veto power and three new two-year term non-permanent members divided among Africa, Asia and Pacific, Europe and Americas. Model (b) provides for no new permanent seats but creates a new category of eight four-year renewable term seats and one new two-year non-permanent and non-renewable seats divided among the major regions of the world.

The world's leaders held a high level plenary meeting at the UN headquarters in New York during 14–16 September 2005.[24] The plenary meeting, however, could not take any decision about strengthening of the Security Council. It, however, indicated a strong and unambiguous commitment by all governments to achieve the Millennium Development Goals by 2015.[25] It also decided to create a peace-building Commission to help countries in the transition from war to peace, backed by a support office and a standing fund. The peace-building Commission will be an inter-governmental advisory body. The main purpose of the peace-building Commission would be to bring together all relevant actors to marshal resources and to advise on and propose integrated strategies for post-conflict peace-building and recovery.

The Report is a reflection of the Bahudhā precept of peaceful co-existence among different societies practising varied lifestyles and adhering to different religious faiths. This can be possible only when an attempt is made to concentrate on the commonalities of cultures and civilizations, along with respect for differences, as every human being shares in the common responsibility of following a pluralistic approach in life. The panelists point out that before suggesting new ways to make the UN function better, in order to handle old and new threats to peace and security, it is important to resolve long-standing disputes like Palestine, Kashmir, and the Korean Peninsula. The Report is a positive verdict on the benefits of collectivism, especially when it comes to security, as the current threats recognize no boundaries—again a reflection of the Bahudhā belief in the ability of human beings across borders to deal with any threats through a pluralistic method. These threats range from poverty, infectious diseases, environmental degradation, war and violence, and terrorism to transnational organized crime. They emanate from non-state actors as well as states, and threaten human security and state security as well.

What emerges clearly is the need to weave together different strands of thought and usher in a collective security system that is effective, efficient, and equitable.[26] The Bahudhā philosophy is central in emphasizing moderation in all things, accommodation of antithetical points of view, and the primacy of a common-sense approach over the rest. Most importantly, the middle path reiterates a harmonious view among conflicting interpretations. It emphasizes that an extreme position does not work well in life. A balanced approach based on magnanimity and equilibrium can work wonders at the world stage.

THE BAHUDHĀ PHILOSOPHY AND THE UN

The United Nations is the highest institutional expression of multilateralism in the world. It is at the General Assembly and/or at the Security Council that the nations of the world come together to contribute their own interpretation of world events, and out of a maze of conflicting thought processes, ideas and opinions, common ground are sought to be found. The world has put its faith in the United Nations and expects leaders to come up with solid, rational policy options which do not compromise or appease conflicting interests but define a plan of action that is based on law and morality. The core philosophy of the UN reflects a pluralistic vision of the world where the aspirations of every state, big and small, can be accommodated. This is in conformity with the Bahudhā philosophy that emphasizes inclusiveness of all people, all societies, and all natural objects.

The Preamble to the UN Charter begins with the words 'We the People of the United Nations'. 'United Nations' could mean a unity amidst the ability to differ and yet to stay united on the course towards world peace. This could also be informed by the central theme of the Bahudhā philosophy that stresses harmony among communities and religions, harmony between nature and humans. Such an approach enables a person to acquire a deep insight into another person's point of view and develop the ability not only to tolerate the differences but also to understand them. Member states of the United Nations could do well not only to accommodate conflicting viewpoints but also understand the reasons for insecurities that a weaker state may experience and exhibit vis-à-vis the stronger powers.

It is also important to understand in today's context why certain states seek WMDs and nuclear weapons. The motivations may not always be for defensive security needs. It may be for gaining national prestige and/or being guided by domestic political pressures to possess nuclear weapons. It is being increasingly believed that mere possession of nuclear weapons would add to a nation's stature in the arena of world politics and also provide intangible security guarantees. In order to counter such a philosophy, there is need for innovative approaches. It is essential to have a legal regime, under the aegis of the UN system, that provides incentives and security to the nuclear 'have-nots' that would prevent an ambitious political or military leadership from acquiring nuclear weapons.

The key to the efficacy of global forums like the UN lies in the fact that nations of the world must learn not to adopt rigid and extreme viewpoints that lead to conflicts and bullying of weaker states. The Bahudhā concept of the middle way is informative as it enables development of the faculty of accommodating antithetical points of view and the primacy of a common-sense approach.[27] The need of the hour is for member states of the UN to find the best possible choice in this environment and live up to it with sincerity, as terrorism is not likely to disappear soon.

In fact, the Bahudhā philosophy that advocates 'so many views, so many ways' and helps in creating an atmosphere in which pluralism blooms and flourishes is the best guide for a new chapter on UN reforms too. There is no denying that the United Nations, since its inception, has been the harbinger of resolution in several conflicts as well as the biggest relief giver in situations that have threatened the harmonious existence of human beings, be it in Asia, Africa, Latin America, or Europe. Most importantly, the UN has played a vital role in informing peoples across the world of food insecurities, environ-mental and man-made disasters, and civil conflicts. This, in turn, has enabled states and peoples across the world to lend a helping hand in such moments of crisis and thus save precious lives and prevent loss of property. The UN provides a platform through which nations across the world can reach out to each other in happiness and in misfortune.

The war on terrorism will be long drawn out and to fight it the US must realize that the UN is the only multilateral forum that could help in combating not only terrorism but also in weeding out the roots of many modern-day malaise, whether social, ideological, religious, or economic. The Bahudhā concept of tolerance and understanding and that every religion has something to offer is of prime significance in nullifying ideas like 'the clash of civilisations' or the 'us versus them' debate that portrays the Islamic world as being in perpetual conflict with the West. The world must learn to respect differences among cultures and civilizational forms and realize that every religion and life pattern has something unique to offer towards the establishment of world peace. It is incorrect to say that the whole Islamic world is always reactionary on the basis of a very militarized interpretation of Islam given by terrorist groups like the Al-Qaeda. Most Muslims believe in love and compassion as do Christians or Hindus, and would love to live a life full of meaning in rhythm with the forces of peace and harmony.

The UN is a world body that has both the structure and the mandate to emerge as the platform that accommodates all religions, civilizations, and nation-states. There is no scope under the Charter to show disrespect or indulge in an act of humiliation to a particular nation or people due to its inadequate military power or economic potential, or even its past conduct. The sovereign equality of nations is a basic feature of the UN system that happily accom-modates special roles for permanent and non-permanent members of the Security Council. In the ultimate analysis, the authority of the Security Council, to use force against derelict member states or non-state actors, is the guarantor that peace shall prevail at all costs. And yet, democracy and ahimsa are the twin principles that alone would enable the world to rise together in fighting the menace of global terrorism and all that accompanies it.

The Bahudhā tenet of 'one truth, many interpretations' enables people to engage with each other not only with tolerance but also with understanding and compassion. It implies that every nation could count on the UN irrespective of the power it wields. Bahudhā sets in concepts of pluralism and liberal democracy and it is this democratic flow of ideas that would enable peace to become a permanent fixture in the realm of world politics. Most importantly all nations, large and small, and even aspiring permanent member nations to the UN Security Council, must have faith and firm belief in the principles and purposes of the UN Charter, and enact them in their conduct of foreign policy and international relations. The UN also needs to reform itself keeping in mind the changing contextual realities of today's world which has moved far ahead of the world that existed in 1945. With new fears of potentially devastating engagements with non-state actors like terrorism, the words of Kofi Annan ring out loud:

Terrorism is a global menace. It calls for united, global response. To defeat it, all nations must take counsel together, and act in unison. That is why we have the United Nations.[28]

THE FUTURE OF UNITED NATIONS

Winston Churchill, one of the architects of the United Nations, had eloquently stated in 1946:

We must make sure that the [United Nations'] work is fruitful that it is a reality and not a sham, that it is a force for action, and not merely a frothing of words, that it is a true temple of peace in which the shields of many nations can some day be hung up, and not merely a cockpit in a Tower of Babel.[29]

Pandits and politicians, diplomats and commentators, concerned citizens and non-governmental organizations have joined the debate on the future of the UN in the wake of the US-led attack on Iraq and also on its ability to effectively respond to the worldwide threat of terrorism. They have spoken about failures of the UN and also about the need to create alternative institutional mechanisms for tackling terrorism and for maintenance of peace. Some are concerned about the UN coming under the influence of Third World countries, being critical of US policies, and marked by a high level of indecisiveness on a moral and political plane contrary to the ideals of the founders of the UN. The founders of the UN wanted it to take sides between a rogue regime indulging in human rights abuse and genocide and people and organizations trying to uphold values of justice and peace. It cannot stand on neutral ground as there is none in such situations.

There is a school of thought that believes that the UN has failed, and goes on to call it a fatally flawed organization that has actually accelerated and spread global chaos. It believes that anti-western forces, dictatorships, state sponsors of terrorism, and America's worst enemies dominate the General Assembly. The UN, which used to be criticized earlier as bureaucratic, ineffective, and undemocratic is also being viewed as 'supine' and 'toothless', 'derelict', and a 'guarantor of nothing'. Dore Gold has argued that:

What is needed to deal with the new security challenges the world is facing is not a revival of the UN but rather the refashioning of the Western alliance.[30]

He goes on to assert that towards this it would make sense to form an organization of democracies committed to the same common values and strategic purposes. The UN could perhaps do humanitarian work. Dore Gold writes:

It is a mistake to make serious aspects of global security dependent on the UN's decisions. The UN cannot take the lead in protecting states' vital national security interests. To be sure, some UN specialised agencies are successful at humanitarian work. The World Food Programme, for example, fed 90 million people around the world in 2000, many of whom would have come close to starvation without its assistance, and the World Health Organisation saved millions of lives by orchestrating the international response to the outbreak of SARS in the Far East and North America. So let the UN give out tents and blankets when international disaster strikes; it simply cannot bear the burden of preventing wars and neutralising aggression.[31]

Several scholars hold the view that the parallel existence of sovereign nation-states and an international political architecture such as the UN, as it is currently constituted, would always be characterized by the political tug of war among them. It is true that the state system has shed its traditional power in view of global trade, the growing volume of international law, and a large number of international organizations. And yet the state system is durable and is most unlikely to become obsolete. It is, therefore, reasonable to expect that in the foreseeable future a delicate balance between the authority of member states and the UN could be necessary. The cordiality of relationship would greatly depend upon making organizations like the Security Council and other allied agencies reflect the new political, social, and economic realities of the present era.

Pragmatism in global affairs would greatly facilitate enduring peace. The ideas, theories, and concerns of global public opinion as are being currently expressed in the case of Iraq and terrorist attacks in different parts of the world are good signals. There should be no attempt to make the UN subserve the national interests of a particular country or of a group of countries. For that will take away the faith of the large majority of the member countries of the UN. The UN has to be the principal instrument for the furtherance of the common interest of member states. This alone can make the UN Charter a living document and the UN a living organization.

There is another school of thought which wants the UN to change— by way of structural reforms and new initiatives in the areas of human rights and poverty removal, peace and security. In a world of global terrorist threats, global markets, and global media, security and prosperity of individuals and nations depend increasingly on an effective multilateral system.[32]

It is being widely appreciated that the founders of the UN could not have envisioned the terrorist attacks and other problems facing the world today. These are woes of enormous magnitude and great complexity. A new approach on collective action is, therefore, called for to eradicate these menaces, particularly from non-state actors. Newton R. Bowles, in his book, *The Diplomacy of Hope*, believes that 'what we need is the anatomy of failure and not the anatomy of hope'. He concludes:

Right now we are lost in a fog of violence, of cynicism, of despair. We need a touch of old-fashioned Utopianism to grow again the Garden of Eden in this bitter Promised Land. Desperate fanatics dream that death is the gateway to beatitude. Where is our hope? It surely is not in neo-liberal unconstrained greed. Is there a better starting point than the UN Charter? . . . It took a bloody war and 50 million lives to give us this Charter. Must there be another? The future is inevitable after it happens.[33]

The US doctrine of pre-emptive self-defence is not compatible with Article 51 of the Charter. The jurists and political commentators have rightly drawn attention to the fact that pre-emptive self-defence also calls for a distinction between prevention and pre-emption. When President George W. Bush delivered the national security concept in September 2002, he clearly decided that the US would act against 'emerging threats before they are fully formed'.[34] This doctrine of preventive war considers the bare existence of a potentially aggressive regime as sufficient for going to war without prior approval of the Security Council—a striking contradiction to the UN Charter.

In the wake of Iraq's invasion of Kuwait in 1990, the Security Council fully supported by the five permanent members and more particularly the United States, showed itself capable of taking decisive action. Its ability to impose comprehensive sanctions and to ensure that they were enforced was clearly demonstrated and so was its capacity to initiate collective military action.

The Security Council must function as the final legal decision-making authority for peacekeeping. And yet, at the same time, it must be realized that legal institutions alone cannot control armed conflicts and maintain peace. Fortunately, growing economic integration, sensitive and influential non-governmental organizations, international tourism, mass media and concerned citizens and leaders are making a valuable contribution to the furtherance of peace in the world. The UN has to take full advantage of this support base.

The quality of national leadership and a degree of commonality in their world views are essential for the efficacy of the UN system or any other international organization. Inis L. Claude Jr. rightly observes:

international organization does not emancipate the world from dependence upon the quality of its statesmanship. Structural apparatus cannot generate its own supply of political decency, discretion, wisdom and moderation. In the final analysis, both the possibilities and the limitations of international organization are set by political forces operative within and among member states. The deficiencies of the United Nations indicate a greater need for review and revision of national policies than of the Charter itself.[35]

The spread of democracies too plays an important role. There is a tendency to view terrorism in terms of Islam. People forget that the two largest Muslim countries in the world are Indonesia and India respectively. Saudi Arabia, Iran, Egypt, Iraq and Pakistan are far behind in terms of Muslim population. There were no Indian Muslims involved in 9/11 or in subsequent terrorist attacks in the West. This has to be seen in the context of a pluralistic democratic society in India. In this democratic context, India provides ample opportunities to its citizens irrespective of their religions, to participate in political, social, economic, and cultural affairs. It is only where Islam is rooted in an authoritarian mould that it gets used as a vehicle of protest because people feel discriminated against in terms of religion rather than in terms of skills and competence.

It is necessary to evolve instruments through which common men and women are led by education and training to dream of a life in which they can realize their potential and experience the joy of living. The more a democratic society provides development opportunities, the more it secures freedom for its people.

In today's increasingly interconnected world, failed states pose an acute risk to global security. States are most vulnerable to collapse immediately before, during, and after conflict. When chaos prevails as the centre cannot hold, terrorism, narcotics trade, weapons proliferation, and other forms of organized crime start flourishing, aided and abetted by warlords, religious fundamentalists and gangsters. The Afghanistan phenomenon is the most apt example of this in contemporary history.

International law presupposes a world of sovereign states, a world where wars break out between countries. In such a world, it is easy for an agency like the UN to broker peace among warring countries operating under diplomatic norms. But conflicts between people and the ruling dictators create altogether another situation where the distinctions between intervention, assistance, and coercion get blurred, and whatever the UN does or seeks to do may well go beyond what the UN Charter provides for.

Stability and peace require more than the maintenance of a balance of power among strong states. The need is to make sovereignty work in all nation-states, and democracies can empower common people rather than making only the ruling elite beneficiaries of economic benefits in a globalized era. The first step must be to prevent conflict from raising its ugly head, failing which, we need to arrive at a meaningful peace agreement when conflict does occur. That is in the interest of everyone.

There is a certain degree of pessimism involved in the domestication of international politics. It is, therefore, necessary to deal with new concepts. The role of the UN has to be viewed not in terms of a world government in the making but as a facilitation centre and an authority that has the necessary wherewithal to resolve conflicts. The *a priori* requirement is the primacy of the rule of law and the cooperation and commitment of the member states in the UN Charter. The UN's monopoly on the use of force, that has been undermined by the US invasion of Iraq, needs to be reiterated by viewing this as an act of aberration not to be repeated.

The war on terrorism needs to be viewed from two interrelated perspectives. Firstly, the war on terrorism is between those states that promote terrorism and those that would exterminate it. In this perspective, the states that harbour terrorist groups and organizations within their borders need to be forced to exercise control over them. Secondly, as regards the non-state actors, the emphasis has to be more on law enforcement than on the military, and on international cooperation in attempts to disrupt the flow of illicit drugs, weapons, money, and people.

The peaceful resolution of any conflict calls for an environment where contending parties would meet and enter into a dialogue with an attitude of accommodation. At the global level, a political architecture based on a Charter drafted and embraced by member states— what the UN is—constitutes a substantive advantage. As Dag Hammarskjold, a former Secretary General, observed:

The United Nations, the creation of which was itself evidence of the resolve of the peoples of the world to substitute the rule of law for recourse to war, is still young and is still growing. The aims and principles laid down in its Charter have yet to be fully accepted and applied to all the problems that confront the world; but it offers the only reliable route to a future where peace and justice can prevail.[36]

This still holds.

It is true that the world continues to have big powers but the UN was never conceived as a great power club. Instead it chose to be a community of equals that included all countries. It needs to be appreciated that the UN system is needed and one should not be blinded to its need and relevance. Anything that we do that contributes to irrelevance and dissolution of the UN may mean change but it will not constitute progress. 'And we ought by now to realize that', as R. G. Collingwood teaches us,

No kindly law of nature will save us from the fruits of our ignorance.[37]

Among concerned citizens and media persons, non-governmental organizations and affected persons, there is considerable appreciation and even a sense of gratefulness for the UN and its agencies for services rendered during times of droughts, famines, floods, resource wars, population movements, economic crises, and regional pandemics. People are genuinely concerned about the future of global political architecture as a peacekeeper in an era of terrorism, civil unrest, and military interventions. There is a growing realization that the world would be a nastier place if the United Nations did not exist. An individual nation-state can never have the authority, moral or political, to bring order or limit the damage. There is also a strong feeling that in the prevailing environment and quality of political leadership it may be difficult to construct altogether a new global institution. The only alternative, therefore, is to strengthen the UN in order that it succeeds in maintaining rule of law agreed to upon by the member states.

The United Nations needs to be empowered to have the capability to weave the aspirations and beliefs of nations. In this quest, the Bahudhā philosophy can provide the approach

   (i) of finding common ground amidst the diversity of opinions and cultures;

  (ii) of the existence of plurality as an idea that can help in understanding cultural diversities, ethnic, religious and linguistic varieties and usher in understanding of others on cultures; and

 (iii) of the Bahudhā approach that can be central to developing the environment for harmony among nations and enable one nation to understand another nation's point of view about life, religion, science and spirituality.

The United Nations could work as a forum for the development of such understanding. Given today's information revolution and its ability to reach millions of people in seconds, it is necessary that the tools of globalization, most importantly the Internet and mass media, build constructive and progressive bridges with various agencies in achieving peace.

NOTES

1. Isaiah, 2:4—written on a plaque in front of the United Nations building in New York.
2. *Washington Post*, National Weekly Edition, 15–21 December 2002.
3. The Dumbarton Oaks proposals of 1944 provided the basis for the UN Charter. In this Conference, the major powers, the USA, Great Britain, the Soviet Union and China agreed on a comprehensive body of criteria that would provide the *modus operandi* for the new organization.
4. The League of Nations formed in terms of the Versailles Treaty of 1919 after the First World War in 1920 was an attempt at collective security. It, however, failed as most of its provisions did not have legal sanction, the major powers lacked political will and, most importantly, the US was not a part of the organization. It is indeed ironical that the idea of

the League was envisaged by US President Woodrow Wilson, as the organization that would celebrate plurality and bring nations together, in order to reduce misunderstandings that bring about devastating conflicts.

5. Bretton Woods is the name of the rural New Hampshire resort hotel in USA where the conference that produced the agreement took place.

6. Joseph E. Stiglitz, *Globalisation and Its Discontents*, W.W. Norton & Company, New York, pp. 233–4.

7. The Soviet Union as well as Eastern bloc nations did not vote against the resolution tabled in this behalf but abstained.

8. The UN intervened in Bosnia-Herzegovina in 1992. After the death of Marshall Tito, Yugoslavia was on the brink of breaking up after various republics showed signs of seceding. On 25 June 1992, the Yugoslav republics of Slovenia and Croatia declared independence from the Yugoslav Federation. Though civil war erupted in these two republics as the Serbian-dominated Yugoslav People's Army marched into Slovenia the conflict soon shifted base and concentrated on the Republic of Bosnia-Herzegovina which contained a majority Muslim population but with significant Serbian and Croatian minorities. Owing to increasing ethnic tensions towards early 1992, the Security Council established a UN Protection Force with headquarters at Sarajevo and its chief task was to provide safe zones to Bosnian Muslims and the Krajina Serbs. Despite such efforts on the part of the UN, Bosnian Serbs attacked the UN-designated safe area of Srebrenica on 11 July 1995, leaving 7,000 Bosnian Muslims dead as well as forcing 30,000 civilians out of the city. The Dayton Peace Accord was signed in late 1995. It set the framework for a shaky peace in strife-torn Bosnia-Herzegovina only with the help of NATO. NATO increased its bombing on the Bosnian Serb forces that ultimately compelled Slobodan Milosevic, the President of Serbia to relinquish office. The United Nations' action was half-hearted and despite its presence in Bosnia, the killings continued.

The genocide in Rwanda stands out as one of the starkest examples of the laxity of the UN despite early evidence of killings and rape. Within a span of two weeks, nearly a million of the Tutsi population were wiped out by the rival Hutu population. The United Nations Assistance Mission in Rwanda (UNAMIR) watched helplessly.

9. Butros Butros-Ghali, *An Agenda for Peace: Preventive Diplomacy, Peace-making and Peace-keeping*, United Nations, New York, 1992, p. 51.

10. Michael Hersh, 'Bush and the World', *Foreign Affairs*, Vol. 81, No. 5 September/October 2002, pp. 18–43.

11. Quoted in Michael J. Glennon, 'Idealism at the United Nations', *Policy Review*, February–March 2005, pp. 3–14.

12. See Preamble to the Charter of the United Nations.
13. According to the second *Arab Human Development Report, 2003,* (UNDP) between 1980 and 1999, Arab countries produced 171 international patents. South Korea alone during that same period registered 16,328 patents. There are just eighteen computers per 1,000 people in the Arab region today, compared with the global average of 78.3 per 1,000. Only 1.6 per cent of the Arab population has internet access while Arab states represent almost five per cent of the world population. The Arab states produce only one per cent of the books and of those the percentage of religious books is high—over triple the world average. According to the International Labour Organisation study, of the eighty-eight million unemployed males between fifteen to twenty-four worldwide, almost twenty-six per cent are in the Middle East and North Africa. Associated Press, 26 December 2004.
14. Fareed Zakaria, *Time,* Hong Kong, 27 June 1955.
15. Newton R. Bowles, *The Diplomacy of Hope, The United Nations Since the Cold War,* IB Tauris, London, 2004, pp. 161–2.
16. Ibid., pp. 166–7.
17. See The National Security Strategy of the United States, White House, Washington DC, 2002, p. 6. This thirty-three-page policy statement spells out the US perception of global security. One significant feature of this document is 'counter proliferation'—the dismantling of fearsome foreign weapons in outlaw states while simultaneously building up a US missile defence system. In furtherance of his fight against terrorism, President Bush also dispatched American special forces to various countries to combat terrorism—including Yemen, Philippines, Georgia, Pakistan, Colombia and many of the former states of the Soviet Union. By 2003, the Bush administration had constructed, renovated, or added to military facilities in Kyrgyzstan, Afghanistan, Pakistan, Bulgaria, Uzbekistan, Turkey, Bahrain, Saudi Arabia, Qatar, Kuwait, and Oman; planned training missions, including some placement of US forces on an open-ended basis, in Georgia, Djibouti, and the Philippines; won airfield landing rights in Kazakhstan; and undertook major military exercises that involved thousands of American soldiers in India, Jordan, and Kuwait. In addition, the Pentagon stockpiled thousands of tons of military equipment in Middle Eastern and Persian Gulf States, including Jordan, Israel, Qatar, and Kuwait. [See C. Uday Bhaskar, K. Santhanam, Uttam K. Sinha, and Tasneem Meenai (eds), *United Nations, Multilateralism and International Security,* Institute for Defence Studies and Analysis (IDSA), New Delhi, 2005, p. 79].
18. Charter of the United Nations, p. 307.
19. The National Security Strategy of the United States, White House, Washington, DC, 2002, p. 18.

20. Tobias Debiel 'Strengthening the UN: Futile Attempt or Feasible Alternative?' in Bhaskar et al. (eds), *United Nations*, pp. 574–91.
21. Quoted in Stephen Schlesinger, 'Return to Multilateralism: The United States and the World', in ibid., pp. 73–87.
22. Report of the Secretary General's High Level Panel on Threats, Challenges and Change, 'A More Secure World: Our Shared Responsibility', United Nations, New York, 2004, paragraph 194, p. 55.
23. Michael J. Glennon, 'Idealism at the UN', *Policy Review*, February–March 2005, pp. 3–14.
24. 2005 World Summit High Level Plenary Meeting, 14–16 September 2005 (Ref: Issued by the UN Department of Public Information, September 2005).
25. United Nations General Assembly draft resolution referred to the High Level Plenary Meeting of the General Assembly by the General Assembly at its 59th Session (Ref: A/60/L.1).
26. High Level Panel Report, Paragraphs 251–53, pp. 67–8.
27. For instance, during the run-up to the Iraq war, the scenes in the meetings of the Security Council became quite ugly. It was indeed necessary and pertinent for permanent members like France and Germany, on the one hand, and the US and the UK on the other, to have adopted less rigid postures and to have respected their commitment to Charter ideals which demanded differences to be resolved and a common way adopted. Instead, all these countries played out their own domestic politics and tried to promote their core national interests. The unilateral decision by the US to wage war against Iraq in the face of explicit denial of that permission by the Security Council constituted an act of grave undermining of the authority of the UN. It is important for the sole superpower like the US to emphasize and uphold that international legitimacy counts and a multilateral forum like the UN provides just that.
28. See UN Press Release, SG/SM/7962, 18 September 2001 at *www.un.org/News/Press/docs2001.*
29. See front page of Dore Gold, *Tower of Babble, How the United Nations has Fuelled Global Chaos*, Crown Forum, New York, 2004.
30. Ibid., p. 233
31. Ibid., p. 238.
32. James P. Muldoon Jr., *The Architecture of Global Governance: An Introduction to the Study of International Organisations*, Western Press, Boulder, 2004, pp. 267–8. In this perceptive work, Muldoon writes of 'reform versus revolution' as the alternatives for global governance in the 21st century. He sees the United States as the advocate of reformism, calling for 'a bit of tweaking' of international institutions to make them 'more efficient, more capable.' He sees 'an amorphous global civil

society' as the chief advocate of the revolutionary perspective, considering the current international governance architecture 'antiquated, outmoded and unrepresentative of today's wired, transnationalised global society; existing international institutions and organisations need to be radically restructured and democratized and new global organizations created.'

33. Newton R. Bowles, *The Diplomacy of Hope, The United Nations Since the Cold War*, IB Tauris, London, 2004, pp. 168–9.

34. See 'Bush's New Security Plan—Strike First. Calls for Shift from Reactive to Proactive Defence against Terrorism, at *www.usgovinfo.about.com/ library/weekly/aa092102a.htm* (9/21/02).

35. Inis L. Claude Jr., *Swords into Plow Shares, Problems and Progress of International Organisation*, Indian edition published by Anupama Publications, Delhi, 1987, p. 446.

36. Dag Hammarskjold's Message for Youth, United Nations Day, 1961.

37. R. G. Collingwood, *The Idea of History*, Clarendon Press, Oxford, 1993, p. 334.

V

The Future of Bahudhā

12

In Conclusion

Children who meet, gladly meet halfway. The power of love makes the
mountain tremble.[1]

—Nadine Gordimer

The issues of globalization, democracy, and peace that have
dominated our lives, especially after 1989, are likely to continue as
the most important global political trends of the twenty-first century
as well.

The dismantling of the Berlin Wall on 9 November 1989 signified
a number of things: the end of the Cold War, the collapse of the
Soviet Union, the strengthening of the forces of globalization,
democracy and peace, and more. It created a new mindset in the
handling of global as well as regional and local issues in the United
Nations, in Europe, and in several parts of the world. Thomas
Friedman, a noted journalist, provides a very apt description:

It tipped the balance of power across the world toward those advocating
democratic, consensual, free, market-oriented governance, and away from
those advocating authoritarian rule with centrally planned economies. The
Cold War had been a struggle between two economic systems—capitalism
and communism—and with the fall of the wall, there was only one system
left and everyone had to orient himself or herself to go one way or another.
Henceforth, more and more economies would be governed from the ground
up, by the interests, demands, and aspirations of the people, rather than
from the top down, by the interests of some narrow ruling clique.[2]

The transfer of Hong Kong to China on 30 June–1 July 1997 meant
the formal ending of colonialism as a style of governance. It also
made a statement that we now live in a democratic age. Fareed Zakaria
in his masterly analysis records:

In 1900 not a single country had what we would today consider a democracy:
A government created by elections in which every adult citizen could vote.
Today 119 do, comprising 62 per cent of all countries in the world. What

was once a peculiar practice of a handful of states around the North Atlantic has become a standard form of government for humankind. Monarchies are antique, fascism and communism utterly discredited. Even Islamic theocracy appeals only to a fanatical few. For the vast majority of the world, democracy is the sole surviving source of political legitimacy. Dictators such as Egypt's Hosni Mubarak and Zimbabwe's Robert Mugabe go to great effort and expense to organise national elections—which, of course, they win handily. When the enemies of democracy mouth its rhetoric and ape its rituals, you know it has won the war.[3]

The destruction of the World Trade Center in New York on 11 September 2001 raised a new mind-wall in international relations. It showed the power of hatred and established, in a dramatic fashion, the strength of terrorism and terrorists. It signalled that religion could and would be used in the pursuit of terrorist goals. It brought fear amongst civilized democratic societies and heralded the beginning of a troubled world. Terrorism has come to occupy the front seat in our discourse among major global concerns of poverty, ignorance, and diseases such as AIDS. Many believe terrorism is a principal threat not only to peace but also to liberty, secularism, and globalization and all that goes with it.

These three major events have generated several positive illusions and myriad fears and all these influence our society and politics. Several questions are being asked: Are we moving into an age of a peaceful world without wars and major conflicts? Are we sure that in coming years religions will not inspire suicide squads, or terrorists will not kill innocent civilians and destroy property in the name of religion? Will terrorism itself disappear from global politics? Are incompatibility and the feeling of distrust among ethnic and religious groups going to decline heralding an era of social harmony? Are we going to have a global political order based on the rule of law and equality?

THE DANGERS OF PEACE

The reputed journalist Robert D. Kaplan, in his widely read essay 'The Dangers of Peace', highlights the fragility of a peaceful world in the context of the United States. He writes:

Of course, there is often nothing worse than war and violent death. But a truism that bears repeating is that peace, as a primary goal, is dangerous because it implies that you will sacrifice any principle for the sake of it. A long period of peace in an advanced technological society like ours could lead to great evils, and the ideal of a world prominently at peace and governed benignly by a world organisation is not an optimistic view of the future but a dark one.[4]

Kaplan may not be alone in his contemplation of the lack of heroism that would characterize a world perpetually at peace. Turning away from military heroism would certainly weaken a nation, even a family. But the way to civilization is the path of peace, gentleness, patience, self-control, dialogue, and justice. The meek, the gentle, the kind, the intelligent are civilized compared to bullies and upstarts.

EDUCATION AND NON-VIOLENCE

Violence in some period of history might have been necessary for human survival. Today, with access to nuclear weapons, it is self-destructive. So non-violence, gentleness, kindness, intelligence, and dialogue are qualities that need to be cultivated. As Robert A. F. Thurman says:

We need schools for self-restraint and gentleness, boot-camps for the battle of self-conquest. We need monasticism and its disciplines to become accessible to the masses, to help them in the form of secular educational curricula, disciplines of behaviour, mind, and intellect.[5]

It is the education system that diminishes the distance between various religious groups, enabling people to share a common social space. Our endeavour should be to strengthen the existing institutions and to build new ones that would facilitate sharing of a common space and imparting of values of harmony and compassion among the youth.

Schools in multi-ethnic, multi-religious societies having children of different faiths, of different social and economic backgrounds, provide a platform where the children begin talking to each other, smiling at each other, and understanding their respective world views. In these encounters, basic human values of respect and tolerance, love and compassion transcend caste, tribe, religion, economics, and politics.

TERRORISM AND FAILED STATES

Terrorism is now a truly global phenomenon and as multinational as Microsoft. It is lethal and cheap. Terrorist attacks could invariably come by stealth, master-minded by some computer whizz-kid along with some science or technology major. There are many players in the field: fanatics, criminals, drug-traffickers, mafia and warlords. It is a highly unconventional war that cannot be successfully fought with only conventional weapons or tactics. The state must learn to be flexible and agile. It calls for and has full scope of cooperation at the global level.

The danger of ineffective handling of terrorism also comes from 'failed' states. The world is threatened less by strong nation-states than by tottering and failing ones. The danger lies in the fact that these 'failing' or 'failed states' have a tendency to establish a nexus with criminals, drug mafia, and fundamentalists. There are several countries in Africa and also in Asia, Eastern Europe, Latin America, and the Middle East which are likely to be in the cycle of civil unrest, conflict and collapse.

Is terrorism a passing phase in the march of humanity towards progress? Would religion ever cease to inspire terrorists among them? As I was pondering over these questions, I read together works by Theodore Dalrymple, British physician and psychiatrist, and Rabindranath Tagore, Indian poet and philosopher.

Dalrymple, in his essay in *City Journal*, the urban policy magazine (Spring 2004), has given a graphic description of what he learnt from his contacts with Muslim youth in British prisons. Dalrymple noted that most schools of Islam treat the Quran as a divinely inspired text that is not open to any literary criticism or creative reinterpretation. It is a sacred book to be memorized, not adapted to the demands and opportunities of modern life. These Muslim boys in British jails are faced with a dilemma: either they abandon their cherished religion, or they remain forever in the rear of human technical advance. Neither alternative is very appealing, and the tension between their desire for power and success in the modern world on the one hand, and their desire not to abandon their religion on the other, is resolvable for some only by exploding themselves as bombs. People grow angry when faced with an intractable dilemma; they lash out.

Rabindranath Tagore too recognizes a dualism in human thought processes. In his book *The Religion of Man*, Tagore calls it 'his existence within the range of obvious facts and his transcendence of it in a realm of deeper meaning'.[6] He goes on to reflect upon human endeavours in the following words:

His achievement of truth goes far beyond his needs and the realization of his self strives across the frontier of its individual interest. This proves to him his infinity and makes his religion real to him by his own manifestation in truth and goodness. Only for man can there be religion, because his evolution is from efficiency in nature towards the perfection of spirit.[7]

One is certain that these Muslim boys in British jails would one day see 'his religion real to him' and it would manifest 'in truth and goodness'. For every religion provides an answer for dilemmas of this kind between hatred and love and eventually doubts melt away in favour of truth and peace.

POST-GANDHI ERA

At the global level, two significant examples of reconciliation in the post-Mahatma Gandhi epoch need to be recommended. These are the efforts of the Dalai Lama of Tibet and Nelson Mandela of South Africa, which lead one to believe that world leaders can play a major role in healing history's wounds.

The Dalai Lama, while demanding Tibetan autonomy and self-respect, insists that the Chinese are his brothers and sisters and wants dialogue with them. He has, during the past five decades, kept his struggle non-violent. The Dalai Lama and his Tibetan followers have still to secure their political goals but the world takes note of this heroic act of non-violent struggle and its resolution of the Tibet issue as the Dalai Lama puts it 'in his lifetime'.

Nelson Mandela, after becoming South Africa's first democratically elected President, invited his white jailor to the inauguration. He and F.W. de Klerk together worked for building a social and political order that would no longer be guided by race and colour. This was possible as Nelson Mandela and his colleagues in the African National Congress (ANC) demonstrated total faith in democracy, dialogue, and reorientation.

MIND WALLS

The collapse of the Berlin Wall had meant not only the end of the Cold War but provided a strong impetus for the spread of democracy and openness, individual liberty, and human rights. There was a new realization that wars, prejudices, and narrow ideologies divide man and woman from each other. The walls built outside are not physical structures but a reflection of mind walls. Minds build such walls and minds alone can pull them down.

The tragedy of 9/11, followed by terrorist attacks on the Indian Parliament and in Madrid, London, Chechnya, Jammu and Kashmir, and Bali has raised new walls.

Historians would be tempted to view the years after 9/11 as the beginning of the era of terrorism. Questions are asked whether the agenda of world politics would continue to be dominated for decades to come by a few hundred international terrorist attacks. It is slowly being recognized that people are not born terrorists as they are born Americans, Chinese or Indians. They may become terrorists in specific political and personal circumstances and might cease to be terrorists when those circumstances change. It has been observed in different parts of the world that the killing of ten terrorists without changing the political circumstances has encouraged that community to give birth to a hundred more. Terror is a means, not an end, except for a few derailed minds. As Timothy Garton Ash says:

There are many divisive walls in today's world. There's the wall being built between Israelis and Palestinians, which in places looks uncannily like the Berlin Wall. There are the high walls of trade protectionism around both Europe and the United States. But behind them are the biggest walls of all: the mind-walls. If we raise our voices, these walls will come down. We are many, and we have not spoken yet. It's up to us.[8]

We all have to realize that there can be no real peace without justice and so long as there is injustice and exploitation, people would rise in revolt.

STATES AND THE UN

States no longer need to pursue military conquest to become rich, as trade, technology, and the market are providing durable means of prosperity. Japan and Germany have emerged as strong economies from the ruins of the Second World War following peaceful policies and economic liberalization.

The state plays a major role in ensuring the freedom of individuals to pursue their interests in diverse areas ranging from employment to religion, from learning to formation of associations. But religious or spiritual freedom as well as scientific or philosophical enquiries cannot be achieved solely by the action of a state. In fact, creative pursuits in arts and literature, philosophy and science, religion and spirituality would be stifled by state intervention. What the state should do is to help create an environment of peace and creativity and refrain from favouring or penalizing a particular person or group. True spiritual freedom can be attained only when each person follows his own 'dharma' with voluntary toleration and respect for beliefs and practices of others in his neighbourhood and beyond.

Undoubtedly, global peace is threatened not only by terrorist activities but also by the acquisition of the technology and Weapons of Mass Destruction by 'rogue' and/or 'failed' states. The UN Charter provides for the legitimate use of military force only to prevent imminent attacks and that does not cover the acquisition of nuclear technology and/or nuclear weapons. This is an area of great concern and it is here that the UN has to be given a role as the final arbiter. But there are several critics of the UN as they believe that the UN would not be able to take timely decision to prevent either the transfer of nuclear technology or the acquisition of nuclear weapons. To quote Kaplan again:

The UN bureaucracy along with others who seek a peaceful world, worship consensus. But consensus can be the handmaiden of evil, since the ability to confront evil means the willingness to act boldly and ruthlessly and without consensus, attributes that executive, national leadership as in far more abundance than any international organization. Though a more powerful UN would serve everyone's interests in the broad field of humanitarian assistance, a really political muscular international organization is undesirable.[9]

The UN is an international institution, especially created for securing global peace and order. In this era of globalization, which calls for closer integration and a greater need for collective action, both the American attitude towards the UN and the UN itself must change. This is not an impossible task as both the UN and the US are committed to global peace and democracy. They can and they should work together.

The United Nations' sixtieth anniversary summit in September 2005 reflected both its strengths and weaknesses in the many areas in which the international community must work together. Success requires diplomacy and patience, and the UN's latest summit continued the march forward in the creation of a community of nations responsible for the well being of all.

The UN needs to be strengthened in several ways: by expanding the Security Council to reflect present day political and economic realities; by funding a permanent peacekeeping force. A strengthened Economic and Social Security Council would also enable the UN to play a more effective role in reforming the global economic and financial system, represented by the IMF, the World Bank and the WTO, to give all nations including the advanced industrial countries, a role in the implementation of the Millennium Development Goals (MDGs).

RELIGION

Was Karl Marx right in holding that 'religion is the opium of the people'? This statement could perhaps be valid if Marx was referring to a specific religious dogma and its impact on a particular community in the context of his own time. It is not true of all religions or even in respect of all eras of Christianity—a religion which he had in mind when he made such a statement. For four thousand years and more, people have been guided by faith in God.

It is, however, true that a small minority of non-believers have rendered yeoman service to the world by accelerating the pace of secularization and modernization in different societies. Fortunately now, thanks to secularists, even believers favourably entertain the idea of separation between the secular role of the state and religious functions of churches, mosques, and temples. A distinct section among believers, popularly referred to as mystics and the Sufis, have been holding the view that God is not another being but dwells inside every human heart. The fundamentalists in different religions, however, are confused about the divinity of humans and instead opt for a literal interpretation of their scriptures. Their adherence to a model code of an age long gone by is, in fact, inadequate in many respects in meeting the demands of modern living.[10]

There is no doubt that in recent years, the concept of secularism based on the principle that the nation is rooted in a secular compact rather than religious and ethnic identities is facing crisis. In many parts of the world, secularism is viewed as a Western cultural construction. Fundamentalists, in particular, do not associate themselves with a secular approach. In their perception, the modernization process would lead to the elimination of religious practices and beliefs. Accordingly, radicals and terrorists do not believe in pluralism and in spiritual and mystical experiences that see the oneness among human beings.

There are fears that the rising tide of terrorism and the self-assertion of various forms of religious, ethnic, and cultural identities, both together and separately, would subvert the democratic order in significant ways. Terrorism will constrict individual freedom, and religious, ethnic, and cultural movement would harm both nationalism and global peace. Several nation-states have declared their identities in terms of religion professed by the majority of their people. Any religion that insists upon adherence to its dogmas and beliefs by all its believers as well as by all its citizens, makes a direct attack on the secular identity that recognizes a commonality that is based on difference. The fact that individuals may hold a variety of different loyalties and ties [of family, village, caste and religion] while being citizens of a country are strong features of a pluralistic secular social order.

FUTURE OF RELIGION

Doubts are also expressed as to whether a secular state and secular society can finally bid goodbye to religion. Such a situation is not likely to emerge as long as religion addresses questions of ethics and spirituality and is not merely confined to dogmas and rituals. In a wider context too, religion would continue to give meaning to life and values that hold society together. In view of the plurality of faiths and the accumulated wisdom of ages, future activities would have the stamp of religious ethics and respect for different views.

A new balance between religion and secularism is likely to emerge in different countries, allowing both to play a meaningful role in the lives of the citizens. The role of the state has to be to provide an environment that secures conditions for the flowering of creative dissent and paves the way for a plurality of beliefs and practices as well as forms of reasoning.

It is likely that religion can increasingly get circumscribed by the rule of law in multi-ethnic and multicultural societies. There can be many religions and cultures living together but there can be only one set of laws in a nation-state. The law must reign supreme whenever it comes into conflict with religious beliefs and practices.

The forces of globalization, ecology, and peace have united each one of us in realistic terms as moulders of 'our common humanity'. The separation of our private sphere of faith and the public sphere of equality before law should form the core of modern living. This is not to minimize the importance of faith and spiritual experiences.

HUMAN SOLIDARITY

We live in a world in which a mutual interaction among traditions and a sharing of knowledge and moral and spiritual experience is taking place. An examination of the way in which people live in multi-religious, multi-ethnic, and multi-racial societies in different parts of the world underscores the need to respect pluralities.

Social solidarity and even national and global solidarity must always be pluralistic in character. Freedom, discipline, mutual help and inter-dependence are interrelated virtues. A non-discriminatory state and a society marked by a religious and spiritual ethos would ensure social solidarity working for the development of human personality.

For achieving such social solidarity, the Bahudhā approach of dialogue and tolerance needs to be cultivated. A tolerance that is genuinely voluntary would be of great help. Arnold Toynbee rightly says:

The fundamental positive motive for toleration is a recognition of the truth that religious conflict is not just a nuisance but is a sin. It is sinful because it arouses the wild beast in human nature. Religious persecution, too, is sinful because no one has a right to try to stand between another human soul and God. Every soul has a right to commune with God in God's and his soul's way and the particular way concerns none but God and the particular soul in question. . . . Toleration does not become perfect until it has been transfigured into love.[11]

Different ideas relevant to the furtherance of social harmony have flourished in all civilizations of the world. The growing knowledge in the world establishes that concepts and principles related to human rights and ecology are not as culture-specific as is often claimed. A new moral imagination and new political imagination should go together to permeate both rationality and respect in our dialogues.

FREEDOM OF SPEECH AND TERRORISM

It was Diogenes [404–323 BC], the Greek thinker, who declared freedom of speech as 'the finest thing in human life'. He led a simple life. The story goes that Plato once saw him washing some lettuce and said, 'if you had paid court to Dionysius, you would not be washing lettuce'. Diogenes replied, 'if you had washed lettuce, you would not have paid court to Dionysius'. It was Diogenes who coined the term 'citizen of the world' providing political clothing to the old Vedic expression 'earth is my mother, I am a son of the world'.

The coming world is not going to be divided between the colonies and the colonized, superior and inferior races but more in terms of modernization and development. Inequalities will persist and the military and industrial complex would continue to make their impact on world politics. But wars and terrorism are not likely to be dominant concerns as we have known them to be in recent years.

DEMOCRACY

Democracy is a way of perceiving power that was premised on the fact that human beings can govern themselves, and do not need gods or kings or despots to run public affairs for them. There are many paths to democracy, globalization, and secularism that are not just an American or western monopoly. There can be unity among various philosophies and ways of living, and a single set of human rights. These human rights, and institutions which guarantee them, have to be based on ideas of preserving and developing human dignity and human potential. Multi-ethnic and multicultural communities and their institutions of governance can facilitate the flowering of the human potential and an acceleration of the pace of modernization. The movement encouraged by globalization can then help to loosen some archaic notions that emphasize exclusiveness, and thereby help in the building of mixed and cosmopolitan communities.

DEMOCRACY AND THE ARAB WORLD

There are democratic stirrings across the Arab world as well. The Palestinian elections, the Iraqi elections, the Qatar elections, the Saudi municipal elections (albeit for men only), Egypt's multi-party elections, and pro-democracy protests in Lebanon are of immense significance. Oman, Bahrain, Kuwait, and Yemen have now elected parliaments. Women are also playing an increasingly active role. The United Arab Emirates, Oman, Qatar, and Yemen have women ministers. Kuwait is moving towards granting women the right to vote. All these developments need to be viewed in the context of a growing desire and support for democracy throughout the world since the 1980s—particularly in South Korea, Taiwan, the Philippines, Indonesia, Central and Eastern Europe, Latin America, and in the former Soviet Union.

There is no doubt that the democratic movement will grow stronger the more it follows local traditions, relates to the Quran, and responds to Islamic initiatives to promote freedom. What is happening now amounts to a rejection of the prejudicial belief that Islam and democracy are antithetical. Up to now, anyone wanting change could only join Islamist organizations. Now there is an alternative to authoritarian rule and radical Islamism—democracy. It is still a tender shoot, but it is already having an impact.

TOLERANCE

The principle of tolerance lies at the heart of the functioning of democracy. The use of religion and caste on the part of an individual and political parties constitutes the greatest abuse of religion and the social system. The need is to consciously move away from this abuse. One can have a political system characterized by reasonably free elections but in the absence of an impartial judiciary and an environment of respect for the other's point of view, the spread of democracy will not mean much to 'life, liberty and pursuit of happiness'.

Ethnic and religious conflicts have generated an attitude of inertia among leaders. This is often reflected in closed-room conversations in catch phrases such as 'nothing can be done', 'let them fight it out among themselves', 'both sides are irresponsible', etc. Characteristics such as exploitation of natural resources, job opportunities in the market, availability of skilled manpower in a particular area, and bad governance are not given adequate attention in attempts to resolve conflicts.

While an attitude of tolerance is central to the reduction of conflict, this does not mean that the standard elements of a developmental strategy—empowerment of the poor (including women), market access, availability of funds, policy reform, and good governance— do not play significant roles in addressing developmental issues. In securing a safer world, no single intervention is likely to be decisive.

Democratic values, ideological openness, freedom of conscience, a positive regard for others who hold different views, as well as the capacity to tolerate even those who remain intolerant, need to be accommodated by every society and by its institutions of governance and social harmony.

BAHUDHĀ AND PUBLIC POLICY

The real question is: can we make the Bahudhā philosophy a global creative venture? Will this attitude help in the process of dialogue among creative minds and in restructuring of the United Nations? The answer is 'yes'. The philosophy of 'one truth, many interpretations' would help people engage themselves in a manner that facilitates creative dialogue for development as well as social harmony.

In the 'one truth, many interpretations' philosophy, as Gandhi expressed it, 'life is an experiment with truth'. We are all imperfect.

All our religions try to show us the path of righteousness and guide us to travel on that path. But one is not superior to another. This attitude alone can lead to equal respect for all religions and all paths[12] and herald a creative relationship between faith, thought, and action—the essential ingredient in the 'pursuit of happiness'.

The Bahudhā culture offers an environment in which, over time, people and nations can learn to respect different points of view and eschew fears and hatred. It can help institute the dialogue process and consolidate the gains. Bahudhā goes beyond the moral realm, and, in practical terms is a cornerstone of the plural society and liberal democracy.

A question is often posed about the role and relevance of the military in the construction of an environment for creative dialogue among civilizations. In the post-9/11 world, it is quite obvious that the ugly face of terrorism has given full justification for a strong military posture. In fact, the rise of terrorist activities in different parts of the world demands it. It, however, does not mean that military intervention can be taken in an arbitrary fashion. It has to conform to international norms and has to have the sanction of the UN system.

The movements for democracy, religious harmony, and good education need not be viewed as separate ideals or goals; these are interrelated. Creative minds, civil society institutions, and global political architecture need to have a unity of purpose. The future of harmonious living demands sharing of a perspective that accommodates different points of view and respect for the ideals of Bahudhā.

The integration of economies and the rapid expansion of information and communications technology in different parts of the world have contributed to the emergence of a global market. But are we a global community? The barbaric attacks of 9/11 have established with great force the idea that we all share a single planet.

There is no doubt that markets must follow a set of rules and that international economic institutions such as the World Bank, the IMF, and the WTO must provide necessary guidelines for this. These rules need to be fair and just. Notwithstanding just and fair rules in the market place, the markets will continue to be an exploitative arrangement and the strong and powerful will always secure more benefits than the weak and the vulnerable. For equity and justice, the world needs to be supported by a global family and the values that accompany it.

We must consciously work for the propagation of the values of a global family, which could reflect a basic sense of decency and quality in which cooperation and support can be a guiding principle against exploitation and enrichment. The IMF, the World Bank, and the WTO, in particular, would have to develop these sensibilities. In short, we need to combine the virtues of 'a secular journey into the outer space of public action', which the market demands, 'with a spiritual pilgrimage into our inner space',[13] which the family provides.

A massive transformation in approach towards religion and social living, towards application of science and new technology, towards harmony among different faiths, and towards cooperation with neighbours and the international community based on the values of democracy, secularism, and dialogue is manifesting itself. Threats are also present—from terrorism, hatred, exploitation, globalization, and one's own narrowness. Amidst these, one has to move collectively as human beings towards a peaceful and harmonious living that demands both rationality and love. On us lies the responsibility to provide these elements.

It is our duty to work together to inculcate the Bahudhā approach in our society, religion, and politics. It is only through dialogue and working together, without sacrificing whatever is viable in our traditions, that a harmonious society can be established. The last hymn of the *Rig Veda* expresses it admirably:

sam gacchadhvam sam vadadhvam, sam so manamsi janatam
samani va akutih, samana hrdayani vah
samanam astu vo manah
yatha vah susahasati [14]

Translated it reads:

Walk together; speak in concord; let our minds comprehend alike, let our efforts be united; let our hearts be in agreement, let our minds be united, that we may all be happy.

NOTES

1. See *http://www.nobel.se/literature/laureates/1991/presentation-speech.html* dated 18 June 2005.
2. Thomas Friedman, *The World is Flat, a Brief History of the Globalised World in the 21st Century*, Allen Lane, an imprint of Penguin Books, London, 2005, p. 49.
3. Fareed Zakaria, *The Future of Freedom*, Viking, Penguin Books, New Delhi, 2003, p. 13.

4. Robert D. Kaplan, 'The Coming Anarchy Shattering the Dreams of the Post Cold War', Vintage Books, New York, 2000, p. 169. Kaplan cites the thesis propounded earlier by Gaetano Mosca, an Italian political theorist in his support. Mosca in his book, *The Ruling Class* (1939) had advocated that universal peace is something to be feared.
5. Quoted in an edited transcript of Robert A. F. Thurman's inaugural address at the Indic Colloquium on 'Completing the Global Renaissance: The Indic Contribution', held on 24–9 July 2002, at the Menla Centre, in the Catskill Mountains in upstate New York.
6. Rabindranath Tagore, *The Religion of Man*, Unwin Books, London, 1961, p. 399.
7. Ibid., p. 127.
8. Timothy Garton Ash, *Free World, America, Europe, and the Surprising Future of the West*, Random House, New York, 2005, p. 232.
9. Kaplan, 'The Coming of Anarchy Shattering the Dreams of the Post Cold War', p. 176.
10. Jews, Christians, Hindus, Muslims, Sikhs and Buddhists are facing problems. For example, believers in Islam are asking questions relating to the Islamic law of inheritance, which allows a widow to inherit only an eighth share, and which gives to sons twice as much as it does to daughters. They resent the law of evidence, which makes a woman's testimony worth only half that of a man. Similarly, Muslim leaders wish girls to be educated in segregated schools, but there is a preference for co-educational schools. Likewise, Muslim divines insist that women dress modestly according to the Hijab code; but the Muslim world is full of women who oppose such strictures. Islam teaches that women should be confined to homes and to child rearing, but Muslim women at several places would like to work in offices.
11. Arnold Toynbee, *An Historian's Approach to Religion*, Oxford University Press, New York, 1956, pp. 250–1.
12. The Vedic Sages called it *sarva dharma sambhava*, i.e., equal respect for all religions.
13. Jagdish Bhagwati, *In Defence of Globalisation*, Oxford University Press, New Delhi, 2004, p. 265.
14. *Rig Veda* IV.IX-X.

सं गच्छध्वं सं वदध्वं सं वो मनांसि जानताम्।

समानी व आकूति: समाना हृदयानि व:।
समानमस्तु वो मनो यथा व: सुसहासति॥

Select Bibliography

Ahmad, Imtiaz and Helmut Reifeld (eds), *Lived Islam in South Asia: Adaptation, Accommodation and Conflict*, Social Science Press, New Delhi, 2004.

Aiyar, Mani Shankar, *Confessions of a Secular Fundamentalist*, Penguin, New Delhi, 2004.

Akbar, M.J., *Nehru: The Making of India*, Viking, London, 1988.

Anzar, Uzma, 'Islamic Education: A Brief History of *Madrasas* with Comments on Curricula and Current Pedagogical Practices', March 2003 (unpublished).

Armstrong, Karen, *Islam: A Short History*, Modern Library, New York, 2002.

————, *Buddha*, Viking Penguin, New York, 2001.

————, *Muhammad—A Western Attempt to Understand Islam*, Victor Gollancz, London, 1991.

Arpi, Claude, *Born in Sin: The Panchsheel Agreement—The Sacrifice of Tibet*, Mittal Publications, New Delhi, 2004.

Ash, Timothy Garton, *Free World, America, Europe, and the Surprising Future of the West*, Random House, New York, 2005.

Assayag, Jackie, *At the Confluence of Two Rivers: Muslims and Hindus in South India*, Manohar, New Delhi, 2004.

Aurobindo, *The Secret of the Veda* (*The Complete Works of Sri Aurobindo*, Vol. 15), Sri Aurobindo Ashram Publication Department, Pondicherry, 1998.

Barret-Brown, Michael, *After Imperialism* (rev. edn), Humanities, New York, 1970.

Basham, A.L., *The Wonder That Was India: A Survey of the Culture of the Indian Subcontinent Before the Coming of the Muslims*, Grove Press, New York, 1954.

Bhagwati, Jagdish, *In Defence of Globalisation*, Oxford University Press, New Delhi, 2004.

Bhaskar, C. Uday, K. Santhanam, Uttam K. Sinha, and Meenai Tasneem(eds), *United Nations, Multilateralism and Inter-*

national Security, Institute for Defence Studies and Analyses (IDSA), New Delhi, 2005.

Blumenthal, Sidney, *The Clinton Wars*, Viking, New York, 2003.

Bouquet, A.C., *Comparative Religion*, Penguin, Harmondsworth, 5th edn, 1956.

Bowles, Newton R., *The Diplomacy of Hope: The United Nations Since the Cold War*, IB Tauris, London, 2004.

Boyd, William and Rawson Wyatt, *The Story of the New Education*, Heinemann, London, 1965.

Brand, Michael and Glenn D. Lowry, *Akbar's India: Art from the Mughal City of Victory*, The Asia Society Galleries, New York, 1985.

Allchin, Bridget and Raymond Allchin, *The Rise of Civilization in India and Pakistan*, Select Book Service Syndicate, New Delhi, by arrangement with Cambridge University Press, London, 1983.

Brown, Judith M., *Nehru: A Political Life*, Oxford University Press, New Delhi, 2003.

Brown, Michael E., Sean M. Lynn-Jones, and Stevan Miller (eds), *Debating the Democratic Peace*, MIT Press, Cambridge, 1996.

Burke, S.M., *Akbar: The Greatest Mogul*, Munshiram Manoharlal, New Delhi, 1989.

Butros-Ghali, Butros, *An Agenda for Peace: Preventive Diplomacy, Peace-making and Peace-keeping*, United Nations, New York, 1992.

Cesari, Jocelyne, *When Islam and Democracy Meet: Muslims in Europe and in the United States*, Palgrave, Macmillan, New York, 2004.

Claude, Inis L., Jr., *Swords, into Plowshares, Problems and Progress of International Organisation*, Random House, New York, [1956], 4th edn, 1998.

Collingwood, R.G., *The Idea of History*, Clarendon Press, Oxford, 1993.

Cotterell, Arthur (ed.), *The Penguin Encyclopedia of Classical Civilisations*, Penguin Books, Middlesex, England, 1995.

Das Gupta, Uma, *Rabindranath Tagore: A Biography*, Oxford University Press, New Delhi, 2004.

Das, Veena (ed.), *The Oxford India Companion to Sociology and Social Anthropology*, Vol. I, Oxford University Press, New Delhi, 2003.

Davids, T.W. Rhys (ed.), *Sacred Books of the Buddhists,* Vol. III, The Pali Text Society, London, 1977.

Dutta, Krishna and Andrew Robinson (eds), *Selected Letters of Rabindranath Tagore,* Cambridge University Press, Cambridge, 1997.

——— (eds), *Rabindranath Tagore: An Anthology,* Picador, London, 1997.

Embree, Ainslie T. (ed.), *Sources of Indian Tradition: From the Beginning to 1800,* Vol. 1, Penguin Books, New Delhi, 1991.

Friedman, Thomas J., *The Lexus and the Olive Branch: Understanding Globalization,* Farrar, Straus, Giroux, New York, 1999.

Friedman, Thomas J., *The World is Flat, a Brief History of the Globalised World in the 21ˢᵗ Century,* Allen Lane (an imprint of Penguin Books), 2005.

'From Surprise to Reckoning', Kargil Review Committee Report, Government of India Publication, New Delhi, 1999.

Fukuyama, Francis, *State Building: Governance and World Order in the Twenty-First Century* (South Asian Edition), Profile Books, London, 2004.

———, *The End of History and the Last Man,* Free Press, New York, 1993.

Fuller, Graham E., *The Future of Political Islam,* Palgrave Macmillan, New York, 2003.

Gandhi, Rajmohan, *Revenge and Reconciliation: Understanding South Asian History,* Penguin Books, New Delhi, 1999.

Garfield, Jay L., *The Fundamental Wisdom of the Middle Way: Nagarjuna's Mulamadhyamakakrika,* Oxford University Press, New York, 1995.

Gerber, William (ed.), *The Mind of India,* Southern Illinois University Press, Carbondale and Edwardsville, 1967.

Gold, Dore, *Tower of Babble, How the United Nations has Fuelled Global Chaos,* Crown Forum, New York, 2004.

Gopal, Sarvepalli, *Jawaharlal Nehru: A Biography* (three volumes), Oxford University Press, Delhi, 1984.

Gottschalk, Peter, *Beyond Hindus and Muslims: Multiple Identity in Narratives from Village India,* Oxford University Press, Oxford, 2001.

Hardiman, David, *Gandhi in His Time and Ours: The Global Legacy of His Ideas,* Columbia University Press, New York, 2003.

Hastings, James (ed.), *The Encyclopedia on Religion and Ethics,* Vol. 2, T&T Clark, Edinburgh, 1981.

Hitti, Philip, *History of the Arabs*, 1937, rev. edn, St. Martin's Press, New York, 1970.

Hobsbawm, Eric, *On History*, Abacus, London, 1997.

Huntington, Samuel P., *Who are We?* Simon & Schuster, New York, 2004.

————, *The Clash of Civilizations and the Remaking of World Order*, Simon & Schuster, New York, 1996.

Hutton, J.H., *Census of India*, Government of India Publication, New Delhi, 1931.

Iyer, Raghavan, B.R. Nanda, Glenn D. Paige, Daisaku Ikeda, Chaiwat Satha-Anand, and B.N. Pande, *Gandhi and Global Non-Violent Transformation*, Gandhi Smriti and Darshan Samiti, New Delhi, 1994.

Jawaharlal Nehru Centenary Volume, Oxford University Press, New Delhi, 1989.

Jawaharlal Nehru: An Autobiography (Sixth impression), Oxford University Press, New Delhi, 1988.

Kaplan, Robert D., *The Coming Anarchy Shattering the Dreams of the Post Cold War*, Vintage Book, New York, 2000.

Kaplan, Robert D., *The Coming Anarchy*, First Vintage Book Edition, New York, 2001.

Karanjia, R.K., *The Mind of Mr. Nehru*, London, 1960.

Keay, John, *India: A History*, Grove Press, New York, 2000.

Kumar, Satish, *The Buddha and the Terrorist: The Story of Angulimala*, The Viveka Foundation: A Centre for Alternative Perspectives, New Delhi, 2004.

Lokeswarananda, Swami (compiled and edited), *The Perennial Vivekananda: A Selection*, Sahitya Akademi, Calcutta, 1992 (reprint).

Madan, T.N. (ed.), *'Religions of India, Plurality and Pluralism'*, in *India's Religious Perspectives from Sociology and History*, Oxford University Press, New Delhi, 2004.

Malik, Jamal and Helmut Reifeld (eds), *Religious Pluralism in South Asia and Europe*, Oxford, Oxford University Press, 2005.

Malleson, G.B., *Rulers of India: Akbar*, Clarendon Press, Oxford, 1890.

Mende Tibor, Conversations with Mr. Nehru, London, 1956.

Menon, K.P.S., *Many Worlds: An Autobiography*, Oxford University Press, London, 1965.

Menon, Nalini (ed.), *The Indian Experience*, Media Transasia Limited, Bangkok, 1997.

Miller, Jeanine, *The Vision of Cosmic Order in the Vedas*, Routledge & Kegan Paul, London, 1985.

Mookerji, Radhakumud, *Asoka*, Motilal Banarsidass, New Delhi, 2002 (reprint).

Muldoon, James P. Jr., *The Architecture of Global Governance: An Introduction to the Study of International Organisations*, Western Press, Boulder, 2004.

Nanda, B.R., *Mahatma Gandhi*, Oxford University Press, New Delhi, 1989.

Nandy, Ashis, 'The Politics of Secularism and the Recovery of Religious Tolerance', *Alternatives*, Vol. XIII, No. 2, 1988, pp. 177–94.

Nehru, Jawaharlal, *The Discovery of India*, Oxford University Press, New Delhi, 1988.

Nicholson, R.A. (trans), *Rumi, Poet and Mystic (1207–1273)*, Unwin Hyman, London, 1978.

Nivedita, Sister, *The Master As I Saw Him*, Udbodhan Office, Calcutta, 1972.

Nussbaum, Martha C., *Cultivating Humanity, A Classical Defense of Reform in Liberal Education*, Harvard University Press, Cambridge, Massachusetts, London, 1997.

Padmarajiah, Y.J., *A Comparative Study of the Jaina Theories of Reality and Knowledge*, Motilal Banarsidass, Delhi, 1963.

Pastor, Robert A. (ed.), *A Century's Journey*, Basic Books, New York, 1999.

Paz, Octavio, *In Light of India*, Harcourt Brace and Company, New York, 1995.

Prabhu, R.K. and U.R. Rao (compiled by), *The Mind of Mahatma Gandhi*, Oxford University Press, London, 1945.

Radhakrishnan, S., *Eastern Religions and Western Thought*, Oxford University Press, New Delhi, 1985.

———, *Rabindranath Tagore: A Centenary Volume (1861–1961)*, Sahitya Akademi, New Delhi, 1961.

———, *Fellowship of the Spirit*, Harvard University Press, Cambridge, Massachusetts, USA, 1961.

———, 'Occasional Speeches and Writings: October 1952 –January 1956', The Publications Division, Government of India, Delhi, 1956.

———, *Gautama: The Buddha*, Hind Kitabs, Bombay, 1945.

Rajagopalachari, C., *Ramayana*, Bharatiya Vidya Bhawan, Bombay, 1989.

————, *Mahabharata,* Bharatiya Vidya Bhawan, Bombay, 1968.
Report of the Secretary General's High Level Panel on Threats, Challenges and Change, 'A More Secure World: Our Shared Responsibility', United Nations, New York, 2004.
Richards, John F., *The New Cambridge History of India: The Mughal Empire,* Cambridge University Press, Cambridge, 1993.
Ridgeon, Lloyd (ed.), *Major World Religions from their Origins to the Present,* Routledge Curzon, London and New York, 2003.
Russell, Bertrand, *Education and the Social Order,* London, Sydney, Wellington, 1932.
Said, Edward W., *Culture and Imperialism,* Chatto & Windus, London, 1993.
Schimmel, Annemarie, *The Empire of the Great Mughals,* Oxford University Press, New Delhi, 2004.
Schlesinger, Arthur M., Jr., *War and the American Presidency,* W.W. Norton & Company, New York, 2004.
Sen, K.M., *Hinduism,* Penguin Books, London, 1961.
Shastri, Vamadeo, *Asiatic Studies,* 2 vols. Cosmo Publications, New Delhi (1882) rpt 1976. Vamadeo Shastri is the assumed name of Alfred C. Lyall.
Singh, B.P., *India's Culture: The State, The Arts and Beyond,* Oxford University Press, New Delhi, 1998.
Singh, K.S., *People of India: An Introduction,* Anthropological Survey of India, Calcutta, 1992.
Smith, Huston, *Islam: A Concise Introduction,* HarperCollins, San Francisco, 2001.
Soto, Hernando de, *The Mystery of Capital: Why Capitalism Triumphs in the West and Fails Everywhere Else,* Basic Books, New York, 2000.
Stiglitz, Joseph E., *Globalisation and its Discontents,* W.W. Norton & Company, New York, 2002.
Tagore, Rabindranath, *The Religion of Man,* Unwin Books, London, 1961.
Thapar, Romila, *Asoka and the Decline of the Mauryas,* Oxford University Press, New Delhi, 1985.
————, *A History of India,* Vol. 1, Penguin Books, Middlesex, 1966.
The 9/11 Commission Report: Final Report of the National Commission on Terrorist Attacks upon the United States, W.W. Norton & Company, New York, 2004.

The Dalai Lama, *Awakening the Mind, Lightening the Heart*, Thorsons
   (HarperCollins), London, 1997.
———, *Kindness, Clarity, and Insight,* tr. and ed., Jeffery Hopkins,
   Motilal Banarsidass, New Delhi, 1997.
———, *A Policy of Kindness: An Anthology of Writings By and About
   the Dalai Lama,* Snow Lion Publications, New York, 1990.
The National Security Strategy of the United States, White House,
   Washington, DC, 2002.
The Way of the Buddha, Publications Division, Government of India,
   New Delhi, 1995.
Toynbee, Arnold, *A Study of History,* the first abridged one-volume
   edition, Strand Book Stall, Bombay and Bangalore, 1995.
———, *An Historian's Approach to Religion*, Oxford University Press,
   New York, 1956.
Vivekananda, Swami, *My India: The India Eternal,* Ramakrishna
   Mission Institute of Culture, Calcutta, 1993.
Weart, Spencer R., *Never at War: Why Democracies Will Not Fight
   One Another,* Yale University Press, New Haven, 1998.
World Bank, *World Development Report, 1998/1999,* Oxford
   University Press, Washington DC, 1999.
Zakaria, Fareed, *The Future of Freedom: Illiberal Democracy at Home
   and Abroad,* Viking by Penguin Books India, New Delhi, 2003.

Index

364

Index

religion and social progress in 67–
72, 78
rituals in 64
social order during 72
villages in 69–71
Versailles Treaty of 1919 328 n4
Vidatha 72, 74
Vikramashila University, in Bihar 205
Vishwa Hindu Parishad (VHP) 258
Vishwamitra, sage 65
Visva-Bharati 133, 144
Vivekananda, Swami xiv, 91, 125–9,
143–4, 182
at Parliament of Religions 125–6,
146 n6
Ramakrishna Mission of 144
Ramakrishna Order of 125
Ramakrishna Paramhansa and 127,
147 n8
Vyasa Maharsi 65, 82 n13
Mahabharata of 55

Wahhab, Muhammad ibn Abd al 47
n20
Wahhabi School 34
Wahhabism 32, 47 n20
Wars of Religion 266–7
war on terrorism 321, 326
see also United States of America
Washington, George 7

Wells, H.G. 184
West Bengal 198–202
Christianity in 198
Hinduism in 198
Renaissance in 198
Wilhelmine Empire, Germany 4
Wilson, Woodrow 329 n4
women, family and status of 68–9
Wood, Gordon 7
World Bank 40, 41, 305, 306, 341,
347, 348
World Health Organization (WHO)
323
World Trade Centre, USA, terrorist
attack on 12, 336
World Trade Organization (WTO) 41,
306, 341, 347, 348

yajnas 54, 90
Yajnavalkya 68
Yajur Veda 72
Yeltsin, Boris 6
Yew, Lee Kwan 40

Zakaria, Fareed 39, 335
Zaynuddin, Makhdum Ahmad 197
Zemin, Jiang 8
Zia ul-Haq 33
Zoroastrianism 26, 256
Zorastrians, in India 193, 194

About the Author

Balmiki Prasad Singh is a distinguished scholar, thinker and public servant. He was the fourteenth governor of Sikkim (2008–13).

Born in Bihar, he was educated in a village school and subsequently at the Universities of Patna and Oxford. He completed his masters in political science from Patna University, gaining record marks and several gold medals. He became a lecturer in political science at Patna University at the age of nineteen.

He was appointed to the elite Indian Administrative Services in 1964. Over the past four decades he has held a variety of important positions in Assam as well as in the Government of India. He has served as Additional Secretary, Ministry of Environment and Forests (1993–95), Culture Secretary (1995–97), and Home Secretary (1997–99) in Government of India.

B.P. Singh also served as Executive Director and Ambassador at the World Bank during 1999–2002, representing India, Bhutan, Bangladesh, and Sri Lanka. He was one of the founder members of the Development Gateway Foundation and member of the Global Environment Facility.

As an intellectual with avid interest in academics, B.P. Singh has held a variety of honorary academic and governmental assignments: Chancellor of the Central University of Tibetan Studies, Sarnath, for six years; Chief Editor of the South Asia Series *Perspectives on Economics, Technology and Governance* of Oxford University Press, New York, for four years; President, Namgyal Institute of Tibetology, Gangtok, for five years; Chancellor, Sikkim Manipal University for five years; and Mahatma Gandhi National Fellow.

He has written seven books, some of which are: *The Problem of Change: A Study of North-East India*; *India's Culture: the State, the Arts and Beyond*; and *The 21st Century: Geopolitics, Democracy and Peace*.

B.P. Singh is an eminent public speaker in English and Hindi and has delivered memorial lectures and speeches at national and global platforms.

He is widely acclaimed as an outstanding administrator of India and also as a public intellectual of eminence in India and beyond for advocating the Bahudhā approach which outlines the path towards a harmonious world, as against the clash of civilizations, and for espousing the cause of ecology, democracy, and peace.